LIFE AND DEATH ON THE MORMON FRONTIER

LIFE AND DEATH ON THE MORMON FRONTIER

THE MURDERS OF FRANK LESUEUR AND GUS GIBBONS BY THE WILD BUNCH

STEPHEN C. LESUEUR

Greg Kofford Books
Salt Lake City, 2023

Copyright © 2023 Stephen C. LeSueur
Cover design copyright © 2023 Greg Kofford Books, Inc.
Cover design by Loyd Isao Ericson
Back cover photo by Gerald Martineau

Published in the USA.

All rights reserved. No part of this volume may be reproduced in any form without written permission from the publisher, Greg Kofford Books. The views expressed herein are the responsibility of the author and do not necessarily represent the position of Greg Kofford Books.

ISBN: 978-1-58958-772-4
Also available in ebook.

Greg Kofford Books
P.O. Box 1362
Draper, UT 84020
www.gregkofford.com
facebook.com/gkbooks
twitter.com/gkbooks

Library of Congress Cataloging-in-Publication Data

Names: LeSueur, Stephen C., author.
Title: Life and death on the Mormon frontier : the murders of Frank LeSueur and Gus Gibbons by the Wild Bunch / Stephen C. LeSueur.
Description: Salt Lake City : Greg Kofford Books, 2023. | Includes bibliographical references and index. | Summary: "This thoroughly researched and vivid account examines a murderous spree by one of the West's most notorious outlaw gangs and the consequences for a small Mormon community in Arizona's White Mountains. On March 27, 1900, Frank LeSueur and Gus Gibbons joined a sheriff's posse to track and arrest five suspected outlaws. The next day, LeSueur and Gibbons, who had become separated from other posse members, were found brutally murdered. The outlaws belonged to Butch Cassidy's Wild Bunch gang. Frank LeSueur was the great uncle of the book's author, Stephen C. LeSueur.
In writing about the Wild Bunch, historians have played up the outlaws' daring heists and violent confrontations. Their victims serve primarily as extras in the gang's stories, bit players and forgotten names whose lives merit little attention. Drawing upon journals, reminiscences, newspaper articles, and other source materials, LeSueur examines this episode from the victims' perspective. Popular culture often portrays outlaws as misunderstood and even honorable men--Robin Hood figures--but as this history makes clear, they were stone-cold killers who preferred ambush over direct confrontation. They had no qualms about shooting people in the back. The LeSueur and Gibbons families that settled St. Johns, Arizona, served as part of a colonizing vanguard for the Church of Jesus Christ of Latter-day Saints, popularly known as Mormons. They contended with hostile neighbors, an unforgiving environment, and outlaw bands that took advantage of the large mountain expanses to hide and escape justice. Deprivation and death were no strangers to the St. Johns colonizers, but the LeSueur-Gibbons murders shook the entire community, the act being so vicious and unnecessary, the young men so full of promise. By focusing the historian's lens on this incident and its aftermath, this exciting Western history offers fresh insights into the Wild Bunch gang, while also shedding new light on the Mormon colonizing experience in a gripping tale of life and death on the Arizona frontier"-- Provided by publisher.
Identifiers: LCCN 2023011240 | ISBN 9781589587724 (paperback) | ISBN 9781589586772 (hardcover)
Subjects: LCSH: LeSueur, Frank, 1880-1900. | Gibbons, Gus, 1874-1900. | Wild Bunch (Gang) | Church of Jesus Christ of Latter-day Saints--Arizona--Saint Johns--History--19th century. | Murder--Arizona--Apache County--History--19th century. | Mormons--Arizona--Saint Johns--History--19th century. | Apache County (Ariz.)--History--19th century.
Classification: LCC F817.A6 L47 2023 | DDC 979.1/04--dc23/eng/20230331
LC record available at https://lccn.loc.gov/2023011240

For Kathy, who knows all the reasons why

CONTENTS

Introduction	ix
1. The Unfolding of God's Plan Across Arizona	1
2. Butch Cassidy and the Wild Bunch	31
3. A Plague of Cowboys and Outlaws	59
4. Pursuing Five Men for Killing a Beef	89
5. Burying Frank and Gus	105
6. Hunt for the Killers	127
7. Called to Another Mission	165
8. A Reckoning for Sheriff Beeler	187
9. Justice Denied	197
10. Serving an Honorable Mission	217
11. Rendezvous with Death	243
Afterword	273
Acknowledgments	289
Works Cited	293
Additional Resources	303
Index	309

INTRODUCTION

Outlaws murdered my great-uncle, Frank LeSueur. Frank and another young man, Gus Gibbons, had been summoned to join a posse chasing suspected cattle rustlers. After a long day in the saddle, all the posse members returned home, except Frank and Gus. Their bodies were found the next day twenty miles outside of St. Johns, Arizona, a small town where the LeSueur and Gibbons families had settled with fellow Mormons. Frank had been shot five times, Gus six, their faces disfigured and blackened with gunpowder after being shot at close range while they lay on the ground, dead or dying. The year was 1900. I was born more than fifty years later in Burbank, a quiet Los Angeles suburb teeming with new housing tracts built for World War II veterans and their families. Frank's murder was well known to my family, but we knew little beyond these meager facts. My grandfather, Karl LeSueur, only five when his older brother was killed, recalled few details. To the best of our knowledge, Frank's death occasioned little notice or consequence. We believed the outlaws were never identified, nor was much effort made to capture them.

We were wrong. In recent decades, historians of outlaws and the West have become quite interested in this episode, largely because the killers were members of Butch Cassidy's Wild Bunch gang. Although there remains room for disagreement regarding which gang members participated, the likely killers were Harvey Logan (alias Kid Curry), Thomas C. Hilliard (alias Tod Carver), Ben Kilpatrick, Will Carver, and Tom Capehart. We know that Butch Cassidy was not with them because, on the day that Frank and Gus were killed, Cassidy was sitting in the St. Johns jail. The sheriff did not record his reasons for detaining Cassidy, but it appears he correctly suspected a connection between Cassidy and the murderers. Cassidy, whose real name was Robert LeRoy Parker, was also a Mormon whose parents emigrated to Utah in the 1850s. How a Mormon boy came to lead a murderous outlaw gang has fascinated and perplexed historians.

In writing about the Wild Bunch, historians have played up the drama of their daring heists and violent confrontations. Their victims serve primarily as extras in the outlaws' stories, bit players and forgotten names whose lives merit little attention. After learning of the Wild Bunch's role in my great-uncle's murder, I decided to examine more closely the accounts left by the families of Frank LeSueur, Gus Gibbons, and other residents of the tight-knit Mormon community in St. Johns. They tell of the outlaws' menacing entrance into St. Johns and of their stopping at a store where Frank's father sold them bullets for their guns. They tell of the minor incident that triggered the call to arrest the outlaws, the subsequent organizing of the posse, the anxious waiting for the men to return, and the missteps that left Frank and Gus alone on the outlaws' trail. Their accounts also describe an aftermath filled with heartache, bitter second-guessing of the sheriff, and an aching desire to find meaning in the young men's deaths.

When writing about Western outlaws, historians must untangle the mythology that surrounds the bandit gangs and gunfighters who were romanticized even in their own time. When Kid Curry was arrested in Tennessee, hundreds of local citizens flocked to the Knoxville jail hoping to get a look at the infamous gunman. They willingly laid down their money when Curry jokingly suggested they pay "ten cents a peep" as they paraded by his cell.[1] Many popular writers portray the outlaws as social bandits and "good badmen," champions of the little guy and symbols of an unsullied frontier making its last stand against encroaching industrialization. Modern popular culture perpetuates many of these themes. The 1969 movie "Butch Cassidy and the Sundance Kid" portrays the two outlaws as affable rogues. In this telling, Butch is as quick with his wit as Sundance is with a gun. Butch eschews violence and aims his larceny primarily at those whose wealth makes them deserving targets. The 1971 to 1973 television series "Alias Smith and Jones" tells the story of Kid Curry and Hannibal Heyes, two likeable young men who, regretting their criminal past, have gone straight and await a promised pardon from the governor. Heyes's smooth tongue and Curry's fast gun help them elude capture by bounty hunters and lawmen, while they use their cunning and violence to protect the vulnerable and innocent. These story lines are consistent with motifs that portray western outlaws as misunderstood and basically honorable men whose station or circumstances have led them to a life of crime. In the case of the Wild Bunch, regardless of what may have initially motivated their turn to crime, we can also add one more character description: the men who murdered Frank LeSueur and Gus Gibbons were stone-cold killers.

---

1. *Knoxville Journal and Tribune*, December 17, 1901, 2.

Still, outlaw myths die hard. Robert Redford, whose role as the Sundance Kid helped propel him to Hollywood stardom, suggested that many Western bandits were just "kids who never grew up or high spirited men whose sense of fun and pranks couldn't be contained by the law."[2] In the movies, yes. But the outlaws' activities, viewed from the perspective of their murdered victims and families, cannot be characterized as playful hijinks. And contrary to outlaw lore, Cassidy and his gang were not necessarily great masterminds.[3] Some of their heists betrayed less than stellar planning and execution. Not everyone got away. Cassidy was positively identified in each of his first two bank robberies. It's also possible Cassidy never actually robbed a train, though he may have helped gang members with the planning. And despite hauls totaling more than a hundred thousand dollars over several years, the outlaws constantly spent themselves broke gambling, whoring, and partying. Butch and Sundance famously interrupted that cycle for a few years when they took up ranching in Argentina, but they eventually returned to doing what they knew best. By all accounts, most Wild Bunch members were crack shots and feared gunmen, but as this history will show, their preferred method of confrontation was ambush. They were not looking for a fair fight; they had no qualms about shooting people in the back.

The LeSueur-Gibbons murders set off a chain of events with long-lasting impacts on both the outlaws and the Mormon families. In the near term, Apache County Sheriff Edward Beeler led posses across five Western states and territories and into Mexico to track down the outlaws, who continued their murderous spree as they fled. The search for the killers eventually sparked the largest manhunt in Utah up to that time. The murders would also spur Dick Gibbons, Gus's uncle, to run for the territorial legislature, where he became a leading proponent of creating a force of Arizona Rangers with the training and expertise to hunt down criminal gangs. During Beeler's chase after the killers, a much-harried Cassidy reportedly sought amnesty for his crimes from Utah Governor Heber Wells. "I want to quit this outlaw business and go straight," Cassidy told his attorney in one version of this story, adding, "I realize now that it's a losing

---

2. Lula Parker Betenson and Dora Flack, *Butch Cassidy, My Brother*, xiii, in Forward by Robert Redford.

3. See, for example, Daniel Buck and Anne Meadows, "The Wild Bunch: Wild, but not Much of a Bunch," 29–31; and Vince Garcia, "The Wilcox, Wyoming Train Robbery—As It Happened," 81.

game."⁴ The amnesty story is likely apocryphal. Nevertheless, Cassidy and Sundance departed for Argentina less than six months later, suggesting that the two men recognized the Wild Bunch's days were numbered.

Many Mormon families living in St. Johns, including both the LeSueur and Gibbons families, left extensive records of their lives in the form of letters, memoirs, and church and county records. A wealth of material is also found in Arizona, Utah, and New Mexico newspapers that covered the murders and search for the killers. As I delved into these records, I realized that the protagonists in this story are not just the outlaws and their immediate victims, but also the St. Johns community. The murders reverberated among the townspeople, altering the trajectory of many lives. Consequently, I broadened the scope of my research to present a clear picture of those affected when their lives intersected with the Wild Bunch. Their interwoven stories provide a new perspective of the Mormon colonizing experience, particularly of the challenges they faced in establishing settlements among the Gentiles (as non-Mormons were called).

Americans are generally familiar with the central role Mormons played in settling Utah, but they are less so with their pioneering efforts in Arizona. The colonizing missionaries sent by Brigham Young to settle St. Johns suffered extraordinary privation in the arid climate and inhospitable frontier environment. They also encountered determined, occasionally violent opposition from the town's existing residents—primarily Mexican-Americans—who saw themselves being pushed aside by the Mormon newcomers. For their part, the Saints wanted to live separately from their gentile neighbors, but survival in that unforgiving region required alliances, and alliances required collaboration and compromise. Both communities had to learn how to live together. Lawlessness along the Arizona frontier exacerbated these challenges. Even as late as 1900, outlaw bands plagued the Western states and territories, where the vast forest and mountain expanses offered safe refuge for murderers, rustlers, and thieves.

In writing about my ancestors, I have been forced to confront cherished family stories of faith and courage. Mythology does not attach itself solely to outlaw history. LeSueur family members recount Frank's murder as a faith-promoting tale. After Frank's death, his brother James reported having a vision in which he saw Frank preaching the Mormon gospel to other deceased spirits in the afterlife. Assisting Frank in this task was a young woman who, James understood, was to be Frank's wife. Shortly

---

4. Charles Kelly, *The Outlaw Trail: A History of Butch Cassidy and His Wild Bunch*, 267.

after James recounted his vision to his parents, a woman from a neighboring town told the LeSueur family that her daughter, Jennie Kempe, had recently passed away and on her deathbed asked to be married to Frank in a posthumous marriage ceremony. Upon seeing Jennie's photo, James proclaimed Jennie to be the girl he saw in his vision. The remarkable circumstances that brought together the LeSueur and Kempe families seemed not only to confirm the reality of James's vision, but also the truthfulness of Mormon beliefs regarding the hereafter. In this telling, the outlaws became mere footnotes in an inspirational story, a story James retold in Church publications and at family gatherings. But crucial aspects of James's story, like outlaw mythology, do not withstand scrutiny. The truth, though less miraculous, is no less compelling.

Various aspects of the Mormon settlement in St. Johns have been examined by William S. Abruzzi, *Dam That River! Ecology and Mormon Settlement in the Little Colorado River Basin* (1993); Daniel Justin Herman, *Hell on the Range: A Story of Honor, Conscience, and the American West* (2010); Charles S. Peterson, *Take Up Your Mission: Mormon Colonizing Along the Little Colorado River 1870–1900* (1973); C. LeRoy and Mabel R. Wilhelm, *A History of the St. Johns Arizona Stake: The Triumph of Man and His Religion Over the Perils of a Raw Frontier* (1982); and Mark E. Miller, "St. Johns's Saints: Interethnic Conflict in Northeastern Arizona, 1880–85" (1997). These works are exemplary, but much information has become available since they were published, adding both color and insight into the Mormon colonizing experience. Historians have written extensively about Butch Cassidy and the Wild Bunch, most recently in Charles Leerhsen, *Butch Cassidy: The True Story of an American Outlaw* (2020). The LeSueur-Gibbons murders have not been overlooked, but neither have they received in-depth attention, except for the purpose of identifying the killers. Apache County Sheriff Beeler also deserves a critical look for his dogged pursuit of the outlaws, which may have helped persuade Cassidy and the Sundance Kid to relocate outside the United States. "Lesueur [*sic*] and Gibbons were my personal friends, and they lost their lives in a well-meant effort to assist me," Beeler told reporters, vowing to follow the outlaws into hell, if need be, to even up the score.[5] Some townspeople blamed missteps by Beeler for the young men's deaths, and the episode cast a dark shadow over his reputation. Looking at these events from both the outlaws' and victims' perspectives contributes sig-

---

5. *Salt Lake Herald*, June 4, 1900, 2 (reprinted from the *Grand Junction Sun*); and *Salt Lake Herald*, June 13, 1900, 2.

nificantly to our understanding of the outlaws and Mormonism, as well as to the history of Arizona and the West.

William "Bill" Gibbons and John "J. T." LeSueur, the fathers of Gus and Frank, overcame many challenges to make a place for themselves and their families in St. Johns. Both would eventually hold office in the Apache County government and become respected leaders in their church. LeSueur also served in the territorial legislature, and by 1900 he was a leading member of the local business community. LeSueur and Gibbons owned extensive herds of sheep. Although deprivation and death were no strangers on the Arizona frontier, their sons' brutal murders shook the entire community, the act being so vicious and unnecessary, the young men so full of promise. The end of the outlaw era was fast approaching, but it did not come soon enough for Frank LeSueur and Gus Gibbons.

Note on the terms "Mormon" and "Zion"

Members of The Church of Jesus Christ of Latter-day Saints have long been known as "Mormons," a nickname that derives from their belief that the Book of Mormon is inspired scripture. Until recently, the Church used the term extensively in its literature and proselytizing materials, such as the "I'm a Mormon" campaign, though always emphasizing the actual name of the church. Today, the Church discourages the use of Mormon and prefers that its members be called Latter-day Saints rather than LDS or Mormons. The change highlights the Church's contention that it is Jesus Christ's true church and its doctrines and teachings represent the restored gospel of Jesus Christ. Because my history examines an era when the term "Mormon" was commonly used by both members and non-members, I use the term throughout both to help portray this time period and provide ease of reading. I also use "Saints" interchangeably with "Mormons."

In biblical times, Zion referred to both the city of Jerusalem and the land of Israel. For nineteenth-century Mormons, Zion represented their New Jerusalem, a place where they gathered in expectation of Christ's Second Coming. Joseph Smith initially identified Independence, Missouri, as the site of the Mormon's Zion, but persecution drove them to Illinois and eventually to Utah, which became their new Zion and place of gathering. Over time, the term "Zion" has taken on many meaning for the Saints, but early Saints were intent on building Zionic communities throughout the Mountain West as part of their effort to establish a righteous kingdom of God to usher in the Millennium.

CHAPTER 1

THE UNFOLDING OF GOD'S PLAN ACROSS ARIZONA

This story begins at the end of the world. The LeSueur and Gibbons families were driven to settle the American West by the same millennial spirit that inspired Butch Cassidy's grandparents to pull handcarts a thousand miles across swollen rivers and interminable prairies to the Great Salt Lake Valley. Like the tens of thousands of Mormons who gathered from North America and abroad, they sought a place of refuge—their Zion—to escape the expected calamities and disasters of the fast-approaching end times. Only Zion and its faithful would be spared God's wrath. The Mormon prophet Joseph Smith had declared in 1835 that "fifty-six years should wind up the scene."[1] Building on Smith's millennial timeline, Apostle (and future Church President) Wilford Woodruff later predicted that "there will be no United States in the Year 1890."[2] Although these deadlines came and passed, the Church's faithful remained confident that Christ's Second Coming lay just around the corner, even if the precise timetable was unknown. Many Latter-day Saints, as they called themselves, fervently believed they or their children would live to see the Savior's return.

The Church of Jesus Christ of Latter-day Saints was founded in 1830 by Joseph Smith. He claimed to be restoring the ancient Christian church and its original teachings, which, according to him, had been corrupted and lost after the deaths of the apostles. In the same year, he published a new book of scripture, the Book of Mormon, which along with the Bible, testifies of Christ's life and mission. Members of the new church became known as "Mormons" because of their belief in the new scripture. As president and prophet, Smith issued revelations, ordained a set of modern apostles to help lead the Church, and began laying plans to build a New Jerusalem or Zion on the American continent. Through his apostles and a growing army of missionaries, Smith sent out the word that God

---

1. Joseph Smith, *History of the Church of Jesus Christ of Latter-Day Saints*, 2:182.
2. Quoted in Charles S. Peterson, *Take Up Your Mission: Mormon Colonizing Along the Little Colorado River 1870–1900*, 228n18.

had restored His true church to earth and called for the faithful to gather together in Zion.

The Mormons didn't simply gather and wait. God's plan called for them to build a righteous kingdom of God to usher in Christ's triumphant return. The impetus for Mormon gathering was theological, but it had economic and political import as well. Once in Zion, the Saints intended to create a political entity that would not only prepare the way for Christ but also serve as the foundation for His millennial governance. Consequently, the Mormons established their own shadow government that would step in and assume power when the day of judgment arrived—and when earthly governments, including the United States, fell by the wayside. But until that time, Church leaders would have to facilitate the well-being of the multitude of converts flocking to Zion from all corners of the globe. A key tenant of Mormon theology also held that Native Americans, as the literal descendants of the Old Testament tribe of Joseph, would play a pivotal role in the unfolding events. From the Church's earliest days, the Mormons devoted enormous resources to proselytize and civilize Native Americans, whose highly anticipated conversion to Mormonism would herald Christ's return.

Following aborted attempts to establish communities in Missouri and Illinois, the Mormons made their headquarters in Salt Lake City in 1847. Utah and the West became their Zion. Brigham Young, Joseph Smith's successor, envisioned a kingdom-building enterprise that would spread far beyond the Great Salt Lake valley to encompass large portions of territory recently ceded to the United States by Mexico, as well as a portion of the Oregon Territory. In 1849, Mormon leaders petitioned the federal government to create a massive new state called Deseret. As drawn by the Mormons, Deseret would comprise two hundred thousand square miles, encompassing present-day Utah, nearly all of Nevada and Arizona, about a third of California (including Los Angeles and San Diego), significant portions of New Mexico, Colorado, and Wyoming, and smaller pieces of Idaho and Oregon.[3] Ultimately, Mormon leaders wanted to establish a Mormon domain that also included Mexico and even South America. When Mormon families were called as colonizing missionaries to settle a particular region or town, their leaders expected them to remain until they were "honorably released" or, as was often the case, they were directed to colonize another frontier outpost. The efficient settling of the West

---

3. Leonard J. Arrington and Davis Bitton, *The Mormon Experience: A History of the Latter-day Saints*, 163.

The Unfolding of God's Plan Across Arizona

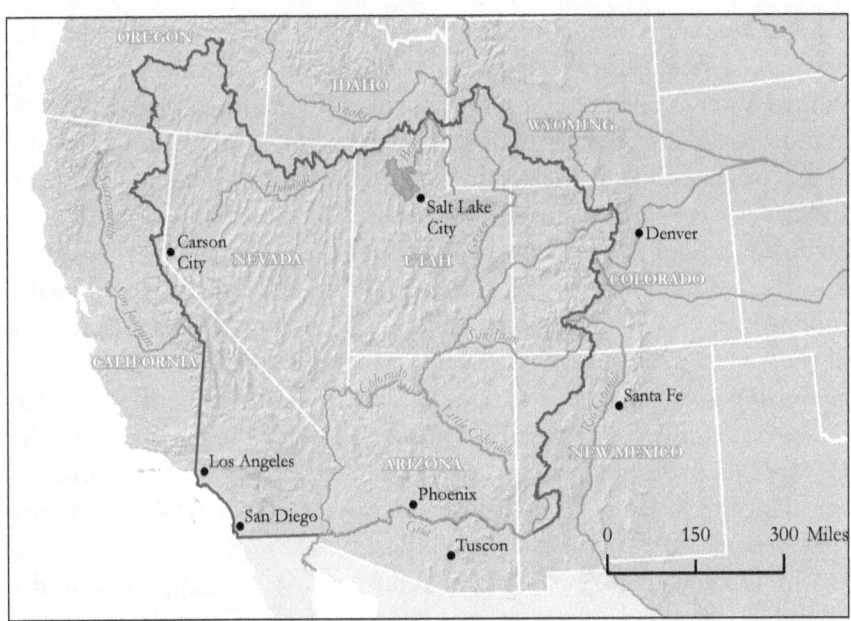

Proposed State of Deseret 1849. Map by Abner Hardy, ThinkSpatial, BYU Geography.

became a theological imperative, a prerequisite for the Second Coming, a sign of God's unfolding plan for his people.[4]

Congress declined to create Deseret, eventually reducing the planned state to Utah's current boundaries. Still, Young's dream of a vast Mormon empire remained undiminished. With methodical intent, the Mormons spread in all directions from their Salt Lake City headquarters. Church leaders established a Perpetual Emigrating Fund to support the mass migration of converts seeking religious and economic salvation in the newly opened western territories. And the converted men, once settled with their families in Mormon settlements and towns, often returned as missionaries to their homelands, where they preached the good news of the true gospel's restoration, creating a perpetual cycle of converts and missionaries to nourish the growing kingdom. Within ten years after their arrival in Salt Lake City, the Mormons had established ninety-six settlements and towns in the West. By 1900, the number totaled at least five hundred.[5] The LeSueur and Gibbons families would be called to serve among Arizona's vanguard.

---

4. Peterson, *Take Up Your Mission*, vi.

5. Leonard J. Arrington, *Great Basin Kingdom: An Economic History of the Latter-day Saints 1830–1900*, 88.

The Mormons started exploring Arizona in 1854, but two decades would pass before serious colonizing began. The intense heat and limited water resources in the remote territory discouraged large-scale emigration, as did the presence of hostile native tribes, particularly the Apache and Navajo. Although Mexico had ceded its claims to this territory, the Indigenous People had not. Nevertheless, Mormon leaders kept an eye on Arizona, hoping eventually to establish a line of settlements extending into Mexico and to the Gulf of California.[6] When US Army troops finally subdued the Navajo and Apache tribes sufficiently to force large numbers of them onto reservations—the Navajos in 1868 and Apaches in 1871—colonizing became much safer for white settlers. Tensions remained, as did occasional conflicts and deadly violence, but with the protection of the US Army, non-natives now had a free hand to appropriate for themselves the choice farm lands, grazing fields, and natural resources surrounding the reservations.

In December 1872, Brigham Young sent a scouting party under Bishop Lorenzo Roundy to explore Arizona's Little Colorado River corridor and other areas to locate possible settlement sites. Although Roundy found the Little Colorado region to be "an inhospitable and forbidding waste," this was not discouraging news.[7] A harsh environment meant less competition for land and resources. "Good countries are not for us," said George Q. Cannon, one of Brigham Young's counselors. "The worst places in the land we can probably get, and we must develop them. If we were to find a good country how long would it be before the wicked would want it and seek to strip us of our possessions?"[8] After a failed colonizing effort in 1873, the Mormons began establishing a series of towns and settlements along the Little Colorado River in 1876, including St. Joseph, Brigham City, Snowflake, and St. Johns.

When Mormon leaders identified St. Johns as a key location for their pathway into Mexico, it was already an established town named San Juan. Its residents were largely Catholic, Spanish-speaking people from New Mexico, many born as Mexican citizens before New Mexico was ceded to the United States. Built on rolling hills along the western bank of the

---

6. Charles S. Peterson, "Arizona, Pioneer Settlements In," 1:66.

7. Peterson, *Take Up Your Mission*, 7. For similar assessments by early Mormon colonists regarding the region's barren conditions, see Kevin H. Folkman, "'The Moste Desert Lukking Plase I Ever Saw, Amen!' The 'Failed' 1873 Arizona Mission to the Little Colorado River," 115–50.

8. Peterson, *Take Up Your Mission*, 9.

Little Colorado River, St. Johns stands at an elevation of nearly 5,700 feet in the White Mountains, high desert prairie that averages less than twelve inches of annual precipitation. Before the Saints' arrival, San Juan had an estimated population of about four hundred, including another two to three hundred in the surrounding villages, with an economy built on small-scale farming, cattle and sheep raising, and freighting supplies to Army encampments in New Mexico and Arizona.[9] The Mormons wanted the entire townsite to themselves. "We would rather buy out the place if we could so as to make a Mormon town of it, and not be mixed with Jews, Mexicans and Gentiles," Apostle Wilford Woodruff wrote regarding Mormon intentions.[10] Mormon leaders instructed Jesse N. Smith, President of the Eastern Arizona Stake, to purchase San Juan, all or in part, and make his home there. But during his visit to San Juan in January 1879, Smith was unimpressed, saying the "water was of very poor quality [and] the settlers seemed low in the scale of intelligence," and so he returned home to Snowflake without making the purchase.[11] Later in the year, Ammon Tenney negotiated a deal with brothers Solomon and Morris Barth to purchase "squatter's rights" to a large portion of the town's land, about 1,200 acres, including substantial water rights to the Little Colorado River. Eventually, the Mormons would pay the brothers 770 cows, 230 calves, and $2,034.60 in cash for an estimated total price of

---

9. The population estimate comes from the 1880 United States Census of the "Village of St. Johns," which was taken in June 1880, by Alfred Ruiz. St. Johns population was 546, including about thirty Mormon families numbering about 150. Most of these Mormons had moved to the area in early 1880 and were living in a section of St. Johns known as Salem. Some Mormon families known to be living in St. Johns at that time were not counted in the census. See also Mark E. Miller, "St. Johns's Saints: Interethnic Conflict in Northeastern Arizona, 1880–85," 72–73.

10. Wilford Woodruff, letter to Brother [Ammon] Tenney, November 24, 1879. Woodruff wrote the letter under the name Lewis Allen, because he was hiding from prosecution for violating federal anti-polygamy laws.

11. Jesse N. Smith, *Journal of Jesse Nathaniel Smith: The Life Story of a Mormon Pioneer 1834–1906*, 232 (January 22, 1879). A few years later when speaking at a St. Johns priesthood meeting, Smith said he thought "the blood of Cain was more predominant in these Mexicans than that of Israel." That is, he thought the St. Johns Mexican-Americans had African-American ancestry and, thus, were not entitled to hold the Mormon priesthood or fully participate in the religion (p. 288, May 6, 1884). This may have also influenced his decision not to purchase St. Johns land and settle there.

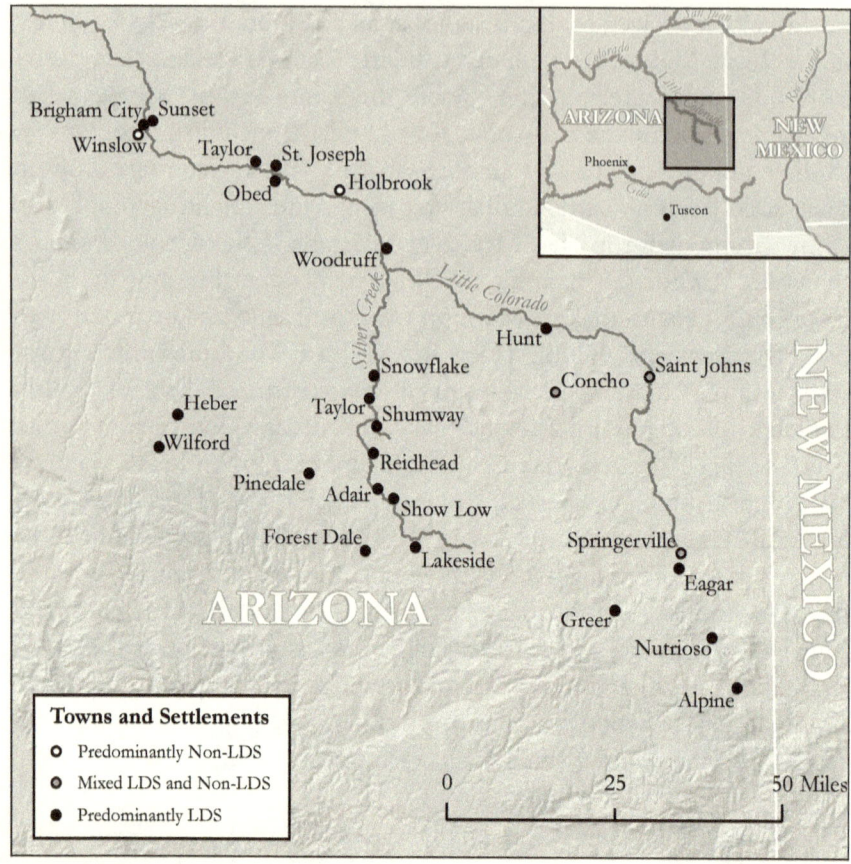

Early Mormon Towns and Settlements Along the Little Colorado River. Map by Abner Hardy, ThinkSpatial, BYU Geography.

$14,734.60.[12] The Mormons kept the deal quiet so that speculators would not jump in and file homestead claims on the townsite before Mormon colonists arrived.

The LeSueur and Gibbons families—both large, extended families—were among the first Mormons to arrive in St. Johns. The LeSueurs in-

---

12. St. Johns Land Records, 114, payment to Barth Brothers. The original bill of sale (November 18, 1879) called for payment of 750 cows, but the quit claim deed, which was written the same day (and signed the next), required payment of 770 cows and $2,000 (C. LeRoy and Mabel R. Wilhelm, *A History of the St. Johns Arizona Stake: The Triumph of Man and His Religion Over the Perils of a Raw Frontier*, 33–36). According to the St. Johns ledger book, the additional 230 calves were paid as interest on the cows, and the additional $34.60 was paid as interest on the $2,000.

cluded brothers John (or "J.T.") and William and two of their sisters, Jane LeSueur Davis and Harriet LeSueur Warner, along with their spouses, children, and sixty-six-year-old mother, Caroline. The four families had immigrated together from Montpelier, Idaho, to Mesa in 1878, but they found the climate too hot for their liking. After fifteen months in Mesa, they packed up their wagons and headed east, looking to settle in either New Mexico or Colorado, or perhaps return to Idaho. However, hostile Native Americans prevented them from traveling any farther east than St. Johns, where they arrived in April 1880. While the LeSueur families were waiting to proceed, visiting leaders from Salt Lake City called them to remain as colonizing missionaries.

The undeveloped countryside surrounding St. Johns initially appeared to have great potential. Unusual rainfall during the past several years had created tablelands and valleys of waist-high grama grass, giving Apache County some of the best grazing pastures in all of Arizona. By 1884, nearly 90 percent of all sheep in Arizona would be raised in Apache. The region's mountains were well-timbered and filled with game. "With its vast deposits of coal, valuable forests of pine, extensive stock ranges and rich farming lands, Apache has all the natural advantages to build up a rich and populous community," wrote Arizona's commissioner of immigration, Patrick Hamilton, who also touted the "many beautiful, clear streams" flowing from the mountains during the spring snowmelt.[13]

Hamilton's job was to promote immigration and economic growth, but with regard to Apache County, his boosterism contained more fantasy than truth.[14] A case in point was the murky Little Colorado River, the main source of water for St. Johns and other Mormon settlements. John Blythe, sent to Arizona to colonize St. Joseph, said the river looked like "a running stream of mud."[15] Another Mormon colonizer described one of the river's tributaries as so thick with red sand that it "looks almost like red

---

13. Patrick Hamilton, *The Resources of Arizona. Its Mineral, Farming, Grazing and Timber Lands; Its History, Climate, Productions, Civil And Military Government, Pre-Historic Ruins, Early Missionaries, Indian Tribes, Pioneer Days, Etc., Etc.*, 95; and 287 (for sheepherding in Apache). See also David King Udall and Pearl Udall Nelson. *Arizona Pioneer Mormon: David King Udall his story and his family 1851–1938*, 71.

14. William H. Lyon. "Live, Active Men, With Plenty of 'Push'": Arizona's Territorial Immigration Commissioners," 149–52.

15. John Blythe, "History of John A. Blythe," 6.

paint, mixed ready for use."¹⁶ The Mormons diverted the Little Colorado for irrigation, but it contained so much sediment that it sometimes damaged the crops. The river and its tributaries ran low in the summer but flooded after downpours, destroying dams and irrigation ditches. When the colonists expressed concern about the river's poor drinking quality, Apostle John Young proclaimed the water to be "wholesome" and promised it would be "palatable" if the Saints faithfully adhered to the Church's health code, called the Word of Wisdom.[17]

St. Johns residents found the water palatable, but barely. A St. Johns Stake history said the river water "was hardly fit for human consumption" and blamed the water for the typhoid and diphtheria epidemics that plagued the Mormon settlements.[18] Kempe family members, who also arrived in 1880, recalled that "when it rained, it was mandatory to put out barrels, dishpans, tubs and buckets to catch the water as it ran off the roofs."[19] It wasn't until the late 1880s that St. Johns resident Mark Hall discovered the McIntosh Spring in the hills about three or four miles east of town. Hall built a home over it and carried the fresh spring water into town three days each week in a large metal tank carried by a horse-drawn wagon, selling the water door to door for five cents per three-gallon bucket. St. Johns residents would rely on the delivery of fresh water via wagon until the town completed a pipeline to McIntosh Spring in 1911.[20]

Water quality wasn't the only problem for Mormon colonists hoping to build a self-sustaining community. Good farmland was scarce. A comprehensive analysis of the climate and soil along the Little Colorado River basin found that the region's elevations above 6,000 feet did not offer reliable growing seasons, while those below 6,000 feet did not receive

---

16. John Tate, "Journal of John W. Tate, October, 1880 to July, 1881," 40–41, (January 8, 1881).

17. Daniel Justin Herman, *Hell on the Range: A Story of Honor, Conscience, and the American West*, 37. After a settler filled a seven-gallon kettle with water from the Little Colorado and allowed the sediment to settle, he found only an inch of water at the top.

18. Wilhelm and Wilhelm, *History of the Saint St. Johns Arizona Stake*, 292.

19. Ellen Greer Rees, "History of Christopher J. Kempe Family," 157.

20. Wilhelm and Wilhelm, *History of the St. Johns Arizona Stake*, 292. Willamelia Smith said her family typically purchased fifteen cents worth of water (nine gallons) from Hall for their drinking and cooking needs, while they used the town's irrigation water (after letting the sediment settle) for washing. From Willamelia Coleman Smith, Interview, June 3, 1985.

St. Johns residents purchased fresh water for five cents a bucket brought in by wagon from a spring four miles away. A pipeline to the town was not completed until 1911. Courtesy Family History Center, St. Johns, Arizona.

sufficient precipitation to produce healthy crops.[21] The thin alkaline soil also limited production. "As a farming country, St. Johns was a flop," said J.T. LeSueur's nephew, Warren Mallory. "The land was full of Salaratus [sic] and the water was full of minerals.'" When his family harvested their wheat, "it was hard to tell whether it was wheat or weeds," Mallory said. "We had to use it for mush and bread. It was so bitter, that we could hardly eat it."[22]

---

21. William S. Abruzzi, *Dam That River! Ecology and Mormon Settlement in the Little Colorado River Basin*, 84. Abruzzi's Chapter 4, "The Little Colorado River Basin," 79–120, provides a detailed examination of the topography, climate, soil, growing season, precipitation, and other environmental conditions in the Little Colorado region.

22. "The Remarkable Memoirs of Warren James Mallory (1868–1945): A Founding Pioneer of Mesa, Arizona, January 18, 1878," 22, 42. Warren Mallory was the son of Charles and Caroline LeSueur Mallory. Caroline, J.T.'s sister, died in Mesa in 1879. Charles moved the family to St. Johns in late 1880 or early 1881, thus joining the four LeSueur families already settled there.

Mormon pioneer Evans Coleman echoed Mallory's assessment, stating that the St. Johns land was "so lacking in fertility one couldn't have raised a disturbance on it with a barrel of whiskey[,] ten Apache warriors and seventeen Texas cowboys. The land surrounding it was no better." Evans Coleman, "Saint Johns Purchase," 1.

The St. Johns Saints, especially in the early days, relied heavily on subsidies and food donations from other Mormon communities to survive.[23] The Mormons eventually planted orchards of fruit trees and grew wheat and other food staples. St. Johns became known for the beautiful poplar trees that lined its streets and served as wind breaks. They also built dams across the Little Colorado River and steered the water to irrigation ditches to water crops. Nevertheless, many farmers struggled for years, even decades, to scratch subsistence in a climate prone to early frosts, prolonged droughts and, when it did rain, destructive floods that destroyed dams and crops. Adding to these challenges, St. Johns and other towns suffered periodic grasshopper infestations that devastated crops. Numerous Mormon settlements along the Little Colorado failed in the early years. All seven of the Mormons' communitarian organizations, called United Orders, eventually disbanded. David K. Udall, the first Mormon bishop in St. Johns, said the region "proved to be a land of extremes, with alternating periods of drouths and floods, undependable seasons, and devastating spring winds."[24]

Despite their hardships, few colonizers doubted the inspired origin of their call to settle the region. If God had purpose in sending them to Arizona and making their work onerous, even cruel, that was His business. It was not theirs to question but to obey and learn, step by step, letting the refiner's fire shape them into more perfect Saints. The four LeSueur families decided to stay in St. Johns rather than continue their journey, because "a call from the Church was not to be ignored."[25]

J.T. LeSueur and his brother, William, built their first home, which their two families shared, by digging a two-room shack into the side of a hill in Salem, the Mormon community located just north of St. Johns's center. They propped up the walls of their new home by setting cedar posts in the ground and filling in the cracks of their front wall with mud.[26] They made do with a dirt roof and floor. For beds, the LeSueurs drove small posts into the ground and wove willows across the posts for

---

23. Joseph Fish, "History of the Eastern Arizona Stake of Zion and of the Establishment of the Snowflake Stake," 68; and Udall, *Arizona Pioneer Mormon*, 74.

24. Udall, *Arizona Pioneer Mormon*, 71.

25. "History of John Davis and His Wife Jane Caroline LeSueur Davis," 3. This history is published in "John and Caroline LeSueur Family."

26. Geneva Greer & Anona C. Heap, "John T. Lesueur [sic] and Geneva Castro [sic]," published in Esther Wiltbank and Zola Whiting, *Lest Ye Forget*, 170.

bedsprings. They would later abandon the dugout when Church leaders directed the Saints to settle on higher ground directly in St. Johns. These were young people: J.T. was twenty-seven years old and his wife, Geneva, twenty-two; William was twenty-three and his wife, Anner Mari, nineteen. Each family had one son, and Geneva was pregnant with another, whom they would name Frank. After getting their families settled, both J.T. and William took off for New Mexico to work on the Atlantic and Pacific Railroad, which was extending its line from Albuquerque to run through Arizona and into southern California. Working separately, they hauled freight, graded roads, sold goods at the railroad commissary, and took on any other work they could find. The construction of the railroad line was a godsend to Mormons throughout the Little Colorado corridor, providing them with needed cash to sustain their new towns and settlements. While the men were gone, Geneva and Anner Mari tended a vegetable garden and corn patch. Geneva made extra cash by knitting clothing for women and babies in St. Johns's Mexican-American community. J. T.'s mother, Caroline, also lived with the family and would stand guard, arming herself with an ax, when strangers came by the house. To cover the family's expenses while he was away, J.T. gave Geneva a package containing $250, which she sewed into her bed tick for safe keeping.[27]

J.T. and William were gone much of the next two years. After the railroad advanced further into Arizona, they were able to work closer to home. When J.T. returned from his last freighting trip in New Mexico, Geneva spotted him as he crossed the valley, and so when he arrived at the shack, she had their two boys, James, four, and Frank, two, standing in front to greet him. J.T. brought $400 in cash. After visiting with his wife, he asked how much remained of the money he had left her. Without answering, Geneva cut open the bed tick with her scissors, pulled out the package, and handed it to her husband. "It was just as I had left it, unopened with the full amount of money in it," J.T. said. "I then decided that if we did not make some success financially, it would not be her fault. . . . I felt that with such a wife I could not fail."[28]

J.T. invested his railroad earnings in the St. Johns Arizona Cooperative Mercantile Institution (ACMI), a Mormon joint-stock store that furnished employment, goods, and credit to local Mormons. He also began working

---

27. "Memoirs of John Taylor LeSueur," published in Don L. LeSueur, comp., *LeSueur Family History: The Descendants of John T. LeSueur and William F. LeSueur* (hereafter refenced as *LeSueur Family History*). J.T.'s memoir is dated June 1, 1938.

28. "Memoirs of John Taylor LeSueur."

After moving to St. Johns in 1880, John "J. T." and Geneva LeSueur lived for more than two years in a two-room dugout they shared with J. T.'s mother and his brother's family. Courtesy Family History Center, St. Johns, Arizona.

at the ACMI, starting out as a salesman and later rising to become the store's supervisor. Over the next fifteen years, he invested in other local businesses as well, often borrowing money to do so. J.T. bought out the St. Johns Drug Store and, with a group of investors, enlarged the operation as the St. Johns Drug Company. In partnership with Bishop Udall and others, he won a mail route contract serving the area. He also went into partnership with two friends to buy and develop a herd of sheep, which he managed with the help of his two oldest sons, James and Frank.

The LeSueur family lived modestly while waiting to see whether these investments would pay off. After J.T. finished working for the railroad, he moved his family from the Salem dugout to a small frame house in St. Johns, papering the walls with illustrated newspapers that provided insulation, decoration, and reading material for the children. Some of the newspapers were pasted upside down, and so James and Frank would stand on their heads to read them.[29] The family made a kitchen table from a large dry goods box and used wooden canned-fruit boxes for chairs. J.T. claimed not to have any exceptional financial ability. "I was cautious in going in debt, only borrowing money when I felt sure I could make

---

29. James Warren LeSueur, "Autobiographical Notes of My Life," 2.

beneficial use of it and could see my way clear to meet my obligation," he said.³⁰ Emerging from the pages of his memoir is a man focused on achieving business success, a man who practiced the virtues of a striving capitalist and entrepreneur: "I am firmly of the opinion that in order to be financially successful[,] it is necessary to carry out in life all these fine grand principles—Industry, Frugality, Economy, Honesty and Temperance."³¹

The call to settle St. Johns would be the last of many colonizing missions served by Bill Gibbons. Born in Kanesville, Iowa, in 1851, Bill was just fifteen years old when Church leaders called him to labor with his father among the Native Americans in St. Thomas, which was then part of Arizona but is now located in Nevada about sixty miles north of present-day Las Vegas. In the winter of 1873, he was called with his father and others to relieve fellow Mormons besieged by hostile Native Americans in Arizona. In the summer of 1874, Bill joined a force of Mormons stationed at Lee's Ferry to prevent hostilities between the Saints and Native Americans. He returned to his home in Glendale after being released in April 1875, but six months later he was called to work among the Hopi in Moenkopi, where he brought his wife and their three young children, including two-year-old Gus. An infant daughter died about a year after their arrival, but two more children would be born in Moenkopi. In the spring of 1878, Apostle Erastus Snow called Bill to do missionary work among the Spanish people in Ramah, New Mexico; Bill would return six months later to help build a woolen factory in Tuba for the Hopi. There he remained with his family until he was called to the St. Johns mission. Quickly able to pick up new languages, he could speak Spanish, as well as the languages of the Paiute, Navajo, Hopi, Ute, and Zuni people.³²

Whenever Bill was called away, his wife, Evaline Augusta Lamb, provided for the family. Called "Gusty" by her family, she raised corn, milked cows, sold butter, and tended a garden, along with whatever else was necessary to sustain the family. Gusty married Bill in 1871 when she was fifteen years old and he twenty. She had their first child less than a month after turning seventeen; their second child, Gus, at eighteen; and her six-

---

30. "Memoirs of John Taylor LeSueur."
31. "Memoirs of John Taylor LeSueur."
32. This biographical information about William Gibbons is found in Andrew Jenson, *Latter-Day Saint Biographical Encyclopedia*, 1:328–329; and Arvin Palmer, comp., *An Arizona Palmer Family History: Selected Sketches of Arthur Palmer and Evaline Augusta Gibbons Palmer and Their Ancestors*, 153.

teenth child, her last, at forty-six. "Sometime he [Bill] would be home two or three months then he would be gone longer than that," Gusty recalled of their early years. "I wonder some time since how we lived."[33] Still, it was a matter of pride with both Gusty and Bill that he never turned down a mission call, no matter how far away or how long he would be gone. "Some of the [Mormon] men would say, 'I will go if some one will look after my family,'" Gusty said. "But he wouldn't do that nor neither would I. I done every kind of work I could get to help things along."[34]

The sacrifices made by the Gibbons family to assist and convert the Moenkopi Hopi reflected the unique place of Native Americans within Mormon theology. Along with the Bible, Mormons believe the Book of Mormon to be a sacred text. The Book of Mormon tells the story of an Israelite family led by God to the American continent in 600 BC. Upon arriving, the family split into two warring factions: the righteous Nephites who followed God's commandments; and the wicked Lamanites, whom God cursed with a dark skin as punishment for straying from His teachings. A thousand years of violent conflict followed. The Lamanites gained the upper hand whenever large numbers of Nephites fell into disbelief; however, Lamanites who repented of their wickedness and returned to God's teachings would see their skins miraculously—and literally—turn white after their conversion.[35] Eventually, the Nephites became as wicked as their Lamanite brothers, and so God allowed the Lamanites to overpower and destroy them. Nineteenth-century Mormons believed that the Indigenous Peoples of North, South, and Central America are the literal descendants of the Lamanites who had been cursed with dark skins. More significantly, they fervently believed that Native Americans throughout the

---

33. Palmer, *Arizona Palmer Family History*, 130.

34. Palmer, 130.

35. Mormons no longer believe that the skins of Native Americans (Lamanites) will turn from dark to white after they embrace Mormonism, but this was not the case for most of the church's history. Even well into the twentieth century, Mormons widely believed and their leaders taught that Native Americans' skins would turn lighter if they converted and obeyed Mormonism's teachings. In the 1981 edition of the Book of Mormon, the Church replaced the phrase "white and delightsome" with "pure and delightsome," based on a change Joseph Smith recommended in 1840. However, other Book of Mormon passages continue to state that God cursed the unbelieving Lamanites with a dark skin, a skin that became white again—"white like unto the Nephites"—after they reconverted. Mormons now interpret the curse and reported change in skin color to be metaphorical or symbolic, rather than literal.

American continents would enthusiastically embrace Mormonism—and become a "white and delightsome" people again—once their true origin as children of Israel was revealed to them through the Book of Mormon. From the Church's earliest days, Mormon leaders sent missionaries to proselytize among Native Americans. Like their Protestant counterparts, the Mormons hoped not just to convert the Lamanites, but also to civilize and turn them into productive farmers and citizens. Mormons expected to succeed where Protestant missionaries had failed, because the Book of Mormon would awaken the Lamanites to their true heritage and destiny. The expected mass conversion of the Lamanite descendants represented one of the signs of the last days.

The Mormons were neither reckless nor naïve when dealing with the Lamanites. Similar to predominant white American sentiments toward Native Americans, the Mormons regarded the Lamanites as savages—mercurial, wild, and prone to thievery and violence. Although Brigham Young famously suggested that it was better to feed Native Americans than fight them, his commitment to peaceful accommodation was not limitless. After just three years in the Utah Territory, Young asked the US government to remove Native Americans from the territory. "We would have taught them to plow & sow, and reap and thresh, but they prefer idleness and theft," Young said.[36] Mormon leaders also tempered expectations of an immediate conversion of Lamanites. Young told Mormon colonists in Utah Valley that the "older Indians would never enter into the New and Everlasting Covenant but that they would die and be damned."[37] In Utah, repeated episodes of conflict and violence were the inevitable result of the competition between Mormons and Native Americans for land and resources.

Nevertheless, the Mormons never completely abandoned their millennial hope to convert and elevate the Lamanites. When the Saints began moving into Arizona in 1876, Young expressed great optimism regarding the redeeming influence the Saints would have upon Arizona's Lamanite tribes. In a July 15, 1876, letter to Mormon leaders in Arizona, the Mormon prophet wrote:

> We desire that the settlements in the Little Colorado be built up to the Lord in righteousness, wherein an example will be set to the surrounding tribes of Lamanites. . . . Treat them with kindness . . . set a proper example. . . .

---

36. Eugene E. Campbell, *Establishing Zion: The Mormon Church in the American West, 1847–1869*, 103.

37. Campbell, 100.

Instruct them in the Gospel. . . . Teach them to live in peace, become free from native vices and become useful citizens in the Kingdom.[38]

Many Arizona Saints shared their prophet's optimism. They interpreted the ancient canal networks, petrographs, and other ruins left by Native Americans as evidence that sophisticated Nephite civilizations had once lived in this region. The Hopi tribe, considered by Young to be of "Nephite blood," seemed a promising prospect for conversion.[39] As late as 1893, the Mormon prophet Wilford Woodruff told a gathering of Saints that he had seen a vision of thousands of Lamanites entering the temple. "They took charge of the temple and could do as much ordinance work in an hour as the other brethren could do in a day," Woodruff said.[40]

The Mormons were well-intentioned. Their missionaries tried to help Arizona's Indigenous People learn useful trades and skills, and they acted as advocates when government promises fell short and mediated disputes with white settlers. But the assistance the Mormons offered—to become Mormons and, essentially, adopt white man's ways—was not assistance Native Americans wanted. It meant abandoning their identity and culture. Mormons who settled St. Johns and the Little Colorado River corridor never questioned government policies that subjugated Arizona's Indigenous People and forced them onto reservations, nor did they question their right to colonize land once populated by Native American nations. The Mormons saw their divine destiny as kingdom builders across the American West. The Native Americans' destiny was to convert to Mormonism. But visions such as Apostle Woodruff's never came to fruition. Only a few hundred Lamanites would be baptized in Arizona. None of them really became part of the Mormon communities or abandoned their native practices and culture.[41]

Despite their lack of proselytizing success, the Lamanite missionaries still contributed to Mormon kingdom building in one important way: they facilitated colonization of the Little Colorado corridor by helping to reduce violence between Mormon settlers and Native American tribes

---

38. Peterson, *Take up Your Mission*, 215.
39. Barry A. Joyce, "The Temple and the Rock: James W. Lesueur and the Synchronization of Sacred Space in the American Southwest," 134. Joyce says that as late as the 1950s, Mesa school children were taught that the regions first settlers "saw in the Salt River Valley many evidences of the truth of the Book of Mormon, covering the passage northward of the Nephites of old" (136n10).
40. Quoted in Jesse N. Smith, *Journal*, 393 (April 8, 1893).
41. Peterson, *Take up Your Mission*, 216.

who had been pushed off their lands.[42] Men like Bill Gibbons developed trusted relationships with local tribes and acted as interpreters who could bridge the language and cultural gap between the Mormons and their Native American neighbors. They helped both sides avoid misunderstandings and intervened to settle disagreements peacefully, creating goodwill that reduced opposition to the Mormons' migration onto traditional tribal lands. Bill's daughter Rhoda Ann, who was born in Moenkopi while her father served there as a missionary, said the Hopi people were visibly upset when the Gibbons family was called to leave Moenkopi and colonize St. Johns. "Mother and Father said the day they loaded up the wagon and were ready to leave, the Hopi came to tell them goodbye and that some of them leaned up against the wagon wheels crying. They didn't want to see them go," she wrote.[43]

Bill Gibbons quickly became a leader within the Mormon's St. Johns community, winning the admiration and friendship of Bishop David K. Udall. Both Udall, age 29, and Gibbons, age 30, had young wives and growing families; both worked unceasingly for the Church, often sacrificing their own well-being to serve the needs of fellow Mormons. Udall selected Gibbons to be one of his two counselors in the bishopric, and in 1887, when Church leaders selected Udall to lead the newly created St. Johns Stake, Udall again chose Gibbons as a counselor. "William H. Gibbons was a zealous, fearless man and understood our Mexican neighbors better than anyone else in our community for he knew their habits and spoke their language fluently. He was town constable and usually carried a six-shooter in his hip pocket, though he never had to use it," Udall said.[44]

During Gibbons's stint as constable, a Mexican-American boy was arrested for murder and placed in the St. Johns jail.[45] One night, Gibbons heard that a mob of white men intended to storm the jail and lynch the boy. He went to the jailhouse, placed his six-shooter across his knees, and waited calmly in the dark with the door unlocked. Fluent in Spanish, he likely offered reassuring company to his young prisoner. Before long, the mob threw open the door, lanterns burning, and started yelling the boy's name. "Stand back," Gibbons shouted. Startled, the mob leader said, "My

---

42. Peterson, 216.
43. Palmer, *Arizona Palmer Family History*, 139.
44. Udall, *Arizona Pioneer Mormon*, 95.
45. Gibbons's daughter, Evaline, describes this incident in two different accounts in Palmer, *Arizona Palmer Family History*, 156, 240.

God, Mr. Bill, I didn't know you were here. Let us have the boy and we will do you no harm."

Gibbons held his ground. "Don't take a step closer or I'll kill the first man that does," he said. The mob backed out, and at the subsequent trial, a jury found the boy innocent.

The Mormons also elected Gibbons as water master to oversee the construction of irrigation ditches that would tap into the Little Colorado River and provide water to St. Johns homes, fields, and gardens.[46] Once the channels were in place, he monitored water usage to ensure that townspeople took only their allotted share. This was no easy task. As Arizona pioneer Joseph Fish noted, the scarcity of water in St. Johns "caused litigation and local strife."[47] People were assigned narrow windows of time for using the water, sometimes taking their "turns" in the middle of the night, and many were tempted to take more than their share when they thought no one was watching.[48] Gibbons often had to apply the skills he honed as a mediator in disputes between Native Americans and Mormons to settle disagreements about water use. "Many times in the night he would be called to go along the city ditch and stop the Mexicans or the Whites from stealing water," one of his daughters recalled.[49]

Through their industry and thrift, Bill and Gusty were building a foundation for economic security when, on August 15, 1888, Bill got a hand caught in the blades of the town's threshing machine.[50] The threshing machine of the 1880s was a noisy, complex, labor-saving device weighing over 2,000 pounds and consisting of wheels, belts, sharp blades, and shaking equipment that removed the husks and chaff as grain moved through the machine. The belts were powered by horses walking on a conveyer belt. Communities and towns often owned a thresher jointly and shared its use due to its expense. Bill felt apprehensive when it was his turn to feed grain into the thresher, as did his wife, Gusty, who was more than

---

46. Udall, *Arizona Pioneer Mormon*, 84–85.

47. Fish, "History of the Eastern Arizona Stake," 66.

48. Warren Mallory recalled, "Water for irrigation was scarce and of very poor quality. We would take the water in turns of a very few hours each. These turns would come at all hours of day and night, and many were the times we got up at 12, or 2, or 3 o'clock in the night to take care of this little bit of water" ("Remarkable Memoirs of Warren James Mallory," 42).

49. Palmer, *Arizona Palmer Family History*, 155.

50. Details of the accident are provided by two of Bill's daughters, Rhoda and Eva, in Palmer, *Arizona Palmer Family History*, 141–42, 155–56, 183–84.

eight months pregnant and haunted by dark dreams and premonitions. She asked him not to do it, but Bill felt it was his responsibility, given that they would be working on a stack of grain at their house. "I'll have to go as they are expecting me," he said.

Shortly after Bill began feeding grain into the thresher, his left hand got caught in the blades and the machine started pulling him in. Two men standing nearby grabbed him around the waist and held on while someone ran to stop the horses. On the other end of the thresher, Will Gibbons, Bill's oldest son, saw his father's bloody glove come through and knew at once something was wrong. He ran around the thresher to find his father sitting on the ground as the other the men desperately tied cloths around his hand to stop the bleeding. The blades had completely mangled Bill's hand all the way to his wrist.

Because Bill's wife was pregnant, the men carried him to his father's house and called for a doctor to amputate the hand. Bill was pale and suffering, having lost a lot of blood, when the Mormon elders administered a healing blessing that evening. The doctor, who was not a Mormon, arrived just as the elders were giving the blessing.[51] Seeing what he regarded as superstition, the doctor turned around and stormed out of the house. As he mounted his horse to leave, one of Bill's friends, also a non-Mormon, tried to get the doctor to return, but he refused. "If they want their Mormon doctors they can have them," the doctor said. Bill's friend angrily pulled the man from his horse and ordered him back into the house. The doctor gave Bill a swig of whiskey to kill the pain, took a large swallow himself, and amputated the hand. Gusty stayed at her in-laws' house so she could care for Bill while he recovered. Two weeks later, she gave birth to a baby girl. Bill insisted that they name her Evaline after her mother.

While Bill convalesced, the family buried the amputated hand, placing it in a padded box with the fingers slighted curled at the second joint, giving it a relaxed look. But sometime afterward, Bill complained of pain in his missing hand, a common phenomenon known as "phantom pain," which occurs in amputated limbs. At Bill's direction, "the box was dug up and the fingers straightened out for the hand to lie flat, as he wanted it to be," his daughter Rhoda said. "After this was done his hand he had lost no longer hurt him."

---

51. The 1880 census lists just one physician living in St. Johns: Benjamin Blake, a twenty-five-year-old man from West Virginia. Whether Blake is the physician is unknown.

Bill and Gusty Gibbons initially struggled but eventually gained a firm financial foothold in St. Johns. In this circa 1893 photograph are (left to right) *Back:* Loman, Rhoda, Will, Gus; *Middle:* Bill, James, Gusty, David; *Front:* Eva, Ione, Junius, John, and Edward. Courtesy Jeanette Hancock.

The Gibbons family struggled in those early years. Gusty sometimes wouldn't eat at mealtime, pretending she wasn't hungry, so there would be enough food for her children. "We came here [St. Johns] and went through some pretty hard times for the want of something to eat and wear," she recalled.[52]

In laboring to establish a viable community in St. Johns, the Gibbons, LeSueurs, and other Mormon families faced not only a hostile desert environment but also implacable opposition from their Mexican-American and non-Mormon white neighbors. The Mormons had purchased the entire west section of St. Johns, along with water rights to the Little Colorado River, from Solomon "Sol" and Morris Barth, German Jews who had married into the Mexican-American community. After emigrating to the United States, Sol worked as a stockman, trader, and freighter providing

---

52. Palmer, *Arizona Palmer Family History*, 130.

grain to the US army in New Mexico and Arizona. He eventually led a group of New Mexican families to the Little Colorado River and established San Juan, where he became the town's leading citizen, owning a mercantile store, freighting business, and hotel, as well as farmland and an extensive herd of sheep. San Juan's name was later anglicized to St. Johns.[53]

Sol and Morris Barth took advantage of the Mexican-Americans' custom of holding their land in common without formal title to the land. The two brothers quietly laid claim themselves to the St. Johns townsite and then sold a large portion of the planned town to the Mormons.[54] To avoid competition with speculators, the Mormons did not publicize their purchase or planned move into St. Johns. Neither did the Barth Brothers, perhaps because their rights to the town's land and river water were highly questionable. It would take years to settle the legal disputes arising from the sale. The town's Mexican-American residents raised no objections when the LeSueurs and other Mormon families settled north of St. Johns in Salem, but they immediately protested when Bishop David Udall arrived in October 1880 and began laying out town lots on the Mormon land adjacent to the established village.[55] The Mexican-Americans had intended to expand their community into the area of town purchased by the Mormons, but now they lay trapped between the Mormons on the west and the river on the east, giving them no room for growth.[56] The burgeoning Mormon population of farmers and ranchers would also siphon away precious water resources and increase competition for grazing land, potentially threatening the livelihoods of the Mexican-Americans.

A few days after Udall began surveying the Mormon town lots, he received a letter signed by thirty Mexican-American citizens demanding

---

53. In justifying the change from San Juan to St. Johns, local postmaster Ebenezer Stover reportedly said, "It is time those Mexicans found out they are living in the United States." Miller, "St. Johns's Saints," 73. Stover would become a member of the anti-Mormon faction.

54. Miller, 74.

55. Udall, *Arizona Pioneer Mormon*, 70–71, said that when he arrived in St. Johns in October 1880, the St. Johns Ward consisted of about fifty Mormon families living in Salem and encompassing the Meadows (ten miles north), Walnut Grove (twenty miles south), and Cebolla, near Ramah, New Mexico.

56. As many as seventeen Spanish-speaking families were already living in the new Mormon section, but, under the terms of the sale, they were allowed to stay. See Wilhelm and Wilhelm, *History of the St. Johns Arizona Stake*, 35; and Tom Beal, "St. Johns hardships legion, but Mormons stood firm," *Arizona Daily Star*, September 18, 2011, 1, 7.

that he stop. The Mormon colonizers would cause "entire and complete damage to our town and the Mexican population," they said.[57] The existing residents wanted to avoid "difficulties and consequences," but threatened to "place all the means in our power and within our reach to impede the establishment of the Mormons in the surroundings of this town."[58]

The Mormons soon recognized that their neighbors had good reason to be aggrieved. "They looked upon us as enemies, who had come to encroach upon their old 'San Juan' settled by them in 1873," Udall said. "The Mexicans resented us and we did not blame them very much. Their 'squatters' rights' had not been properly respected by those who sold the land to our people."[59]

Still, the Mormons had no intention of leaving. After receiving the call to colonize St. Johns, they had sold their farms, homes, livestock, and other possessions to raise money for the wagons, teams, and provisions needed to immigrate, often traveling hundreds of miles across rugged mountains and desert wastelands. The Church had already made a significant down payment on St. Johns, with a final installment due soon.[60] Mormon leaders regarded St. Johns as a key outpost in the expanding Mormon kingdom. Except in extraordinary circumstances, Mormons would not abandon their colonizing mission. The calls as colonizing missionaries "were as binding as calls to foreign missions and they were not free to leave until released," wrote Evans Coleman, whose family was called to settle the Apache County town of Alpine.[61]

More than a little irony attaches to the attitudes of the Mormons and Mexican-Americans. Each wanted the town for themselves; each regarded the other as an undesirable neighbor. The Mexican-Americans, who viewed the Mormons as blindly obedient fanatics, joined with the Anglos to deny funding for Mormon public schools and exclude Mormons from teaching

---

57. Marcus Baca et al. to D. K. Udall, October 26, 1880, in Udall, *Arizona Pioneer Mormon*, 78.

58. Udall, 79.

59. Udall, 77.

60. The St. Johns Saints would eventually repay church headquarters for the money paid to the Barth brothers.

61. Evans Coleman to Dear Dave, May 2, 1946. Coleman said his father, who was the Alpine bishop, eventually asked for and received an official release from the Mormon prophet, Lorenzo Snow, allowing the family to move from Apache County.

positions due to their illegal practice of polygamy.[62] Many Mormons considered the old San Juan community of whites and Mexican-Americans to be of "the worst element " and "low filthy habits," as well as "low in the scale of intelligence."[63] Although it would be wrong to say the Mormons harbored no prejudices against people of Mexican descent, their initial desire to buy out the entire Mexican-American community derived primarily from their desire to live, as much as possible, separately from the corrupting influence of the outside world. They established their own cooperative businesses, often traded only among themselves, and voted as a bloc to protect their interests and increase their power. Mormons did not want to live among "Gentiles" of any ethnic group or race, including whites. The Mexican-Americans could also be insular, with a desire to maintain their own religious and cultural practices in the face of an encroaching American culture. Their wariness of living among the Mormons is understandable. Not only were the Mormons hemming them in against the river, but the Mormons' large numbers and clannishness threatened to marginalize the Mexican-American community, both politically and economically. Subsequent actions by both groups exacerbated rather than relieved tensions.

Although it was the Barth brothers who deceived the Mexican-American people by secretly selling the entire west side of St. Johns, the Mexican-Americans directed their anger at the Mormon newcomers. Sol Barth, after inviting the Mormons to settle in St. Johns, also turned against them. Barth and other local businessmen had anticipated brisk sales and burgeoning profits when the newcomers arrived, but they quickly saw that the Mormons' growing numbers would threaten their own economic and political interests. Not only did the St. Johns Saints establish jointly held businesses—including the ACMI mercantile store, a flour mill, and a stock raising company—but they primarily patronized their own stores, making non-Mormon business owners feel as if they were competing against the corporate Church. To counter the Mormon influence, Barth helped lead a

---

62. Jed Woodworth, "Public Schooling in Territorial Arizona: Republicanism, Protestantism, and Assimilation," 116. In St. Johns, local authorities made the teacher qualifying exams intentionally impossible for Mormon applicants to pass.

63. Fish, "History of the Eastern Arizona Stake," 62, 67; and Jesse N. Smith, *Journal*, 232 (January 22, 1879).

coalition of Apache County's non-Mormon and Mexican-American citizens that controlled local political offices and the courts through the mid-1880s.[64]

The Mormons contended that their chief opponents—known as the St. Johns Ring—held a firm grip on power through rampant fraud and corruption. The St. Johns Ring also used that power to bring nuisance lawsuits and issue judgments against the Mormons. Sol Barth often served as foreman on grand juries that indicted Mormons for such crimes as unlawful assembly, larceny, and perjury.[65] In 1884, Mormon opponents founded the St. Johns *Apache Chief* under publisher George McCarter, who called for the violent expulsion of the Saints. "How did Missouri and Illinois get rid of the Mormons? By the use of the shot gun and the rope," McCarter wrote in May 1884, adding, "In a year from now the Mormons will have the power here and the Gentiles had better leave. Don't let them get it. Desperate diseases need desperate remedies. The Mormon disease is a desperate one and the rope and shot gun is the only cure."[66]

The anti-Mormon fervor in Apache County flourished amid broader efforts, primarily led by the Republican Party, to diminish Mormon political influence and root out polygamy in the Western territories.[67] In an 1884 Independence Day speech, Arizona Chief Justice Sumner Howard warned that the growing Mormon population threatened to put Arizona "under the vicious influence of a political polygamous priesthood at Salt Lake City."[68] At the same time, Arizona Governor F. A. Tritle called for a crackdown on Mormon polygamists; territorial lawmakers obliged by passing legislation that required Mormon voters to disavow belief in polygamy.[69] Antagonisms boiled over in 1885 when Arizona authorities convicted five polygamists of violating the territory's anti-bigamy laws and sentenced three of the men to four years of imprisonment in the Detroit

---

64. Miller, "St. Johns's Saints," 66–99, provides a detailed examination of the early conflict between the St. Johns Mormons and their neighbors. See also, Scott E. Fritz, "Merchants of St. Johns, 1876–1885: A Study in Group Formation, Bigoted Rhetoric, and Economic Competition." The list of jointly held Mormon businesses in St. Johns comes from Fish, "History of the Eastern Arizona Stake," 66.

65. Miller, "St. Johns's Saints," 83–84.

66. *Apache Chief*, May 30, 1884, quoted in Peterson, *Take Up Your Mission*, 229.

67. Edward Leo Lyman, "Elimination of the Mormon Issue from Arizona Politics, 1889–1894," 205–28; and JoAnn W. Bair and Richard L. Jensen, "Prosecution of the Mormons in Arizona Territory in the 1880s," 25–46.

68. *Apache Chief*, July 18, 1884, quoted in Peterson, *Take Up Your Mission*, 230.

69. Lyman, "Elimination of the Mormon Issue in Arizona Politics," 207–8.

House of Correction. Mormon Bishop David Udall had been one of the chief targets of the prosecution, but he escaped conviction because his second wife went into hiding and could not be found to testify against him. Udall's opponents next charged him with perjury in an unrelated case, using trumped up evidence to secure conviction. Udall received a three-year sentence to be served in the Detroit House of Correction, where he arrived September 2, 1885, handcuffed to a convicted counterfeiter.

After helping orchestrate Udall's conviction, the St. Johns Ring began losing its influence within Apache County. The honorable bishop's prosecution won him sympathy even from many of the Mormons' enemies, who believed they had gone too far with their manufactured charges.[70] Several Ring leaders, including John Lorenzo Hubbell, Charles Gutterson, and Alfred Ruiz, sent letters to Democratic President Grover Cleveland requesting a pardon for Udall. The Mormon bishop served less than four months in the Detroit prison before he and the imprisoned polygamists received pardons from President Cleveland, allowing the men to return to their Arizona homes. Meanwhile, members of the Ring got caught up in their own scandals. In 1887, Solomon Barth was convicted of destroying county records and forging county warrants.[71] He was sentenced to ten years in the Yuma prison, though he was pardoned after serving two years. That same year, Francisco Baca was convicted of embezzling more than $11,000 while serving as Apache County deputy treasurer; and in a civil and criminal case, Nathan Barth was fined $500 and ordered to pay Morris Barth's widow $9,000 as part of a settlement in which he also agreed to leave the territory.[72] Mormon relations with their neighbors, including the Mexican-American community, gradually improved as Sol Barth, Hubbell, and other ringleaders began accepting the reality of the Mormon presence in St. Johns.

The breakup of the St. Johns Ring opened economic and political opportunities for many Mormon colonizers. The Gibbons family encountered tough times after Bill lost his hand in the thresher, but their fortunes improved when he was elected county treasurer in 1891 and

---

70. Peterson, *Take Up Your Mission*, 237; and Miller, "St. Johns's Saint," 97.

71. The county warrants were essentially checks or promises to pay, which the county issued when cash was short. Barth was accused of fraudulently increasing the value of warrants, such as taking a $90 warrant and changing it to $190 (by adding a one) and depositing the "raised" warrant in his bank account.

72. *St. Johns Herald*, September 22, 1887, 3.

again in 1893. He also served on the Apache County Board of Supervisors in 1895 and 1897. It probably helped that the two oldest Gibbons boys, Will and Gus, who turned eighteen and sixteen years old in 1890, were old enough to contribute to the family's livelihood. Like other families, the Gibbons maintained a garden and fruit orchard on their town lot.[73] Bill also purchased a herd of sheep and operated a ranch west of Springerville, which steadied the family income and provided work for Gusty and their children, who spent the summers at the ranch tending sheep and spinning yarn from the wool.[74]

J.T. LeSueur probably benefited the most from the improving relations. In October 1886, Apache County's Citizen's Ticket nominated him for treasurer as part of an effort to clean up the county's finances that had been plagued by fraud and theft. Not only had cash gone missing in prior years, but the county's finances were in such disarray that its warrants—that is, its promises to pay—were getting only sixty-five cents on the dollar. In touting LeSueur's candidacy, the *St. Johns Herald* praised "his modest worth, honorable record and stirling [sic] business qualifications."[75] LeSueur received 65 percent of the 902 votes cast to win the 1887–1888 term as Apache County treasurer.[76] "There never was any trouble about county moneys or accounts being well kept with him [LeSueur] in there," said George Crosby, who later served as the county's district attorney and worked closely with LeSueur in both church and government settings.[77]

After serving a two-year term as county treasurer, J.T. was elected Judge of the Superior Court and then Democratic representative to the territorial legislature. After that, he never again ran for office in Apache County, joking that he didn't want to jeopardize his winning streak. Still, LeSueur continued to wield considerable influence. His fellow citizens called upon him to lead numerous government, business, and commu-

---

73. *St. Johns Herald*, September 13, 1888, 3, praised the flavorful taste of peaches from Gibbons's St. Johns orchard.

74. In July 1900, Gibbons owned 250 sheep and fifteen acres of land in Eagar, according to the minutes of the Apache County Board of Supervisors, July 9, 1900, 89.

75. *St. Johns Herald*, October 21, 1886, 1.

76. *St. Johns Herald*, November 18, 1886, 3.

77. George H. Crosby, Jr., "As My Memory Recalls: Stories of the Colonizing of the Little Colorado River Country," 43. This reminiscence is a collection of newspaper columns that Crosby wrote for local newspapers and compiled by his daughter, Laprele Crosby Nunnery.

John "J.T." and Geneva LeSueur invested in numerous business projects to provide for their nine children. Two more boys would follow. In this circa 1897 photograph are (left to right) *Back:* Ray, Frank, Alice, James; *Front:* Nelle, Paul, Geneva, John, Karl, Charley, Leo. Photograph in author's possession.

nity projects, and he served as a Mormon Stake High Councilman from 1887 to 1900. "As long as he stayed in Apache County he was a power in local politics, by odds the strongest man in the Democratic party—close-mouthed, clear-headed and with lots of influence, and never flying off on a tangent," Crosby said.[78]

LeSueur enjoyed even greater success in business, where he saw many of his earlier investments pay off handsomely. These included a thriving sheep business, mail routes, a drug store, and the Mormon's ACMI co-operative store, where he held dividend-paying stock and rose to become the store's supervisor. In 1897, after the weekly *St. Johns Herald* (formerly the anti-Mormon *Apache Chief*) fell into mortgage foreclosure, he purchased the paper and ran it as the proprietor. He sold it for a profit eighteen months later. In September 1899, the *St. Johns Herald* identified J.T. LeSueur as the sixth richest taxpayer in Apache County with an assessed

---

78. Crosby, 43.

J.T. and Geneva LeSueur lived with their eleven children across the street from the Mormon chapel in one of St. Johns's most elegant homes. The home was built in 1891. Courtesy Arizona State Library, Archives and Public Records, Archives Division. No. 96-2106.

property valuation of nearly $18,000. Four of the five taxpayers listed ahead of him were business operations.[79]

For all their good fortune, J.T. and Geneva LeSueur could not escape the harsh realities of the region's punishing environment. They still had to purchase fresh water by the bucket from the water wagon and put out pots and pans to catch rainwater, just like everyone else. Their home had no electricity, running water, or flush toilets. Like other frontier families, they emptied and washed bed pans daily, scoured and scrubbed floors from their knees, and washed clothes by hand. Their family wasn't perfect. One of their sons, thirteen-year-old Charley, was convicted of petty larceny in December 1898 after he and four other boys broke into several stores, certainly an embarrassment for such a prominent family.[80] Another time, J.T. stepped in after his oldest sons, James and Frank, had let a family horse run in a race held by raucous cowboys. One of the cowboys wanted to run the horse in another race with Frank riding as the jockey, but he

---

79. "Who Pays the Taxes?" *St. Johns Herald*, September 30, 1899, 4. In July 1900, LeSueur owned 800 sheep, according to the minutes of the Apache County Board of Supervisors, July 10, 1900, 93.

80. Charles P. Anderson, *Journal of Charles P. Anderson: Writings from 1856–1913*, 28 (December 22, 1898). Anderson served as the St. Johns bishop for eleven years beginning in 1892.

couldn't find anyone willing to bet against Frank. It's unclear whether J.T. stopped further racing to protect his horse or keep his sons away from the horse-racing crowd.[81] But overall, by 1900, J.T. and Geneva had carved out a niche as major contributors to their religious and civic communities. When they moved to St. Johns as young parents in 1880, they lived in a cramped dugout with a dirt floor and ceiling. Twenty years later, J.T. and Geneva lived in the center of town across the street from the ward chapel in one of St. Johns's largest and most elegant homes. They had ten children, with one more to come.

---

81. James Warren LeSueur, "My Recollection of Pioneer Days," in *LeSueur Family History*.

CHAPTER 2

BUTCH CASSIDY AND THE WILD BUNCH

While the LeSueur and Gibbons families labored as colonizing missionaries in St. Johns, another Mormon, Butch Cassidy, was making a name for himself as the leader of one of the West's most notorious outlaw gangs. After his release from a Wyoming prison in 1896, Cassidy and fellow gang members executed a series of high-profile bank and train heists over the next several years, making off with hundreds of thousands of dollars in stolen currency. Although a few of the outlaws were captured, Cassidy always escaped, adding to his reputation as a master criminal. Lawmen throughout the Western states and territories watched eagerly for their chance to capture the elusive bandit, while detectives with the Pinkerton National Detective Agency worked undercover to expose Cassidy and his gang. Neither the lawmen nor the Pinkertons were having much success until early 1900, when a Pinkerton agent discovered that Cassidy was working as a trail boss at the WS Ranch in Alma, New Mexico. The unmasking of Cassidy's identity would set in motion the events leading to the murders of Frank LeSueur and Gus Gibbons by his Wild Bunch gang. The story of the Wild Bunch and the murders naturally begins with Butch Cassidy.

Robert LeRoy Parker was born April 13, 1866, in Beaver, Utah, to Maximilian "Maxi" and Ann Gillies Parker.[1] Both his parents had emigrated with their families from the United Kingdom and travelled with Mormon pioneers to Salt Lake City in 1856. Maxi, who was twelve years old at the time, helped pull and push the Parkers' handcart. The Gillies family traveled with a traditional wagon company that got caught up in a snowstorm and had to be rescued along with other handcart companies. Ann, who was ten, would have walked alongside the wagon much of the way. After arriving in Utah, Maxi's father, Robert, was called to settle in Beaver to help establish a woolen mill, while Ann's father, also named Robert, was called to Beaver as a skilled carpenter and cabinet maker.

---

1. Some sources have "Maximillian," but a birth registration record on ancestry.com, as well as other documents, suggest that "Maximilian" is the correct spelling.

In 1862, at age eighteen, Maxi returned twice to St. Louis to help guide emigrating Saints to Utah. He subsequently met Ann and married her on Ann's nineteenth birthday, July 12, 1865. They first settled in Beaver and later moved to Circle Valley, near the town of Circleville, in 1879.[2]

Much of what is known about Cassidy's youth comes from his sister, Lula Betenson. She was born in 1884, the year Cassidy left home, and so she did not know her brother personally, gleaning her information from her parents and siblings. Called "LeRoy" by his parents and "Bob" by his siblings, Butch was the oldest of thirteen children. He grew up in a poor but stable family. Like many pioneers, Butch's father took up a variety of jobs to provide for his family. In Beaver, Maxi delivered mail. After moving to Circle Valley, he planted wheat, hauled wood, and worked for mining companies, often at locations far from home. The family lived in a cramped, two-room cabin, and like many of their Circle Valley neighbors, they struggled to make a successful go of farming. The spring winds blew so hard across the valley that sandstorms pulled the seeds from the ground, forcing Maxi and other farmers to replant their seeds two and sometimes three times.[3] Ann was a devout Church member who strived to raise their children as active Mormons. Maxi may have been equally faithful in the early years of their marriage, because on November 14, 1868, he and Ann travelled to Salt Lake City to be sealed together as husband and wife in the Endowment House.[4]

In Beaver, which had two Mormon wards (or congregations), the Parker family would have enjoyed the same opportunities to attend church meetings as did the LeSueur and Gibbons families in St. Johns.[5] Bob would have heard inspirational stories of Mormonism's founding prophet, Joseph Smith, and his successor, Brigham Young. He would have been taught Christian beliefs from the New Testament and Book of Mormon and

---

2. For Butch Cassidy's family and his youth in Utah, see Lula Parker Betenson and Dora Flack, *Butch Cassidy, My Brother*, 7–51; Bill Betenson, *Butch Cassidy, My Uncle: A Family Portrait*, 29–34; Thom Hatch, *The Last Outlaws: The Lives and Legends of Butch Cassidy and the Sundance Kid*, 9–41; Charles Leerhsen, *Butch Cassidy: The True Story of an American Outlaw*, 33–53; and Richard Patterson, *Butch Cassidy: A Biography*, 1–11.

3. See Betenson and Flack, *Butch Cassidy, My Brother*, 33; and Rodney Garth Dalton, "From Knights to Dreamers: The Journey of Our Utah Dalton Family from Early 1100 AD to 2007 AD and Beyond," vol. 3, ch. 9.

4. Parker family records at familysearch.org.

5. Bob Goodwin, who is preparing an article on Butch Cassidy's early years, helped me sort through details of Cassidy's childhood.

urged to study and pray so that he might one day be a missionary and serve in other church callings. However, after the family moved to their remote Circle Valley ranch when Bob was thirteen, the opportunities to fellowship with other Saints were limited. In fact, a Mormon ward was not established in nearby Circleville until after Bob left home. Over time, Maxi's faith also wavered. He attended church irregularly, if at all, and drank and smoked, both violations of the Mormon health code. Maxi nearly turned against Mormonism following a land dispute with a fellow church member. In those days, Mormons took their civil disagreements to their bishops, rather than to court, and Maxi's bishop ruled against him. Whether the Parkers were actually cheated or treated unfairly is difficult to verify, but Maxi believed he had been wronged. "He was so hurt, he would have left the church if it hadn't been for Mother," Maxi's daughter recalled.[6]

The Parker boys largely followed their father's example and as they got older made themselves scarce at meeting times. Mormonism never seemed to take root in Bob or many of his siblings. Bob eventually stopped attending church. Still, he was hardworking and industrious, and as a teenager he took outside jobs to help support the family when he wasn't needed at home. In the evenings at the isolated Parker ranch, the parents and children entertained themselves by telling stories and singing, with Bob playing the harmonica.

Bob longed for more than Circle Valley or his family could provide. At about age thirteen, he was accused of stealing a saddle.[7] Not too long after, he became friends with a minor rustler, Mike Cassidy, who taught Bob how to use a gun, ride, rope and brand horses and cattle, and rustle livestock.[8] In June 1884, shortly after he turned eighteen and while his father was away on business, Bob announced that he was leaving Circle Valley, saying he wanted to go somewhere that had higher paying jobs. "There's no excitement around here," he told his mother. When she countered that he could have a bright future in Circle Valley, Bob vigorously disagreed. "I look at the struggle you and Dad have had, and it don't look very good to me," he said. Still feeling bitter about the bishop's decision against his father, Bob added, "Always somebody to cheat you out of what you've got coming—like the time you lost the homestead. If it isn't some

---

6. Betenson and Flack, *Butch Cassidy, My Brother*, 34.

7. Charles Kelly, *The Outlaw Trail: A History of Butch Cassidy and His Wild Bunch*, 11; *Eastern Utah Advocate* (Price), May 19, 1898, 1; and Pinkerton's National Detective Agency records, Box 89, Folder 8.

8. Patterson, *Butch Cassidy*, 7.

righteous saint getting the best of you, then it's the weather that's agin you, freezing the stock or the crops."[9]

Bob left the next morning with a couple of friends. He raised the cash for the trip by selling rustled cattle to two neighbors. The Parkers were convinced that those neighbors, who were cohorts of Mike Cassidy, had rustled the cattle themselves and then claimed they bought them from Bob to throw suspicion on him. In the family lore, Bob took the fall for a crime he did not commit. But the more likely explanation is that Bob indeed rustled the cattle, and that's why he hurried out of town, even if it meant not saying goodbye to his father.[10] He didn't want to be around when the crime was uncovered.

Without the constraints of family or Mormonism, Bob began exploring a new life and persona as Roy Parker. He had grown to 5'9" inches, athletic and strong at 165 pounds, with light brown hair, blue eyes, and a friendly, open face. His Pinkerton card notes that Cassidy "has a remarkably square jaw." He rambled around, working on ranches in Utah, Wyoming, and Colorado for several years before landing in Telluride, where he found work leading pack mules laden with ore down the mountain from the mines.[11] The work was onerous and offered little reward, and so he drifted into other jobs as well. His sister said he sent home some of his earnings. He gambled on horses and became friends with Matt Warner, who also grew up as a Mormon cowboy in Utah.[12] Both young men expressed disdain for the profligate "smart alecks" they met in Telluride, which Warner described as "a surprising place of saloons, gambling dives, dance halls, and board sidewalks, where thousands of strange, crazy people we didn't like at first, swarmed, pulled amazing scads of money out of their pockets, and tried to gamble it off or throw it away on drinks and dance-hall girls as fast as they could, and who tricked, robbed, shot, and stabbed each other to an amazing extent."[13]

Roy told Warner, "I feel like you do about these lady-fingered city sneaks."[14]

---

9. Betenson and Flack, 45.

10. Matt Warner, *The Last of the Bandit Riders*, 107, said that Butch fled Circleville and was chased into Colorado because he rustled cattle *and* stole some horses from a neighbor.

11. Betenson, *Butch Cassidy, My Uncle*, 37–41.

12. Warner's birth name was Willard Erastus Christiansen. He was born April 12, 1864, in Ephraim, Utah.

13. Warner, *Last of the Bandit Riders*, 106.

14. Warner, 107.

Roy and Warner had a high time racing and betting on horses, spending liberally at saloons and bawdy houses. If Warner is to be believed, they also shared liberally with neighbors and friends, and eventually ran through their earnings. After five years away from home, Roy was again broke with no prospects for work—at least, none that he cared for. Roy's past crimes in Utah had been relatively minor. He had perhaps stolen a saddle and couple of horses, and engaged in some rustling and rebranding of cattle, making him what Warner called a "half-outlaw."[15] Petty rustling and thievery were not uncommon in the West, nor were such activities out of step in a Gilded Age characterized by corrupt politicians and rapacious Robber Barons.[16] But on June 22, 1889, Roy and Warner teamed up with Warner's brother-in-law, outlaw Tom McCarty, and a fourth man to rob Telluride's San Miguel Valley Bank. Warner said the young men understood the robbery would turn them into full-fledged outlaws with virtually no chance of turning back. "But the stakes looked so big we was willing to take that chance," Warner said. "The adventure seemed so great it purty [sic] near took our breaths away."[17]

The four bandits were assisted by others, including Dan Parker, Roy's twenty-one-year-old brother, who may have cut the telegraph wires and held the relay horses.[18] The bandits made off with more than $20,000 in a brazen daylight robbery. Unfortunately, an acquaintance identified them during their flight, and so posses chased them into Utah, knowing precisely whom they were looking for. They hid in Brown's Park, Utah, and Star Valley, Wyoming, both known gathering spots for outlaws. Eventually, Roy split off from the others and settled in Wyoming's Fremont County, where he made his home for most of the next six years. He first adopted the alias "George Parker," then "George Cassidy," presumably a nod to Mike Cassidy, the man who taught him how to wrangle and rustle livestock. Some say he acquired the nickname "Butch" because he worked in a butcher shop, though no one knows for sure. He continued using a variety of aliases throughout his career, but he would become known to his friends—and law officers—as Butch Cassidy.

Once resettled in Wyoming, Cassidy appears to have resumed the life of a "half-outlaw." He and a new friend, Al Hainer, started a ranch as horse dealers on Horse Creek in north Fremont County. Whatever money Cassidy had brought with him from the Telluride heist was quickly ex-

---

15. Warner, 117, 123.
16. Leerhsen, *Butch Cassidy*, 54.
17. Warner, *Last of the Bandit Riders*, 118.
18. Betenson, *Butch Cassidy, My Uncle*, 48.

Robert LeRoy Parker, alias Butch Cassidy, was a popular, skilled cowboy, but the young Mormon couldn't resist the easy money that came with rustling and robbing. In this 1894 prison photo, the twenty-eight-year-old Cassidy displays what the Pinkertons called his "remarkably square jaw." Courtesy Wyoming State Archives, Wyoming State Penitentiary Photo Collection, No. 187, Butch Cassidy, Mug Shot.

hausted, likely gambled away, thus necessitating the new venture.[19] Cassidy and Hainer soon gained reputations as horse thieves who rarely purchased horses but always had plenty to sell.[20] Cassidy also legitimately acquired a handful of steers and horses with Hainer and another friend, Jacob Snyder,

---

19. Leerhsen, *Butch Cassidy*, 106, states that Cassidy deposited $17,500 in a Lander bank and went flat broke after a month. However, the amount greatly exceeds what would reasonably have been Cassidy's share of the Telluride bank robbery.

20. Kelly, *The Outlaw Trail*, 53.

apparently to build his own ranch and herd. At various times, he also worked for some of the larger cattle outfits, gaining a reputation as a top cow hand. But rustling's easy money was hard to resist, and so Cassidy and Hainer continued stealing and selling other people's horses.

The rampant horse stealing by Cassidy and others eventually created a backlash among Wyoming's big ranchers.[21] It's impossible to determine how many horses were stolen during this period, but the final straw came in November 1891 when more than four hundred horses went missing from several ranches. Although Cassidy and Hainer were probably minor players compared to others with whom they associated, they were among more than a dozen men targeted by lawmen and local ranchers. During the next eighteen months, at least nine suspected horse thieves were killed, while another eight to ten were arrested or fled the state.[22] Cassidy and Hainer kept up the business anyway, reportedly because both had gambling habits that needed feeding. They likely thought they were safe: they had plenty of friends in the area watching out for them, and convictions were hard to come by. In June 1893, Cassidy and Hainer were acquitted of horse-stealing charges, but a jury in a second trial convicted Cassidy while acquitting Hainer. The Mormon outlaw was sentenced in 1894 to two years of hard labor in the Wyoming State Penitentiary in Laramie. Cassidy's family, however, thought the trial was a frameup and that he may have been sold out by Hainer.[23] "Several times my brother expressed his bitterness for being sent to prison for the theft of a horse valued at $5.00," Lula Betenson said.[24]

Cassidy had cause for complaint. Although there exists little doubt he was a horse thief, newspaper reports and court records also suggest that local officials, recognizing they had a weak case, engineered his conviction with questionable witnesses and possibly a stacked jury. Having grown weary of Cassidy's rustling activities, they made sure the second trial achieved the desired outcome.[25]

---

21. The best treatment of these events is Mike Bell, "Butch Cassidy and the Great Western Horse Thief War," unpublished paper, which updates his book, *Incidents on Owl Creek*.

22. These deaths and arrests are described in Bell, "Butch Cassidy and the Great Western Horse Thief War," 16–22.

23. Betenson, *Butch Cassidy, My Uncle*, 80–81; and Betenson and Flack, *Butch Cassidy, My Brother*, 92–95.

24. Betenson and Flack, 92.

25. Mike Bell, *Incidents on Owl Creek: Butch Cassidy's Big Horn Basin Bunch and the Wyoming Horsethief War*, 163–64, 198–99. More recently, Bell examined

Cassidy was a well-behaved prisoner, and after serving eighteen months, he received a pardon from Wyoming Governor William A. Richards.[26] Cassidy's petition for early release had drawn support from several prominent Fremont County citizens, including the judge who sentenced him to prison, District Court Judge Jesse Knight. Judge Knight thought Cassidy was guilty of rustling but also acknowledged to the governor that Cassidy did not get a fair trial. Expressing hope that a pardon might turn the outlaw into a law-abiding citizen, Knight said, "Cassiday [sic] is a man that would be hard to describe—a brave, daring fellow and a man well calculated to be a leader, and should his inclinations run that way, I do not doubt but that he would be capable of organizing and leading a lot of desperate men to desperate deeds."[27] Historian Charles Kelly asserts that Governor Richards personally interviewed Cassidy, asking the outlaw to "go straight" and "quit rustling" as a condition of his pardon.[28] According to Kelly, Cassidy told the governor he could make no such promise, because he had gone too far down the outlaw trail to turn back. Instead, Cassidy pledged to stay out of Wyoming, which was sufficient to satisfy the governor and gain release. The story appears to be fanciful myth.[29] Cassidy would have been smart enough to agree to any conditions requested, regardless of whether he intended to comply. Three months after granting the pardon, Governor Richards defended his decision, telling a rancher who was fearful of Cassidy that "he assured me at the time of his pardon that he had no quarrel with you or anyone else in Fremont County, that he had enough of Penitentiary life and intended to conduct himself in such a way as to not again lay himself liable to arrest."[30]

While Butch was serving time in prison, his younger brother Dan, who had assisted Butch in the Telluride bank robbery, was arrested and charged with robbing a stagecoach of US mail sacks containing several hundred

---

Cassidy's arrest and trials in *Wyoming Outlaws: Butch Cassidy in Wyoming: 1889–1896*, 211–30, 301–7, 319–30, 383–89.

26. For Cassidy's imprisonment in the Wyoming State Penitentiary, see Bill Betenson, *Butch Cassidy: The Wyoming Years*, 93–106; Leerhsen, *Butch Cassidy*, 147–54; and Thomas B. Moy, "Butch Cassidy in Wyoming State Prison," 56–63.

27. Betenson, *Butch Cassidy, My Uncle*, 91. Knight's letter was dated September 28, 1895. See also Bell, *Incidents on Owl Creek*, 163–64.

28. Kelly, *The Outlaw Trail*, 60.

29. Patterson, *Butch Cassidy*, 77–78; and Hatch, *The Last Outlaws*, 145.

30. Letter from Governor Richards to Hon. J. L. Torrey, March 16, 1896. Quoted in Betenson, *Butch Cassidy: The Wyoming Years*, 105–6.

dollars. The crime carried an automatic sentence of life imprisonment.³¹ A jury found Dan guilty and, at just twenty-two years old, he began serving a life sentence in the Detroit House of Correction. Although there is little doubt that Dan participated in the stagecoach robbery, his parents started a letter-writing campaign to have him pardoned, asserting that Dan was at home with them in Circleville when the holdup was committed. Butch had received no such support from his parents after his conviction; they probably didn't even know he was imprisoned. They also may have blamed him for Dan's turn to criminality. Butch, having adopted the alias George Cassidy, had told prison authorities he was born in New York, had no religious affiliation, and could provide no information about his parents or any relatives. It was as if Robert LeRoy Parker had never existed.

Cassidy was released from the Wyoming prison on January 20, 1896. Now twenty-nine, he headed straight for Brown's Park, which remained a popular gathering spot for dubious characters. Some, like Cassidy and Matt Warner, had grown up as Mormons but itched for more excitement. Many Western outlaws freely used three locations—Brown's Park, Hole-in-the-Wall, and Robbers Roost—as waystations where they would hide following robberies and plot their next heist. Robbers Roost was located within the steep canyons of southeastern Utah's high desert country between the Dirty Devil River and Green River in Millard County, offering outlaws numerous places to defend themselves from curious lawmen. At Hole-in-the-Wall, anyone wishing to enter the outlaws' haven had to make a rugged climb through a long, narrow pass that was flanked by formidable, red-rock mesas, making unwanted intruders easy to spot and defend against. Numerous gangs erected cabins in the mile-high Hole-in-the-Wall valley, where they brought stolen horses and cattle to graze, and lived by a code of "honor among thieves" that enabled them to share the valley. Brown's Park was nestled in an isolated mountain valley along the Green River in Utah's northeastern corner near Vernal. The location gave outlaws escape routes into Colorado and Wyoming. Upon returning to Brown's Park, Cassidy abandoned the half-outlaw life and began recruiting men for what would later be called the Hole-in-the-Wall, or Wild Bunch, gang.

Cassidy reportedly wanted to name his outlaw band "The Train Robbers Syndicate," a name that suggests serious intent.³² This claim is

---

31. Betenson, *Butch Cassidy, My Uncle*, 51–59, discusses Dan Parker's criminal activities and trial.

32. For a discussion of the origin of the Wild Bunch name, see Patterson, *Butch Cassidy*, 123–24; and Daniel Buck and Anne Meadows, "Butch Cassidy and the

likely apocryphal. Cassidy's initial heists were bank and payroll robberies, and, as will be seen, it's possible he never participated directly in a train robbery. Newspapers sometimes tagged the group as the "Hole-in-the-Wall Gang," as "Robber's Roost Gang," or as Cassidy's or Logan's gang. The name by which they eventually became known, "Wild Bunch," was slang that had multiple meanings. It could describe a group of cowboys on a spree, a herd of unbroken horses, or an outlaw gang. Newspapers and lawmen applied the term "wild bunch" informally to different gangs throughout the West, including Cassidy's gang.[33] For example, in June 1899, the *Salt Lake Herald* referred to Cassidy and fellow outlaw Elzy Lay as "members of the 'wild bunch.'"[34] Later that year, the newspaper reported that "frequent visitations of the 'wild bunch'" had, for a time, discouraged the establishment of a bank in Vernal.[35] This latter reference lends support to the theory that saloonkeepers in and around Vernal popularized the name—calling the outlaws "that 'wild bunch' from Brown's Park"—based on their rowdy behavior whenever they came into town. Cassidy's gang probably became the one-and-only Wild Bunch after the Pinkerton National Detective Agency gave them that name in a 1902 memorandum to the American Bankers Association. Although the gang was largely broken up by then, the name Wild Bunch caught on in the press and is now commonly used to describe Cassidy's outlaw gang.

No one knows for sure how many outlaws joined the Wild Bunch or participated in its robberies. Some historians have estimated that dozens belonged, but the number is probably closer to fifteen to twenty, including girlfriends and close associates, such as those who held their relay horses.[36] Not all the men who frequented Brown's Park or the other hideouts rode with Cassidy's gang, though they may have been part of the boisterous cowboys that tore up local towns with drinking sprees. The Wild Bunch operated as a loose collection of criminals who were not strictly bound together as an exclusive gang. Outlaws moved in and out of the gang, participating in robberies with Wild Bunch members when it suited

---

Sundance Kid," 63–70.

33. For other outlaw gangs referred to as the "wild bunch," see *Daily Oklahoma State Capital* (Guthrie), September 9, 1895, 1; *Salt Lake Herald*, July 26, 1897, 7; *St. Johns Herald*, April 23, 1898, 4; and *Indian Chieftain* (Vinita, Oklahoma), April 29, 1897, 3.

34. *Salt Lake Herald*, June 13, 1899, 5.

35. *Salt Lake Herald*, September 2, 1899, 5.

36. Leerhsen, *Butch Cassidy*, 182, makes a similar estimate.

their purposes. Among the gang's best-known bank and train robbers were O. C. "Deaf Charley" Hanks, Elzy Lay, Henry "Bub" Meeks, George "Flatnose" Currie, Harvey "Kid Curry" Logan, Lonie Logan, Tom O'Day, and Harry "Sundance Kid" Longabaugh. Two other prominent members, Will Carver and Ben Kilpatrick, joined up in the late 1890s after their previous outfit, the Ketchum Gang, fell apart.

Cassidy is popularly regarded as the Wild Bunch leader, though Harvey Logan may have wielded just as much or even more influence. Nevertheless, Cassidy is credited with devising carefully planned robberies that used strategically stationed relays of fresh horses to outrun pursuers following a robbery. The posses' horses would usually give out long before they could catch the bandits. In a typical Wild Bunch robbery, three or four outlaws would team together on a train or bank heist and, after a successful escape, would lie low at a far-away locale for a year or more. A few months after the robbery, a different combination of gang members would hold up a bank or train in another location, keeping authorities guessing as to when and where the outlaws would strike. The bandits hid some of their loot along their escape routes to speed their get-away and returned later to pick it up. However, not every robbery worked according to plan. Some were thwarted and resulted in members being arrested; other robberies netted little money.[37] Successful or not, they pulled off enough lucrative heists and caused enough trouble to raise the ire of bank and railroad owners. Wild Bunch members kept their identities well-hidden by using multiple aliases, hair dyes, and other disguises. They also blew through their money quickly, spending it on women, alcohol, and gambling with the same alacrity as Telluride's "lady-fingered city sneaks" who had so disgusted Cassidy when he first left home.

Cassidy would later gain a reputation as a gentleman bandit, even a Robin Hood who shared liberally with the poor. Cassidy's younger sister, Lula Parker Betenson, portrays her brother as a social bandit, an enemy of giant cattle companies, ruthless banks, and domineering railroads. "He was not a killer either by nature or reputation, but his friendly, singular charm and his interest in people—the struggling people—won for him

---

37. For example, when the gang held up the Southern Pacific No. 1 near Humboldt, Nevada, on July 14, 1898, the bandits—reportedly the Sundance Kid, Harvey Logan, and Flatnose Currie—got only $450 for their efforts. See Daniel Buck and Anne Meadows, "The Wild Bunch: Wild, but not Much of a Bunch," 29.

their protection from the law," Betenson said.[38] According to her version of events, whenever Cassidy was arrested or jailed, it usually resulted from a misunderstanding or trumped-up charge, causing him to become disillusioned and resentful.[39] Cassidy reportedly avoided bloodshed—his meticulous planning of robberies was designed to preclude the need for gunplay—and he was said to be proud that he never killed anyone. Even the Pinkerton file noted that "he has never been suspected of, or charged with murder, although he was a fearless man and a good revolver-shot."[40] Cassidy's friends and acquaintances interviewed by Charles Kelly told him the outlaw "never drank to excess, was always courteous to women, was free with money when he had it, and extremely loyal to his friends. All old-timers interviewed for this [Kelly's] biography, including officers who hunted him, were unanimous in saying, 'Butch Cassidy was one of the finest men I ever knew.'"[41]

Cassidy's generosity with his abettors is likely true. It gained their gratitude and assistance when the law crowded him too closely. The historical record also suggests he was personable and well-liked by those who knew him. But it's also true that Cassidy began stealing and rustling at an early age. After leaving home, he moved with relative ease, even enthusiasm, from rustling to robbing banks. When he robbed his first bank in 1889, he faced no personal crisis or dire need for money, other than that he and his comrades had recklessly spent all their money. And whatever Cassidy's aversion to bloodshed, he teamed up with some of the West's most notorious killers, including Harvey "Kid Curry" Logan, who eventually was wanted on warrants for fifteen murders.[42] Like his fellow bandits, Cassidy pointed guns at his victims and threatened to kill them if they didn't hand over the money. Even if Cassidy was disinclined to shoot, he knew his comrades were not.

The Cassidy-led gang committed its first major robbery eight months after his release from prison. On August 13, 1896, Butch, Elzy Lay, and Bub Meeks robbed Idaho's Montpelier Bank of $7,165 in order to pay the attorneys who were defending Matt Warner for murder. Like Cassidy and Warner, Meeks was a Mormon. He grew up in Fremont County, Wyoming,

---

38. Betenson and Flack, *Butch Cassidy, My Brother*, xv.

39. For example, see Betenson and Flack, 48–50, 54–56, 74, and 96.

40. Pinkerton's records, Box 89, Folder 8, Names and aliases of the Wild Bunch, 6.

41. Kelly, *The Outlaw Trail*, 4.

42. Hatch, *The Last Outlaws*, 162–63.

and probably first met Cassidy at the outlaw's Horse Creek Ranch, which was located near Meeks's family property.[43] Soon after the Montpelier robbery, Warner's wife revealed to authorities the identities of all three men and their intent to use the money for Warner's legal fees.[44] Despite their efforts, Warner was convicted of voluntary manslaughter and sentenced to five years in the Utah State Penitentiary.[45] The next significant Wild Bunch heist occurred on April 21, 1897, when Butch, Lay, and perhaps Meeks and Joe Walker stole $9,860 from the mine payroll in Castle Gate, Utah. Newspapers again identified Cassidy as one of the culprits.

The Wild Bunch committed probably just a handful of robberies over the next two to three years, though it's impossible to determine the precise number. Law enforcement and newspapers often blamed them for robberies that may have been committed by others; similarly, some of their robberies might not have been reported or were attributed to other gangs. The men likely continued stealing horses, both for their own use and to sell, and they didn't hesitate to kill a stray cow when they got hungry.

In late 1898, Cassidy and some of the gang moved their operations south, and by early 1899 they were working at the WS Ranch in Alma, New Mexico. Using the alias James Lowe, Cassidy became a trusted ranch hand and eventually was made a trail boss. In addition, he reportedly became part owner of a saloon, where he occasionally tended bar. Other gang members drifted into Alma and were hired by Cassidy to work with his cowboy crew. Cassidy's outlaw pal, Elzy Lay, who went by the name William "Mac" McGinnis, joined on as a bronco buster. William French, manager of the WS Ranch, described Lowe as a "fair complected" and stoutly built man of middle height who "had a habit of grinning and showing a very even row of small teeth when he spoke to you."[46]

French considered all Lowe's friends to be reliable hands, and so it puzzled him that Lowe's crew turned over so frequently. "There was hardly a trip we made to the road that two or three of them didn't want to quit—called away on some unexpected emergency."[47] Another thing also puzzled him. When new cowboys were hired to replace those who quit, the newcomers acted as strangers to each other when they arrived, but "I frequently saw them together in the dusk of the evening sitting under a

---

43. Patterson, *Butch Cassidy*, 86–87.
44. *Salt Lake Herald*, September 9, 1896, 1.
45. Patterson, *Butch Cassidy*, 97.
46. Captain William French, *Recollections of a Western Ranchman*, 258.
47. French, 259.

fence in close confab like long-lost brothers," French said. He discussed this with one of the other managers, who thought something suspicious was going on, but "as long as things were going so well it was no affair of ours to inquire into it."[48]

What was going on with Jim Lowe and his friends? They were using the WS Ranch as a base of operations. The ranch not only served as a place to plan new robberies, but it also served as a clever hideout that provided more freedom and entertainment than an isolated, mountain retreat. When Cassidy and his fellow bandits went into hiding for several months after the Castle Gate holdup, they grew bored and restless at their Robbers Roost hideout, despite the cheery presence of prostitutes.[49] Working as WS Ranch hands enabled the outlaws to keep their identities well-hidden while still enjoying the town's many diversions. The unexpected emergencies requiring their absence were undoubtedly trips to plan or execute robberies.

One of those robberies occurred June 2, 1899, when three to six men robbed the Union Pacific westbound train near Wilcox, Wyoming. The likely three were Flatnose Currie, Harvey "Kid Curry" Logan, and the Sundance Kid. Others who may have participated were Lonie Logan, Ben Kilpatrick, and Logan's cousin Bob Lee. Newspapers also named Cassidy as a suspect, but scant evidence supports this conclusion—though he likely helped plan the heist.[50] To get at the train's safe, the outlaws blew open the express car, destroying the car and nearly killing the Wells Fargo messenger inside. The bandits stole as much as $50,000, but during the getaway they got into a shoot-out with a trailing posse and killed Converse County Sheriff Josiah Hazen. The spectacular holdup made the Wild Bunch nationally famous and persuaded Union Pacific officials to hire the Pinkerton National Detective Agency to help put a halt to the gang's activities.

Less than six weeks after the Wilcox train robbery, Elzy Lay joined forces with two former members of the Ketchum gang, Sam Ketchum and Will

---

48. French, 260.

49. Kelly, *The Outlaw Trail*, 159.

50. Details of the Wilcox train robbery are found in Vince Garcia, "The Wilcox, Wyoming Train Robbery—As It Happened," 65–84; Hatch, *The Last Outlaws*, 184–87; Patterson, *Butch Cassidy*, 143–48; and Mark T. Smokov, *He Rode with Butch and Sundance: The Story of Harvey "Kid Curry" Logan*, 92–113. All cast doubt on or flatly reject Cassidy's presence at the robbery, as do Betenson, *Butch Cassidy, My Uncle*, 144; and Jeffrey Burton, *The Deadliest Outlaws: The Ketchum Gang and the Wild Bunch*, 351. Leerhsen, *Butch Cassidy*, 188–90, places Cassidy at the scene, but offers no additional evidence supporting this assertion.

Carver, to rob the Colorado and Southern Railway train near Folsom, New Mexico. It is unclear whether Butch helped mastermind the July 11 heist, but two of his ranch hands, Bruce "Red" Weaver and Tom Capehart, assisted by holding the relay horses for the outlaws. The bandits made off with $50,000 to $70,000.[51] During their escape, a posse found the three men at their hideout in Turkey Creek Canyon, New Mexico, and engaged them in gunfire, seriously wounding both Ketchum and Lay. The outlaws wounded two posse members and killed two others, Deputy Sheriff Henry M. Love and Sheriff Edward J. Farr of Huerfano County, Colorado. Farr had joined the chase as part of a special force brought in by train to New Mexico. Eventually, both Ketchum and Lay were captured. Ketchum died in custody, while Lay was convicted of second-degree murder for Farr's death. The judge sentenced Lay to life in the New Mexico territorial prison in Santa Fe.

As Lay's involvement in the robbery became known, William French, his boss at the WS Ranch, began to wonder "how many members of what was usually alluded to as the 'Wild Bunch' I had in my employ."[52] Still, he said nothing to local authorities. In fact, he told Lowe he was willing to attest to Lay's good behavior and use his influence to mitigate Lay's sentence. In early March 1900, just a few months after Lay's conviction, French received a visit from Frank Murray, the assistant superintendent of Pinkerton's Denver office. Murray was investigating reports that bank notes from the Wilcox train robbery were circulating in Alma and nearby towns. In fact, Ben Kilpatrick, going by the name Johnny Ward, had recently joined the WS Ranch outfit and was apparently passing the notes. While questioning French, Murray showed him a photograph of three or four men and asked him if he recognized any of them. French pointed to one of the men, saying his name was Jim Lowe. Murray informed French that Lowe was actually Butch Cassidy, "the brains and leader of the best-organized gang of outlaws that had appeared in the country for more than a lifetime."[53]

French said nothing about his own suspicions, instead telling Murray that "all I knew about him [Lowe] was that he was the best trail boss I had ever seen and one of the best men that the WS had in their employ since I had known them."

Murray replied that despite French's good report of Cassidy's character, "there was hardly a State or a territory south of the Canadian line that

---

51. Details of the Folsom train robbery are found in Burton, *Deadliest Outlaws*, 162–68; and Hatch, *The Last Outlaws*, 188–89.

52. French, *Recollections of a Western Ranchman*, 266.

53. Quotes from French's discussion with Murray in French, 273–74.

wasn't anxious to get hold of him." Nevertheless, Murray insisted he had no intention of arresting Cassidy. "I'm not such a fool as to attempt it in this neighborhood," he said, stating that his only business in Alma was tracking the stolen bank notes.

When Lowe returned to the ranch, French informed him of Murray's visit, saying the detective claimed he was Butch Cassidy. Confronted with the accusation, Lowe "only grinned," French said.[54] Lowe told French that he and Capehart had already spotted Murray in the bar and bought him a drink, so they could find out why he was snooping around Alma. Without admitting his identity, Lowe told French he would pull out soon to avoid trouble. This was disappointing news to French, who did not plan to fire Lowe despite his lengthy criminal record.

After Cassidy and Capehart informed other gang members of Murray's investigation, some wanted to kill him, but Cassidy intervened and helped Murray get safely out of town, according to Pinkerton detective Charlie Siringo.[55] "Lowe said he didn't have the heart to see Frank Murray killed," Siringo said.[56] If true—and Siringo is the only person who tells this story—it speaks to Cassidy's reputed desire to avoid bloodshed. Regardless, the outlaws recognized that Cassidy's cover was blown, making it impossible to continue their anonymous operations in Alma. It would be only a matter of time before more Pinkertons and lawmen began showing up. Consequently, the outlaws decided to quit the WS Ranch, and in mid-March 1900, five members of the gang began riding north, likely heading for one of their hideouts in Utah or Wyoming.[57] Neither Butch Cassidy nor the Sundance Kid rode with them. Sundance had already left the ranch, while Cassidy stayed behind to sell his stake in the saloon and wrap up his affairs in Alma.[58] Cassidy and Red Weaver left March 24, stopping

---

54. French, 274.

55. Charles A. Siringo, *A Cowboy Detective: An Autobiography*, 354–56, 367. Siringo, who referred to Murray as both "Murray" and "Curran," said he was told by two different people that the Wild Bunch ran Murray out of town.

56. Siringo, 356.

57. Some people later speculated that the outlaws were on their way to rob the Santa Fe Pacific Railroad (for example, *St. Johns Herald*, May 5, 1900, 3). However, the outlaws had departed the WS Ranch abruptly to avoid discovery, and given the continuing turmoil from their previous robbery, they probably had neither the time nor inclination to plan a new robbery. Their conspicuous ride through New Mexico and Arizona towns also suggests they were not concerned about maintaining the stealth that might precede a robbery.

58. Siringo, *Cowboy Detective*, 355; and Burton, *Deadliest Outlaws*, 272.

first at a neighboring ranch to steal its entire herd of saddle horses—sixteen horses and a mule—before hurrying on their way to catch up with the rest of the gang.[59]

Historians have long puzzled over the identities of the five outlaws who rode north toward St. Johns. Each used an alias as they passed through the small New Mexico and Arizona towns. None of the subsequent reward notices had their real names, except for Tom Capehart's. Among those thought to have been responsible for the murder of the St. Johns men were gangs led by Squint Jones, Red Pipkin, Bronco Bill Walters, Bill Smith, and the Ketchum brothers—all incorrect suppositions. In recent years, researchers have carefully tracked the movements and physical characteristics of known outlaws, eventually enabling them to identify the outlaws' identities with a high degree of certainty. The accumulated evidence suggests that the five outlaws who rode out of Alma ahead of Cassidy and Weaver were Tom Capehart, Thomas C. Hilliard, Ben Kilpatrick, Will Carver, and Harvey Logan.[60]

Some people say that Tom Capehart took up the outlaw life after being mistreated by Deputy Marshal George Scarborough.[61] Born in Texas in 1874, Capehart was "a noted bronco stomper" who wasn't afraid to ride

---

59. New Mexico Territory vs. Bruce Weaver and James Lowe, April 27, 1900, "Larceny of horses." French (*Recollections of a Western Ranchman*, 276) said the theft of horses by Lowe and Weaver induced the rancher, whom they did not like, to sell his ranch. Leerhsen (*Butch Cassidy*, 200) said the outlaws stole about thirty horses, some bearing the WS brand, but I have been unable to verify this assertion. The indictment charges them with stealing four horses, four geldings, four mares, four colts, and a mule belonging to B. F. and W. S. Ashby.

60. The academic quest to identify these five outlaws began in earnest with Philip J. Rasch's groundbreaking "Death Comes to St. Johns," 1–8. Others who followed refined his insights, including Burton, *Deadliest Outlaws*; Robert K. DeArment, *George Scarborough: The Life and Death of a Lawman on the Closing Frontier*; Donna B. Ernst, "A Deadly Year for St. Johns Lawmen," 18–21; and Smokov, *Harvey "Kid Curry" Logan*. My conclusions about the identities of the five outlaws align with Burton's.

61. Information about Capehart can be found in Donna B. Ernst, "The Real Tom Capehart," 38–41; DeArment, *George Scarborough*, 175–85, 237–40; Burton, *Deadliest Outlaws*, 9–10, and throughout; and Joseph "Mack" Axford, *Around Western Campfires*, 22–26.

For many years, some historians, supported by contemporary accounts, believed that Capehart was Harvey Logan, who was using "Tom Capehart" as an

the wildest horses. Among the cowboys at the Arizona and New Mexico ranches where he worked, many considered him a hero, one of the best at breaking horses. Capehart gained even more notoriety when he was accused of participating in the attempted robbery of the Southern Pacific Railroad at Steins Pass, New Mexico, in December 1897. One of the actual bandits, Tom Ketchum of the Ketchum Gang, had accidently dropped his handkerchief with the embroidered initials "TK" during his escape.[62] A posse arrested Capehart, thinking the initials stood for "Tom Kephart." Scarborough and some of the other lawmen pistol-whipped Capehart in an unsuccessful attempt to beat a confession out of him.[63]

Capehart spent more than two months in jail before he and five others were brought to trial on February 25, 1898. After a two-week trial, a jury deliberated less than one-half hour before issuing a "not guilty" verdict for Capehart and two others. Unhappy with the verdict, the district attorney filed new charges to hold Capehart and the others without bail, and so Capehart languished in jail eight more months until the charges were finally dismissed. Once free, he worked briefly for the Wabash Cattle Company in Apache County and then moved to the WS Ranch in Alma, probably not too long after Cassidy and fellow gang members were hired on at the ranch.[64]

Was Capehart truly innocent in the Steins Pass robbery? No solid evidence ties him to the holdup, but it seems highly coincidental that shortly after his release from jail, Capehart began working at the ranch hideout with members of both the Wild Bunch and Ketchum gangs. And just six months after his release, Capehart assisted in the gang's Folsom train robbery. If not a criminal before his jailing, Capehart certainly threw in quickly with leading Western desperadoes. It was also said he swore vengeance against Scarborough for the beating the lawman inflicted on Capehart.

As the five outlaws passed through the New Mexico and Arizona towns, Capehart used the alias "Bud Wilson" and perhaps "Smith" as well.[65] No

---

alias. However, Ernst and Burton argue convincingly that the "Tom Capehart" who participated in these events was, in fact, the real Tom Capehart.

62. Leonard Alverson, "Reminiscences of Leonard Alverson," 19. Leonard Alverson Personal Correspondence, 1933–1939, Box 1, folder 2.

63. DeArment, *George Scarborough*, 179.

64. *St. Johns Herald*, April 21, 1900, 3.

65. The descriptions of Capehart and his aliases can be found in Pinkerton's records, Box 89, Folder 4, memo, January 28, 1902, on "Tom Capehart, alias Bud

known photograph of Capehart has been found, but he was said to be 5'10" tall and about 175 to 180 pounds, with a red face, especially at the point of his nose, probably from so many years cowboying in the sun. Despite his use of aliases, Capehart would be easily recognized in Apache County, where he had a reputation as an expert bronco buster.

Thomas C. Hilliard was better known by his alias, Tod Carver. Most recently, he had worked as a cowboy and bronco rider in Arizona and New Mexico. Like Capehart, he had acquaintances among the local cowboys and ranchers. He also had a distinguishing physical feature that would make him easy to identify and remember, even by those who had never seen him before: the forefinger of his right hand was missing, either all of it or in part.[66] But other aspects of his personal life, especially his connection to the four other riders, are unclear. He was born February 12, 1874, in San Saba County, Texas, the second of at least seven siblings.[67] His parents, William and Amanda Hilliard, were farmers. Carver grew up in the same county as the Ketchum brothers and was likely acquainted with their family, and he once worked with Tom Ketchum and Tom Capehart at the Hashknife cattle outfit in Holbrook, Arizona.[68] The Pinkerton's dossier on Carver described him as a train robber, holdup man, and rustler, but there is no evidence tying him to any of the previous crimes committed by either the Ketchum Gang or the Wild Bunch. This may have been the first time he rode with the gang.

Carver had just turned twenty-six years old when the outlaws left Alma. He had a dark complexion—"almost swarthy," according to the Pinkerton's file—with black hair, dark eyes, and a thin, dark mustache. He was slender and of medium height, probably about 5'7" and 150 pounds.[69] The Pinkerton's file said Carver had "small feet, active move-

---

Wilson, Train Robber"; and *St. Johns Herald*, April 21, 1900, 3, reward circular.

66. Some sources, such as the Pinkerton's records, say the right forefinger was missing at the second joint, while others, such as the newspaper reward notices and the St. Johns jail record, simply say the forefinger was "off."

67. See 1880 and 1900 census records for San Saba County, Texas, precinct No. 3, under William Hilliard, head of the household. See pages 260–61 below for additional evidence linking Thomas C. Hilliard to Tod Carver.

68. Pinkerton's records, Box 89, Folder 5, Tod Carver; and Donna B. Ernst, "Unraveling Two Outlaws Named Carver," 30.

69. Tod Carver's height and weight were variously estimated from 5'7" and 145 pounds to 5'10½" and 175 pounds, but in his 1918 draft registration card (as Thomas C. Hilliard), he was described as being of medium height and slender build.

Thomas C. Hilliard, alias Tod Carver, was regarded as law-abiding by some and a lawless desperado by others. This photograph was likely taken in June 1901 while he was being held in the St. Johns jail for the murders of Frank LeSueur and Gus Gibbons. Courtesy Library of Congress, Pinkerton's National Detective Agency Records.

ments, [and] talks very fast," suggesting a slightly built, nervous man. He had a mixed reputation among those who knew him. "Tod Carver is well known among the cattle men of eastern Graham county," said an Arizona newspaper. "By some of our most substantial citizens he is regarded as a law abiding man, while by others he is regarded as a lawless desperado."[70]

---

70. *Graham Guardian*, January 10, 1902, 4.

The tall and handsome Ben Kilpatrick was known as a "lady killer." He abandoned his wife and two children when he ran into trouble in Texas and rode with the Ketchum Gang in New Mexico before joining up with the Wild Butch. Courtesy Library of Congress, Pinkerton's National Detective Agency Records.

It came as little surprise to Ben Kilpatrick's neighbors that Ben, along with two of his brothers, became outlaws. "Ben, Ed and George [Kilpatrick] were natural born criminals who started their careers as boys in their early teens by robbing sheep camps," said John Loomis, a cattle rancher who lived near the Kilpatrick farm in Coleman County, Texas.[71] Loomis considered their father to be honest and industrious, but said their mother encouraged her sons' criminality. Born January 5, 1874, Ben married at age eighteen, had two children, and then, less than three years into his marriage, abandoned his family when he and his brother George ran into some local trouble.[72] After moving west into Arizona and New Mexico, Ben and George found comfortable companionship among outlaws, including Will Carver, Harvey Logan, and the Ketchum brothers.

---

71. John A. Loomis, *Texas Ranchman: The Memoirs of John A. Loomis*, 67.

72. Biographical information about Ben Kilpatrick's early life and a description of his physical appearance is found in Burton, *Deadliest Outlaws*, 9, 53–55; Pinkerton's records on Kilpatrick; Arthur Soule, *The Tall Texan: The Story of Ben Kilpatrick*, 1–12; and *St. Johns Herald*, June 2, 1900, 3, reward notice.

Ben Kilpatrick, now twenty-six, stood almost six feet tall and weighed about 180 pounds. The Pinkertons would later tag him with the name "the Tall Texan," but it doesn't appear that he or any of his friends used that moniker. Rather, "the Tall Texan" appears to have been the invention of a newspaper writer who drew it from a description given by a police chief. The catchy nickname was subsequently used by the Pinkertons and picked up by historians.[73] Kilpatrick was a handsome man—a "lady killer," according to fellow outlaw Harvey Logan[74]—with dark hair, gray blue eyes, and a light complexion. He used the alias "Mack Steen" as he rode north. He was known to be boisterous and temperamental.

Will Carver's descent into the outlaw life appears to have been triggered by the death of his wife. Born September 12, 1868, in Sonora, Texas, Carver worked for several ranches in the San Angelo area and was considered "a fine roper and horseman, and a crack shot with a six shooter, using either hand with equal facility," according to the local newspaper.[75] One of the ranches where he worked belonged to the Ketchum family, and for a short time, he and Sam Ketchum ran a gambling room. In February 1892, Carver married seventeen-year-old Viana Byler. By all accounts, the future outlaw was devoted to his young bride, but less than six months later, Viana died due to the complications of pregnancy. Their baby was stillborn.

Seaton Keith, a rancher who employed Carver, said he was "a good, quiet, steady boy" who "seemed to go all to pieces" after the death of his wife and baby.[76] Another rancher, John Loomis, concurred, saying Carver was "devoted to his wife" and "had a nice personality and everybody liked him" during the years he worked as a cowboy, but he also "was naturally a wild reckless fellow who drifted in with the wrong crowd" after Viana died.[77] Even years later, Carver remained "very melancholy over the death of his wife," a fellow cowboy said.[78]

Nothing stands out about Carver's physical appearance, though his photo seems to capture the sadness noted by many who knew him. Now thirty-one years old, he was five feet, six or seven inches in his boots and

---

73. See Mark Boardman, "A Tall Order? What we don't know about Wild Bunch member Ben Kilpatrick."

74. James D. Horan, *The Authentic West: The Outlaws*, 240, 244.

75. *San Angelo Standard*, April 13, 1901, as quoted in John Eaton, *Will Carver, Outlaw*, 130.

76. Burton, *Deadliest* Outlaws, 7.

77. Loomis, *Texas Ranchman*, 66.

78. Alverson, "Reminiscences," 9.

Will Carver was a "good, quiet steady boy" who "seemed to go all to pieces" after his wife and baby died, according to those who knew him. Courtesy National Portrait Gallery, Smithsonian Institution; gift of Pinkerton's, Inc.

had a somewhat stocky build, weighing about 150 to 160 pounds.[79] He often went by the name G. W. Franks or just Franks, an alias he used as he rode through the Apache County towns of Springerville and St. Johns.[80]

---

79. Burton, *Deadliest Outlaws*, 7.
80. Siringo, *Cowboy Detective*, 371, said a Wild Bunch associate told him that Carver had used "Franks" as an alias when he rode with the Ketchum Gang.

In popular culture today, he is known as Will "News" Carver, allegedly because he liked to see his name in the newspaper. However, there is no contemporary evidence suggesting he had such a nickname (or desire to read about his own exploits). This appears to have been a dramatic invention of the movie, "Butch Cassidy and the Sundance Kid." The local newspaper where he was known described Carver's personality in almost the opposite terms: "He was a plain, unassuming, quiet sort of desperado, of a very retiring disposition, and rather shunned than courted notoriety."[81] Still, he was considered fearless, had already killed at least one lawman, and would not hesitate to kill to avoid capture.

Harvey "Kid Curry" Logan was considered the most violent and dangerous member of the Wild Bunch.[82] "His motto is 'Kill a sheriff now and then and make them respect you,'" said Pinkerton detective Lowell E. Spence. "He fears no man, and sets a very cheap price on human life, including his own."[83] Logan's reputation as a bloodthirsty killer is perhaps exaggerated, but he had a vicious temper and quickly became violent, particularly when drinking.[84] He was prepared to kill—and people did get killed—when he felt threatened.

Harvey Logan was born in Tama County, Iowa, in 1867, one of five brothers and a sister. After his mother died in 1876, Harvey and four of his siblings were sent to Dodson, Missouri, to be raised by an aunt and uncle. When Harvey was sixteen or seventeen years old, he and three of his brothers moved to Montana, started a ranch, and adopted the name "Curry."[85] The brothers were hard workers, but after their brother Hank

---

81. *San Angelo Standard*, April 13, 1901, as quoted in Eaton, *Will Carver, Outlaw*, 129.

82. Biographies of Logan include Smokov, *Harvey "Kid Curry" Logan*; and Gary A. Wilson, *The Life and Death of Kid Curry: Tiger of the Wild Bunch*. Although Burton, *Deadliest Outlaws*, does not focus on Logan alone, the book also provides excellent details about Logan and his activities.

83. *Knoxville Sentinel* (TN), December 17, 1901, 1. A similar assessment is provided in Pinkerton's records, Box 87, Folder 1, *Illustrated Police News*, "Tough Terrors" (undated), which said Logan, when being chased, "will plan to assassinate his pursuers, or if cornered, if not overpowered, will promptly commence shooting," while Cassidy and other gang members "will first try all means of escape before shooting or murdering."

84. Smokov, *Harvey "Kid Curry" Logan*, x–xii.

85. Contrary to popular belief, Harvey did not change his name to honor fellow outlaw George "Flatnose" Currie. Smokov said both Harvey and his brother Hank adopted Curry long before Harvey met Flatnose. Logan family members

Harvey Logan, alias Kid Curry, was wanted for as many as fifteen murders. "The very devil showed in his eyes," said a man who knew him. Pictured with his girlfriend, prostitute Annie Rogers, Logan caroused and spent lavishly following successful robberies. Courtesy Library of Congress Prints and Photographs Division, Washington, DC.

died, Harvey, John, and Lonie began drinking excessively, shooting up saloons when drunk, and getting into brawls that landed them in court on assault charges. Wyoming pioneer William Harmon described John and Lonie as "mean, bull-dozing cusses," adding that "the very devil showed in [Harvey's] eyes."[86] Trouble followed the brothers everywhere. On December 27, 1894, Harvey shot and killed neighboring rancher Pike Landusky during a saloon fight. The evidence suggests that he acted in self-defense, but Harvey didn't expect to get a fair trial, and so he fled. It wasn't long before he was rustling cattle and committing petty holdups with Flatnose Currie and other Hole-in-the-Wall outlaws.

Harvey Logan stood 5 feet, 7 ½ inches tall and had a medium build, weighing 145 to 160 pounds. He had a dark complexion, dark eyes, and a prominent nose. A journalist who later visited Logan in jail described the

---

later speculated that Hank adopted a new to name so the wife he left behind in Missouri couldn't track him down. Harvey, due to his youth, was subsequently called "Kid" at one of the ranches where the brothers first worked. See Smokov, *Harvey "Kid Curry" Logan*, 6–8.

86. Smokov, *Harvey "Kid Curry" Logan*, 23.

outlaw as "a man of strong physique, cool head and wonderful nerve and a strong face."[87] An attending doctor said the jailed outlaw "gives every indication of having done much hard riding. . . . Logan hasn't a half pound of superfluous flesh on his body and could give anybody a hard fight."[88] A skilled marksman, Logan once impressed onlookers by using his pistol to shoot the rings around a target at a shooting gallery. Moody and given to fits of sullenness, he could also be boisterous and combative when drinking. Following a successful robbery, he would spend lavishly on alcohol, fancy clothes, gambling, and prostitutes, blowing through his share of the take as if an endless line of banks and trains stood waiting to be robbed.

As the five outlaws rode north from Alma, Logan and his companions were probably still flush with cash from the Wilcox train robbery, but they could not have been in a good mood. Their last two robberies had triggered intense shoot-outs and narrow escapes from trailing posses. They had killed three lawmen, while one of their own, Sam Ketchum, had been slain. Another, Elzy Lay, had survived near-fatal wounds only to be captured and sentenced to life in prison. Tom Ketchum, Sam's brother, had been convicted of attempted train robbery and was slated to hang in Clayton, New Mexico.[89] Bob Lee had recently been arrested for his participation in the Wilcox train robbery, while Bub Meeks was serving a thirty-five-year sentence in the Idaho State Penitentiary in Boise.[90] Nosy Pinkerton agents had forced the outlaws to abandon what had been an ideal setup at the WS Ranch for planning robberies and hiding in plain sight. Worst of all, on February 28, 1900, about two weeks before they left the WS Ranch, Logan's brother Lonie was shot and killed as he ran from a posse that had tracked him to his aunt's house near Kansas City. News of Lonie's death likely would have reached Alma before the outlaws' departure. Retribution could not have been far from Harvey Logan's mind.

After leaving Alma, the outlaws rode north to Luna, where they were seen purchasing arms and provisions.[91] From Luna, they headed west at

---

87. *Louisville Courier-Journal*, December 29, 1901, 9.

88. *Knoxville Journal and Tribune* (TN), December 17, 1901, 2.

89. Acting alone, Tom Ketchum had tried to rob the train near Wilcox just one month after his brother and other Wild Bunch members had successfully pulled off their robbery. Tom was shot and captured in the attempt.

90. Betenson, *Butch Cassidy, My Uncle*, 104–5. Meeks, who was convicted for his participation in the Montpelier bank robbery, died in the Wyoming State Mental Hospital in 1912.

91. *El Paso Herald*, April 12, 1900, 1.

a leisurely pace into Apache County and took the trail north, probably passing through the Mormon communities of Alpine and Nutrioso before arriving in Springerville on Sunday, March 25. The total distance along today's roads from Alma to Springerville is about eighty miles. The men shopped at one of Springerville's stores for additional provisions and stopped at the post office to leave a letter for Jim Lowe, whom they expected to come by in a day or two.[92] Springerville residents would certainly have been curious regarding where these men came from and where they were going, but there's no indication anyone asked, nor that the men volunteered the information. Townspeople provided few details regarding the men other than their general physical appearance and their names, all aliases. Tom Capehart gave his name as "Wilson," but he was recognized by those who had seen or worked with the bronco buster the previous year at the nearby Wabash Cattle Ranch. People also noticed that one of the men was missing all or part of his right forefinger. After finishing their business in Springerville, the outlaws, who pulled twelve extra horses, rode a few more miles and camped for the night on the open prairie.

The next day, Monday, March 26, the men packed up their gear and began riding toward St. Johns, where they intended to purchase more supplies. Along the way, they stopped to kill a cow for lunch. They butchered and dressed the cow in a ravine, keeping out of site to prevent discovery, but the cow's calf bawled loudly for its mother and would not be quieted. The mail carrier en route from St. Johns to Springerville, Lyman "Duane" Hamblin, heard the agitated calf and decided to investigate. The county had suffered a raft of cattle thefts in recent months, and Apache County Sheriff Edward Beeler, who was Hamblin's uncle, had instructed his nephew "to keep watch while on his mail route for any men who might look suspicious."[93] Hamblin, however, merely thought the calf was in distress, and so he drove his mail buggy over to the ravine to help. Looking down the embankment, he saw several men dressing the cow as it hung from a tree, while one of them attempted to drive away the noisy calf. Realizing he had blundered onto outlaws—and fearful he had been seen—Hamblin

---

92. *Arizona Republican* (Phoenix), May 7, 1900, 4.

93. This account of Hamblin's discovery comes from his daughter, Lois, in Lois Hamblin Golding and Delma Golding Johnson, *Our Golden Heritage: The Duane and Addie Noble Hamblin Family*, 56. Lyman Duane Hamblin Sr. (1872–1951) was the son of Lyman Stoddard Hamblin (1848–1923), who was the youngest child of Jacob and Lucinda Taylor Hamblin.

turned and drove his buggy quickly to Springerville, where he reported to Sheriff Beeler what had transpired.

Did Beeler guess these were the same rough-looking men who had ridden through town the previous day? It was only one cow, perhaps not worth tangling with experienced gunmen. But this was cattle country. Looking the other way when cows were pilfered, even just one, would set a bad precedent—and cattle rancher Henry Barrett, owner of the butchered beef, was not one to look the other way. Known to be hot-tempered, Barrett also had reputation as a "tough old rooster" who was "fearless and nervy" in tracking suspected rustlers.[94] He still carried with him the high-powered Mauser rifle he had captured from the Spanish while serving with Teddy Roosevelt's Rough Riders in Cuba. Barrett's herd had suffered in recent years from depredations by cattle rustlers, particularly the Bill Smith Gang, and so he immediately signed on when Sheriff Beeler began gathering a posse to follow and arrest the men who killed his beef. After finishing their meal, the five outlaws continued north to St. Johns, leaving behind the partially eaten carcass of the slaughtered cow.

---

94. For description of Barrett's pugnacious personality, see *Coconino Sun* (Flagstaff), July 25, 1903, 1; and Ray McKnight, "The Battleground Shootout—Arizona Rangers Fight Smith Gang," 46.

CHAPTER 3

A PLAGUE OF COWBOYS AND OUTLAWS

When James LeSueur was six or seven years old and loose upon the town, he wandered into a cowboy dance at a local St. Johns celebration. Upon seeing the curious boy, a drunken cowboy decided to enliven the festivities by ordering him to dance a jig. LeSueur refused, and so the cowboy pulled out his pistol and shot near his feet. "I danced the best I could," recalled LeSueur, who performed "the double shuffle and a few other jigs" his father had taught him.[1] On another occasion, LeSueur looked inside Sol Barth's barn and saw two cowboys strung up from the rafters, victims of vigilantes who meted out swift justice to suspected outlaws.[2] Extralegal violence, of course, was a territory-wide phenomenon—one historian tallied more than one hundred lynchings by Arizona citizens too impatient for a courtroom verdict—but Apache County achieved ignominious distinction in this regard.[3] "It is a common thing at present in Apache county, Ariz., to come across the bodies of horse and cattle thieves dangling from trees," the Flagstaff *Arizona Champion* reported in September 1887.[4]

---

1. James W. LeSueur, "My Recollection of Pioneer Days."
2. Larry D. Ball, *Desert Lawmen: The High Sheriffs of New Mexico and Arizona, 1846–1912*, 133, says vigilantes hanged two county prisoners in St. Johns in 1881 at a time when Sheriff Stover was "conspicuously absent." Ove C. Oveson also mentions the hanging of two men in the county jail in the fall of 1881 ("Sketch of the Life of Ove Christian Oveson," 56). However, James LeSueur would have been only three years old at this time, so he may have been "remembering" something that was later told to him. It's also possible that more than one St. Johns hanging occurred. C. LeRoy and Mabel R. Wilhelm, *A History of the St. Johns Arizona Stake: The Triumph of Man and His Religion Over the Perils of a Raw Frontier*, 47, says, "Occasionally, a lone figure was found hanging in the main entrance of the pioneer jail, the victim of a summary execution conducted during the night by persons unknown."
3. Lori Davisson, "Arizona Law Enforcement: A Survey from the Collections of the Arizona Historical Society," 326.
4. *Arizona Champion* (Flagstaff), September 3, 1887, 1.

Apache County in those days attracted hundreds of Texas cowboys, many of them rootless young men who came to Arizona to help manage the growing herds of cattle that fed on what was, at least for a time, the region's lush prairie grass. Bored, intoxicated, and looking for excitement after long stretches of eating beans and cattle dust, cowboys made life both interesting and dangerous when they came into town. From the Mormons' point of view, none were more troublesome than the cowboys who worked for the Aztec Land and Cattle Company. "Their cowboys would ride through the town shooting and yelling," LeSueur said. "They set up gambling dens and bawdy houses in St. Johns and Holbrook. Drunkenness together with its attendant crime flourished in the very doors of the Saints."[5]

LeSueur may have exaggerated, but only slightly. Apache County was plagued by rustlers and thieves, men with made-up names and mysterious backgrounds, men who were trying to build their own herds of cattle or horses without any means except the branding irons that hung from their saddles. Some were thought to be desperadoes driven into Arizona from Texas or New Mexico.[6] The Black River valley in southeast Apache County served as a well-known haven for rustlers and outlaws, including William "Bronco Bill" Walters, Dan "Red" Pipkin, and the Bill Smith Gang. After the gunfight at Tombstone's OK Corral in 1881, brothers Ike and Phineas Clanton moved to the southern part of Apache County near Springerville, where they reportedly rustled Mormon cattle and drove them to Mexico for sale. The Apache County sheriff and his deputies had the impossible task of enforcing the law against such men in a county that, until 1895, was larger than the combined states of New Hampshire and Vermont. Situated in Arizona's northeastern corner, Apache County shared a border with New Mexico that stretched more than two hundred miles across badlands and offered numerous safe havens for outlaws to elude pursuing lawmen. The appearance of the five Wild Bunch desperadoes riding north toward St. Johns, while certainly intimidating, was not entirely surprising. The county overflowed with such characters. "Of all the places I have ever

---

5. James W. LeSueur, "Trouble with the Hash Knife Cattle Company," in *LeSueur Family History*.

6. Jeff Guinn, *The Last Gunfight: The Real Story of the Shootout at the O.K. Corral—And How It Changed the American West*, 91–92; Joseph Pearce, *Line Rider: A True Story of Stampedes, Gamblers, Indians and Outlaws Written by Arizona Ranger Joseph Pearce 1873–1958*, 23–24; and Jim Bob Tinsley, *The Hash Knife Brand*, 57–59.

been [and] in all my association with bad men, I had never seen as bad a collection as was in Apache County," said Charley Kinnear, a Springerville saloonkeeper and Clanton associate.[7]

J.T. LeSueur had his first encounter with outlaws only a year or two after moving to St. Johns. Three highwaymen accosted LeSueur and Milford Allred while they were hauling freight for construction of the new Atlantic and Pacific Railroad near Winslow.[8] While the bandits made their escape, they were spotted by John Eagar, another Mormon freighter, who was standing on a hill above them. Eagar called for help and two other railroad men came running with their guns. Each man gave a pistol to LeSueur, and the five men gave chase, soon trapping the bandits behind a rocky ledge. The bandits opened fire, but after some skirmishing, LeSueur and the railroad men maneuvered themselves to get clear shots at the thieves. "As we reached the ledges they threw up their hands and begged for their lives," LeSueur said.[9]

They turned their prisoners over to the railroad company, which sent them to Prescott under strong guard. All three bandits pleaded guilty and were sentenced to several years in the territorial prison at Yuma.[10]

Not all such incidents ended without bloodshed. Two years after the Mormons began settling in St. Johns, the town was the scene of a massive shoot-out between Mexican-American men and Mormon cowboys from the Greer ranch.[11] The Greers, one of the most prominent Mormon fami-

---

7. Evans Coleman, "Nesters, Rustlers and Outlaws," 179. Coleman spelled Kinnear as "Caneer," but this undoubtedly was the Charley Kinnear who ran a Springerville saloon frequented by the Clantons. Joseph Fish, "History of the Eastern Arizona Stake of Zion and of the Establishment of the Snowflake Stake," 40, lists "Charles Kenner" of Springerville as one of the Mormons' chief persecutors.

8. Neither account of this event—one by J.T. LeSueur and the other by Allred's family—said how much money was taken. See "Memoirs of John Taylor LeSueur," in *LeSueur Family History*; and Dona Lucile Johnson Cooper, "A Combination of Simple Biographies, Autobiographies and Histories of the areas They Settled and the Part They Played in Opening Up the Arizona Territory," 2011. The account of this incident was apparently provided by Samuel "Sam" Johnson, one of the subjects of this family history.

9. "Memoirs of John Taylor LeSueur."

10. LeSueur says they received six-year sentences, while Johnson's account said four.

11. Accounts of this incident are provided by Nathaniel "Nat" Greer in Errol G. Brown, comp., *The Greer Family and A Look Into The Past*, 37–44; Mary Farr in the *Ogden Herald* (UT), July 31, 1882, 3; Ammon Tenney in the *Deseret Evening*

lies in the region, owned a 160-acre spread about eighteen miles northwest of St. Johns, where they ran large herds of horses and cattle across northeastern Arizona grasslands. The Greer patriarch, Thomas, died in 1881, leaving his wife and sons to manage operations. Originally from Texas, the Greer men brought with them a Southern swagger and propensity for confrontation. In the competition for rangeland, they often tangled with Mexican-American sheepherders, sometimes driving off the Mexican-Americans' herds and sometimes having their own camps dispersed. In the spring of 1882, after losing a large number of horses and cattle to rustlers, Nat Greer caught a young Mexican-American man stealing one of their horses, and so he cut an earmark on the man to brand him as a thief. Greer considered this light punishment. "We always, in the days of open range rights, considered stealing of cows and horses as a 'capital offense,'" he said. "I have known of several cases in Texas, when a known thief was taken to the nearest tree and strung up."[12]

On June 24, 1882, Nat (25) and his brothers Dick (18) and Harris (16) attended the annual San Juan Day celebration in the Mexican section of St. Johns. Five cowboys from the Greer ranch rode with them to the celebration, which featured musicians, acrobats, and a bull fight. Nat said the Mexican-Americans had invited them to look over some cattle and horses that would be on sale, but Joseph Fish, a contemporary chronicler of Mormon activities in Arizona, said the Greer boys were warned to stay away. "The Mexicans had ill feelings toward the Greers on account of their running and scattering their sheep herds. The Greers were advised not to go to St. Johns upon this occasion as the Mexicans would make them trouble," Fish said.[13] Refusing to be scared off, the young cowboys came armed. They arrived shortly after 10:00 a.m. but were told the cattle and horses they had come to examine were still on the way. They were also asked to turn in their guns, because the Mexican-American community wanted only the festival police to carry guns during the holiday celebration.

News, July 29, 1882, 3; Christopher Kempe in *Deseret Evening News*, August 30, 1882, 1; Joseph Fish in "History of the Eastern Arizona Stake," 34, 67; and Fish, "History of the Arizona Territory," 629–30. Joseph Fish Papers, Box 1. In addition, James LeSueur, although just four years old at the time, offers accounts of the incident in "How Saint Johns was Settled," 3–4; and "Autobiographical Notes," 2. Also useful are Lorenzo Hill Hatch, Journal, 128 (June 25 and July 10, 1882); and Wilhelm and Wilhelm, *History of the St. Johns Arizona Stake*, 45–47.

12. "Greer Family," 40.
13. Fish, "History of the Arizona Territory," 629.

The request was not unusual. Western communities routinely prohibited men from bringing guns to roundups, dances, and other public events to remove temptation from trigger-happy cowboys. Some frontier towns banned altogether the open carry of weapons within the town's limits to prevent an impetuous and perhaps drunken resort to violence when tempers flared.[14] However, the Greer cowboys, fearing a setup, refused to disarm because they saw that "many of the [Mexican] men there had their guns on them, as we did," Nat Greer said.[15] A policeman gave the men one hour to either give up their guns or leave the town, but rather than depart, the Greer men stopped at a store to get something to eat.[16] It was a show of bravado demonstrating more valor than discretion, because soon after entering the store the cowboys looked out the window and saw the festival police marching toward them accompanied by twenty to thirty Mexican-American men armed with rifles and pistols. The cowboys now decided to leave. Four exited out the back door and four through the front, each group trying to quietly slip away. Someone fired at them from across the street. In an instant, the street rang with gunfire.

"Bullets by the dozens flew through the streets," said Fish, as men, women, and children fled the celebration in disorderly confusion.[17] Ove Oveson was helping Mexican-American friends build a coral when a bullet struck the pole he was holding. "That is anof [enough]," he told himself. "I ran for home."[18] Oveson could hear the bullets whistling around him, with one striking the ground between his legs as he dashed away. The Greer men who bolted out the back door were able to jump on their horses and escape, though one of them, seventeen-year-old Hyrum "Hi" Hatch, caught a bullet in his left shoulder.[19] The other four cowboys—the three Greer brothers and James Vaughan—took cover in an unfinished house and exchanged gunfire with the Mexican-Americans, who scrambled to the Barth Hotel about one hundred yards away. The Greers wounded one

---

14. For an example of the banning of firearms at a sheep rodeo, see *St. Johns Herald*, July 28, 1900, 2. For a discussion of laws and practices prohibiting the carry of firearms within towns, see Robert Dykstra, *The Cattle Towns*, 112–48; and Adam Winkler, *Gunfight: The Battle Over the Right to Bear Arms in America*, 160–73.

15. "Greer Family," 41.

16. *Deseret Evening News*, July 29, 1882, 3; and *Ogden Herald*, July 31, 1882, 3.

17. Fish, "History of the Eastern Arizona Stake," 67.

18. Oveson, "Sketch," 56.

19. Lorenzo Hatch, Journal, 128 (June 25, 1882). Lorenzo Hatch, the father of Hi Hatch, estimated that forty or fifty shots were fired at the four escaping cowboys.

"Bullets by the dozens flew through the streets" of St. Johns when an ongoing feud between the cattle ranching Greer family and Mexican-American sheep owners erupted in a deadly shootout. Among the Greer cowboys pictured here—(left to right) Joseph T. Woods, Jeff Tribet, Nat Greer, Hi Hatch, and Albert F. Potter—all but Potter were present at the shootout. Some Mormons regarded the Greer cowboys as courageous defenders of their rights in a lawless land, while others thought the Greers' roughneck style exacerbated tensions with their gentile neighbors. Courtesy Arizona State Library, Archives and Public Records, Archives Division. No. 97-9493.

of the attackers, but their assailants seized the advantage by pouring in rifle fire from the hotel's second floor. "The four of us in the house had only our six guns, plenty of bullets in our belts, but our shooting wasn't too effective at that distance," Nat said.[20] Vaughan was struck by three bullets to his body but continued firing until a rifle shot from the hotel window pierced his neck and severed his jugular vein, causing a gush of blood. The twenty-year-old Vaughan stuck a finger in the wound to slow

---

20. "Greer Family," 41.

the bleeding and kept firing until he was too weak to hold his pistol.[21] He died a few minutes later. Another shot wounded Harris Greer in the hand.

After an hour, Nathan C. Tenney walked up the street carrying a white flag. "For God's sake, quit firing," Tenney shouted as he held up his hand.[22] Tenney, a sixty-four-year-old Mormon, spoke fluent Spanish and was well-liked by the Mexican-Americans. Sol Barth persuaded the Mexican-American men to stop shooting while Tenney spoke to the Greers, who also agreed to a cease fire. Tenney then arranged for the young men to surrender to Sheriff Ebenezer S. Stover, so they could be escorted to safety. But as Stover was handcuffing the boys, someone fired from the loft of the Barth Hotel, instantly killing Tenney with a shot likely meant for one of the Greers. The sheriff got the brothers safely to the jail, where they were locked up on charges of assault with a deadly weapon with intent to murder.

Not everyone in the Mexican-American community was assuaged by this outcome, and the threat of lynching intensified as night approached. J.T. LeSueur, Dick Gibbons, and other Mormon men guarded the jail with the sheriff for several nights until the Greer brothers were sent to Prescott for trial. Non-Mormons accused the cowboys of being the aggressors, having come to St. Johns "for the purpose of running the town and enacting another Mountain Meadows Massacre on a small scale."[23] Nat Greer and Joseph Fish said the cowboys were eventually acquitted; other accounts say they were found guilty but given light punishment. Their weapons and more than $125 in cash were confiscated at their arrest and never returned. Fish said the Greers also paid about $1,500 in legal fees. Not one of their assailants was charged with a crime.

Violent conflict over rangeland, of course, was not unique to the Greers and Mexican-Americans. The forced removal of Native Americans to reservations had opened up Arizona's abundant grasslands for cattlemen, and the new Atlantic-Pacific Railroad line attracted large cattle outfits seeking to monopolize the open range. The Aztec Land and Cattle Company, also known by its brand, the Hashknife, dominated the Little Colorado River corridor. In 1884, the New-York based Hashknife purchased a million

---

21. *Ogden Herald*, July 31, 1882, 3; and Robert Greer, "San Juan Dia 1882," 8. A note says this account was written by Robert Greer. James H. Vaughan Phelps was born October 15, 1861, in Hill, Texas, to Macajah H. and Martha Ann Phelps.

22. James W. LeSueur, "Autobiographical Notes," 2.

23. *Daily Arizona Citizen* (Tucson), July 6, 1882, 2. The article's author signed his name "Gentile."

acres of Atlantic-Pacific land south of the railroad line in Apache County and brought in more than 32,000 Texas cattle. Mormon and non-Mormon homesteaders who had hoped to purchase their homestead claims from the railroad now found themselves competing with the Hashknife for grazing lands. Some were forcibly driven from their homes by aggressive cowboys seeking to enforce the Hashknife's property rights. Many of the cowboys were good men, but a significant number were roughshod cowboys and even criminals who had been chased out of Texas and New Mexico and now were harassing Mormon settlers while rustling cattle from their Hashknife employers.[24] Robert Carlock, a former president of the Aztec Land and Cattle Company, disputes claims that Hashknife cowboys carried out a widespread purge of Apache County's small cattle ranchers and farmers, but there is no question that some Mormon families were driven from their homesteads or, in other instances, lost animals that strayed onto Hashknife land.[25] Several Mormon men were pistol-whipped. More than a few rustlers and thieves worked at various times for the Hashknife, including Tom Capehart, Tod Carver, and Tom Ketchum. Even as late as 1898, Hashknife owners were struggling to expel the criminal element among their cowboys.[26] The Hashknife's arrival also hastened the end of the Mormons' isolation, exposing their communities to the worldly influences they had sought to escape. As a result, the Mormons tended to blame the Hashknife for problems that troubled cattle towns throughout the West, such as drunkenness, gambling, prostitution, rustling, and banditry.

---

24. Tinsley, *The Hash Knife Brand*, 58–71.

25. Robert H. Carlock, *The Hashknife: The Early Days of the Aztec Land and Cattle Company, Limited*, contends that Mormon claims of mistreatment by Hashknife cowboys were exaggerated. Company executives, headquartered in New York, held no personal animus toward the Saints nor directed a vendetta against them, he said. Only a handful of Hashknife cowboys, if even that, physically beat Mormons or jumped their homestead claims. Moreover, it was the Mormons who stood on the wrong side of the law, having established farms, ranches, and even towns on land owned by the Hashknife. The Mormons "seemed to have had a need to feel persecuted and put upon," he concluded (182).

In contrast, both Daniel Justin Herman (*Hell on the Range: A Story of Honor, Conscience, and the American West*, 114) and Tinsley (*Hash Knife Brand*, 58–71), along with numerous settlers and cattlemen from that period, state that Hashknife cowboys harassed the Saints with threats of violence and sought to drive them from Hashknife lands.

26. Tinsley, *Hash Knife Brand*, 78–79.

Hashknife grazing lands lay west of St. Johns, but the conflict occasionally spilled over into the town, where the Mormons already faced determined opposition from Mexican-Americans. In April 1884, a group of non-Mormons tore down a fence on a Mormon's property in St. Johns and attempted to "jump" the claim by moving a small wooden home onto the lot. When Bishop David Udall and several Mormons tried to intervene, their skirmishing drew other townspeople into the fray. "In no time Mormons, Mexicans, Jews, and 'Gentiles' assembled on the spot and feelings ran riot," Udall said.[27] In the face of Mormon resistance, the non-Mormons brandished their guns to show they meant business. Exasperated, Udall told his friends he was going home to get his gun. As he turned to cross the street, Andrew Gibbons, Bill's brother, put a hand on Udall's shoulder to hold him back. "Bishop, you must keep your cool," Gibbons said. "Much depends on you today." Recognizing that Gibbons was right, Udall called out loudly, "Men, let us all go home." The Mormons left and soon the entire crowd dispersed, including the claim jumpers.

The Mormons gained a small victory, but Apache County Sheriff John Lorenzo Hubbell subsequently arrested Udall and several other Mormon men involved in the skirmish.[28] Although the Mormon men were later acquitted, Hubbell took no action against the men who had destroyed and trespassed on Mormon property. This pattern repeated itself throughout Apache County, whose sheriffs and courts often failed to protect Mormon settlers from Aztec cowboys.[29] Joseph Fish expressed the prevailing Mormon view when he complained that Hubbell won the 1884 election for county sheriff because he "entered into a compact with the leading horse and cattle thieves of the county, pledging himself to shield them in their freebooting business for their support at the election, which he got."[30] Evans Coleman, a Mormon cattleman, said many of the nesters—that is, squatters—who inhabited the county's remote mountain areas targeted Mormon cattle for rustling. "The nesters boasted that they killed only Mormon cattle. Some of those non-Mormon cowmen never ate anything but Mormon beef. On a round-up, they dropped out every

---

27. Udall, *Arizona Pioneer Mormon*, 92.

28. Fish, "History of the Eastern Arizona Stake," 67; and Mark E. Miller, "St. Johns's Saints: Interethnic Conflict in Northeastern Arizona, 1880–85," 81–82.

29. Herman, *Hell on the Range*, 89–120, describes the Mormons' contentious relations with cowboys from the Hashknife and other outfits.

30. Fish, "History of the Eastern Arizona Stake," 37.

Mormon-owned cow they could find," he said.³¹ The squatters knew that when they stole Mormon beef, they wouldn't face the deadly reprisals typically meted out to rustlers. "Even if a nester was caught killing an animal, it was a hundred miles to Solomonville, where he would be tried. He would have a dozen witnesses, and would pay his expenses out of Mormon beef, to boot," Coleman said.³²

Appealing to the law could have deadly consequences. James Hale, a sixty-one-year-old Mormon polygamist, was gunned down outside a Springerville store on December 25, 1886, when he went to town to buy food for a Christmas dinner.³³ The *St. Johns Herald* initially said his death was an accident resulting from the reckless firing of pistols "during a holiday jollification" outside a local saloon. However, prior to the shooting, Hale had reported to authorities the activities of rustlers he had seen operating in the area, which had led to a number of arrests. The man who allegedly shot Hale, Billy Evans, was said to be part of the rustling gang.³⁴ Witnesses claimed the drunken Evans fired his .44 pistol at Hale with an intent to kill. At least one witness reported that prior to shooting Hale, Evans said he wanted to see if a bullet would go through a Mormon. Two days later, a posse captured Evans, who was shot in the groin trying to flee, and brought him back to stand trial. Evans, who used both "Diamond"

---

31. Coleman, "Nesters, Rustlers and Outlaws," 178.

32. Coleman, 178.

33. The *St. Johns Herald*, December 30, 1886, 3; and January 6, 1887, 3, published accounts of this incident. County court records related to Hale's shooting are republished in LaReah H. Toronto, comp., "To These, Our Grandparents." See also *Apache County Critic* (Holbrook, AZ), July 9, 1887. Secondary accounts of this incident are found in: Winkie Crigler, *Beans 'N' Things*, 55–56; Herman, *Hell on the Range*, 153–54; Wilhelm and Wilhelm, *History of the St. Johns Arizona Stake*, 245; and in Esther Wiltbank and Zola Whiting, *Lest Ye Forget*, 67.

34. In Apache County court records of this incident, Evans is listed as "J.W. Dimon alias W.M. Timberline." The *St. Johns Herald* refers to him as Diamond, who goes by "Ace of Diamonds" or "Jack of Diamonds." However, the *Apache County Critic* claimed his real name was Billy Evans, who went by Jack Diamond or Jack Timberline. The Tucson *Arizona Daily Star* (July 17, 1887, 4) also said that Timberline was an alias for Bill Evans. Joseph Fish listed "Jack Evans" of Springerville as one of the Saints' chief persecutors in Apache County (Fish, "History of the Eastern Arizona Stake," 41). Wilhelm and Wilhelm (*History of the St. Johns Arizona Stake*, 245) appear mistaken in identifying him as Tom Tolbert; Herman (*Hell on the Range*, 153) appears mistaken in identifying him as C. W. Johnson, alias Kid Swingle.

and "Timberline" as aliases, recovered and was released two weeks later due to insufficient evidence. Hale's death left a family of orphaned children. It also sent a clear message regarding the risks of informing on or testifying against rustlers and bandits.

As the Mormons' leader in St. Johns, Bishop Udall felt especially vulnerable to violent reprisals. Bill Gibbons, a constable and second counselor in the bishopric, would secretly follow Udall after their nighttime meetings, gun in his hip pocket, to make sure Udall made it home safely.[35] And during the heightened antagonisms surrounding the polygamy trials in the mid-1880s, Nat Greer stayed at Udall's house and served as his bodyguard.[36]

Mormon men did not typically carry weapons when they first began settling the Little Colorado River basin.[37] When highwaymen held up J.T. LeSueur and Milford Allred, the two men were unarmed; so too was Bishop Udall when Aztec cowboys tried to push Mormons off a St. Johns lot. Over time, the Mormons' commitment to legal processes placed them at a disadvantage in confronting Arizona's growing lawless element. Many Mormons had ambivalent feelings about the Greer brothers. The Greers were quick to resort to violence but didn't let anyone push them around. On the one hand, the Greers' ongoing feud with Mexican-American sheepherders undermined Mormon efforts to develop peaceful relations with their neighbors. Some may have also viewed the Greers' attitude and activities as contrary to the Mormons' religious principles. That's why Joseph Fish, in his account of the San Juan Day gunfight, carefully noted that the Greer brothers were not Mormons, which was technically correct, because they had not yet been baptized.[38] Fish's effort to distance the Mormons from the Greers reflected the discomfort many felt about the Greers' aggressive embrace of the cowboy ethos.

But the Greers also had defenders within the Mormon community, people who appreciated their roughneck style. During a discussion of the Greer family, a Mormon man complained about the rowdy brothers, saying, "Now if the Greer boys were like everyone else and they would go on missions, then all our troubles would be over."[39]

---

35. Udall, *Arizona Pioneer Mormon*, 95–96.
36. Ellen Greer Rees, comp., "Greer Men and Ellen C. Greer."
37. Herman, *Hell on the Range*, 76.
38. Fish, "History of the Eastern Arizona Stake," 34.
39. "Greer Men," 31. Quotation edited for clarity.

"Missions! Missions! Go on missions!" Charley Riggs replied. "Do you think what might happen to us if they went on missions? Who would we have to fight for us?"

By the mid-1880s, as the county's criminals grew increasingly bold, large numbers of the Mormon men started arming themselves in case of trouble. "The feeling was so bitter against the saints that the saints felt under the necessity of carrying fire arms," Joseph Fish said.[40]

Still, the Mormons did not abandon their commitment to finding non-violent solutions. Shortly after the claim-jumping incident in St. Johns, visiting Mormon authorities from Salt Lake City counseled the Saints to let God fight their battles for them.[41] "We should cultivate a spirit of forbearance and not fight with carnal weapons," said Apostle Brigham Young, Jr., at a May 16, 1884, meeting.[42] Young said the Saints would prevail by living righteously. "When we go before the Lord properly our enemies melt away. We must trust the Lord implicitly and keep our tempers," he said.[43] Referring to President Taylor's recently announced plan to send additional families to reinforce the St. Johns mission, Apostle Francis M. Lyman said, "We expect this difficulty here to be settled by the steady growth of our people. The better element will predominate."[44] To keep the Mormon community pure and strong, Young and Eastern Arizona Stake President Jesse N. Smith reiterated their counsel against mixing with outsiders, fearing especially for Mormon girls who went to work for non-Mormons.

On Sunday, May 18, following two days of preaching, the St. Johns congregation held a special fast and prayer meeting in which they beseeched God to "release us from the bonds and persecutions of our enemies."[45]

---

40. Fish, "History of the Eastern Arizona Stake," 68. See also, Wilhelm and Wilhelm, *History of the St. Johns Arizona Stake*, 50, who said the Mormons began arming themselves at all times.

41. Jesse N. Smith, president of the Eastern Arizona Stake Mission, provides the most details of this conference in his *Journal of Jesse N. Smith: The Life Story of a Mormon Pioneer 1834–1906*, 288–290 (May 16–18, 1884). Other accounts are provided in Maria S. Ellsworth, editor, *Mormon Odyssey: The Story of Ida Hunt Udall, Plural Wife*, 70; Joseph Fish, "The Life and Times of Joseph Fish: Mormon Pioneer," 236; Hatch, Journal, 141; and Udall, *Arizona Pioneer Mormon*, 93–95.

42. Smith, Journal, 288 (May 16, 1884).

43. Smith, Journal, 288 (May 16, 1884).

44. Smith, Journal, 288 (May 16, 1884).

45. Diary of Ida Hunt Udall (one of Bishop Udall's plural wives), as quoted in Ellsworth, *Story of Ida Hunt Udall*, 70.

After the meeting, the visiting authorities and St. Johns's leading men held a solemn prayer meeting at Bishop Udall's home. Stake President Smith described their prayers:

> We named the names of a number of the more prominent of our enemies in this country before the Lord, praying that if it were possible that they might repent of their wickedness against us and do so no more, but that if they would not repent that He would deprive them of their power to further injure us.[46]

Each person present prayed in a similar manner, imploring God to intercede on their behalf against their enemies.

Mormons were not pacifists. They armed themselves and would fight, even kill, if necessary, to defend themselves. But their leaders cautioned against provoking their enemies or instigating violence. Prayers "are the weapons for us to fight with," Elder Young asserted. "We must be in the right and have God on our side. We must never take the law into our own hands."[47] Over the years, the Mormons would hold additional fast and prayer meetings pleading for relief from their enemies.[48]

A decisive turn for the St. Johns Saints came in 1886 when Hashknife managers formed a coalition with Mormons and others to act against suspected rustlers and bandits operating in Apache County. The Pleasant Valley War that raged for most of the 1880s was just the largest of several Arizona conflagrations in which cattlemen and sheepherders battled for rangelands once fertile but now shrinking due to overgrazing and drought. When a depression sent cattle prices downward, Hashknife owners could no longer ignore the rustlers, including some in their own outfit, whose activities threatened the company's existence. Growing banditry of rail-

---

46. Smith, Journal, 289 (May 18, 1884).

47. Smith, 289 (May 17, 1884).

48. In his incisive examination of the Pleasant Valley War, Mark Herman argues that the conflict over Arizona's rangeland often pitted an ethos of honor against an ethos of conscience. "Honor trended toward assertion, strength, fierceness, combat," Herman said. "Conscience trended toward restraint, modesty, sympathy" (*Hell on the Range*, xxii). Honor was especially prominent among the Texas cowboys who came to dominate the American West, as reflected by their propensity for gambling, drinking, whoring, and violence, especially in using violence to defend reputation. Honor demanded that men demonstrate physical courage, even dominance, and, above all, "save face" when their manliness was challenged. Maintaining law and order while upholding the values of conscience presented a difficult challenge to Mormons and other Arizona settlers.

roads and stagecoach lines added to these problems.[49] The county's stock growers grew increasingly frustrated with Sheriff John Lorenzo Hubbell, who seemed uninterested in pursuing horse and cattle thieves. And so the Hashknife and other large cattle companies, including the powerful Apache County Stock Growers Association, joined with the railroads, Mormons, small ranchers, and sheepherders to promote law-and-order candidates in the November election. This coalition formed the Citizen's Ticket and pushed a slate of candidates to replace allegedly corrupt officials dominating the county offices. For example, the Citizen's Ticket convention nominated J.T. LeSueur as treasurer to restore the integrity of the treasurer's office and put the county on firm financial footing. But the most important reform candidate—and most controversial figure on the party's ticket—was sheriff's candidate Commodore Perry Owens, who promised to clean up Apache County and drive out the outlaws.

Owens was born July 29, 1852, on a small farm in eastern Tennessee and later moved with his family to Indiana.[50] He left home at the age of sixteen for the Indian Territory, working on ranches in what is now Oklahoma, where he honed his shooting skills. He settled in Navajo Springs, Apache County, in the early 1880s and gained a reputation as a man of bold action defending Anglo cattle and sheep from Navajo raiders who refused to stay put on their reservation. On September 15, 1883, while working on the ranch of James Houck, Owens shot and killed a young Navajo herding horses. Owens claimed he was defending himself after being shot at by three Navajos, but the slain man's companions said Owens fired at them without provocation.[51] The Navajo agent, D. M. Riordan, had Owens arrested for murder, but Owens was eventually released, leading Riordan to complain that Houck and Owens were "dangerous to the peace and good order of the region."[52] In an 1880 photo, Owens wears cowboy chaps, a holstered long-barreled pistol, a belt full of ammunition, and a wide-brim hat over his long, flowing, reddish-blond hair. With a heroic name, Winchester rifle, and hair that hung well below his shoulders, Commodore Perry Owens struck the pose of an adventur-

---

49. Larry D. Ball, "Commodore Perry Owens: The Man Behind the Legend," 27.

50. For details of Owens's early life, see Ball, "Commodore Perry Owens," 27–33; and David Grasse, *A Killer is What They Needed: The True, Untold Story of Commodore Perry Owens, A Sheriff of the Arizona Territory*, 1–32.

51. Grasse, *A Killer is What they Needed*, 17–22, provides the most detailed examination of this incident.

52. Grasse, 22.

Apache County Sheriff Commodore Perry Owens could "stand twenty feet from an empty tomato-can and keep it rolling and jumping with alternate shots from his two guns." Mormon pioneers praised Owens for driving out the outlaws plaguing the county, but residents eventually soured on his aggressive approach. Unapologetic, he said, "They refused me a second term because I was a killer, but a killer was what was needed then." Photo circa 1886, courtesy Arizona Historical Society, No. 100-0004056.

ous Western cowboy. "Owens nearly always carried two revolvers, and could draw either with his right hand or his left with wonderful speed," said Will Barnes, who was then secretary of the Apache County Stock Association. "Several times on the round-ups I had seen him stand twenty feet from an empty tomato-can and keep it rolling and jumping with alternate shots from his two guns until it was torn to pieces."[53] Owens also carried a Winchester and could fire it rapidly and accurately from the hip, giving him an edge in a showdown.

In the runup to the November 1886 election, the *St. Johns Herald* threw its support behind Owens, warning would-be lawbreakers that their days were numbered. "Thieves have only two more months in which to work in Apache County," the *St. Johns Herald* proclaimed on October 28.

---

53. Will C. Barnes, *Apaches and Longhorns: The Reminiscences of Will C. Barnes*, edited by Frank C. Lockwood, 147.

After escaping injury at Tombstone's famous Gunfight at the OK Corral, Ike Clanton moved to Apache County, where he and his brother Phin allegedly rustled Mormon cattle. Six years later, Ike was gunned down at his ranch by a deputy claiming Ike had resisted arrest, while Phin was convicted of rustling. Courtesy of Arizona State Library, Archives and Public Records, Archives Division. No. 97-7485.

"Two more months for the rustler and assassin."[54] Owens garnered 55 percent of the votes to defeat incumbent Sheriff Hubbell.[55]

Owens's election ushered in an open season on suspected rustlers and thieves. In early March 1887, a grand jury issued indictments against twenty-five alleged criminals, and in April arrest warrants were issued for Ike and Phin Clanton, who had long been suspected of rustling Mormon cattle. On June 1, Apache County Deputy Jonas Brighton shot and killed Ike for resisting arrest, while Phin was convicted of rustling and sentenced to ten years in prison for stealing a cow.[56] Later that month, Jack Evans, the man accused of killing James Hales on Christmas Day, was shot and killed by Charlie Thomas, a rancher who said he caught Evans and a man named Sprague stealing his horses. Thomas did not admit to killing Evans and Sprague, but merely said "they would never steal any more horses

---

54. *St. Johns Herald*, October 28, 1886, 2. See also, *St. Johns Herald*, October 21, 1886, 1.

55. *St. Johns Herald*, November 18, 1886, 3.

56. Ball, "Commodore Perry Owens," 39; and *St. Johns Herald*, June 9, 1887, 3; September 22, 1887, 3; and September 29, 1887, 3.

from him."⁵⁷ A third member of Evans's rustling crew, Lee Renfro, was shot and killed by Brighton under questionable circumstances shortly after. "Unlawful killings are always to be regretted," said the *St. Johns Herald* regarding the shooting of Renfro, "but in this instance the county enjoys a happy riddance without the expense of a prosecution."⁵⁸ Also early in the year, Sol Barth was found guilty of forging county warrants and sentenced to prison. Although the court proceedings against Barth began before the Citizen's Party swept into power, his conviction reflected Apache County's dramatically altered political power structure.

In the late summer, Owens rode to Holbrook to take on Andy Blevins, who was better known as Andy Cooper.⁵⁹ Cooper, as the oldest of the Texas-born Blevins boys, headed up a family rustling gang causing trouble among the area's ranchers and Navajos. He and his brothers had also jumped the land claims of several Mormon families when the Hashknife was seeking to push the Saints off Hashknife lands.⁶⁰ Twenty-five years old and unmarried, Cooper had a reputation as a gunslinger, earned in part for his active defense of the Graham family in the Pleasant Valley War. His father, Mart Blevins, and brother Hamp had recently been killed in the bloody range feud. The *St. Johns Herald* called the Blevins crowd "a desperate gang of cattle thieves" who "openly boasted that the officers of the law were afraid to undertake to arrest them."⁶¹ In fact, an arrest warrant for Cooper had been issued nearly a year before Owens took office, but Sheriff Hubbell and his deputies had not attempted to make the arrest. When rumors began circulating that Owens, now eight months on the job, was afraid to deliver the long-standing warrant, he decided to act. In August, Owens warned Cooper that he had a warrant charging him with stealing a horse, and on September 4, Owens went to the Blevins home in Holbrook to make the arrest. Deputy Frank Wattron offered to

---

57. *St. Johns Herald*, June 30, 1887, 3. The editor of the *St. Johns Herald* would later question whether the reports of the killing were a ruse to allow Evans and Sprague to escape. Regardless, they were never heard from again.

58. August 11, 1887, 3. See also Ball, "Commodore Perry Owens," 39; and *St. Johns Herald*, July 21, 1887, 3.

59. The most detailed examination of this episode can be found in Grasse, *A Killer is What They Needed*, 77–118. I also drew upon Ball, "Commodore Perry Owens," 43–48; Herman, *Hell on the Range*, 157–63; and Wilhelm and Wilhelm, *History of the St. Johns Arizona Stake*, 234–37.

60. Herman, *Hell on the Range*, 107–9.

61. *St. Johns Herald*, September 8, 1887, 3.

accompany Owens, but the sheriff declined. "If I take a posse down there it is almost sure that several men will be killed," Owens said. "But if I go alone they can only kill one man."[62]

Wattron and several other men watched from the railway platform across the street as Owens, Winchester rifle in hand and six-shooter by his side, approached the Blevins home. Crowded inside the 600-square-foot house were eleven people: Andy Cooper; his brothers John and Sam Houston; their mother, Mary; John's wife, Eva, and their infant son; a Blevins sister; another woman with her two young girls; and a man named Mose Roberts.[63] As Owens stepped onto the porch, he peered inside a window, where he saw some of the people gathered inside. Owens called for Cooper to come out and watched through the window as both Cooper and John got out their pistols. John took a position by a door about four feet to Owens's left while Cooper came to the door where Owens was standing. Cooper opened the door only wide enough to stick out his head.

"I have a warrant for you, and I want you to come along with me," Owens told Cooper.[64]

"What warrant is it, Owens?" Cooper replied.

Owens said it was the warrant for horse theft he had previously mentioned to Cooper. Cooper didn't answer right away, as if he were thinking it over. "Are you ready?" Owens asked.

"Wait," Cooper said, his head still sticking out the door. "In a few minutes."

"No! Right away," Owens demanded.

"I won't go," Cooper replied. He raised his six-shooter, perhaps preparing to fire. Owens didn't wait to find out. He shot Cooper with his rifle, knocking Cooper back into the house with a gaping stomach wound. The ball exited near his spine.

Seeing Owens shoot his brother, John pushed open the side door and fired wildly at Owens, missing the sheriff but killing Cooper's horse behind him. Owens whirled and shot John in the shoulder, driving him back. Owens retreated onto the street so he could get a better view of movements

---

62. Wilhelm and Wilhelm, *History of the St. Johns Arizona Stake*, 235.

63. Roberts is called "Mote" in some accounts.

64. Two similar versions of the conversation between Owens and Cooper are contained in the *Apache County Critic*, September 10, 1887 (republished in Grasse, *A Killer is What They Needed*, 102–4); and Owens's sworn statement at the coroner's inquest, September 6, 1887 (republished in Wilhelm and Wilhelm, *History of the St. Johns Arizona Stake*, 235–36).

within the house. Seeing Cooper through a window, he fired again, this time hitting Cooper in the hip. At that moment, Mose Roberts jumped out a bedroom window and ran from the house, attempting to escape the mayhem. Roberts had a six-shooter in his hand, Owens said, and so, after maneuvering for a direct line of sight, he shot Roberts in the back as he fled. The ball struck Roberts in the left shoulder and passed through his left lung, tearing away part of his left collarbone as it exited the body. Owens reloaded his rifle and turned his attention back to the house, while Roberts made his way back inside through a rear door. Roberts fell to the floor in a pool of his own blood. While Owens studied the house, fifteen-year-old Sam Blevins jumped onto the front porch, brandishing Cooper's pistol. Behind Sam, his mother, Mary, screamed. She grabbed Sam, frantically trying to drag him back inside the house. She was too late. Owens shot the boy, who collapsed at his mother's feet with his legs sticking out the door. "I stayed a few moments longer," Owens said. "I see no other man so I left the house."

That was largely Owens's version of the encounter. Mary Blevins claimed Cooper was not armed when he answered the door. John Blevins's wife, Eva, said Cooper was not resisting arrest. According to Eva, Owens shot Cooper after saying only, "I want you, Andy."[65] Some also claimed Roberts was unarmed when he ran from the house.

The shooting had unfolded so quickly—lasting just a minute or two—that the men watching from across the street had little time to react. Deputy Wattron grabbed his shotgun and ran to assist Owens, but the shooting had already stopped when he reached the sheriff. "Did you get them?" Wattron asked.

"Yes," Owens coolly replied. "When ever I draw a bead I know I have got them."[66]

Owens had fired just five shots from his Winchester. Sam Blevins died almost immediately. Andy Cooper crawled around on the floor, bleeding painfully, begging for someone to kill him. He died that evening. Mose Roberts, whose connection with the family remains unclear, died eleven days later. Only John Blevins survived. None of the others inside the home were injured, but they did not escape the horror. "Dead and wounded in every room, and the blood over the floors, doors and walls," said an observer who went inside after the shooting. "One little child, seven years of age, was literally bespattered with clots of human gore. The agonizing groans of the wounded, the death rattle of the dying, mingled

---

65. Herman, *Hell on the Range*, 159.
66. Ball, "Commodore Perry Owens," 47.

with the screams of the females made a sight that no one would care to see a second time."⁶⁷ Owens came under criticism from some quarters for his quick trigger, but the men who witnessed the action from across the street largely substantiated his version of the incident. The inquest that followed ruled that Owens had acted in self-defense. "Outside of a few men, and very few men at that, Owens is supported by every man, woman and child in this town," wrote a Holbrook resident in a letter published in the *St. Johns Herald*. The *Herald* editor praised Owens for his "good work" in "ridding the Territory of two, and perhaps three, of the worst characters that ever infested any country."⁶⁸ John Blevins was subsequently arrested and convicted of attempted murder for shooting at Owens.

The swift and violent measures taken against the Clantons, Blevins, and others sent a clear message to Apache County's criminals. Will Barnes, secretary and treasurer of the Stock Growers' Association, said the county's bad men "fairly burned up the roads and tore the mountains down" fleeing the county before their number came up.⁶⁹ Those who didn't get the message, such as the Clantons' brother-in-law, Ebin Stanley, were warned to leave or face similar trouble.⁷⁰ The *St. Johns Herald* reported in September 1887 that Stanley and his family planned to move to Chihuahua, Mexico. "They have the best wishes of many friends for their prosperity in their new home," the paper's editor noted with no hint of irony.⁷¹

One man who refused to leave was Jamie Stott, a Massachusetts native who had established a ranch about forty miles south of Holbrook.⁷² Stott was first accused of harboring horse thieves and then of murder. Many also thought he had close connections with the Graham faction in Pleasant Valley, but what may have sealed his fate is that he once insulted Apache County Deputy Sheriff Jim Houck, a volatile and violent man who reportedly coveted the grassland on Stott's ranch.⁷³ On August 11,

---

67. Quoted in Herman, *Hell on the Range*, 159.
68. *St. Johns Herald*, September 8, 1887, 3.
69. Barnes, *Apaches and Longhorns*, 134.
70. *St. Johns Herald*, September 22, 1887, 3, says that Stanley was given the alternative of leaving the territory or standing trial.
71. *St. Johns Herald*, September 29, 1887, 3.
72. Herman, *Hell on the Range*, 167–96, provides an account of the lynching of Stott and his two associates.
73. Grasse, *A Killer is What They Needed*, 15–17, provides a short sketch of Houck, thought by many to be a sociopathic killer but who nevertheless served as a lawman and was elected to the Thirteenth Arizona Territorial Legislature.

1888, Houck arrested Stott at his home, though he had no warrant, and handed Stott and two of Stott's associates—Jim Scott and Jeff Wilson—to a mob of nearly thirty men from Apache County and Pleasant Valley. The mob first hanged Scott and Wilson, both twenty-four years old, who begged for their lives. Hoping to force a confession from Stott, the mob constantly raised and lowered him with a noose around his neck, but Stott, also just twenty-four, vigorously proclaimed his innocence until he finally died from the numerous mock hangings. The evidence suggests that Stott was, indeed, innocent. The other two young men, Scott and Wilson, were primarily guilty of being his friends, though Houck may have also held a grudge against Scott.[74] Although no Mormons were known to have participated in the mob action, several Mormon leaders knew and approved of the carefully planned lynching. They believed the men were guilty and deserving of punishment.[75] "This hanging probably did more to run out the cattle and horse thieves than any other," wrote Mormon chronicler Joseph Fish. "No amount of shooting could terrorize the cowboy element as this lynching did."[76] Fish acknowledged that the hanging was an "unlawful act," but said "public sentiment was so strong" in support of the lynch mob "that nothing was done."[77] No charges were ever filed against the vigilantes. Houck reportedly later used Stott's land to graze his sheep.

Apache County eventually soured on Sheriff Owens. Among the problems that surfaced during his term were a rapid turnover of deputies, whom he occasionally blamed for his own shortcomings, poor record keeping, and an inordinate number of prisoner escapes. In addition, Owens was absent from St. Johns chasing criminals more often and for longer stretches than previous sheriffs. Even the *St. Johns Herald*, once Owen's leading cheerleader, joined the chorus of critics. After John Blevins was convicted of

---

74. Carlock, *The Hashknife*, 197–200, suggests that Scott, a Hashknife foreman and "a natural Texas fighter" (197) may have been targeted because it was he, not Stott, who had a run-in with Houck. Wilson, a former Hashknife cook, had been accused of a minor theft earlier that year.

75. Herman, *Hell on the Range*, 187–94, examines evidence of Mormon complicity, as well as Mormon attitudes about the lynching.

76. Fish, "History of the Arizona Territory," 690.

77. Fish, "History of the Eastern Arizona Stake," 75. Will Barnes (*Apaches and Longhorns*, 163) also states that support for the vigilantes was so strong that no Apache County jury would have convicted them. "In my judgment any attempts to punish these men would have resulted only in more bloodshed, and would have accomplished nothing," he said.

attempted murder, Owens insisted on taking Blevins to the Yuma prison, although everyone knew a governor's pardon was on the way. The *St. Johns Herald* excoriated Owens for humiliating Blevins in this manner, stating, "Sheriff Owens has been guilty of perpetrating an act of injustice and assumption of authority which surprised even his most partial friends."[78] Most significant was the *Herald's* about-face on the strong-arm tactics used by Owens and his deputies. In contrast to the paper's enthusiastic defense of Owens's bloody takedown of the Blevins family, the paper now declared its opposition to such methods. Without mentioning Owens by name, the *Herald* seemed to be taking direct aim at the sheriff:

> The common people are beginning to think that our Territory has had enough of desperadoes as "peace" officers, who parade about with abbreviated cannon strapped to their hips. What the country most needs, is not so much a class of officers who shoot people, simply because they have "the drop," but men possessing some brains, coupled with a little executive ability. The trouble with the desperado-class of officers is that they shoot whom they please, and are acquitted on the plea that their victims "had it in for 'em," and the shooting was in self-defense. Experience proves that nine out of every possible ten, of this class of murderers, are arrant curs with not a spark of true bravery in their composition.[79]

As would be shown in the upcoming election, the *Herald* was speaking for the majority of Apache County's voters.

What caused citizens to become disenchanted with Owens? Owens's introverted nature made him poorly suited to the sheriff's job, which required an outgoing personality and ability to address issues through negotiation and tact, as well as with the gun. Among the complaints lodged against Owens, he was said to be a poor administrator whose distrustful nature caused heavy turnover among his deputies.[80] But the main problem seemed to be a growing recognition of overreach. Just as county officials quickly regretted railroading Bishop Udall into prison, they likewise may have felt that those recently convicted were too harshly punished. Solomon Barth subsequently received a governor's pardon, as did John Blevins. Apache citizens, including J.T. LeSueur and other county officials, would later petition the governor to pardon Phin Clanton after the chief witness against Clanton admitted

---

78. *St. Johns Herald,* November 8, 1888, 3.
79. *St. Johns Herald,* June 14, 1888, 3.
80. Ball, "Commodore Perry Owens," 48–49; and Grasse, *A Killer is What They Needed,* 72, 156.

that he had lied under oath.[81] It was also reported that Jonas Brighton, the deputy who killed both Ike Clanton and Lee Renfro, was secretly on the payroll of the Stock Growers' Association, thus raising questions whether Brighton was carrying out a private vendetta for the region's cattlemen—and whether Brighton's victims were really resisting arrest when he shot them.[82] Owens had relatively little support when the 1888 election rolled around. The Citizens Party that previously nominated Owens for sheriff was now disbanded, and Apache County voters divided into traditional Democratic and Republican camps. Neither party put Owens on its ballot.

Owens believed he had been unfairly discarded after he had done exactly what the voters had elected him to do: Aggressively root out and eliminate the criminals infesting Apache County. He was unapologetic. "They refused me a second term because I was a killer," he told George Crosby, "but a killer was what was needed then."[83]

Owens may have been unwanted, but he was not unappreciated. Mormons came to view his two-year tenure as an answer to their prayers. Owens was "providentially sent from Tennesse [sic] to assist in getting rid of the thieves," said his friend, John Bushman.[84] James LeSueur, J.T.'s oldest son, echoed this sentiment. In recalling how the Saints dealt with the criminals infesting the county, LeSueur said, "The Saints called a day of Fasting and Prayer for the Lord to bring about a change. A man by the name of Commodore Owens was elected sheriff."[85] Whether LeSueur was referring to the May 1884 solemn prayer meeting or a subsequent prayer meeting is unclear, but his point is not: God sent Owens to help fight the Saints' battles. Joseph Fish also praised Owens for ridding the county of the Blevins family, saying "this was one of the best things that ever happened and had the effect of breaking up the worst gang of thieves that there was in the country."[86] Bishop Udall did not mention Owens in his

---

81. Herman, *Hell on the Range*, 163–65.

82. Evidence suggesting that the Apache County Stock Growers Association hired Brighton to kill Ike Clanton and possibly others is presented in Herman, *Hell on the Range*, 152–54; and Grasse, *A Killer is What They Needed*, 69–70.

83. George H. Crosby, "As My Memory Recalls: Stories of the Colonizing of the Little Colorado River Country," 5. See also Ball, "Commodore Perry Owens," 51.

84. Quoted in Ball, "Commodore Perry Owens," 51.

85. LeSueur, "Trouble With the Hash Knife Cattle Company."

86. Fish, "History of the Eastern Arizona Stake," 77. Fish, "Manuscript," 689, also praises Owens's feat as "one of the most daring and successful that was ever accomplished."

memoir, but he also believed God brought about the deaths of the Saints' enemies. "Within two years after the special fast, and the solemn prayer meeting, five of the six ringleaders, one by one, met with violent deaths, and none of them at the hands of their Mormon neighbors," Udall said.[87] However, as far as can be determined, none of the major Ring leaders had actually died or been killed.[88] Udall wrote his memoir more than forty years after these events, so he likely was thinking of the cowboy outlaws killed during Owens's term, such as Ike Clanton, Billy Evans, and Andy Cooper, who were considered enemies of the Saints. James LeSueur, who was just eight years old when Owens was elected sheriff, was probably not speaking from personal knowledge so much as he was reflecting the Mormon community's views that he absorbed while growing up in St. Johns. "A great debt of gratitude is due Commodore Owens for his brave and efficient service as sheriff," LeSueur said.[89]

The degree to which Apache County's crime rate subsided under Sheriff Owens remains a subject of debate. Shortly after the Blevins shootout, Apache County was hit by a wave of mail-coach and train robberies. Eventually new criminals drifted into the territory and filled the void left by those who had been chased out. The same geographical conditions that attracted thieves and robbers remained. The large desert expanses and high mountain country, all in a county the size of two states, provided too many avenues for escape and too many remote, easy-to-defend places to hide. In the coming years, several factors would reduce the unusually elevated levels of violence that characterized the 1880s—the Pleasant Valley

---

87. Udall, *Arizona Pioneer Mormon*, 95.

88. The so-called St. Johns Ring was a fluid group, making uncertain which six Ring leaders Udall was referring to. Ten of the most likely candidates are: Albert F. Banta, Solomon Barth, C. I. Gutterson, John Lorenzo Hubbell, Benigno Lopez, George McCarter, William Milligan, Tomas Perez, Alfred Ruiz, and Ebenezer F. Stover. Udall states that Hubbell, who later became a friend of the Saints, was the only ringleader who wasn't killed. However, records show that Banta (d. 1924); Barth (d. 1928); Lopez (d. 1954); and Perez (d. 1893) also lived through this period. I could not discover what happened to Gutterson, McCarter, Milligan, or Stover.

89. LeSueur, "Trouble With the Hash Knife Cattle Company." There is no conclusive tally of how many alleged rustlers and outlaws were killed during the period when Owens and other Arizona sheriffs were trying to clean up their counties. LeSueur said as many as thirty-eight were killed, while Joseph Fish stated about twenty-one "had been killed in a very short time which improved things very much for the honest stock raisers" ("History of the Eastern Arizona Stake," 30). Both numbers appear extremely high.

War finally wound down, and the Hashknife outfit sold its cattle business—but Apache County would remain a favorite outlaw haunt through the turn of the century.

Still, the Citizens Party's short-lived existence brought about one notable change in Apache County: Mormon, Mexican-American, and non-Mormon Anglo communities began working together toward shared goals. It is unclear whether J.T. LeSueur was the first Mormon elected to county-wide office, but after his election as treasurer, the election of other Mormons followed. Prime T. Coleman, a Mormon cattleman, served on the county's Board of Supervisors in 1888, while Nat Greer succeeded LeSueur as county treasurer. County voters elected Bill Gibbons to two terms as treasurer (1891 and 1893) and two terms on the county's Board of Supervisors (1895 and 1897). Having won acclaim for his running of the treasurer's office, LeSueur was elected Judge of the Superior Court in 1889 and representative to the Arizona Territory Legislature in 1891.[90] Other Mormons also won elective offices, including David Udall. The Mormon bishop, previously prohibited from voting because he was a polygamist, was elected to the Territory Council in 1899. The integration of Mormons into the county leadership forced both Mormons and non-Mormons to find common ground in public safety and economic matters, thus dislodging former prejudices. Mormon men were increasingly called upon to take leading roles in civic enterprises, such as water projects and quarantining during disease outbreaks. To be sure, old antagonisms did not completely disappear. The Mormons continued to form business alliances primarily among themselves and in 1889 established their own school, the St. Johns Stake Academy. But even some of their most bitter enemies, notably John Lorenzo Hubbell and Sol Barth, eventually softened and lived harmoniously with the Saints. Speaking years later about Hubbell, Udall said, "When he came to know us and we know him, we became true friends."[91]

A number of Mormons, including J.T. LeSueur and Bill Gibbons, went into the sheep business, creating a Mormon community consist-

---

90. Among other elected officials that I could identify as Mormons: A.V. [Andrew] Gibbons (Bill's brother), Board of Supervisors, 1898–1900; Willard Farr (J.T.'s colleague at the ACMI), Superior Court Judge, 1895–1896; Lee Roy Gibbons (Bill's brother), Superior Court Judge, 1897–1898; J. B. Patterson (one of J.T.'s partners in the sheep business), representative to the territory legislature, 1897–1898; and Charles Jarvis, Recorder, 1891–1892.

91. Udall, *Arizona Pioneer Mormon*, 181. Before Barth died in 1928, at age eighty-six, he asked that his funeral be held in a Mormon church.

ing of both cattle and sheep owners. Mormon diaries and memoirs do not indicate trouble between the two groups, suggesting that their shared religion made it possible to address conflicts over grazing land, if there were any, without resorting to violence. It would have been unthinkable for two Mormon factions to raid each other's camps and kill livestock, as often occurred when cattlemen and sheep owners feuded. In addition, LeSueur and others hired both Mexican-American and Mormon sheepherders to manage their flocks, thus strengthening economic ties between the two groups. Mexican-American sheep owners likely benefitted from dampened hostilities between cattle and sheep owners.

Mormon men also became accustomed to carrying weapons as necessary accoutrements of a Western wardrobe. A photograph of a Mormon youth outing, taken about 1900, illustrates this point. Although the occasion is a picnic, the five young men wore belts of ammunition and holstered pistols. All but one, Will Gibbons (second from left), carried a rifle. Presumably, they knew how to use their weapons. Of course, some Mormon men, such as the Greer brothers, carried a cowboy swagger from the beginning. Twenty years later, these young men appear to be cut from that same cloth.

Lawlessness and violence could be ameliorated, at least to some extent, by sustained community action. The harsh environment could not. No amount of fasting and praying could halt the punishing droughts, destructive floods, or early and late frosts. The soil refused to produce more than a modicum of crop yield. Some people flourished, like Nat Greer with his large cattle herd and saloon, and J.T. LeSueur with his multiple business investments. The sheep business provided a good living for many. In town, people grew vegetable gardens and fruit orchards to supplement their family income. While waiting for their crops to grow, men took jobs hauling freight, putting up fences, and other laboring jobs. Women sewed, taught school, and took in washing. But building flourishing communities along the Little Colorado River proved too much for the local environment. Newcomers came but many left disappointed. Oldtimers sometimes gave up as well.

Two months before the Wild Bunch rode through Springerville, the Mormon-owned Salt Lake City *Deseret Evening News* published an anonymous dispatch from a St. Johns resident bluntly describing the many problems still facing the Mormon colonizers. Due to a continued drought, "some of our farmers look forward with sad misgivings as to what the future

When the Mormons first settled in St. Johns, the men did not always carry pistols or rifles, but by 1900 they came well-armed even to a picnic of young adults. Courtesy Apache County Historical Society.

has in store for them," the St. Johns writer said. "It has been very difficult to maintain the settlements in this Stake. . . . Uneasiness prevails, dissatisfaction is quite general, and the spirit of unrest is abroad in the land."[92]

Drought wasn't the only problem. Dry spring winds, alkaline water, and heavy county debt and taxes, as well as economic depression, were causing widespread hardship, the writer said. Many colonizing missionaries had exhausted their resources trying to coerce the desert soil into submission. Some of the local Saints were predicting that the St. Johns Stake would be disbanded and the colonizers called away to new missions. "One by one many of our good citizens have left us and 'moved on' or back," the dispatch said. "Some have gone to the Salt River valley, some to the Gila, some to New Mexico and Colorado, some to Idaho, and others have returned to Utah."[93]

Mormon leaders in Salt Lake City were well aware of the turbulence and uncertainty gripping the St. Johns mission. Even before the *Deseret Evening News* published the dispatch from St. Johns, the Mormon prophet, Lorenzo Snow, had sent a delegation of Church authorities to Arizona

---

92. *Deseret Evening News*, January 31, 1900, 7.
93. *Deseret Evening News*, January 31, 1900.

for a special conference of the St. Johns Stake. Leading the team were Apostles Heber J. Grant and Rudger Clawson, who carried written instructions from President Snow releasing the St. Johns Saints from their colonizing mission.[94] The Church's leaders had decided, Snow said, "that the good people of St. Johns be given their full liberty to either move away from that place or remain, as they may choose."[95]

On January 29, 1900, the third day of the conference, Apostle Grant read the prophet's letter granting a release to the entire St. Johns Stake. Grant then surprised the colonizers by telling them that, despite the release, the Lord actually wanted them to stay:

> I went to your Stake feeling that St. Johns ought to be abandoned, but I came away convinced that it was not the mind and the will of the Lord that the country should be abandoned. Looking at things naturally I would say that it was a mistake to maintain a foothold in such a country, but the inspiration of the Lord to me as well as to my associates during our recent visit to your place was exactly opposite to this.[96]

Apostle Clawson and J. Golden Kimball, another visiting authority, echoed these sentiments, promising St. Johns would prosper "if we would pay our tithing[,] keep the word of wisdom and the Commandments of God," said St. Johns Bishop Charles Anderson.[97] Clawson prayed that "the waters would be healed, and that the late [and] Early frosts would cease and that the rains would come in season." Elder Kimball said their children would not be led astray.

At a priesthood meeting that immediately followed, the St. Johns men took up the question of whether to accept the release. "Many recounted the hard times they have had in Arizona," Anderson said, but when "an expression of the people was called for the majority was in favor

---

94. Details of this special conference are provided in Charles P. Anderson, *Journal of Charles P. Anderson: Writings from 1856–1913*, 30; *Deseret Evening News*, February 9, 1900, 7; and February 12, 1900, 7; and Lorenzo Brown, "The Journal of Lorenzo Brown, 1823–1900," 264. This conference was not the regular quarterly stake conference, which had been held in late December 1899.

95. Lorenzo Snow to Elders Heber J. Grant and Rudger Clawson, January 24, 1900. The letter is contained in Anderson, *Journal*, 30 (January 29, 1900).

96. Heber J. Grant to David K. Udall, May 8, 1900. Udall Family Correspondence Collection, 1859–1950. Microfilm. Grant's description of his feelings aligns with Anderson's journal account.

97. Anderson, *Journal*, 30.

of staying."[98] In a letter discussing the conference, Apostle Grant said, "I know that God is able to temper the elements to the good of the people in St. Johns."[99] The Church also would be sending aid to provide relief and give new life to their projects, he said, adding, "I think your difficulties are mainly past and that prosperity has now set in."

Two months later, as Apache County Sheriff Ed Beeler gathered a posse to ride north in pursuit of suspected rustlers, the Mormon community was still feeling the exhilaration and optimism emanating from the conference. Life would continue to be hard, but their leaders' promises and prayers gave renewed hope. St. Johns was a frontier town, its economy dominated by cattle and sheep. The dust of their hooves clouded main street when they were driven through town and across the bridge spanning the Little Colorado River. Automobiles and paved streets and airplanes and radios existed only in an unimagined future. Still to be solved was how to bring running water to the town. Like floods and frosts, rustling and thievery were a constant nuisance. In his first year on the job, Sheriff Beeler had won praise for his willingness to take head-on the county's bad men. Beeler wasn't combative, but he didn't back down. When five men passed through Springerville and killed a rancher's cow, it was expected that the sheriff would pursue them and bring them to account. It was expected that the community would support him.

---

98. Anderson, *Journal*, 30.
99. Grant to Udall, May 8, 1900.

CHAPTER 4

PURSUING FIVE MEN FOR KILLING A BEEF

After the outlaws finished eating the steaks carved from Henry Barrett's cow, they rode toward St. Johns, about twenty-eight miles north of Springerville. They arrived in the early evening. Having been on the trail for perhaps a week, the hardened men with dark beards, heavy mustaches, and sun-beaten faces couldn't help but attract attention when they rode into town trailing twelve extra horses. They carried the most advanced rifles, including smokeless Mausers and .30–40 Winchesters that fired high-velocity bullets preferred by gunmen because of their powerful impact. Each man had a full complement of six shooters. Canvas bags filled with cartridges hung from their saddle horns.[1] They stopped at several St. Johns stores and purchased more ammunition and supplies. One of those who waited on the outlaws at the Mormon's ACMI general store was its superintendent, J.T. LeSueur, whose son, Frank, would join the posse the next day.[2] The outlaws apparently presented a menacing demeanor, because the local paper reported that some merchants were surprised the men actually paid for their purchases.[3]

The outlaws were still shopping when Apache County Sheriff Ed Beeler showed up after dark with part of his posse, including cattleman Barrett and mail carrier Duane Hamblin, who had guided the posse to Barrett's slaughtered cow.[4] Some residents later questioned why Beeler didn't try to arrest the men on the spot, but Beeler had neither a numerical advantage nor a sufficient element of surprise. Any attempt to arrest them could have triggered a shootout, possibly in the busy store itself, resulting in multiple casualties and even deaths. Beeler did not press the matter and the five strangers rode out of town without incident.

---

1. Sheriff Beeler provided many of these details about the outlaws' guns and ammunition in *Salt Lake Herald*, June 4, 1900, 2.

2. John T. Crosby, interviewed by Carl W. LeSueur, January 16, 2002. Crosby was the son of Alice LeSueur Crosby and nephew of Frank LeSueur.

3. *St. Johns Herald*, March 31, 1900, 3.

4. Lois Hamblin Golding and Delma Golding Johnson, *Our Golden Heritage: The Duane and Addie Noble Hamblin Family*, 56.

Writing more than three decades later, Clarissa Gibbons, Gus's aunt, said Beeler and his posse promptly went about "drinking and gambling all of the night" and didn't pursue the men until the next morning.[5] However, her recollections were perhaps clouded by her anger at Beeler's later missteps, as well as by the years that had passed. In his contemporary journal, Bishop Charles Anderson said the posse left St. Johns about 11:00 p.m. in pursuit of the men.[6] A newspaper account published a few days later also said Beeler and his men left that night. The posse, which now numbered at least five men, followed the trail for much of the cold and windy night, finally catching up with the outlaws at sunrise about three miles outside of town, near the county bridge, where they had set up camp.

It is puzzling why the outlaws had camped so close to town and seemed in no hurry to go. They appeared unaware, or were unconcerned, that the mailman had seen them butchering the cow. They perhaps were also unaware of the posse's arrival in St. Johns while they purchased supplies. And they may have lingered to wait for Butch Cassidy and Red Weaver, who couldn't be far behind. Whatever the reason, when the posse spotted the outlaws' camp, Sheriff Beeler was not eager to start the action. He recommended sending to town for reinforcements and waiting until they had superior numbers to engage the outlaws, but Barrett, perhaps fearing delay would allow the outlaws to escape, wanted immediate engagement.[7] He may have thought they were chasing an old nemesis, the Bill Smith Gang of rustlers, and so looked forward to settling accounts. At Barrett's urging, the posse moved in.

Clarissa Gibbons contended that Beeler's posse, rather than trying to arrest the men, "fired at the outlaws without any warning and stirred them up like a nest of hornets."[8] However, contemporary newspaper accounts say the outlaws saw the sheriff and his posse as they approached and opened fire from long range.[9] Although Gibbons appears to be wrong

---

5. Clarissa Isabell Wilhelm Gibbons, "A Short Sketch of My Life," 14 (January 18, 1934).

6. Charles P. Anderson, *Journal of Charles P. Anderson: Writings from 1856–1913*, 31 (March 27, 1900). Anderson wrote, "A lot of desperados passed through here last night. At 11 Oclock p.m. the Sheriff with a posse of men followed." Similarly, the Salt Lake City *Deseret Evening News* said, "The Sheriff, with a posse started in pursuit that night" (April 4, 1900, 1).

7. *Salt Lake Herald*, June 4, 1900, 2.

8. Gibbons, "Short Sketch of My Life," 14.

9. *St. Johns Herald*, March 31, 1900, 3; and *Deseret Evening News*, April 4, 1900, 1.

about who fired first, she correctly surmised the outlaws' state of mind. A furious gun battle ensued and, for a time, the posse seemed to have the advantage. They shot two of the outlaws' horses and apparently wounded one of the outlaws in the stomach. Beeler said they later found a bloody rag from the wound on the trail.[10] But the outlaws, rallied by "a tall, nervy leader," soon evened the odds with accurate fire from their powerful rifles.[11] Beeler, who had taken cover beside a large, thick tree, said one of their bullets went in one side of the tree and out the other. The withering fire from the outlaws' guns prevented the posse from advancing closer.[12]

Recognizing that he had engaged skilled gunmen, Beeler sent one of his deputies back to St. Johns to raise another posse and return as fast as possible with reinforcements. In the meantime, the five desperadoes were able to saddle up, gather their extra horses, and make their escape, though they were forced to leave behind some of their bedding, one dead horse, and another horse that would soon die. Beeler gave chase with the rest of his posse, and the two sides fought a running gun battle for twelve to fifteen miles. The outlaws lost more horses along the way. "When their horses were killed, they quickly changed to fresh ones," Beeler said.[13]

Back in St. Johns, at about daybreak, Dick Gibbons was lying in bed, listening to the clamoring wind and not in any hurry to start work. "While I was thinking about getting up, someone yelled, 'Dick' outside," he said.[14] It was Ben Crosby, the deputy sent by Sheriff Beeler to recruit reinforcements. Crosby told Dick about the gun battle raging by the bridge and asked him to join the posse. Dick agreed, though first he went out to milk his cow. About that same time, Dick's nephew, Gus Gibbons, came by the house on his way to pick up the mail in town. Dick asked Gus to get his mail too. Dick's wife, Clarissa, was celebrating her thirtieth birthday, and so before Gus left, she invited Gus and his wife, Pearl, to join them at dinner that night. When Gus returned with Dick's mail, he told

---

10. *Salt Lake Herald*, June 4, 1900, 2.
11. *St. Johns Herald*, April 21, 1900, 3, from the reward circular.
12. *Salt Lake Herald*, June 4, 1900, 2.
13. *Salt Lake Herald*, June 4, 1900, 2.
14. Richard Gibbons, "Diary of Richard Gibbons, Copied from His Own Daily Journal and Covering the Time from March 16, 1888 until His Death on January 1, 1924," 258–59 (March 27, 1900). Other primary accounts include Clarissa Gibbons, "Short Sketch of My Life," 13–15; *St. Johns Herald*, March 31, 1900, 3; and *Deseret Evening News*, April 4, 1900, 1.

Dick Gibbons made the fateful decision to split his posse in two, unaware that the group with Frank LeSueur and his nephew Gus Gibbons would be the only one trailing the outlaws. Dick and his wife, Clarissa, sit with their three children (from left) Mabel, Edward, and Wilhelm in this photo from about 1900. Courtesy JoAnn Wilcox.

Clarissa that he had been persuaded to join the manhunt and was going home to find a horse and saddle.[15]

Frank LeSueur also joined the posse somewhat by happenstance. He had been inspecting his family's sheep camps in the mountains south of Springerville when the outlaws passed through that town. After selecting a location for shearing the sheep, Frank rode to Springerville and was purchasing supplies on Monday, March 26, when Sheriff Beeler summoned him to join the posse.[16] Frank agreed to help but said he first needed to return home. The next day, he joined the posse being organized by Ben Crosby and Dick Gibbons. By eight o'clock on the morning of March 27, Crosby and Gibbons had assembled a posse of seven men, including Frank, and rode off for the bridge.

Gus was still getting his gear together when the posse left. His wife, Pearl, said he had a cup of coffee but was too nervous to eat breakfast. Before leaving, Gus stopped by his parents' house. His father was away at the family's sheep camp, but his mother and sisters were still home. They

---

15. Gibbons, "Short Sketch of My Life," 13.
16. James W. LeSueur, "A Patriarchal Blessing and its Fulfillment," 124.

watched Gus retrieve his father's rifle, kneel on the kitchen floor, and load the bullets. Gus stood and kissed each of them. "I'll soon be back," he said with perhaps more cheerfulness than he actually felt.[17]

"We watched him ride away waving goodbye," said his sister Eva, who was then eleven.

Gus rode to his uncle's house to get directions from his Aunt Clarissa regarding where to meet up with the posse. "He was pale and very much excited," she said.[18]

With Gus, the posse now numbered eight men: Ben Crosby, Dick Gibbons, Will Harris, Antonio Armijo, Francisco Ruiz, Gus Gibbons, Frank LeSueur, and possibly James Murry or St. George Creaghe.[19] When they assembled at the bridge, they were met by one of Beeler's deputies, who apprised them of the situation. They could see for themselves the dead horses and the shell casings scattered about. The deputy told them that one of the outlaws was wounded. The wild shoot-out at the bridge should have alerted the new posse to the dangerous game that was afoot. They would be chasing skilled gunmen who, if pressed, would shoot to kill. But it is unclear whether any of them realized at the time—or even afterward—that they were trailing one of the West's most notorious criminal gangs, a gang whose members had already committed numerous murders. Beeler's man pointed the direction that the outlaws and posse had taken, and Dick Gibbons's group rode swiftly in pursuit. "The sheriff had

---

17. Arvin Palmer, comp., *An Arizona Palmer Family History: Selected Sketches of Arthur Palmer and Evaline Augusta Gibbons Palmer and Their Ancestors*, 137, 237.

18. Clarissa Gibbons, "Short Sketch of My Life," 13.

19. In one instance, Richard Gibbons ("Diary," 259) refers to the eighth posse member as "Murry." James Murry, a fifty-two-year-old farmer, resided in the Springerville census precinct. Murry, who was married and had five children, previously had served as a constable. However, Gibbons later refers to the eighth man as cattleman "George Seath," a name that cannot be found in the 1900 Arizona census. It's possible that Gibbons actually wrote "St. George Creaghe," but the person who created the typescript from Gibbons's diary could not decipher the name. Creaghe, who previously served two terms as Apache County sheriff, had recently moved to Lamar Town, Colorado, where he listed his occupation as "stock dealer." However, he still owned one hundred head of cattle in Apache County, according to the Apache County Board of Supervisor minutes, July 6, 1900, 84. If he was visiting Arizona on business, he may have been persuaded to join the posse, given his experience as a lawman. Creaghe was married with nine children still at home.

left word for us to come as quickly as possible for he intended to follow the outlaws and get them if it took all summer," Gibbons said.[20]

Dick Gibbons, age forty-one, appears to have taken charge of the eight-man group, which was riding two hours or more behind the sheriff's posse. After following the trail northeast for about fifteen miles, Dick thought the outlaws might be taking a long route to the G-Ranch, an area he also called Cedro, and so he decided to divide his posse in half. He would lead half the men along a shortcut that would enable them to head off the outlaws and prevent their escape, while the other four men would stick to the trail until they caught up with Sheriff Beeler's posse. If the plan worked, the outlaws would be squeezed between the two posses.

Dick took with him the older, more experienced men: Ben Crosby, Will Harris, and the unidentified posse member. Crosby, thirty-one, was a farmer and married, but had no children. Harris, thirty-five, was a cattleman, married, and had three children, including a newborn. The fourth member was either James Murry, fifty-two, a Springerville farmer and former constable, or St. George Creaghe, sixty-one, a cattleman and former county sheriff. In contrast, Gus Gibbons, at twenty-six, was the oldest member of his group. Gus had been out of the country on a two-year Mormon mission and had been back just four months. He was married and working for his Uncle Dick. Antonio Armijo, twenty-three, was single and worked as a bartender and typesetter. He also served as a St. Johns constable.[21] Francisco Ruiz, twenty-two, had previously served as a deputy sheriff and listed marshal as his occupation in the June 1900 census.[22] Ruiz was married with a one-year-old daughter. Frank LeSueur, nineteen, managed his family's sheep business but was planning to leave soon on a two-year foreign mission similar to the one Gus had just served. Dick Gibbons did not explain his reasoning for dividing the posse in this manner, but he may have wanted the more seasoned men to undertake what could be the more dangerous mission. The younger posse members, sent to link up with the sheriff's posse, would participate more safely as part of a larger group with experienced leadership. Besides, Ruiz and Armijo had some law

---

20. Gibbons, "Diary," 259.

21. *St. Johns Herald*, December 3, 1898, 4; and *St. Johns Herald*, May 26, 1900, 4. The 1900 census had Armijo living with his parents and listed his occupation as a bartender.

22. *St. Johns Herald*, August 26, 1899, 4. The *Herald* refers to Francisco as "Frank," as does the 1910 census for St. Johns. Ruiz's father was Alfred Ruiz, Apache County district attorney and one-time member of the anti-Mormon St. Johns Ring.

enforcement under their belts. Dick also told LeSueur and the others that if they didn't meet up with Beeler's posse by the time they reached a certain place on the trail, they should wait for Dick's group before riding further.

LeSueur's group of four continued following the outlaws' trail. Although they didn't see the sheriff, they talked to a sheepherder who told them that the outlaws, five in number, had just passed by a half hour earlier. The sheepherder showed them the route the outlaws had taken, and Frank's group spurred their horses to catch up. Meanwhile, Dick Gibbons's posse reached Cedro, where they had hoped to block the outlaws' retreat. After finding no sign of either the outlaws or Beeler's men, "we hurried to meet the boys who were still on the trail," Gibbons said.[23] But when they arrived at the pre-arranged meeting place, LeSueur's group had already left. Gibbons also learned from the sheepherder that the outlaws had passed through heading in the direction of a long mesa, and "the [four] boys were close upon them."[24]

It was now early afternoon. Gibbons and his men had been riding hard since about 8:00 a.m., stopping here and there but also hurrying, first to catch up with Sheriff Beeler and then to meet up with LeSueur's group. By the time they reached the sheep camp, their horses were "played out," Gibbons said. It was useless to push them any further, and so they decided to return to St. Johns. Gibbons brushed aside worries about LeSueur and the others. "We went on home, thinking that the boys would be all right, as Sheriff Bealer [sic] was still on the trail," he said.[25] Gibbons's decision to abandon the chase was understandable, but, as the editor of the *St. Johns Herald* noted, "this left four inexperienced boys on the field alone, not having a leader even among themselves."[26]

Those boys had also been riding hard, and the new trail was taking them deeper into rough country. About 4:00 p.m., Francisco Ruiz's horse grew tired and fell behind. When he called for the others to stop, the young men broke off the chase to talk about what to do.[27] They were about twenty miles from St. Johns and it was getting late, too late to return home; but if they continued on, they were looking at a rugged climb up a steep mesa. Initially, everyone but Frank LeSueur wanted to turn back, but LeSueur

---

23. Gibbons, "Diary," 259.
24. Gibbons, 259.
25. Gibbons, 259.
26. *St. Johns Herald*, March 31, 1900, 3.
27. *St. Johns Herald*, March 31, 1900. *Deseret Evening News*, April 4, 1900, 1, said that Antonio Armijo's horse also gave out.

eventually persuaded Gus Gibbons to continue with him. Antonio Armijo and Francisco Ruiz said they would go back to Cedro and stay the night at the sheep camp. LeSueur and Gibbons planned to ride to the top of the mesa, which provided a good vantage point for seeing if they could spot the others. After that, they would follow the trail as far as Joe Carns's ranch. If they hadn't found the sheriff by then, they intended to stay at the ranch for the night.[28] Armijo and Ruiz tried to persuade LeSueur and Gibbons to ride back with them, but LeSueur was adamant about pushing forward. "Let us go on," he said. "The sheriff is ahead and will need our help."[29]

While the posses trailed the outlaws, friends and loved ones at home worried about their safety. Dick Gibbons's wife, Clarissa, said she tried to eat some breakfast with her three children, but she was so anxious that she "already felt full without anything to eat."[30] Soon she heard a knock at the door. It was Gus's wife, Pearl. "She was crying and so was I," Clarissa said. The two women had a large field glass and spent much of the day scanning the mountains and ridges to see if they could see the posses. "The wind was blowing a heavy gale," Clarissa said.

Much to their surprise, at about 10:00 a.m., they spied Sheriff Beeler and his posse riding back into town. Both horses and men were worn out. Beeler's posse had ridden more than twenty-five miles from Springerville to St. Johns the previous day, and after a short rest in St. Johns, had been out all night—since about 11:00 p.m.—tracking the outlaws. After the early morning gunfight at the county bridge, they chased the bandits in a running gun battle for fifteen miles until their horses finally gave out. In an unfortunate twist of fate, Beeler's posse returned to town on a different trail than the one taken by Dick Gibbons's posse, and so the two posses never saw each other. Seeing Beeler's posse return without their husbands made the waiting even more painful. "I never could experience a worse thing I know," Clarissa said.

The waiting also gave the two women time for some morbid pondering. "Clara, I've been thinking," Pearl said. "If one of the boys should happen to be killed, which one of them would it be best to get it?"

---

28. The discussion among the young men is contained in the *St. Johns Herald*, March 31, 1900; *Deseret Evening News*, April 4, 1900; and Dick Gibbons. "Diary," 260. Gibbons said Armijo also initially wanted to go on with LeSueur but changed his mind during their discussion.

29. *Deseret Evening News*, April 4, 1900, 1.

30. Gibbons, "Short Sketch of My Life," 13.

After considering the question, Clarissa replied, "It would be better for my husband to be the one, for I had three sweet little children to comfort me." If Gus died, she pointed out, Pearl would be alone.

Pearl disagreed, precisely because she had no children. Without a husband, Clarissa would have to care for three little ones all by herself. "But we were both feeling fearful," Clarissa said, "and the wind kept blowing hard all day, adding to our unrest."

Later that day, Francisco Ruiz's father, Alfred, tried to persuade Sheriff Beeler to go back out and see about the eight posse men who were still on the trail. Beeler saw no need to worry, given the outlaws' huge head start. "The boys wouldn't even see the outlaws' dust," Beeler assured him.[31]

Why didn't Sheriff Beeler go back out? Beeler and his men were undoubtedly exhausted after more than twenty-four hours trailing the outlaws. Besides, Beeler was now preoccupied with a new concern. Sometime after returning to St. Johns, he arrested two suspicious looking men, James Lowe and Bruce Weaver, both well-armed and carrying a string of six extra saddle horses.[32] The two outlaws apparently had sold or traded the other horses and mule they had stolen when they left Alma. No charges against Lowe and Weaver are listed in the Apache County Jail Record, but Beeler apparently surmised, correctly, that they were associates of the five outlaws. Just two days after the murders, a dispatch from nearby Navajo Springs reported that Beeler arrested Lowe and Weaver "en route for the scene of the trouble, and are supposed to be members of the gang" he was chasing.[33] Lowe, who was really Butch Cassidy, insisted that he was an honest cowboy who had just finished working for Captain William French of the WS Ranch. He claimed not to know Weaver, who, he said,

---

31. Gibbons, 14.

32. *Arizona Republican*, May 7, 1900, 4.

33. The March 29 dispatch was published in the *Arizona Bulletin* (Solomonville), April 6, 1900, 6. In addition, Beeler told a reporter for the *Grand Junction Sun* that he arrested Lowe and Weaver for cattle rustling, further evidence that he connected them with the five outlaws who killed Barrett's cow (article reprinted in the *Salt Lake Herald*, June 4, 1900, 2). However, the reporter mistakenly said Beeler arrested Lowe in Springerville. The reporter repeatedly confused Springerville with St. Johns. For example, the article mistakenly states that the gunfight with the outlaws occurred near Springerville and that the posse returned to Springerville after the pursuing the outlaws. St. Johns was the actual location in both instances. It's possible that Beeler arrested the men in Springerville before riding to St. Johns, but then the date of their incarceration would have been March 26, rather than March 27, as listed in the jail record.

had joined him along the trail.³⁴ Lowe said that if Beeler telegraphed French in New Mexico, French would confirm his story. Apache County's jail record listed Lowe as twenty-eight years old (he was actually thirty-three) and 5'8¼" tall (actually 5'9"), with grey eyes, light brown hair, and a light complexion.³⁵ Weaver was listed as twenty-five years old (his actual age) and 5'11¾" tall, with blue eyes, red hair, and a light complexion. The two men spent the night of March 27 in the St. Johns jail while Beeler arranged to telegraph French.³⁶

Meanwhile, Gus's wife, Pearl, continued to brood. She tried to persuade Clarissa to go with her to see Beeler, but Clarissa said it wouldn't do any good, because Beeler had already told Mr. Ruiz that he wasn't going back out. Eventually, Pearl went to town anyway to see if anyone had heard news about the boys. When she came back, she reported that Beeler and his men had gone to bed. The sheriff's supposition that the second posse would not catch up to the outlaws was not unreasonable, but he did not consider the deadly consequences if, by some unlucky turn of fate, he were wrong.

Dick Gibbons and his group arrived back home at dusk, much surprised to learn that Sheriff Beeler had been in town most of the day. When Gibbons told his wife and Pearl that four boys, including Frank and Gus, were still on the trail, the two women feared the worst. Pearl stayed the night and slept in the bedroom with Clarissa, while Dick slept in the front room. Dick knew the young men had been closing in on the outlaws when he left them, but he didn't mention this to Clarissa or Pearl, nor did he try to wake Sheriff Beeler to form a new posse. It would have been nearly impossible to find the boys in the dark. "None of us slept much that night," Clarissa said.³⁷

J.T. and Geneva LeSueur didn't sleep well either. Early the next morning while it was still dark, J.T. called at the Gibbons's home and got Dick out of bed to discuss what to do about the four boys, who still hadn't returned. "Someone should go out and see what was the matter," Gibbons said, and then, after eating breakfast, he organized a search party.³⁸ He was

---

34. William French, *Recollections of a Western Ranchman*, 277.

35. Apache County Jail Record, 1900, 2.

36. There was no telegraph office in St. Johns at this time, and so Beeler likely sent the message to Holbrook's telegraph office.

37. Gibbons, "Short Sketch of My Life," 14.

38. Gibbons, "Diary," 259. See also Clarissa Gibbons, "Short Sketch of My Life," 14.

joined by three others: Sheriff Beeler; Frank's best friend, Will Sherwood; and Gus's older brother, Will Gibbons. Before he left, Dick tried to assure Pearl that the boys were all right, telling her that their horses had probably given out and forced them to camp overnight. "Although I tried my best, I could not reconcile her," he said.[39]

The four men left at about 8:00 a.m. and split into two groups to expand their search, agreeing to meet at Dick Greer's windmill. When they arrived back together, the two Wills—Will Gibbons and Will Sherwood—reported that they had met Antonio Armijo and Francisco Ruiz returning home after spending the night at Cedro. Antonio and Francisco told the men where they had last seen Frank and Gus. The searchers were subsequently joined by two unnamed men from the Mexican-American community, and the group of six began following the same trail the young men had taken the day before. Along the way, they spotted quilts and other items the fleeing outlaws had discarded to lighten the load on their horses.

At about noon, the men neared the trail where Frank and Gus had climbed the mesa with their horses. Dick Gibbons said:

> I saw an object on the steep hillside that startled me. It looked like the body of a man, but I would not admit it to myself. It was still to [sic] far away to be identified and while I was thinking about it, I saw another object that looked like a quilt that had been thrown away by the outlaws and had been rolled up by the wind and lodged in the wash, where it now lay, but as we drew nearer, I saw that it was the body of a man and upon closer inspection, I recognized it as the body of my nephew Gus Gibbons. It was lying in the bottom of a little draw, with the head downhill and the face upwards, with three ghastly bulletholes [sic] thru his head.[40]

"Oh my God, they have killed my brother," Will Gibbons exclaimed when he came upon the body.[41] He was so startled that his horse nearly stepped on Gus.

"We well knew what the other object was that we had noticed laying on the hillside," Dick Gibbons said. Frank LeSueur lay face down about seventy-five yards above where Gus had fallen. Frank, like Gus, was shot multiple times, his face mangled by a shot between the eyes. Gus's face was also badly disfigured. One of the bullets had entered Gus's mouth and exited through the back of his neck; another entered his left ear and exited below his mouth, breaking his lower jaw. Both men had powder marks on

---

39. Gibbons, "Diary," 260.
40. Gibbons, 260–61.
41. Palmer, *Arizona Palmer Family History*, 138.

their faces, indicating they had been shot at close range. After killing the young men, the outlaws had turned their pockets inside out and stolen everything of value. Dick Gibbons could not his contain his outrage:

> The sight was horrifying to the senses. To see the two boys lying there that I had known since they were in the cradle and had watched grow up and were just in the pink of manhood, and for them to be ambushed and shot down like dogs, without even a chance to fight for their lives, made me sick. It was murder in its worst form and there is not another crime beneath the roof of heaven that can stain the soul of man with a more infernal hue than an assassination such as this.[42]

The sight of Frank's mutilated corpse devastated Will Sherwood. The Sherwood and LeSueur families had arrived in St. Johns at about the same time, and Will and Frank grew up together in the small town. "Will had but one very close pal," said Erma Udall Sherwood regarding Will's friendship with Frank. "It took Will years to get over this tragedy."[43]

Still in shock, the men began the terrible task of caring for the bodies. They were twenty miles outside of St. Johns, much too far away to carry two stiffening bodies draped over horses while two men walked alongside. Sheriff Beeler volunteered to stay with the bodies while others fetched a wagon, but Dick Gibbons demanded that Beeler "face the townspeople" and deliver the awful news himself.[44] Consequently, four of the men, including Sherwood and Beeler, returned to St. Johns. Dick and Will Gibbons stayed behind with the bodies. Even then, Dick and Will had to transport the bodies more than two miles down the steep canyon draw and through the badlands to a point on the trail where a wagon could reach them. Because Will's horse was the gentlest of their two horses, Will and Dick lifted Frank onto Will's horse and carried him down to where Gus lay. They put Gus on the same horse, lashed the bodies tightly, and began making their way to the wagon road.

Clarissa and Pearl Gibbons again waited anxiously all day, hoping for news that the young men were safe. The entire community buzzed with tension and dread. Everyone knew what was going on—the desperados who had come through town, the shootout at the bridge, the posse's chase,

---

42. Gibbons, "Diary," 261.

43. Susan Inez Sherwood Arnett, ed., "The Life History of William Wellington and Erma Udall Sherwood & Their Descendants," 15. Will and Erma, the daughter of St. Johns Stake President David Udall, were married March 2, 1907, in the LeSueur's former home.

44. Palmer, *Arizona Palmer Family History*, 238.

and now the four missing boys. Neighbors dropped by Clarissa's home throughout the day to chat and help pass the time. This scene likely repeated itself at the LeSueur home, where worried family members waited for news while concerned neighbors checked on the boys' status ("any news yet?") and offered assurances ("I'm sure they're all right"). Antonio Armijo and Francisco Ruiz rode into town about noon, raising hopes that Frank and Gus were also safe. Finally, at about 4:00 p.m., Gus's twenty-year-old brother, Loman, came running toward the house. The women were sitting just inside the house, and as they watched him approach, they knew he was bringing news of some kind. Clarissa said, "He came to the door as pale as a sheet, stepped up on the door step, staggered back and said 'Dead!'"

That was all Loman said. Both women knew what he meant. "Pearl gave a scream and threw herself on the bed and would not be comforted," Clarissa said.[45]

When Clarissa was told that her husband had stayed with the bodies until the others could return with a wagon, she also became distraught. "My feelings were something awful for I was afraid that the robbers would stay near where they had killed the boys and maybe kill the rest who came to look for the boys' bodies," she said.[46] While the LeSueur and Gibbons families had gotten the worst news possible, Clarissa's worries continued.

Meanwhile, Dick and Will Gibbons were left on their own for eleven frightening hours. Both feared the outlaws were still lurking nearby and, at least once, they scrambled for cover behind rocks after hearing suspicious sounds. At sundown, with the late March night growing cold, they gathered wood and built a fire to keep warm. Finally, at about 10:30 p.m., more than ten hours after the bodies had been found, Will Sherwood returned with a buckboard wagon, bringing along Seth Russell, Warren Mallory, and Joseph B. Patterson to help with the bodies. Mallory, Frank's thirty-one-year-old cousin, was the son of Charles and Caroline LeSueur Mallory. Patterson was one of J.T. LeSueur's business partners and a close family friend. Upon seeing the men pull up in the buckboard, "we hailed them with joy," Dick Gibbon said, "for the prospects of spending the whole night here was not attractive in the least to us. They brought us some water and a good lunch and we ate with a great relish."[47]

---

45. Gibbons, "Short Sketch of My Life," 15.
46. Gibbons, 15.
47. Gibbons, "Diary," 262. Seth Russell was Amasa Seth Russell, born in 1862 or 1864. He may have been a neighbor of the LeSueurs, as he is listed next to J.T. LeSueur's family in the 1900 federal census.

They got underway at about midnight but stopped at 3:00 a.m. at the house of Jose De Los Reyes Bustamente.[48] The men woke up Jose and asked him to heat some water so they could wash the bodies and faces, which were bloody and riddled with bullet holes. "It did not improve their looks much," Dick said.[49] They finally arrived in St. Johns at 4:00 a.m., where they dropped the bodies off at the Jarvis Photo Gallery for a coroner's inquest and preparation for burial.[50] Dick went to the home of his brother, Bill Gibbons (Gus's father), to comfort the family. "It was heart rending to hear their sobs and to see the grief so clearly portrayed on their faces," he said.[51]

Dick's reunion with Clarissa was bittersweet. She had begun the previous day planning a birthday celebration with Gus and Pearl. Now she prepared to attend Gus's funeral. "My wife," Dick said, "met me at the door in her nightclothes, with as sad an expression on her face as any of the other mourners."[52]

When Dick and Will Gibbons rolled into St. Johns with the young men's bodies in the dark morning hours of Thursday, March 29, family members were already making preparations to hold the funeral at 3:00 p.m. on that very day. News of the murders spread rapidly across Mormon communities in Arizona and the mountain west. Stake President David Udall, who was in Springerville at the time, was notified by wire, as was Snowflake Stake President Jesse Smith. Telegrams were also sent to towns in New Mexico to alert friends and relatives. E. S. Perkins, publisher and business manager of the *St. Johns Herald*, began interviewing posse members and townspeople for an article he would publish in the next issue of the weekly paper. John W. Brown, the principal of the Mormon-run St. Johns Academy, was also interviewing participants and family members for a dispatch that would be published April 4 on the front page of the Salt Lake City *Deseret Evening News*. Shortly after returning with the bodies, Dick Gibbons attended a

---

48. According to the 1900 federal census, Jose De Los Reyes Bustamente, age fifty-three, was a farmer, married, and had five children living at home in the St. Johns precinct.

49. Gibbons, "Diary," 262.

50. Charles Jarvis, a dentist, also owned a photograph studio or gallery that, at least in this instance, served as a mortuary. See C. LeRoy and Mabel R. Wilhelm, *A History of the St. Johns Arizona Stake: The Triumph of Man and His Religion Over the Perils of a Raw Frontier*, 272; and "Charles Godfrey Defriez Jarvis."

51. Gibbons, "Diary," 262–63.

52. Gibbons, 263.

coroner's jury at the Jarvis Gallery, where they concluded that the boys were killed by the same outlaws they had been trailing. Sheriff Beeler began organizing another posse to track down the murderers.

Amid these activities, the boys' bodies were prepared for viewing. Frank was shot five times, Gus six times, their faces blackened with powder burns by shots fired at close range. Andrew Gibbons, Gus's uncle, said the boys were shot up "almost beyond recognition," while a long-time Arizona resident observed that he had "never witnessed such mutilation, not even by the savages."[53] Anderson said he worked all day with Charles Jarvis and Solomon Waite, right up until the funeral started, "washing and dressing the bodies and getting them in proper shape to be looked at by the sorrowing families."[54]

All these events occurred while Gus's father, Bill, was working at his Blue Springs sheep ranch about twelve miles west of Springerville. When news reached St. Johns of Gus's death, David Overson was dispatched to inform Bill in time for him to return and attend the funeral. It was a long horseback ride, and Overson thought the entire way about how best to break the news. It was well after dark when he reached the Gibbons ranch. When Bill heard the knock at the door, he called out, "Who is there and what is wanted?"

Startled by Bill's brusque command, Overson forgot his carefully prepared speech and blurted out, "Gus has been shot dead."[55]

---

53. *St. Johns Herald*, May 5, 1900, 3.
54. Anderson, *Journal*, 31.
55. This incident is recounted by Gus's sisters in Palmer, *Arizona Palmer Family History*, 142–43 (Rhoda) and 238–39 (Eva). "Overson" is also spelled Oveson in some documents.

CHAPTER 5

BURYING FRANK AND GUS

Frank LeSueur and Gus Gibbons were adored by their younger sisters. For Alice LeSueur, Frank was "the handsome older brother who always took her to the dances and was her best pal," said Alice's daughter.[1] While Frank was away from home attending Brigham Young Academy, Alice, two years younger, sent letters emanating the cheerful friendship of close confidantes. She recounted family news, local politics, and social gossip, including rumors about a pair of neighbors who "are getting along like cats and dogs" and heading for divorce.[2] She inquired whether Frank saw much of one of their friends, Pearl, at the academy; and she encouraged him to write to a hometown friend who wanted to be more than a friend. "Lavinia said for you not to forget to write her (I believe she likes you very much)," Alice wrote.[3]

Gus had similar close relationships with his younger sisters, particularly Rhoda, who was three years younger, and Eva, who was more than fourteen years younger. Just as Frank often escorted his sister Alice to dances, Gus would take Rhoda to community and church dances. "I thought they were the handsomest pair I had ever saw," Eva said of Gus and Rhoda.[4] But Eva most vividly remembered when Gus took her to a dance, probably when she was just seven or eight years old. Gus had offered to bring Eva so that his parents could go to the dance on their own. Eva said she was planning to watch people dance, but Gus had other ideas.

"I can't dance," Eva protested when Gus took her hand.

---

1. Anona Crosby Heap, "Mother of Mine."
2. Alice LeSueur to Frank LeSueur, November 10, 1898, in *LeSueur Family History*.
3. Alice LeSueur to Frank LeSueur, February 15, 1899, in *LeSueur Family History*. Alice may have been referring to Lavinia Berry, who lived in St. Johns and was about the same age as Frank.
4. Evaline Gibbons Palmer, "Gus Gibbons," in Arvin Palmer, comp., *An Arizona Palmer Family History: Selected Sketches Of Arthur Palmer And Evaline Augusta Gibbons Palmer And Their Ancestors*, 137.

"You are my partner," he replied and, much to her delight, led her to the floor.[5]

Andrew Augustus "Gus" Gibbons was born February 16, 1874, in Glendale, Utah, the second of sixteen children. His family moved to Tuba City in 1876 when his father was called to serve a mission to the Hopi and help them build a wool factory. His family moved again in 1879 when his father, along with his grandparents and several uncles, was called by the Mormon Apostle Wilford Woodruff to colonize St. Johns. Little is known about Gus's early years, but they were often a time of deprivation for the Gibbons family.

When Gus was called to serve a mission to Great Britain, Bishop Anderson recommended him highly, describing Gus as "quite intelligent" but noting that "his opportunities for education has [sic] been quite limited."[6] Gus had attended the Mormon-run St. Johns Academy for two years after it opened in 1889, but given that the Gibbons family struggled financially for a time after Gus's father lost his hand in a thresher accident, Gus may have been needed to work at home rather than continue his schooling.[7]

In early 1896, Gus went to work for David and Ida Udall on their farm in Round Valley. Ida had five young children, the oldest ten and the youngest less than a year old. As a plural wife, Ida often had to manage the children and the farm by herself, and so David hired Gus to live in the home and assist with whatever was needed, including mentoring the boys, Grover, 8, and John, 6. Their older sister, Pauline, marveled at how well Gus got along with her younger brothers, getting them to help around the farm when she could not.[8] Gus's success in winning over the boys was not surprising. His sister Eva recalls that on the family's wash days, Gus would cheerfully help the women by fixing dinner, often making codfish balls and sopapillas. "I was always thrilled when Gus was home," Eva said. "He always had a kindly word or pat on your shoulder."[9]

---

5. Palmer.

6. Charles P. Anderson to Wilford Woodruff, August 2, 1887, in Charles P. Anderson, *Journal of Charles P. Anderson: Writings from 1856–1913*, 25.

7. St. Johns Academy administrative records (in the LDS Church History Library) show that Gus was enrolled at the academy in 1889 and 1890, probably for grades nine and ten, in the school's "preparatory" department, or beginning track.

8. Pauline Udall Smith, "The Memoirs of Pauline Udall Smith," 27.

9. Palmer, *Arizona Palmer Family History*, 137.

It was apparently while working in Round Valley that Gus met Priscilla Smith in 1897. Twenty-year-old Priscilla was the daughter of Snowflake Stake President Jesse N. Smith, a polygamist with five wives and, eventually, forty-four children. Smith, a cousin of the Prophet Joseph Smith, helped colonize settlements in Utah and Arizona, eventually becoming one of Mormonism's most influential men in the Arizona Territory. Priscilla learned to sew from her mother and earned income by sewing for others. Along with some of her sisters, she played the guitar, and together they entertained at dances and parties with their singing and playing. The young Priscilla was the "belle of the town of Snowflake with her long, almost black auburn hair and gay, dark eyes, and trim waistline," said her daughter, Emily Parker.[10]

Despite her strict upbringing, Priscilla pushed the boundaries of acceptable behavior. "Priscilla was a fun-loving girl—high-spirited and gay, and prone to raise the ire of her parents," Parker recalled. "She dared to pierce her ear-lobes and cut her bangs against her mother's wishes."[11] Equally disconcerting, Priscilla would violate Church rules against "round dancing" in which a man placed his arm intimately around a woman's waist as they danced across the floor. Although forbidden by her father to dance the waltz and similar "wanton" dances, Priscilla would slyly "balance" against her partner's arms in the square-dance corner, "innocently forgetting her father's definite rule concerning 'round dancing,'" Parker said.[12]

As a young woman, Priscilla often stayed in the homes of her married sisters to help them with their children, who called her "Aunt Pearl." She met Gus during one of these visits to a sister in Eagar, and so Gus and his family also came to call her "Pearl."[13] Gus wasted no time in getting acquainted. "The first day I met him he asked me to go to the big

---

10. Emily S. Parker, "Priscilla Smith Gibbons Smith." This version is slightly more detailed than the reprinted version in Oliver R. Smith and Dorothy H. Williams, eds., *The Family of Jesse Nathaniel Smith, 1834–1906*, 145–47.

11. Parker, "Priscilla Smith Gibbons Smith."

12. Parker, "Priscilla Smith Gibbons Smith." During 1881 to 1900, Jesse N. Smith's journal records numerous instances in which he and other church authorities voiced strong opposition to round dancing. See *Journal of Jesse Nathaniel Smith: The Life Story of a Mormon Pioneer 1834–1906*, 258, 259, 275, 346, 385, 388, 436.

13. Gibbons family reminiscences refer to Gus's wife as "Pearl," as did the *St. Johns Herald* when they married, while Smith family reminiscences refer to her as Priscilla. Pearl said she met Gus while staying in Eager with her sister Susan "Susie" Smith Jarvis (1868–1960), wife of Heber Jarvis (1860–1953).

Sunflower Dance," Pearl said.[14] It is unknown whether Pearl "balanced" in Gus's arms that night, but they soon fell in love and arranged to get married, despite Gus's plans to go abroad on a two-year mission. Gus's sister Rhoda was heartbroken by the news of their engagement, knowing her close relationship with Gus would change. "I think I cried as much the day he married as I did at the time he was killed," Rhoda said.[15]

Gus and Pearl were married in her mother's home in Snowflake on September 1, 1897. Pearl's father, Jesse Smith, performed the marriage ceremony. The couple held celebrations in Snowflake and St. Johns, where the local newspaper wished "Gus and his fair bride a long and happy married life."[16] On September 26, Gus spoke briefly in his St. Johns ward. "I intend to leave on my mission in a few days," he told the congregation. "It is quite a task, though it is my desire to go and fulfill an honorable mission."[17] Pearl accompanied Gus to Salt Lake City so they could be sealed together—that is, married for eternity—in the Mormon temple. From there, Gus left for his mission in Great Britain, while Pearl returned to Arizona, splitting her time between her mother's home in Snowflake and Gus's parents' home in St. Johns.

In Great Britain, Gus joined other Mormon men, young and old, in an important rite of passage that tested character and strengthened faith. "It has been one desire of my life to go and preach the gospel to those who sit in darkness," he told Church President Wilford Woodruff when accepting his mission call.[18] Gus worked closely with other missionaries, preaching among strangers, supporting local congregations, and, most importantly, seeking converts who could build up the church in Utah and the surrounding states and territories. As late as 1890, more than 25 percent of Utah's population was foreign born, most of them converts from Europe.[19] Missionaries paid their own way, and so the costs presented a real hardship to the missionaries and their families, both in terms of lost wages and expenditures, but it was a hardship they bore as an opportunity and obligation. In a mission photograph, Gus has a confident, earnest look. With his groomed mustache, double-breasted coat, top hat, and umbrella, he could be mistaken for a businessman or banker. One would

---

14. Parker, "Priscilla Smith Gibbons Smith."
15. Palmer, *Arizona Palmer Family History*, 142.
16. *St Johns Herald*, September 4, 1897, 4.
17. St. Johns Ward General Minutes, 3:402.
18. Andrew A. Gibbons, letter to Wilford Woodruff, July 28, 1897.
19. William G. Hartley, "Coming to Zion: Saga of the Gathering."

Gus Gibbons (right) departed on a two-year mission to Great Britain just one month after marrying Pearl Smith. "If he has an enemy in the world, I do not know it," Bill Gibbons said of his son, Gus. With Gibbons are Elder Jepson and Elder Brown. Courtesy Church History Library, Andrew A. Gibbons photographs, PH 281.

not guess that he hailed from a remote Arizona town where he had worked variously as a sheepherder, farmer, and day laborer, and would return to that hardscrabble life after completing his mission.

Rhoda Gibbons became engaged while Gus was away but waited to get married until he returned in November 1899. She married Frederick Davis two days later. Eva, now eleven years old, was also happy to see her brother but said, "I was so hurt to think when he came home he went to Snowflake first to see Pearl before he came home to see us."[20]

Gus and Pearl began the happy task of becoming reacquainted as they made a life for themselves in St Johns. Gus worked for his Uncle Dick, a stockman with five hundred head of sheep, while Pearl tended house. They were especially close with Dick and his wife, Clarissa. Gus Gibbons did not appear destined for greatness, but he was kind and decent and loved by all who knew him. "Gus has been a good boy all the days of his life," his father said. "And if he has an enemy in the world, I do not know it."[21]

Frank LeSueur was born September 4, 1880, in the one-room shack his father had dug into the side of a hill in Salem, where the family first settled before moving into St. Johns proper. Gus Gibbons's grandmother, Rizpah Gibbons, likely served as the midwife attending Frank's birth, because she was the only Mormon midwife in St. Johns for many years.[22] Frank was close to his sister Alice but even closer to his older brother, James. The two were much alike: They performed chores together, spent many hours together fishing, swimming, hunting, and horse racing, and took an interest in studying business and making something of themselves. Their parents encouraged them to read great works of fiction, such as Dickens and Shakespeare, as well as books written by Mormon leaders, which were available at the church library.[23] At home, the two boys helped their mother with housework and the garden, for which she rewarded them with ice cream and other treats. Later, they both worked at the store J.T. managed and tended the family's sheep. "She [Mother] taught us thrift, honesty, love

---

20. Palmer, *Arizona Palmer Family History*, 137.

21. *Deseret Evening News*, April 4, 1900, 1.

22. Genevieve J. Long, "Laboring in the Desert: The Letters and Diaries of Narcissa Prentiss Whitman and Ida Hunt Udall," 291.

23. James W. LeSueur, "Autobiographical Notes," 4. James said he read every book in the library.

"Frank and I were like David and Jonathan in our affections," said James LeSueur (left) regarding his younger brother Frank in this undated photo. Courtesy Family History Center, St. Johns, Arizona.

for God and the [Church] authorities," James said. "Father was very strict and would not stand for any wrong doing on our part."[24]

Frank eventually grew lanky and strong, even taller than James, with heavy eyebrows and dark features. The brothers enjoyed dancing, having learned from their father, and they liked to joke and tease. Frank's sense of humor sometimes tended toward irreverence and, at least when he was younger, aimed at poking fun at his more strait-laced older brother. When Frank became a deacon at age twelve, James was the president of the deacons quorum. At Frank's first meeting with the deacons, James asked him to give the opening prayer. Bowing his head, Frank said, "Amen, Brother Ben, shot a crow and killed a hen. Amen." James never again asked Frank to pray.[25]

A firm believer in entrepreneurial principles, J.T. promoted thriftiness in his sons by matching any money they put into savings to pay for schooling and missions. The LeSueur family was well off, one of the richest in the county, and lived in the grandest home in St. Johns, but

---

24. LeSueur, 5.
25. Walter B. LeSueur, "My Brother Frank, Killed By Outlaws," in *LeSueur Family History*.

J.T. and Geneva also had ten children to provide for and would later add another. They did not lavish extra spending money on their children. J.T. continually sought to guide Frank's moral and educational development, advising his son to "cultivate wisdom, self denial and do nothing that you will some day be ashamed of."[26]

Frank entered St. Johns Stake Academy in 1890 at age ten, just one year after Gus Gibbons. The Mormon-run academy opened in 1889 and attracted dozens of young Mormons throughout Apache County, ranging in ages from eight to twenty-two. The school was held in the upper rooms of the Church tithing office and had two departments, "preparatory" for less advanced students and "intermediate" for those with more schooling. Gus Gibbons was still a preparatory student when Frank began his schooling, and so they might have had the same teachers and been in the same classroom together, despite their six-year age difference. The classroom setting was not fancy—students shared a single dipper with which to drink from a bucket of fresh water—but it enabled Mormon youth to participate together in extracurricular activities such as music, drama, dancing, and sports. For students who moved into the intermediate department, the school took them through the first two years of high school.

Students spoke highly of their principal, John W. Brown, and their teachers, who did not spare the rod when enforcing discipline and ensuring that students remained attentive. It was not unusual for teachers to deliver a hard rap with a ruler on the hands or head to bring students into line, but one teacher, Samuel Moore, used a willow switch with exceptional ferocity. One day he whipped a boy so hard that a classmate, Will Harris, stood up and demanded he stop. When Moore kept at it, Harris called out, "Come on, boys!" and charged the teacher. Several of the larger boys followed. They pinned the teacher on his desk while Harris delivered his own whipping until Moore begged him to stop. "It was one day I enjoyed in school," said Frank's older brother, James.[27]

Principal Brown called Frank "gifted" and "a big-hearted, noble young man."[28] Upon graduating from St. Johns Academy, Frank attended Brigham Young Academy to finish high school. The night before he left,

---

26. J.T. LeSueur to Frank LeSueur, December 2, 1898, in *LeSueur Family History*.

27. "My Recollection of Pioneer Days." LeSueur called both Brown and Moore "good teachers and brilliant men."

28. *Deseret Evening News*, April 4, 1900, 1. Brown was the unnamed author of the article.

J.T. and Geneva LeSueur held a farewell party for their son at their home. The next day, Frank rode a bicycle more than fifty miles to Holbrook to catch the train to Utah, saving the six-dollar stagecoach fare.[29] He was just shy of seventeen years old.

Frank liked spending time with the ladies and may have had at least one steady girlfriend: Pearl Udall. Pearl was the oldest daughter of David Udall, leader of the St. Johns Saints. Around the time Frank was killed, he and Pearl were very close, according to Maria Ellsworth, who said Pearl was deeply affected by Frank's death. "Frank was Pearl's sweetheart, and they would likely have married had he lived," Ellsworth said.[30] If this is true, then Pearl Udall was probably the "Pearl" that both James and Alice LeSueur mentioned in their letters to Frank. "Be good to Pearl," James advised his brother, suggesting that Frank and Pearl may have been more than just friends.[31]

When Frank took the train to Provo for his second year at Brigham Young Academy, he began flirting with fellow passenger Charlotte "Lottie" Kempe, a first year-student from Concho. Lottie and Frank were probably already acquainted, because Lottie's five half-sisters—her polygamous father's other family—lived next door to the LeSueurs in St. Johns. "He liked me," Lottie said regarding Frank's attentions, but Frank may have thought the attraction wasn't mutual, and so "he asked me if I had a sister as sweet as I."[32]

---

29. *St. Johns Herald*, September 4, 1897, 4.

30. Maria S. Ellsworth, ed., *Mormon Odyssey: The Story of Ida Hunt Udall, Plural Wife*, 201.

31. James LeSueur to Frank LeSueur, September 26, 1898, in *LeSueur Family History*. Frank and Pearl Udall both attended Brigham Young Academy during the 1898–1899 school year, along with seven other students from the St. Johns Stake. See *St. Johns Herald*, January 7, 1899, 4, letter from Charlotte Kempe, December 18, 1898.

Also of note, in April 1900, less than a month after Frank was killed, Pearl Udall wrote to her parents in Salt Lake City alluding to an incident that has brought "a gloom over us. Oh it does seem so sad. When I read it the night before I ran up to my room and offered a silent prayer for the dear bereaved people." Pearl almost certainly was referring to the murders of Gus and Frank. Unfortunately, the first page of this letter is missing, so we don't know what else she might have said, particularly whether she and Frank had been dating. Pearl Udall to DK Udalls [sic], April 1900.

32. Charlotte "Lottie" Kempe Magnum wrote two accounts of this conversation: "The TRUE Story of Jennie Kempe," in Ruth L. DeWitt Wake, comp., "Our Heritage Book II: Christopher Jensen Kempe; Wives: Anne Ongerod, Olene Olsen, Anna Dorthea Johnson; Daughter: Ruth Leila (Kempe) DeWitt," 84–85;

Yes, Lottie said, "I have the sweetest, prettiest sister one ever saw." She then told Frank about her fourteen-year-old sister, Jennie.

"Save her for me," Frank replied. It would be more than a year until he saw Lottie again.

Frank wasn't without faults. As a teenager, he pushed hard against the limits established by his parents. "I have a number of boys, whom I am trying to raise up to be good citizens and useful members in the church," J.T. LeSueur wrote in a July 1897 letter to the Church headquarters. "One of them, who is 17 years of age, is somewhat inclined to be wild and at times [neither] his mother nor no one except myself can control him."[33] J.T. was writing to Mormon leaders because, two weeks earlier, he received what he thought was a call to serve a two-year proselytizing mission. J.T. said he was both financially able and willing to serve, but he worried that Frank would drift into serious trouble while he was gone. "I have some fears as to what course he might take if I was entirely out of reach," he said.

A few years earlier, J.T. and Geneva had sent Frank to Kemper Military School in Boonville, Missouri, in hopes of taming his unruly nature. None of the LeSueurs mentioned Frank's stint at Kemper in their reminiscences, and so it is unknown when or for how long he attended the school. Evidence of his attendance is found in a surviving photograph of Frank in his Kemper uniform. A baby-faced Frank, perhaps thirteen or fourteen years old, stares into the camera, inscrutable, his eyes fixed under dark eyebrows. A note with his photo states, "Frank LeSueur at Kemper Military School in Mo to learn discipline." J.T.'s subsequent letter to Church authorities indicates that the school did not temper Frank's wild streak—at least, not to his parents' satisfaction.

J.T. did not provide any examples of Frank's defiant behavior, but the Arizona frontier offered numerous temptations and opportunities for mischief. St. Johns Mormons generally sought to steer their sons and daughters away from the influence of the cowboys who dominated Arizona towns. Young Mormon boys were not immune to the masculine allure of the swaggering cowboy culture on full display at local rodeos, horse races, and shooting matches, as well as on the streets and in the saloons. In fact, Frank, who was an excellent horseman, trained one of the family's horses,

---

and "The True Story of Jennie's Sealing to Frank," in Ellen Greer Rees, "History of Christopher J. Kempe Family," 162.

33. J.T. LeSueur, letter to Elder George Reynolds, July 12, 1897. Frank was actually seven weeks shy of his seventeenth birthday.

Considered wild and unruly by his parents, Frank LeSueur was sent to Kemper Military School to learn discipline. He was probably thirteen or fourteen years old in this undated photo. Courtesy Leo M. LeSueur.

Joe, for racing. During one local race, he was recruited to ride Joe against other cowboys, much to his father's displeasure.[34] Evans Coleman, who would later serve a Church mission, said he and other young Mormon men would often "tank up" at a St. Johns saloon before attending church dances, where alcohol was not permitted.[35] The siren call of adventure that induced Butch Cassidy to leave his confining life on the Parker farm could have the same effect on St. Johns young men. They understood the harsh realities that lay ahead for those who toiled along the Little Colorado River, and they could see what must have seemed like exciting alternatives to the constricting requirements of Mormonism. "I have thus far been able to keep my son away from bad company, and have great hopes, (mingled with fears) in his behalf," J.T. said.[36]

Just a few weeks after expressing these concerns, J.T. sent Frank to attend Brigham Young Academy, probably hoping the Mormon school would help rein in his son's impulsive tendencies. Less than a month after his arrival, Frank received a letter from his brother James scolding him for

---

34. James Warren LeSueur, "My Recollection of Pioneer Days."
35. Evans Coleman, "Do You Remember," 1.
36. LeSueur, letter to Elder George Reynolds, July 12, 1897.

not associating more closely with fellow Apache County students at the academy. James accused Frank of thinking he was too good for them. "You must not treat your home people slightingly," James wrote. "If we intend to remain in St. Johns, which I think we do, we must make friends with everyone."[37] Frank's parents recognized his rough edges, saying he "was very outspoken," sometimes giving offense, but they added that he was also "just as tender-hearted, always willing to make amends for any injury he [had] done another, or to render help in the time of need."[38]

Frank's rebellious behavior appears to have subsided significantly during his two years at the Provo school. He focused on his studies and apparently caused no more problems for his parents. In addition, his father was not called away from home. The mission assignment J.T. thought he had received was actually intended for his son, James, who subsequently left for Great Britain in January 1898.[39] After completing his schooling in Provo, Frank returned home in the spring of 1899 and assisted his father in the family businesses. In December 1899, he attended a dance being held in conjunction with the St. Johns Stake conference, which brought in young Mormons from outlying settlements and towns. It was likely at this dance that Frank saw Lottie Kempe from Concho. Remembering their train ride together, Frank approached Lottie and asked, "Where is that sweet sister you were to save for me?" Lottie introduced him to Jennie, who, now fifteen years old, was home visiting from Brigham Young Academy. Frank was immediately attracted to the fair-skinned girl with dark hair and an open face. "He danced with her several times," Lottie recalled.[40]

---

37. James LeSueur to Frank LeSueur, September 26, 1898, in *LeSueur Family History*.

38. *Deseret Evening News*, April 4, 1900, 1.

39. After receiving J.T. LeSueur's letter, church authorities informed him that the mission call was intended for his son, James. "Let the son be called and not the father, he is really needed at home," Apostle Joseph F. Smith wrote in a note on the back of J.T.'s letter to Elder George Reynolds, July 12, 1897. See also James LeSueur, letter to George Reynolds, July 29, 1897.

40. Lottie Kempe Mangum accounts of Jennie and Frank are found in Wake, "Our Heritage Book II," 84–85; and Rees, "History of Christopher J. Kempe Family," 162. James LeSueur thought Frank and Jennie "kept company" at Brigham Young Academy, but their attendance at the school never overlapped. Frank attended the Provo school from September 1897 to May 1899, while Jennie, who was more than three years younger than Frank, left for Brigham Young Academy in June or July 1899. By that time, Frank was already home, having completed his schooling.

Following the dance, the young women had a slumber party at the Udall's house, where Jennie told her sister—and perhaps the other girls, as well—how much she liked Frank. "That Frank LeSueur is the swellest guy I ever saw," she said. "I shall set my cap for him."

Frank was equally taken with young Jennie. The morning after the dance, he came into the kitchen and said, "Mother, that little Jennie Kempe from Concho is the sweetest girl I ever saw."[41]

Their chance meeting at the dance would have important ramifications for both the LeSueur and Kempe families, but whether Frank and Jennie saw each other again is unknown. Soon after the dance, Jennie returned to Concho and then to Brigham Young Academy in Provo, where, as it turns out, Pearl Udall was also attending school. Were Pearl and Frank still sweethearts, as Maria Ellsworth contends? That is unknown as well. Frank was busily engaged at home during the weeks following the conference. In January, his father took his mother, Geneva, to Chicago for a major operation, and he gave Frank responsibility for managing all the LeSueur household and business affairs during the four weeks they were gone.[42] In February, the Mormon prophet Lorenzo Snow called Frank to serve a foreign mission, which Frank readily accepted. "I feel grateful to my Heavenly Father for the privilege of being called to perform a mission for our Grand and Noble Church and I hope and pray that I may go and be able to fulfill an honorable one," he told Snow in reply.[43]

Rather than leave right away, Frank waited to notify the prophet when he could depart, because he didn't want to leave until after his brother James returned from his mission in the spring. "These brothers were very much attached to each other," said John Brown, their principal and teacher at St. Johns Academy. "And as they had not been in each others' [sic]

In Lottie's account, she says she and Jennie were attending a conference and an associated dance. In fact, a quarterly stake conference was held in St. Johns on December 9 and 10, 1899, with a stake dance held Monday, December 11. If Jennie and Lottie had come home from Provo during a term break, this could have been the conference and dance. A diary kept by Leila Kempe, who lived with her half-sister Jennie in Provo at that time, indicates Jennie returned to Provo on or before December 21. See Wake, "Our Heritage Book II," 179.

41. Quotes from Lottie Kempe, "The TRUE Story of Jennie Kempe," in Wake, "Our Heritage Book II," 84–85; and "The True Story of Jennie's Sealing to Frank," in Rees, "History of Christopher J. Kempe Family," 162.

42. "Memoirs of John Taylor LeSueur," in *LeSueur Family History*.

43. Frank LeSueur, letter to President Lorenzo Snow, February 18, 1900.

society much since they were grown, Frank desired to meet and visit James before he left."[44]

In the days before joining the posse, Frank was inspecting the family's sheep camps, working with the sheepherders, and selecting locations for the spring shearing. Frank's parents had been impressed by the way he had managed the sheep business during their absence. Frank was "well adapted" to the occupation, his father said, "and I intended he should have full management of our sheep business as soon as he returned from a two years missionary service which he had accepted."[45] It was only by chance that Frank happened to be traveling through Springerville on Monday, March 26, 1900, the day Sheriff Beeler was organizing a posse and summoned Frank to join. Given Frank's impulsive nature, his parents undoubtedly urged him with stern warnings to follow orders and be careful.

Early that same Monday morning, Gus Gibbons dropped by the home of his uncle Dick Gibbons, and together they went to town to get the mail. After breakfast, Gus helped his uncle set fence posts until about noon, and in the afternoon, they deepened Dick's well.[46] He and Gus planned another workday on the following day, Tuesday. The two men also intended to have dinner together Tuesday evening with their wives in celebration of Clarissa Gibbons's birthday. However, by the time Gus came by Tuesday morning to begin work, Dick had already agreed to join the posse. Gus was asked to join the posse shortly after.

In calling upon Frank, Gus, and other men, Sheriff Beeler was invoking *posse comitatus* ("the power of the county") to assist in the apprehension of suspected criminals. Arizona territorial law required all able-bodied adult males to comply with the request of a sheriff, deputy-sheriff, coroner, or constable for assistance, or be subject to a fine. A citizen posse—essentially, amateur lawmen—had its drawbacks. Despite a familiarity with horses and guns, the average frontiersman lacked the experience needed to track criminals on long-distance pursuits and was often ill-equipped to confront skilled gunmen.[47] However, it's not surprising that more than a dozen Apache County men joined Beeler's call for assistance. Many in the

---

44. *Deseret Evening News*, April 4, 1900, 1.

45. "Memoirs of John Taylor LeSueur."

46. Richard Gibbons, "Diary of Richard Gibbons, Copied from His Own Daily Journal and Covering the Time from March 16, 1888 until His Death on January 1, 1924," 258.

47. Larry D. Ball, *Desert Lawmen: The High Sheriffs of New Mexico and Arizona, 1846–1912*, 209–10.

Frank LeSueur (right) with his boyhood friend, Will Sherwood. Frank was said to be outspoken, rebellious yet tender-hearted, and more courageous than cautious. Courtesy Family History Center, St. Johns, Arizona.

county raised cattle or sheep. The local economy depended heavily on their success. At least two members of the posse were cattlemen. And given the county's long struggle to stamp out rustling, it's not surprising that they reacted swiftly to the killing of just one cow. Tolerating small-scale pilfering would only embolden thieves. Both the LeSueur and Gibbons families raised sheep, and so Frank and Gus may have felt obligated to support a fellow livestock owner, just as they would hope for similar support if their families' sheep were threatened. The law required them to join the posse when summoned by the sheriff, but community ties and a sense of duty probably weighed more heavily in their decision to participate.

Gus and Pearl Gibbons had been married for just four weeks before Gus left on his mission to Great Britain. Separated for more than two years, they still were like newlyweds, having been back together less than four months when Gus joined the posse. Gus was nervous, Pearl was scared. When she went over to Dick Gibbons's house that morning to wait with Aunt Clarissa while their husbands were gone, she was already crying and fearing the worst.

Frank LeSueur grew up in an environment where young men learned to ride, hunt, and hit what they aimed at. A photograph of Frank with his boyhood friend, Will Sherwood, shows them standing together, each with a rifle, holstered pistol, and ammunition belt. Against the backdrop of rugged boulders and brush, the young men have the appearance of seasoned cowboys, capable of handling anything the frontier sent their way. But a familiarity with horses and guns did not necessarily make them skilled—or even moderately competent—lawmen. Frank, being young and single, may have been more than eager to join the posse, despite any misgivings by his parents. "He knew nothing of fear," they said. "And we never could impress upon him the necessity of caution."[48]

The double funeral for Frank and Gus was the largest ever held in St. Johns.[49] The Mormons' log meeting house could not accommodate everyone who came to attend. Five men spoke at the funeral. Three of them, Andrew Peterson, Elijah Freeman, and Bishop Charles Anderson, assured mourners that the young men had been called to new missions in the "spirit world" or afterlife. "When sacrifices are required, the purist are taken," Peterson said. "God has another mission for them to perform."[50]

Andrew Gibbons, Gus's uncle, praised the boys for their willingness to lay down their lives in support of the county sheriff. "They felt that they had to support the sheriff whom they supposed to be ahead, and did not feel to desert him, and so went even to death," Gibbons said.[51] St. Johns Stake President David Udall said he knew both boys well. Gus had even lived in his home and worked for him. He looked upon them as his own and had, on many occasions, talked to them as a parent to a son. Udall acknowledged that Frank and Gus were not perfect, but said they were as pure as mortals can be. "These young men are worthy of salvation," he said.[52]

Reassuring words could not dispel the gloom. Something precious had been taken. "Our town is overwhelmed with sadness and two homes are bursting full of grief," wrote E. S. Perkins, editor of the *St. Johns Herald*.[53]

---

48. *Deseret Evening News*, April 4, 1900, 1.
49. Details of the funeral can be found in "Funeral Services Held March 29, 1900," St. Johns Ward General Minutes, vol. 3 (1887–1902), 518–19; Joseph O. Stradling, Jr., Family Papers, Box 13; and Anderson, *Journal*, 31.
50. "Funeral Services," 518.
51. "Funeral Services," 519.
52. "Funeral Services," 518.
53. *St. Johns Herald*, March 31, 1900, 2. Bishop Anderson (*Journal*, 31) echoed this observation in his journal, saying "the most profound grief & sorrow prevaled [*sic*]" at the funeral.

In his dispatch about the murders to the Salt Lake City *Deseret Evening News*, John Brown spoke of the "grief and . . . piteous cries of a wife, fathers and mothers, sisters and friends."[54] Mourners were especially outraged by what they viewed as the gratuitous violence perpetrated after the boys were killed. "With fiendish delight . . . the murderers, not content with taking life, must mutilate in horrible manner the bodies of their victims," Perkins wrote.[55]

At the close of the funeral, the choir sang "Farewell, All Earthly Honors," with these first and closing verses:

> Farewell, all earthly honors, I bid you all adieu,
> Farewell, all earthly pleasures, I want no more of you;
> I want my union grounded in the eternal soil,
> Beyond the pow'rs of Satan, where sin can ne'er defile
> There Christ himself has promised, a mansion to prepare,
> For all who serve him faithful—the cross the crown shall wear;
> Bright palms shall there be given to all the ransomed throng,
> And Glory, glory, glory, shall be the conqueror's song.

The boys' remains lay in two white caskets on a raised stage. After the benediction, the mourners came up to the stage along the two outside aisles and filed by the caskets. Years later, Joseph O. Stradling Jr., who was just nine at the time, vividly recalled seeing the bodies. "Frank was dressed in a white suit and Gus in what I long afterwards learned was Temple burial clothes," Stradling said. "Both men had been shot in the head and strips of court plaster covered the bullet holes."[56] A train of thirty vehicles followed the remains to the cemetery.

How were Frank and Gus killed? None of the murderers left a record of the killing, but four days after the funeral, Dick Gibbons and Dick Greer rode back to the murder site and "looked the spot over thoroughly" to ascertain what happened, Gibbons said.[57] The two men examined the locations of the empty shell casings, the positions of the bodies when they were found, their wounds, and other evidence. Their observations suggest that once the outlaws realized they had outrun Sheriff Beeler's posse, they changed directions and headed south toward a long mesa that would give

---

54. *Deseret Evening News*, April 4, 1900, 1.
55. *St. Johns Herald*, March 31, 1900, 2.
56. Joseph O. Stradling, Jr., Family Papers, Box 13.
57. Gibbons, "Diary," 264.

A modern view from the mesa top shows that the outlaws who killed Frank LeSueur and Gus Gibbons could watch their approach for miles across the desert prairie below. Photo by Stephen C. LeSueur.

them a good vantage point to monitor their pursuers and, if necessary, defend their position. When the outlaws reached the base of the mesa, they were forced to dismount and lead their horses up the steep draw. In addition to the horses they were riding, they still had about eight extra horses, the others having been shot. It would have been slow going, but the posse was nowhere in sight. Once atop the mesa, the outlaws had a bird's-eye view of the prairie below. Even without binoculars, they could see for miles across the sage and sandy trails, making it easy to spot any dust kicked up by horses in the distance. The safety of the high mesa allowed them to rest themselves and their horses, drink from their canteens, dress the wound of the man reportedly shot at the bridge, and eat a piece of jerky or other food stuffed in their saddlebags.

Riding about a half hour behind the outlaws, Frank, Gus, Antonio, and Francisco were five hundred yards from the mesa when Francisco's horse tired and fell behind. The five outlaws, hidden behind cedars, bushes, and boulders at the mesa's crest, watched their every move. They watched the boys wend their way up the trail and stop to let Francisco catch up, then talk among themselves, perhaps passing around a canteen

This contemporary photo shows the rugged terrain where Frank LeSueur and Gus Gibbons were murdered as they walked their horses to the mesa top. Courtesy Family History Center, St. Johns, Arizona.

as they debated whether to go on. They watched Antonio and Francisco turn and head back to the sheep camp.[58] They watched Frank and Gus continue up the trail. As Frank and Gus approached, the outlaws moved their small herd of horses a safe distance away so that the boys' horses would not be alerted by their smell. The outlaws then crept into position and readied their weapons.

The climb to the mesa top was rocky and steep. Eventually, Frank and Gus dismounted and walked their horses up the hillside, battling the wind as they picked their way through the rocks. Frank walked in front, pulling his horse, with Gus following behind. A lawman experienced in tracking outlaws would have recognized his vulnerability—that he would be completely exposed and defenseless—while climbing the mesa. He would not have done it, not without first sending a scout around one of the flanks to

---

58. James H. McClintock stated that LeSueur and Gibbons had been "deserted by six Mexican members" of the posse. This is incorrect. The two Mexican-Americans accompanying them, Francisco Ruiz and Antonio Armijo, turned back only after one of their horses gave out. See James H. McClintock, *Mormon Settlement in Arizona: A Record of Peaceful Conquest of the Desert*, 292.

climb the mesa and ensure no ambush waited at the top.[59] No evidence suggests the boys even considered the danger. After all, they believed the sheriff's posse was ahead. Maybe the boys chatted blithely about cattle or sheep or Frank's anticipated mission service or how tired their backs were as they strained to pull their horses up the narrow draw. If they didn't meet up with the sheriff, they would have to find a place to camp for the night. Gus would have bemoaned the fact that he would surely miss the birthday celebration planned that evening for his Aunt Clarissa. Would Pearl stay up worrying about him? Frank and Gus were about ten to twenty feet from the top when the outlaws opened fire. The thunderous blast would have blinded the boys and frightened their horses, which likely had not been trained or used around gunfire. The startled horses would have reared up and whinnied and jerked free from the reins, scattering dust as they galloped from the danger. At the first volley, Frank was struck by several bullets and fell to the ground, instantly killed. Gus was also wounded, but not as badly, and so he turned and scrambled back down the hillside amid the hail of bullets. He had been shot in the stomach and was starting to bleed. Although he must have been panic-stricken, he had the presence of mind to take off his handkerchief and place it over his wound as he frantically sidestepped rocks and brush.

While Gus ran for his life, the outlaws came out from hiding and continued firing. Gus got about seventy-five yards down the hill before he was felled by a bullet in the back. One of the outlaws walked up to Frank and put a bullet through his head. Others ran down to where Gus lay, his face turned to the sky. He may have still been alive, struggling for breath and looking up at the outlaws as they fired two or three more bullets into his head. With both boys lying dead on the ground, the murderers loosened their pants and rifled through their pockets for food and money. They recaptured the horses and took the young men's guns, belts, and saddles. The fierce wind said to be blowing that day would have swallowed the noisy bursts of gunfire. Antonio and Francisco, perhaps but a mile away, would have heard only a hissing wind racing across the ruddy plain.

When the search party found Gus the next day, he was lying at the bottom of the draw with his head downhill, his face looking up. Gus's handkerchief, caked in blood, lay beside his body. Frank was lying face down with his head resting on one of his arms and his legs partly doubled

---

59. Joe Pearce, an Arizona Ranger, describes the proper technique for tracking outlaws up a mesa or canyon draw in Joe Pearce and Richard Summers, "Joe Pearce – Manhunter: Some Adventures of an Arizona Ranger," 254.

under him. Powder burns scarred their faces.⁶⁰ On the rugged hilltop, among the bushes and boulders where the killers had lain in wait, searchers found seventeen empty shell casings in five separate places, indicating that all five outlaws had fired at the unsuspecting boys. On the ground was an abandoned saddle. A blanket, neatly folded, rested in a small cedar tree.⁶¹

When Dick Gibbons and Dick Greer returned to the murder site, they found Frank's hat lying near where he fell. Gibbons knelt beside the crimson soil where Gus had fallen and dug out the bullets that passed through Gus's head when the outlaws, standing above him, fired their last shots.⁶²

---

60. The damage caused by the point-blank shooting of the boys' faces probably led to the account in the *El Paso Daily Herald*, April 12, 1900, 1, which reported that the outlaws stomped the dead men's "heads into a jelly." But it was the outlaws' bullets, not boots, that mutilated the faces.

61. Details of the articles left by the outlaws are from Gibbons, "Diary," 261.

62. Gibbons, 264.

CHAPTER 6

HUNT FOR THE KILLERS

On the morning of the funeral, while friends and relatives prepared the remains of Frank LeSueur and Gus Gibbons for burial, Sheriff Edward Beeler led a posse out of town on what would become an obsessive quest to bring back the murderers, dead or alive. Along with saddlebags packed with ammunition and supplies, Beeler carried a heavy load of guilt. Many local citizens believed he had mishandled his sheriff's duties: first, in failing to arrest the outlaws when he caught up to them in St. Johns; and then, in failing to return to the chase while part of his posse remained in the field. "The sheriff was blamed considerable for letting them [Frank and Gus] go on as they did," Joseph Fish, a prominent Arizona Mormon, wrote shortly after the murders. "They were expecting the sheriff to join them, but from some cause he did not go."[1]

The Gibbons family was especially angry. Writing many years later, Gus's sister Eva and his Aunt Clarissa castigated Beeler with embellished accounts of his malfeasance. Eva said that when the outlaws arrived in St. Johns, they rode through the town unchallenged, causing trouble for much of the night.[2] Clarissa said when the outlaws finally left town, Beeler and his men went to a local saloon to drink and gamble and didn't resume their pursuit until the next morning.[3] Eva said Beeler had been drinking before he led the chase and got drunk and went to bed when he returned to St. Johns.[4]

No evidence supports these assertions about Beeler and his posse. Nevertheless, many in the community were understandably upset by Beeler's decision to leave the second posse alone on the trail. He too quickly dismissed the possibility that the other posse members would catch up to what were clearly skilled gunmen and the danger that posed. He might

---

1. "The Life and Times of Joseph Fish, Mormon Pioneer," 417 (March 27, 1900).
2. Arvin Palmer, comp., *An Arizona Palmer Family History: Selected Sketches of Arthur Palmer and Evaline Augusta Gibbons Palmer and Their Ancestors*, 237.
3. Clarissa Isabell Wilhelm Gibbons, "A Short Sketch of My Life," 14.
4. Palmer, *Arizona Palmer Family History*, 237.

Apache County Sheriff Edward Beeler was a "nervy looking man . . . as hard as nails," said a Utah reporter. Beeler won high praise as an aggressive but fair lawman until his missteps contributed to the murders of Frank LeSueur and Gus Gibbons. Courtesy Marlin and Nonie Harmon.

not have found the boys in time, but he didn't even try. At the funeral, Gus's uncle Andrew said Frank and Gus were killed because they would not desert the sheriff. Left unspoken was a growing feeling that they were killed because the sheriff had deserted them. Beeler may have shared this belief. "Lesueur [sic] and Gibbons were my personal friends, and they lost their lives in a well-meant effort to assist me," he said.[5]

Until this incident, Beeler had been a popular sheriff, known to be plainspoken, energetic without being overly aggressive, and persistent in tracking down and arresting suspected criminals. He was praised for his ability to maintain law and order in a county that still attracted more than its fair share of rustlers, bandits, and shifty characters. Edward Beeler was born May 5, 1864, in Polk County, Tennessee, to Dr. Milton W. Beeler and Mary Hannah Delaney Cameron. Genealogical records show that his mother died when Ed was two or three years old, and his father died when he was ten.[6] Beeler left Tennessee at age nineteen and headed west. Little is known about his activities, but in September 1887, he wrote to his brother and one of his two sisters from Patterson, New Mexico, where he was working for a cattle company. He wrote briefly but with affection,

---

5. *Salt Lake Herald*, June 4, 1900, 2.
6. Familysearch.org.

telling his siblings that "my girl has gon [*sic*] back on me . . . but it does not bother me much as I am having a great big time with a mexican [*sic*] Girl."⁷ He later moved to Arizona and in 1894 was working as a range foreman for Henry Huning, a Show Low cattleman and store owner.⁸ However, Beeler had ambitions beyond being a cowboy tending other men's cattle. He settled in Springerville, a rough cattle town, and purchased 120 acres of land a few miles east of the town, probably with an eye toward cattle ranching. In January 1896, he joined a group of partners to establish the Round Valley Water Storage Company and build a reservoir on the Little Colorado River.⁹ While living in Springerville, he also met and fell in love with Mary Hamblin, a young Mormon woman from the nearby town of Nutrioso.

Mary Elizabeth Hamblin was born September 25, 1872, in Kanab, Utah, to Jacob and Sarah Hamblin. Her father, ordained by the Mormon Prophet Brigham Young as an "Apostle to the Lamanites," was renowned for his efforts to proselytize and develop peaceful relations among many of the Western tribes.¹⁰ Jacob was also a polygamist with five known wives, including at least one Native American woman, having followed Young's advice that Mormon men should take Lamanite women as polygamous wives to help bring about the conversion of their people. Jacob died in 1886, and Mary was living with her mother in Nutrioso when she and Beeler courted. Mormons typically did not like their sons and daughters marrying outside the faith, but there is no indication that Hamblin family members objected to Beeler. Subsequent events would suggest they liked the hard-working Tennessean. One of Mary's brothers, Jacob Hamblin Jr., and her cousin, Duane Hamblin, would later become lawmen themselves. Jacob Jr. performed the marriage service in a ceremony held in the Hamblin home on September 27, 1896.¹¹

---

7. See his September 2, 1887, letter in "Letters Written by Ed Beeler to His Family in 1887 & 1898," RoundValleyAZ.com.

8. *St. Johns Herald*, March 1, 1894, 4.

9. Apache County deed records show that he purchased the land on October 8, 1895. See also the *St. Johns Herald*, January 11, 1896, 4; and March 6, 1897, 1. An Apache County assessment in July 1897 showed that he owned an unspecified number of dairy cows and two work horses (*St. Johns Herald*, July 17, 1897, 1).

10. See Todd M. Compton, *A Frontier Life: Jacob Hamblin, Explorer and Indian Missionary*, 435, for Hamblin's 1876 ordination by Young.

11. Edward Beeler and Mary Elizabeth Hamblin Marriage Certificate, September 27, 1896, familysearch.org.

Beeler's affection for Mary was real. "I wish you could see my Darling[.] I know you would like her," Beeler told his sisters. "I never realized I had a heart until I met my Wife."[12] Mary returned Ed's love with equal fervor, as evidenced by the anguished journal entries she would write after he was killed in an ambush. "He was a big man and handsome, too," said Rhoda Gibbons, adding that Mary was "a very pretty girl."[13]

Beeler was elected Apache County Sheriff on the Democratic ticket in November 1899, winning 54 percent of 487 votes cast for sheriff.[14] As sheriff, he was responsible for law enforcement in a county larger than the state of Maryland but with a population of just 8,300 inhabitants residing mainly along the Little Colorado River corridor.[15] The county seat and largest town, St. Johns, had a population of about 550, with another 300 or so residents in the town's census district. Beeler had part-time undersheriffs, deputies, and jailers he could call upon for assistance, but ultimately, policing the county was his responsibility. As with most Western sheriffs, his duties went far beyond just arresting suspected law breakers. He oversaw the boarding of prisoners and maintenance of the county jail, served arrest warrants, managed foreclosures, enforced quarantines during disease outbreaks, escorted prisoners to judicial venues and convicted felons to the territorial prison in Yuma, and, if required, carried out executions. He also served as the county assessor for the purpose of levying county taxes. For these services, Beeler received an annual salary of $1,880, which included his duties as "jailor and janitor." He also received additional funds for mileage and expenses incurred while tracking criminals, transporting prisoners, and performing other sheriff-related duties.[16]

---

12. See his January 11, 1898, letter in "Letters Written by Ed Beeler to His Family in 1887 & 1898."

13. Palmer, *Arizona Palmer Family History*, 143.

14. Apache County Board of Supervisors Minutes, November 26, 1898, 450, inserted page. Beeler received 265 votes and his opponent, Antonio Gonzales, received 222 votes.

15. When originally established in 1879, Apache County measured more than 21,000 square miles. In 1895, Navajo County was split from Apache County, making Apache County about 11,200 square miles, the size it is today. The population estimate comes from the 1900 census.

16. For discussions of the diverse responsibilities of the western sheriff, see Larry D. Ball, *Desert Lawmen: The High Sheriffs of New Mexico and Arizona, 1846–1912*, 265; and Frank Richard Prassel, *The Western Peace Officer: A Legacy of Law and Order*, 46–47.

The sheriff's job also carried the prospect of deadly confrontations. In the twenty years prior to 1900, at least twenty-five Arizona peace officers were killed in the line of duty, probably more, and even greater numbers were injured in gun battles and brawls.[17] During his first year in office, Sheriff Beeler energetically pursued cattle rustlers and other criminals, and often traveled to remote county outposts and even across state lines to arrest lawbreakers, sometimes accompanied by a deputy but more often riding alone.[18] Long-time Apache County resident Bert Colter said the Smith brothers, a brazen gang of rustlers operating south of Springerville, once threatened Beeler, saying they would kill him if he tried to arrest them. One day, the three brothers and a fourth gang member rode defiantly into Springerville, guns at their sides, and took prominent seats on the sidewalk in front of Gustav Becker's general store. The outlaws positioned themselves so they could see up and down the street if trouble came. To counter their move, Beeler quietly placed five or six men with shotguns above and to the sides of where the gang was sitting. In unison, Beeler and his men shouted for the outlaws to raise their hands and then partially showed themselves to demonstrate to the outlaws that they were surrounded, said Colter, who witnessed the arrest.[19] Beeler disarmed the men and rushed them to St. Johns until their trial, where they were sentenced to the territorial prison. Colter may have embellished his story, but the many newspaper reports of Sheriff Beeler's activities leave no doubt that he was extremely effective in carrying out his duties. "Mr. Beeler is a man suited for the position he holds and is doing some good work in hunting the outlaws down that have raided Apache county for several years past," wrote the editor of the *St. Johns Herald* just six months into Beeler's term.[20]

---

17. This figure comes from "Arizona Line of Duty Deaths," Officer Down Memorial Page. Neither Frank LeSueur nor Gus Gibbons, who were deputized posse members, are listed on this website, so it appears that the number of Arizona peace officers who were killed in the line of duty, including those who were assisting them, is undercounted. Still, the website serves as a valuable resource.

18. Beeler's activities were reported in the *St. Johns Herald*, May 27; June 10 and 17; July 29; August 5, 19, and 26; and September 9, 1899 (page 4 in all issues); and *Arizona Republican*, May 28, 5; August 1, 2; August 8, 4; October 14, 3; and October 22, 1899, 8.

19. C. LeRoy and Mabel R. Wilhelm, *A History of the St. Johns Arizona Stake: The Triumph of Man and His Religion Over the Perils of a Raw Frontier*, 176. Colter, born January 25, 1887, would have been twelve or thirteen years old at the time.

20. June 10, 1899, 4. Two months later, the *St. Johns Herald* editor praised Beeler and his undersheriff, C. H. Sharp, following the arrest and trial of a

In January 1900, Ed and Mary Beeler moved from Springerville to St. Johns, making it easier for Ed to perform his sheriff's duties from the county seat.[21] About two weeks later, their St. Johns neighbors held "a surprise on Mr. & Mrs. Beeler," most likely a party welcoming them to the community.[22] As a devout Mormon, Mary would have attended Sunday services regularly and participated in the women's Relief Society and other church organizations. Whether Ed also attended services is unknown, but he was well known among the Mormons and worked closely with many of them, including the LeSueur and Gibbons families, in carrying out his responsibilities. In a studio photograph, Beeler wears a suit and sports a trim mustache with just a hint of a handlebar, his dark hair pressed neatly to his scalp. By many accounts, he presented an imposing figure. "Sheriff Beeler is a nervy looking man nearly six feet tall, and physically seems to be as hard as nails," wrote a reporter for a Utah newspaper.[23] Beeler told a reporter for the *Phoenix Gazette* that when he traveled from St. Johns to a big town like Phoenix, "everybody looks at me as much as to say, 'there's a fellow from the mountains.'"[24] The reporter wasn't surprised:

> It is no wonder that people look at Sheriff Beeler when he comes to town. He is worth looking at, and if a man actually hungered for a real live Fourth of July scrap to last to a finish, he might select Beeler and feel certain that he would have no chance to tell about a disappointment afterwards—that is, if the ability remained to speak about it at all.[25]

Beeler made clear his preference for small-town living. When a reporter for the *Arizona Republican* asked whether life in St. Johns wasn't rather

---

suspected rustler, saying, "Sheriff Beeler and Under Sheriff Sharp are doing a great deal to discourage the unlawful handling of cattle" (August 19, 1899, 4).

21. *St. Johns Herald*, January 20, 1900, 3.

22. Amanda Christina Kempe Hastings, "Memorandum" book, February 6, 1900, 6. Amanda and her family were next-door neighbors of J.T. LeSueur and family.

23. *Salt Lake Herald*, June 4, 1900, 2. Evans Coleman also described as Beeler as a tough character, saying Beeler understood the kind of men the outlaws were because "Beeler was raised with that class of men. He talked their language; knew their motives, and that life meant nothing to them—neither their own or anothers [sic]." Coleman was the brother of Prime T. Coleman, who later became Beeler's ranch partner. See Evans Coleman to The Arizona Pioneers' Historical Society, February 7, 1953.

24. The *Phoenix Gazette* article was published in the *St. Johns Herald*, August 12, 1899, 1.

25. *St. Johns Herald*, August 12, 1899, 1.

monotonous, Beeler shook his head. "No," he said. "I suppose it depends on how a man's raised. We never hear anything there until some fellow comes in and tells about it as a reminiscence. We've got so we don't care anything about news."[26]

The unpretentious sheriff impressed the big-city reporters. Despite his sturdy appearance, "it should not be understood that Sheriff Beeler looks like a scrapping man," the *Phoenix Gazette* said. "Just the contrary. He looks like a mild, easygoing individual and one who would live many years before seeking trouble. He is gentlemanly and intelligent, and altogether conveys the impression that he is a splendid good fellow to tie to either in peace or war."[27]

Beeler's easygoing nature would be tested following the murder of his two friends. Immediately after reporting their deaths, he began organizing a posse to capture the outlaws, eventually enlisting ten men. Dick Gibbons named six of those who joined the posse: Will Harris, who had served in the eight-man posse with LeSueur and Gibbons; former Apache County sheriff William W. Berry; Earnest Barrett, a cousin of Henry Barrett, whose cow the outlaws had killed; Elijah Holgate, Dick Gibbons's nephew; Ryan Heart; and a man named Snider.[28] The four unnamed men were from the Mexican-American community. Beeler and his deputies also interviewed witnesses—people who had seen or talked with the outlaws in Springerville and St. Johns—to identify the murderers. Their names and descriptions were published in the next issue of the *St. Johns Herald* and wired to towns throughout the Mountain West.[29] Beeler offered an $850 reward for the arrest of five suspects identified as:

- John Hunter, who is about 30 years old, dark complexion, black mustache, about 5 ft. 7 in. high, wore a black hat and dark sack coat. This man is also known as Skeet Jones and lived at Ft. Wingate last year.
- Bob Johnson, is supposed to be much like Hunter.

---

26. *Arizona Republican* (Phoenix), August 8, 1899, 4.
27. *St. Johns Herald*, August 12, 1899, 1.
28. Richard Gibbons, "Diary of Richard Gibbons, Copied from His Own Daily Journal and Covering the Time from March 16, 1888 until His Death on January 1, 1924," 263. According to census records, Elija[h] Holgate was a single, thirty-year-old farmer, and Earnest Barrett was a single, twenty-five-year-old laborer living with Henry Barrett. I could not find Ryan Heart or Snider listed in the 1900 census for Apache County.
29. *St. Johns Herald*, March 31, 1900, 3.

- Wilson, alias Smith, who worked for Wabash Cattle Company for a short time [in] April 1899, in this county. He is about 5 ft. 10 in. high, weighs about 175 lbs., has slightly dark complexion, dark hair and mustache, had short black beard when last seen, is stoop shouldered but quite well appearing, has blue eyes, and is of very pleasing address, but not over talkative, has a peculiar way of ducking his head from side to side when he talks and he usually smiles a great deal when talking. He is an expert bronch [sic] trainer.
- Coley with right forefinger shot off.
- Unknown man.

The *St. Johns Herald* bemoaned these "indefinite and incomplete" descriptions, but over the next two months Beeler would continue talking to witnesses and other lawmen to refine the descriptions.[30] The weekly *St. Johns Herald* published the reward circular with updated descriptions in every issue for the next three months. The Apache County reward quickly grew to $2,000, which included $1,000 offered by the county ($200 for each murderer); $250 from the Gibbons family; $500 from the LeSueur family; and $250 from Beeler himself.[31] Arizona Governor N. Oakes Murphy, responding to public pressure, would later contribute an additional $500 in territorial funds for the arrest and conviction of the murderers.[32]

Butch Cassidy and Red Weaver remained in the St. Johns jail on charges of horse theft at this time.[33] Arrested under the alias Jim Lowe, Cassidy claimed that his former boss at the WS Ranch, William French, would verify that he was a trustworthy cowboy. Beeler had sent French a wire asking him to confirm Lowe's story, but he had not received a reply before he left, so he put one of his deputies in charge "with the instructions to run the office the best he knew how."[34] On Thursday, March 29, sometime in the morning before the funeral, Sheriff Beeler and his posse of ten deputies rode south, taking trails that would lead them southeast into New Mexico and to the Mexico border. In his dispatch to the *Deseret*

---

30. *St. Johns Herald*, April 21, 1900, 3.

31. *St. Johns Herald*, April 21, 1900, 3. Some reward circulars said that William Gibbons and J.T. LeSueur offered $750 jointly, but other circulars (for example, *St. Johns Herald*, June 9, 1900, 3) said that of the $750, Gibbons offered $250 and LeSueur $500.

32. *St. Johns Herald*, May 19, 1900, 3.

33. The *St. Johns Herald*, March 31, 1900, 3, reported that "Jim Lowe and 'Red' Weaver are in the county bastile [sic] here awaiting an investigation."

34. *St. Johns Herald*, May 12, 1900, 3.

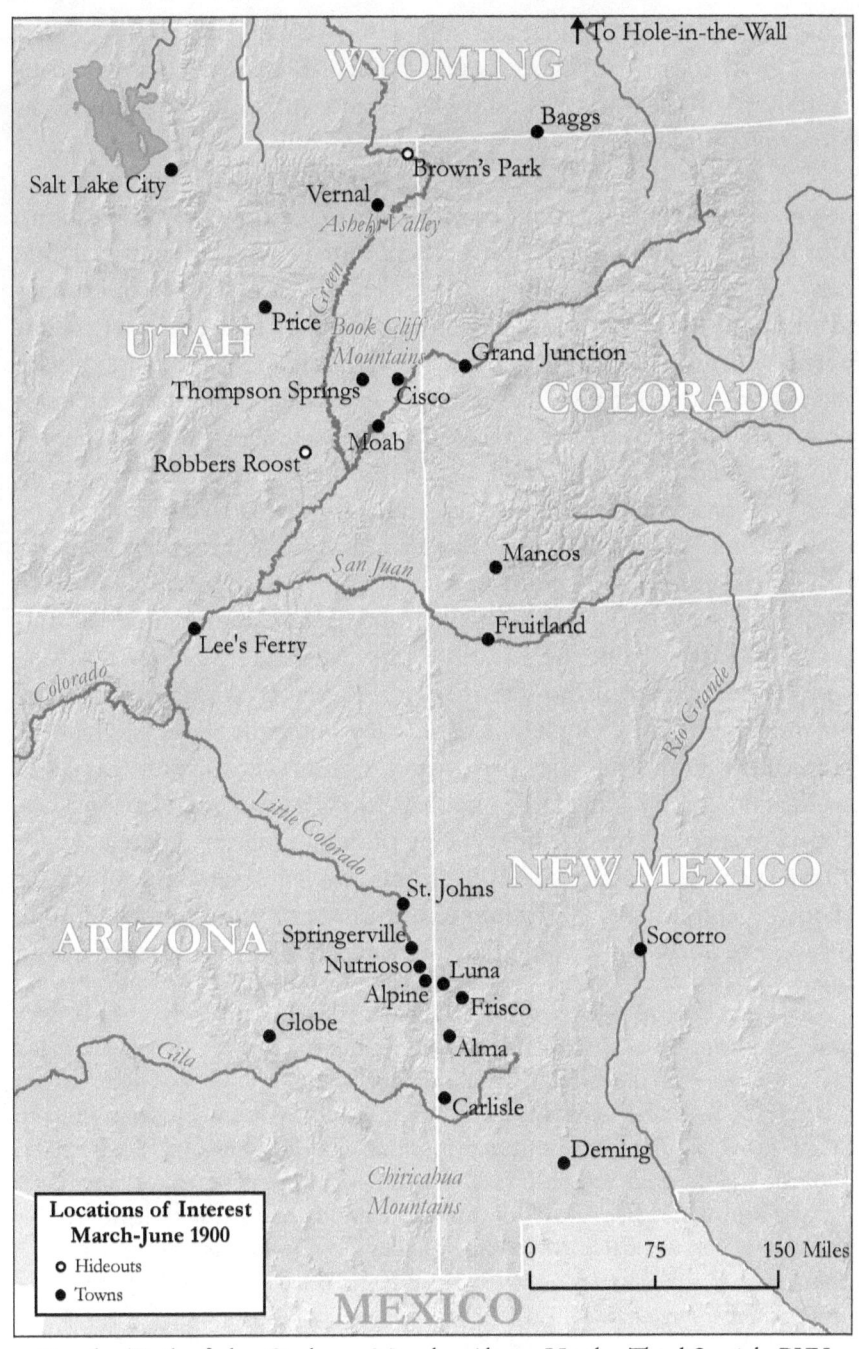

On the Trail of the Outlaws. Map by Abner Hardy, ThinkSpatial, BYU Geography.

Evening News, St. Johns resident John Brown noted that the murderers had a head start of thirty-six hours, making it unlikely they would be overtaken.[35] Beeler, however, said "he did not intend to return until he brought a prisoner with him."[36]

While the outlaws' escape route cannot be traced with precision, newspaper reports of sightings provide clues to their possible whereabouts over the next several days. The outlaws initially headed southeast into New Mexico and on the night of March 29, stole seven horses in Frisco, a town southwest of Reserve.[37] Jimmy Gettling, one of the ranchers whose horses were stolen, said he and the other victims were acquainted with the outlaws. The outlaws "didn't want to steal our horses, for they knew how badly it would inconvenience us," Gettling recalled, "but they figured a posse would be on their trail and if [they] themselves didn't take our horses the posse would, and they sure didn't want any fresh-mounted men on their trail."[38] The bandits were headed for Mexico, he said.

The horse thefts triggered a pursuit by a Frisco posse. By Sunday, April 1, Beeler's posse was reportedly riding just an hour behind the outlaws at Jim Crow Mine, near Carlisle, New Mexico. The *Arizona Bulletin* said the posse, recognizing that the outlaws carried "splendid arms," did not press them close enough for a fight.[39] Undoubtedly, Beeler and his men proceeded cautiously as they narrowed the gap with their prey, careful to avoid another ambush like the one that felled LeSueur and Gibbons. The outlaws were seen that evening passing through Duncan, Arizona, where Tom Capehart stopped to talk with several people he knew, thus providing another identification linking him to the murders.[40] On Monday, April 2, the outlaws rode south, killing and eating part of a cow along the way,

---

35. *Deseret Evening News*, April 4, 1900, 1. It is unclear precisely when Beeler's posse left town. If the outlaws had a thirty-six-hour head start, this would mean that the posse left in the early daylight hours of March 29. However, Dick Gibbons ("Diary," 263) said Beeler was still organizing the posse around breakfast time, so the posse may not have left until mid-morning. The *St. Johns Herald* (March 31, 1900, 3) said the posse left on Friday, March 30, but this appears to be incorrect, because Brown said Beeler and his posse had already left by the time he sent his dispatch, which was dated March 29. Charles P. Anderson, *Journal of Charles P. Anderson: Writings from 1856–1913*, 31, also says the posse left March 29.

36. *St. Johns Herald*, May 12, 1900, 3.
37. *Holbrook Argus*, April 14, 1900, 5.
38. Evans Coleman to Arizona Pioneers' Historical Society, January 22, 1953.
39. *Arizona Bulletin*, April 13, 1900, 7.
40. *Arizona Bulletin*, April 13, 7.

just as they had done a week earlier in Apache County. They camped that night on the Triangle Ranch, eighteen miles northwest of San Simon and near the northern edge of Cochise County. They resumed their southward retreat the next morning and headed into Arizona's Chiricahua Mountains.

At least two posses continued following the outlaws' trail, but newspapers often carried hearsay and unconfirmed reports, making it difficult to track their movements with confidence. For example, the *El Paso Herald* said, "It is reported that the posse from Frisco, N.M., was waylaid near Duncan and three of them killed."[41] The report was not true. A later false report received in St. Johns said Sheriff Beeler had been killed in a skirmish with the outlaws.[42] The ambush of an Arizona prospector was also blamed on the outlaws by newspapers and lawmen, as was the murder of two men and wounding of a third near the Mexico border, but these also were rumors rather than fact.[43]

As he pursued the outlaws, Beeler consulted with other Arizona and New Mexico lawmen. One of those was George Scarborough, who two years earlier had helped break up the Bronco Bill gang that had been using Apache County's Black River valley as one of its hangouts.[44] Now a range detective for cattle companies, the forty-year-old Scarborough was a tenacious tracker known for his aggressive tactics when dealing with suspected rustlers and criminals—too aggressive, according to some of the men he arrested. Tom Capehart was allegedly beaten by Scarborough after his arrest for the 1897 Steins Pass train robbery. Scarborough himself was tried and acquitted for murder three times for killings he committed as a lawman. Beeler said he warned Scarborough about the LeSueur-Gibbons killers when Scarborough was in Lordsburg, New Mexico, though it is unclear whether Beeler talked with him directly or sent him a wire.[45] Just a day or two later, Scarborough was called to investigate the cow slaughtered by the five outlaws near the Triangle Ranch.

---

41. *El Paso Herald*, April 12, 1900, 1.

42. *St. Johns Herald*, April 28, 1900, 3.

43. *St. Johns Herald*, April 28, 1900, 3. The prospector, who was thought to be murdered, actually recovered from his wounds. The *Herald* (May 19, 1900, 2) later reported that he had been attacked by Native Americans.

44. For a biography of Scarborough, see Robert K. DeArment, *George Scarborough: The Life and Death of a Lawman on the Closing Frontier*. Utah newspapers said Scarborough was working as a Wells Fargo detective at this time, but DeArment (210) said he was a range detective for cattle companies.

45. *Salt Lake Herald*, June 4, 1900, 2.

The beef was discovered at the outlaws' abandoned campsite by the ranch's manager, Walt Birchfield.[46] On April 2, Birchfield wired Scarborough in Deming and asked him to help find the perpetrators. Beeler thought it was his warning to Scarborough that had put the detective on the outlaws' trail, but Birchfield's comments afterward suggest that neither he nor Scarborough understood that these were the same men Beeler was pursuing. "If I had known that outlaws had killed the beef . . . I wouldn't have sent for [Scarborough]," Birchfield said, "as I wouldn't have tackled them just for the beef."[47]

Scarborough and Birchfield followed the outlaws' tracks high into the Chiricahua Mountains. When they spotted the outlaws the next day, Scarborough decided to open fire without warning. "There was no use to call on them to surrender," he said.[48] Scarborough got off three or four shots and Birchfield just one, all missing, and the outlaws scrambled for safety behind some rocks. Scarborough fired two more times when he saw a head pop up, but after a half hour of quiet waiting, he and Birchfield decided to get back on their horses and find a better position. As they made their move, the outlaws opened fire from about 350 yards away. One of the bullets found its mark, striking Scarborough in the right thigh and knocking him from his horse. The force of the bullet from the high-powered rifle completely smashed the bone. As the outlaws poured fire on the men, Birchfield managed to crawl to Scarborough and build a protective mound of rocks around him. The bullets splintered into pieces when they hit the rocks, cutting the men on their arms and head. One of the ricocheting pieces also wounded Birchfield painfully in his left shoulder. At dark, with the outlaws silent and presumably gone, Birchfield rode seventeen miles through rain, sleet, and snow to San Simon, where he recruited several cowboys to return with him in a buckboard to retrieve Scarborough. Someone wired news of the skirmish to Deming and requested a doctor. Birchfield and the men reached Scarborough at daybreak on April 4. He was cold and weak but conscious and begging for

---

46. DeArment, *George Scarborough*, 222–29; and Jeffrey Burton, *The Deadliest Outlaws: The Ketchum Gang and the Wild Bunch*, 260–66, describe the hunt for the outlaws by Scarborough and Birchfield and their subsequent gunfight.

47. DeArment, *George Scarborough*, 223. Burton (*Deadliest Outlaws*, 261) says that Scarborough would have known of the LeSueur-Gibbons murders by wire from Silver City to Deming, but he probably did not see the connection with the men he was following.

48. DeArment, *George Scarborough*, 224.

water. When they brought Scarborough back to San Simon, waiting at the railroad station were a doctor, Scarborough's son, Ed, and Sheriff Beeler and two of his deputies. Beeler had heard about the shooting and came to talk with Scarborough and Birchfield.

Scarborough was still conscious and able to speak, but it's not known what information about the outlaws, if any, he passed on to Beeler. However, Beeler learned at least one important detail from Birchfield, who said he recognized the voice of cowboy Tom Capehart among the outlaws. When the outlaws brought down Scarborough with the long-range shot, "there was a big yell, and it was old Capehart," said Birchfield, who had once been Capehart's boss at the Diamond A horse ranch. "I would have knowed him anywhere."[49] Other evidence also pointed to Capehart as the suspect initially identified as Wilson, and so Beeler added Tom Capehart's name to the reward circular.[50] Details about the outlaws who shot Scarborough and Birchfield, such as their weapons, equipment, and horses, persuaded Beeler and others that these were the same men who had murdered LeSueur and Gibbons. Scarborough was placed on the next train to Deming, where the doctor removed shattered pieces of bone from his leg, but Scarborough died in the early morning hours of April 5. Although it is doubtful that Capehart or the other outlaws would have recognized whom they were shooting at from such long distance, many people came to believe that Scarborough's killing was an act of revenge by Capehart for the arrest and beating he had suffered at Scarborough's hands. "Capehart got off clear, and swore then he would kill Scarbel [Scarborough] before he died," Beeler said. "He has done it, and killed a brave man, too."[51]

At the time Scarborough was killed, Beeler's was the only posse pursuing the outlaws. Within a week, three more posses had joined the field, including a posse of six led by Sheriff Jim Blair of Grant County, New Mexico, and a party led by former Cochise County Sheriff John Slaughter.[52] Birchfield remained with Beeler in San Simon to help organize and join the pursuit. The lawmen followed the outlaws south toward the Mexico border, even crossing into Mexico before turning north and

---

49. DeArment, 239–40.
50. *St. Johns Herald*, April 21, 1900, 3.
51. *Salt Lake Herald*, June 4, 1900, 2.
52. *Deseret Evening News*, April 19, 1900, 4; *Arizona Republican*, May 7, 1900, 4; and Burton, *Deadliest Outlaws*, 268. Dick Gibbons ("Diary," 266) also reported that four posses were trailing the outlaws.

chasing them into Colorado.⁵³ According to the *Graham Guardian*, Beeler employed ten Navajo men to help him track the outlaws.⁵⁴ Another report said the outlaws received the help of a local guide to pilot them through New Mexico's canyons and plains. "Their camps were made in places so nearly inaccessible that it would have been impossible to have taken them by surprise," the *El Paso Daily Herald* said.⁵⁵ Several reports said the outlaws continued to steal horses from ranches along the way, giving them an advantage with fresh mounts.⁵⁶ The outlaws typically traveled in two groups, Beeler said, with one or two men riding a day behind to monitor their pursuers. Soiled bandages found at each of the outlaws' deserted campsites provided further confirmation that one of the outlaws had been wounded at the initial shootout by the St. Johns bridge.⁵⁷ Although Beeler undoubtedly benefited from the experience of the fifty-eight-year-old Slaughter, the posse never got close enough to engage the outlaws in a fight. Scarborough's murder and the horse stealing brought new posses into the field, while lawmen throughout many parts of Arizona and New Mexico watched carefully for signs of the outlaws. Together, they dogged the murderers as they fled through the Western badlands and mountains, giving the outlaws little rest and forcing them into desperate, uncomfortable lives on the run while tending to a wounded companion.

Sometime in late April, Sheriff Beeler received word that one of the alleged killers had been seen hauling wood into Globe, Arizona, and so Beeler left the chase to investigate.⁵⁸ The suspect, William "Coley" Morris, had been incorrectly identified in the first reward circular as missing his right forefinger. The second known circular, which was published three weeks later, corrected the error and accurately assigned the missing fore-

---

53. *Salt Lake Herald*, June 4, 1900, 2; and *Arizona Republican*, May 7, 1900, 4.
54. *Graham Guardian*, June 22, 1900, 1.
55. *El Paso Daily Herald*, April 12, 1900, 1.
56. *Graham Guardian*, June 22, 1900, 1, said the outlaws stole twenty horses from the WS Ranch in Alma, which, if true, was the same ranch where Cassidy and other gang members had worked. The *Albuquerque Citizen*, June 20, 1900, 3, said the outlaws stole ten horses near Wilcox and another thirty horses north of the White Mountains. It is impossible to verify whether these thefts were committed by the five fleeing outlaws.
57. Lois Hamblin Golding and Delma Golding Johnson, *Our Golden Heritage: The Duane and Addie Noble Hamblin Family*, 57.
58. *Arizona Republican*, May 7, 1900, 4.

finger to a different suspect, Tod Carver. Beeler found Morris on May 2 on a ranch outside of Globe where he was working. Morris gave his name as Bill Morris but said he was sometimes called Coley Morris. He offered no resistance when Beeler arrested him, saying he would accompany the sheriff to St. Johns without trouble, because "he was not the man wanted."[59] A wire report stated, "Morris admits being an acquaintance with members of the gang, but says he was not interested," an odd admission suggesting he may have been invited—or, at least, had the opportunity—to join the outlaws.[60] Morris also contended that he could easily prove his alibi. Beeler arrived in St. Johns with Morris on Monday, May 7. Beeler had returned to town with a prisoner, just as he had vowed when he left more than a month earlier.[61]

During Beeler's absence, both Jim Lowe and Red Weaver had been released from the St. Johns jail, though on different days and for different reasons. Lowe had told Beeler that Weaver "was a stranger he had picked up on the road," and that William French, foreman of the WS Ranch in Alma, could confirm his identity.[62] It's unknown what Weaver told the sheriff, but he apparently went along with Lowe's story to prevent Beeler from discovering Lowe's identity. French said he received a wire from the Apache County sheriff asking about Lowe and Weaver.

The telegram presented French with a dilemma. He clearly knew that Lowe was the infamous Butch Cassidy, leader of a gang that had committed numerous robberies and murders. Yet, French liked Lowe and considered him an excellent trail boss. French said that neither he nor Lowe thought much of Weaver. "I afterwards heard that Jim was anxious to get rid of him [Weaver] as he regarded him as merely a bluffer with no definite claim to be classed as a member of the 'Wild Bunch,'" French said. Lowe claimed Weaver "lacked the necessary courage or sand when it came to a show down."[63] Weaver wanted to be considered a member of the Wild Bunch, but he served primarily as a messenger, not as someone who could be trusted to carry off a robbery. "They always paid him well for his services," French said, "with instructions to keep his mouth shut if he didn't want to hear from them unpleasantly."[64]

---

59. *Arizona Republican*, May 7, 1900, 4.

60. Reprinted in the *San Francisco Call*, May 7, 1900, 1; *San Francisco Chronicle*, May 7, 1900, 3; and *St. Johns Herald*, May 12, 1900, 3.

61. *St. Johns Herald*, May 12, 1900, 3.

62. Captain William French, *Recollections of a Western Ranchman*, 277.

63. French, 277.

64. French, 277.

Perhaps French also feared that he would hear unpleasantly from the outlaws if he revealed Lowe's identity, but more likely he was adhering to the Western code of minding your own business. If an outlaw wasn't stealing *your* money or rustling *your* cattle, then his activities were none of your affair. French said Beeler's telegram merely asked whether he knew Jim Lowe and Bruce Weaver. "After thinking the matter over I sent him a reply saying I did," French said.[65] With that information, the district attorney authorized the release of Lowe on March 31, two days after Beeler left St. Johns with his posse.[66] With his decision to keep Lowe's identity a secret, rather than reveal to Apache County authorities that they had arrested Butch Cassidy, French helped prolong Cassidy's criminal career and possibly abetted the deaths of additional lawmen who crossed paths with the Wild Bunch.

French was apparently mistaken in his recollection that he vouched for both Lowe and Weaver, because the Apache County district attorney kept Weaver locked up pending further investigation. Lowe, who claimed not to know Weaver, probably also claimed he knew nothing about how Weaver acquired the extra horses, thus letting the Wild Bunch wannabe take the fall for the stolen horses. An investigation by Apache County officials discovered that the horses were indeed stolen. On April 8, Socorro County Deputy Cal Ashby picked up Weaver from the St. Johns jail and returned him to Socorro, where he was jailed on charges of horse stealing.[67] Two newspapers reported that during the journey, Ashby "extracted a partial confession" from Weaver implicating him in the LeSueur-Gibbons murders.[68] Weaver's reported confession was—or should have been—a significant development in identifying the killers, because Weaver could have provided the names of the five men who rode through Springerville

---

65. French, 276. French (277) said Apache County officials allowed Lowe to take the stolen horses with him, but this is unlikely. If Apache officials had determined the horses were not stolen, they would not have had any reason to hold Weaver. It is more logical to believe that they detained both Weaver and the horses, which they turned over to the Socorro County deputy when he escorted Weaver back to Socorro County.

66. Apache County Jail Record states that James Lowe arrived on March 27, 1900, and was released March 31 by the authority of the district attorney.

67. Apache County Jail Record states that Weaver arrived on March 27, 1900, and was released April 8 into the custody of a Socorro County deputy. *The Socorro Chieftain* (New Mexico), April 14, 1900, 1, identifies the deputy as Cal Ashby.

68. *Las Vegas Daily Optic* (New Mexico), April 16, 1900, 2; and *Albuquerque Daily Citizen*, April 19, 1900, 3.

and St. Johns. But the article contains no additional details as to what Weaver told Ashby, nor does there appear to have been any follow-up to find out what Weaver might have known. Sheriff Beeler had suspected that Weaver and Lowe were connected to the outlaws. That's why he arrested them. But there is no indication that Beeler was informed of Weaver's alleged confession. That Weaver could have been persuaded to reveal the identities of the five murderers is doubtful, given the likely retribution from his comrades, but under questioning, he might have inadvertently provided information helpful in tracking down the killers.

On April 27, a Socorro grand jury indicted both Weaver and Lowe for horse stealing, although only Weaver was present.[69] After being released from the St. Johns jail, Lowe made his way quietly to Utah, trying his best to avoid the firestorm ignited by his gang. He had no intention of returning to Socorro County to face the horse-stealing charge and risk identification.[70] Weaver pleaded not guilty and requested his trial be postponed so he could secure witnesses who would confirm his alibi and testify that Lowe told Weaver and others that he (Lowe) had purchased the stolen horses from the owner.[71] On May 4, Weaver posted bail of $1,000 and was released from jail.[72] However, the 1900 census shows Weaver again sitting in the Socorro County jail in mid-June, though it is unknown whether the incarceration was related to this charge or a new one.[73] Subsequent events would show that he was released again before his trial.

Meanwhile, Sheriff Beeler kept Bill "Coley" Morris jailed while he investigated his alibi. The nature of his alibi is unknown, but after a few days, Apache County authorities began to doubt Morris's guilt. District Attorney Alfred Ruiz could not find any witnesses who could identify

---

69. New Mexico Territory vs. Bruce Weaver and James Lowe, April 27, 1900, "Larceny of horses"; and *Socorro Chieftain*, April 28, 1900, 1. A plea of not guilty for the two men was entered April 28, according to *Socorro Chieftain*, May 5, 1900, 1.

70. Burton, *Deadliest Outlaws*, 269, states that Cassidy (Lowe) appeared in person for the April 27–28 Socorro County court proceedings. However, there is no record of Lowe being jailed or posting bail, as is the case for Weaver. It is highly unlikely that Cassidy would have voluntarily returned to Socorro County to face a charge of horse stealing after he was released from the St. Johns jail, especially given the general excitement over the recent killings in Arizona and New Mexico. The risk of discovery would have been too great.

71. New Mexico Territory vs. Bruce Weaver and James Lowe, April 27, 1900, "Larceny of horses."

72. *Socorro Chieftain*, May 12, 1900, 1.

73. US 1900 Census for Socorro County, New Mexico.

Morris as one of the five outlaws who rode through St. Johns, and on May 12 the *St. Johns Herald* reported: "Sheriff Beeler informs us that it is very probable that his man, captured near Globe, is not one of the murderers of Lesueur [sic] and Gibbons."[74] Soon thereafter, Beeler reached the definite conclusion that Morris was innocent and released him. The next reward circular published in the *St. Johns Herald* dropped Morris as a suspect. He was never again listed or sought in connection with the murders.[75]

Why was Morris mistakenly identified as a one of the killers? Wild Bunch members used multiple aliases, sometimes adopting the names of cowboys they knew. This threw suspicion onto others while causing confusion as to their real identities, especially if they resembled in some way the men whose names they borrowed. One of the five outlaws, perhaps Tod Carver, may have used Coley as an alias when they travelled through Apache County, thus creating the desired confusion and wasting of resources tracking down the wrong man. Some historians have mistakenly asserted that Morris was, in fact, Tod Carver, leading them to conclude that Beeler arrested and then unwittingly released one of the probable murderers.[76] It's true that the initial reward circular identified Coley as missing his right forefinger; however, even before Beeler arrested Coley Morris, the updated reward circular stipulated that it was Tod Carver, not Morris, who had the missing forefinger. When the *Arizona Republican* reported on Morris's arrest, the paper incorrectly said he was missing his right forefinger, probably relying on the initial circular's description of him.[77] After Morris secured his release and his name was removed from the Apache County reward circular, the subsequent circulars continued to list "Tod Carver, with right forefinger off," as a suspect.[78] The close attention given to this particular detail in the evolving reward circulars shows that Beeler and other Apache County authorities clearly understood that they were looking for a man who was missing a forefinger—and Morris was not that man.

---

74. *St. Johns Herald*, May 12, 1900, 3.

75. *St. Johns Herald*, May 19, 1900, 3.

76. See, for example, Burton, *Deadliest Outlaws*, 268; Mark T. Smokov, *He Rode with Butch and Sundance: The Story of Harvey "Kid Curry" Logan*, 140; Donna B. Ernst, "Unraveling Two Outlaws Named Carver," 30; and Donna B. Ernst, "A Deadly Year for St. Johns Lawmen," 20.

77. *Arizona Republican*, May 7, 1900, 4.

78. *St. Johns Herald*, May 19, 1900, 3.

With Coley Morris now ruled out as one of the killers, Beeler published an updated list of suspects:

- Tom Capehart, alias wilson [sic], who worked for Wabash Cattle Company, in Apache County, Arizona, a short while in 1899. He is about five feet ten inches tall, weighs about 175 pounds, has slightly dark complexion, dark hair and mustache, had short black beard when last seen, is stoop shouldered but quite well appearing, has blue eyes, and is of very pleasing address, but not very talkative, has a peculiar way of ducking his head from side to side and at the same time forward while he talks, and he usually smiles a great deal when talking. He is an expert bronch trainer.[79]
- Tod Carver, with right forefinger off, slender built, about five feet ten and one half inches high, weight about 175 pounds, has black eyes and moustache, is very active, but is not talkative. He is thought to wear a five and one half boot.
- Jess Black, alias Franks, is five feet eight or nine inches in height, has very dark complexion, black beard, and black eyes, and weighs about 175 pounds. He is very quiet.
- Mack Steen alias Bob Johnson, six feet high, weighs about 180 pounds, is light complexioned with light blue eyes, and very heavy sandy mustache, and is of a very quiet and reserved disposition.
- Also a fifth and unknown man, who is very dark complexioned, has black, straight hair, is low heavy set, and is also very quiet.[80]

The list of names corresponded well with the aliases the outlaws were known to use. Tom Capehart, of course, was known in the county and identified by his real name. Tod Carver was an alias used by T.C. Hilliard, but he too had punched cows in Arizona and New Mexico and was readily identified by his missing forefinger. Will Carver often used "G.W. Franks" as an alias, while Ben Kilpatrick, the tallest of the group, would have been Mack Steen. Harvey Logan, also known as Kid Curry, was likely the unnamed fifth man, as he had recently journeyed with Kilpatrick to Alma. The physical descriptions correspond roughly to the named outlaws,

---

79. This description of Capehart aligns well with an 1899 Cochise County sheriff's log, which described Capehart as "5 ft 10 in, 170 lbs, dark complexion; black hair inclined to baldness at the front, black moustache, not heavy, not very talkative. When he laughs it is very loud" (Donna B. Ernst, "The Real Tom Capehart," 40).

80. *St. Johns Herald*, May 19, 1900, 3.

who disguised their appearance by dyeing their hair and growing varying lengths of beards and mustaches, which they also dyed.

Some later accounts identified Bill Smith and his gang as the murderers, but Smith, like Capehart and Tod Carver, was no stranger to Apache County citizens.[81] In fact, two years earlier, Smith had been arrested and jailed in St. Johns on charges of rustling Henry Barrett's cattle. If his gang had been involved, he or a fellow gang member would certainly have been recognized when they stopped to buy supplies in Springerville and St. Johns prior to the killings. Barrett and Sheriff Beeler, who may have initially thought they were chasing Smith, also would have recognized him during the shootout at the bridge. Yet Beeler and other local authorities did not consider Bill Smith to be a suspect. In contrast, multiple pieces of evidence point to the five Wild Bunch outlaws. Four were known to have been together in Alma: Capehart, Will Carver, Kilpatrick, and Logan. How and when Tod Carver joined the group is unclear, but his identification as a participant is well supported. The fact that the five men left a letter in Springerville for Cassidy and Weaver also bolsters their identification as Cassidy's Wild Bunch comrades. Subsequent events during the posse's chase also strengthen this conclusion. Logan's identification as a participant is not as strong as the other four, but his close connection with the group at this time, as well as the violent course they pursued as they travelled north, suggest a murderous and vengeful intent not inconsistent with Logan's character. Beeler himself later came to believe that Logan was one of the LeSueur-Gibbons murderers.[82]

Morris's release meant Sheriff Beeler was no closer to capturing any of the murderers than when he had begun his pursuit six weeks earlier. Given Beeler's obvious desire to avenge his friends' murders and satisfy an aggrieved community, it is to his credit that he did not try to beat a con-

---

81. *Arizona Republic*, August 16, 1988, C7. Another gang sometimes mentioned in connection with the murders was the "Bronco" Bill Walters gang, which included Red Pipkin. But that gang had broken up the previous year. At the time LeSueur, Gibbons, and Scarborough were murdered, Walters was imprisoned in the New Mexico Territorial Penitentiary, serving a life sentence for second-degree murder, while Pipkin was in jail awaiting trial for grand larceny, a charge for which he would be convicted. See Karen Holliday Tanner and John D. Tanner Jr., *The Bronco Bill Gang*, 155–64.

82. Pinkerton's records, Box 89, Folder 4 (Tom Capehart), memo, January 28, 1902, on "Tom Capehart, alias Bud Wilson, Train Robber."

fession out of Morris or push to prosecute an innocent man. Or maybe Morris had an alibi that was too airtight to ignore.

When Beeler left the chase to arrest Morris, most of the various lawmen and deputies who had joined his posse following Scarborough's murder returned home. County sheriffs were typically responsible for paying a posse's expenses and afterward getting reimbursed by their county governments, which were not always swift or dependable in paying such expenses, especially if the manhunt failed.[83] And many county governments, often cash-strapped if not broke, were reluctant to fund lengthy pursuits of criminals. New Mexico lawmen remained on the alert after Beeler's departure, but it is uncertain whether any were actively pursuing the outlaws. Beeler, however, was determined to capture the murderers. After releasing Morris, he rode back into the field on May 18 with two or three deputies whom he continued to pay out of his own pocket.[84] Remarkably, Beeler picked up the outlaws' trail as they headed north through New Mexico. Riding hard, Beeler and his men were rapidly closing the gap on the desperadoes when heavy rains stopped them at the ferry crossing at the San Juan River near Fruitland. Locals informed Beeler that the outlaws had already crossed the river. Three of the murderers took the ferry, while the other two, perhaps arriving later in the midst of a rising river, shoved their horses into the water and swam across holding onto their horses' tails.[85] Continuing rain forced Beeler to wait three days before he could renew his pursuit. While waiting, Beeler wrote a letter to Grand County Sheriff Jesse Tyler in Moab, Utah, providing descriptions of the five outlaws who had already killed three lawmen. As it turned out, Sheriff Tyler and one of his deputies, Sam Jenkins, had recently run down another Wild Bunch member, George "Flatnose" Currie.

Both Jesse Tyler and Samuel Jenkins were born to large Mormon families, though it is unclear whether either man was an active churchgoer. The forty-three-year-old Tyler was born in the southern Utah town of Beaver, spent his formative years in Fillmore and, at about age thirty-three, moved to Grand County.[86] Single and apparently never married,

---

83. Ball, *Desert Lawmen*, 212–13.

84. Dick Gibbons ("Diary," 270) states that his nephew Elijah Holgate was among those in Beeler's posse.

85. *Salt Lake Herald*, June 4, 1900, 2.

86. *Grand Valley Times* (Moab), June 1, 1900, 1. The US Census has Tyler's family living in Beaver in 1860 and Fillmore in 1870.

Tyler had lived in Grand County for ten years after moving from Fillmore. People who knew him described him as an "Honest Jack" and "a man above reproach" with "sterling integrity."[87] Elected to his first term as Grand County Sheriff by one vote in November 1898, Tyler had gained the respect of local citizens as a hard-working, effective lawman.[88] "He was always fearless in the discharge of his duty," said the *Grand Valley Times*. "He has probably done as much to put down the outlaws as any other man in the state in the time he has been sheriff." [89]

Samuel F. Jenkins was born and raised in Ogden, the tenth of thirteen children. He had married Joanna Reynolds in 1878, but she either died or they divorced before having children.[90] The forty-six-year-old Jenkins was now single but engaged to be married. A small-time rancher with a band of horses and about twenty cattle, he served regularly as a deputy to Sheriff Tyler. He also owned a hotel in Park City. Like Tyler, Jenkins was well known and popular among local residents, particularly the area's Ute Native Americans, who regarded Jenkins as a "warm friend."[91]

Tyler and Jenkins were tracking cattle rustlers when they encountered Flatnose Currie. Currie, then twenty-eight or twenty-nine, was a longtime partner of Harvey Logan and Logan's brother Lonie. The trio began as cattle and horse thieves before joining up with the Wild Bunch as bank and train robbers. Those who knew Currie said he was an outstanding marksman with both a pistol and a rifle and described him as "always genial and a 'good fellow.'"[92] George Bissell, a Wyoming rancher who employed Currie as a cowboy for four years, said Currie "was the best he ever saw."[93] Currie was also a killer, as was his former protégé, Harvey Logan. Among those killed in shoot-outs with the two outlaws were Johnson County Deputy Sheriff William "Billy" Deane in 1897 and Converse County Sheriff Josiah Hazen in June 1899.[94]

---

87. *Grand Valley Times*, June 1, 1900, 1.
88. *Moab Times Independent*, December 22, 1949, 1.
89. *Grand Valley Times*, June 1, 1900, 1.
90. Marriage details from familysearch.org.
91. *Salt Lake Tribune*, June 1, 1900, 1; and *Salt Lake Tribune*, May 29, 1900, 2.
92. *Salt Lake Herald*, April 23, 1900, 2.
93. *Salt Lake Tribune*, April 22, 1900, 1; and *Salt Lake Herald*, April 23, 1900, 2.
94. Smokov, *Harvey "Kid Curry" Logan*, 54–56, 103, describes the likely roles of Currie, Kid Curry, and their compatriots in the killing of sheriffs Deane and Hazen.

Hazen was killed while pursuing Currie, Logan, and the Sundance Kid after they robbed a Union Pacific train of up to $50,000 near Wilcox, Wyoming. Following the holdup, Currie split off from fellow Wild Bunch outlaws and rustled cattle with Tom Dilley in Utah's Green River country. Their activities caught the attention of Sheriff Tyler and Uintah County Sheriff William Preece, and the two sheriffs joined forces to track down the duo. On April 16, their combined posse, which also included Sam Jenkins, came upon Currie in the Book Cliff Mountains while he was on foot and called for him to surrender. "D—m if I will. I will die first," Currie shouted before firing at Preece.[95] Still without a horse, Currie fled to the Green River, which he crossed that night under cover of darkness, and then took refuge behind some boulders on a hill near the river. The posse surrounded Currie's hiding place the next morning, April 17, and after exchanging gunfire into the afternoon, they killed the outlaw with four bullets that found their mark, including a shot to his right temple.[96] Currie's Winchester was still cocked and ready to fire when a deputy took it from the dead man's hands.[97]

The lawmen didn't immediately know whom they had killed, but once the dead man was identified as the wanted train robber and alleged murderer George Currie, Salt Lake City newspapers reported enthusiastically on the gun battle that led to his death. In addition, the Pacific Express Company of the Union Pacific had offered a $3,000 reward for Currie's capture—dead or alive—following the Wilcox train robbery. Tyler, Jenkins, and four other posse members were now slated to receive equal shares of $500 each for their roles in bringing him down.[98] A few weeks after the incident, Sam Jenkins was visiting Salt Lake City and stopped at Zang's saloon to talk with an old friend, Frank Lambert, who was employed at the saloon.[99] Their conversation flowed to Jenkins's recent service as a deputy, and Jenkins recounted the gunfight with Currie.

---

95. *Salt Lake Herald*, April 23, 1900, 2.

96. Salt Lake City newspapers published numerous accounts of the gun battle and identification of Currie, including the *Deseret Evening News*, April 21 and 23, 1900; *Salt Lake Herald*, April 21, 22, 23, and 30, 1900; and *Salt Lake Tribune*, April 20, 21, 22, and 23, 1900.

97. "Testimony of R.D. Westwood," April 21, 1900, at the Coroner's Inquest for Flatnose Currie, published in Colleen Pitt Preece, "Thomas William Preece aka Sheriff 'Billy' Preece," 58.

98. *Salt Lake Tribune*, April 22, 1900, 1.

99. *Deseret Evening News*, May 29, 1900, 1.

"Well, Sam, you want to be careful of those fellows," Lambert said, "or they are liable to get you one of these days."

"If they do, Frank, they'll get me by shooting me in the back, for they can't kill me any other way," Jenkins replied.

A week or two after Currie was killed, three rough-looking men rode into the Thompson Springs area, a railroad station stop also known as Thompson's about thirty-five miles north of Moab. The men freely admitted to a ranch hand at the Webster City Cattle Company that they had been holdup partners with Currie and were now looking for $8,000 in robbery money they believed he had cached in the mountains.[100] Subsequent events would strongly suggest that these were three of the men who killed LeSueur, Gibbons, and Scarborough. Following their conversation with the ranch hand, the outlaws rode south through Moab and returned to New Mexico, apparently to join their other two compatriots. The outlaws had been able to move about somewhat freely during this time because Beeler had broken off the chase to investigate Coley Morris. But after dismissing Morris as a suspect, Beeler and his deputies returned to the field, quickly found the outlaws' trail, and chased them across the San Juan River and back into Utah.

The same three outlaws were seen again on Wednesday, May 23, passing through Moab on their way to Thompson Canyon. Local townspeople, who took careful note of the brands on the men's horses, said the strangers frequently asked questions about where Currie had been killed and the name of the sheriff who had killed him. Meanwhile, sheriffs Tyler and Preece continued hunting for Currie's rustling partner, Tom Dilley. On Saturday, May 26, after the posse split into two groups, Tyler's posse, which again included Jenkins, came across three men wrapped in blankets and huddled around a campfire on the Book Cliffs near Hill Creek. The men looked like Utes that Tyler had helped cross the creek the previous day, and so he decided to stop to ask whether they had seen the rustlers. Tyler and Jenkins rode up to the men and dismounted without their weapons, intending just to talk with them. The other two posse members,

---

100. *Deseret Evening News*, May 29, 1900, 1; and *Salt Lake Tribune*, May 29, 1900, 1. The newspapers said the outlaws talked to the ranch hand just five days after Currie's murder, but other evidence suggests their conversation took place nearer to the month's end.

Deputy Sheriff Herbert Day and a young man named Mert Wade, waited about fifty yards away.[101]

"Hello, boys," Tyler said cheerfully as he approached the campfire.[102]

"I'll hello you, you s— of a b—!" one of the men replied. "Following us up are you. I'll teach you to keep out of here and leave us alone after this." The three men dropped their blankets to reveal Winchester rifles they were holding underneath.

Tyler and Jenkins turned and ran for their horses. They were both killed by a barrage of bullets fired into their backs. Jenkins fell instantly, while Tyler was spun around and staggered backwards a few steps before collapsing. In addition to the shots coming from the three strangers, two shots were fired from the surrounding brush, according to Day, leading him to believe there were at least five men. After shooting the unarmed Tyler and Jenkins, the outlaws turned their fire on Day, who fled on horseback as bullets whistled by. Wade, who had been sitting on a boulder as he watched the ambush unfold, ran for cover in the brush. Neither Wade nor Day was injured.

When Deputy Sheriff Day found Preece's posse about three miles away, he rode up "waving his hands, yelling at the top of his voice and behaving like a crazy man," said Robert Fullerton, a local ranch manager and member of Preece's posse.[103]

"What's the matter, Day?" Fullerton asked.

"They've killed 'em both. They, them!" Day exclaimed.

Still confused, Fullerton said, "What are you talking about man?"

"Jesse and Sam have bitten the dust; they are both dead, shot by outlaws, and I saw them fall," replied Day, who began weeping.

Because Day had counted as many as twenty horses in the camp, he thought there might be more than five outlaws, and so Preece returned to Thompson's to gather reinforcements. Preece also telegraphed news of the murders to nearby sheriffs and to Utah Governor Heber M. Wells, who telegraphed the governors of Wyoming, Colorado, and Arizona. Posses would soon begin gathering throughout the region.

---

101. Among the many accounts provided by Day and Wade of the killing of Tyler and Jenkins are the *Deseret Evening News*, May 29, 1, and June 5, 1900, 2; *Salt Lake Herald*, May 28, 1–2, and May 29, 1900, 1–2; *Salt Lake Tribune*, May 28, 1, and May 29, 1900, 1–2; and *Grand Valley Times*, June 1, 1900, 1.

102. *Deseret Evening News*, June 5, 1900, 2.

103. *Deseret Evening News*, May 29, 1900, 1.

When a posse of six men retrieved the bodies of Tyler and Jenkins early the next morning, they found them riddled with lead and horribly mutilated by pistol and rifle shots. Some posse members believed the two men had been shot after they lay dead, just as the outlaws had done to LeSueur and Gibbons.[104] However, while all accounts said the bodies were mutilated by the gunfire, not all claimed the outlaws continued firing after the two men were killed. None of the accounts reported the presence of powder burns on the bodies, as was the case in the LeSueur-Gibbons murders, so it is equally likely that the initial volley of bullets, which were fired at close range, created the ghastly wounds as they entered and exited the bodies. "The bullets used by the outlaws were of the soft-nose variety," the *Salt Lake Herald* reported. "And where they came out there are holes almost large enough for a man to insert his fist."[105]

The outlaws stole the lawmen's horses and other small valuables, leaving behind some of their bedding, two saddles, sixteen horses, and, oddly, two Winchester rifles, suggesting they were well stocked with weapons. The posse strapped the two dead men onto mules and carried them fifty miles to Thompson Springs, where they were placed on ice for preservation before embalming. Tyler's remains were carried thirty-five miles by wagon to Moab, while Thompson's officials waited for Jenkins's brother to retrieve his remains for burial in his hometown of Ogden.[106] "Tyler was a poor man and his family will be left with practically nothing," the *Salt Lake Tribune* said.[107] Sheriff Beeler's letter to Tyler warning him about the outlaws arrived in Moab the day after his murder.[108]

When the outlaws opened fire on Tyler and Jenkins, Deputy Sheriff Day, sitting fifty yards back on his horse, thought he heard Jenkins yell, "Dilley," leading to an initial supposition that rustler Tom Dilley and his men were the killers. However, Wade, sitting next to Day, said he didn't hear Dilley's name called and thought Day had just imagined it.[109]

---

104. *Salt Lake Herald*, May 29, 1900, 2. Strangely, the same account says that Jenkins's body had six or seven bullet holes and Tyler's just two, which would appear to contradict the assertion that "the men had been riddled with lead after they lay dead upon the ground."

105. *Salt Lake Herald*, May 28, 1900, 1.

106. *Salt Lake Tribune*, May 29, 1900, 2; and *Salt Lake Herald*, May 30, 1900, 2, for the transportation, embalming, and burial of the bodies.

107. *Salt Lake Tribune*, May 29, 1900, 2.

108. *Salt Lake Herald*, June 4, 1900, 2.

109. *Salt Lake Herald*, May 29, 1900, 2.

Subsequent investigation quickly led authorities to conclude that Dilley had not been in the area and could not have been among the killers. Meanwhile, mounting evidence pointed to the men Beeler was pursuing. Five days after the murder, the Moab *Grand Valley Times* reported:

> Letters received here from Arizona officials giving a description of horses and their brands taken form [sic] there by a party of three men who are wanted there for the murder of a Sheriff and two Deputies, leaves no doubt whatever but that they are the party who passed here, a week ago Wednesday and also the party at whose hands Sheriff Tyler and Sam Jenkins met death.[110]

Upon hearing of the lawmen's murder, Sheriff Beeler took the train to Thompson Springs from Mancos, Colorado, arriving May 31.[111] After consulting with Utah lawmen and getting a description of the outlaws, weapons, horses, accoutrements, and other details, Beeler was equally convinced these were the same men who murdered LeSueur, Gibbons, and Scarborough. "They answer the description of the men wanted by him in every particular, and the brands on the horses are the same, so there is no doubt but that the same parties committed all the murders," he told a reporter.[112]

Were these the same five men—or three of the five men—who killed LeSueur, Gibbons, and Scarborough? After Tom Dilley was ruled out, suspicion fell on Butch Cassidy, who many believed had partnered with Flatnose Currie and Harvey Logan on the Wilcox train robbery the previous June. "Descriptions of the men as given by Herbert Day, who saw them, to persons here who have known Cassidy, make it appear almost certain that the well-known train robber is of the gang," said the *Salt Lake Herald*.[113] Adding to suspicions about Cassidy's participation, a cowboy at a ranch on the Green River reportedly spotted Cassidy in the area around the time of the murders.[114] But Utah newspapers continued to raise other possible suspects, such as Lewellen C. Lewellen, who was wanted for the murder of two policemen in Denver. Another major suspect, rustler Joe (or Jim) Rose, "is the kind that shoots a man in the back," said Vernal Mayor E. W. Davis.[115] Coincidentally, Ben Kilpatrick often used the surname "Rose" as one of his aliases, and so, in this instance, Rose and Kilpatrick may have been the same person.

---

110. *Grand Valley Times*, June 1, 1900, 1.
111. *Salt Lake Tribune*, June 1, 1900, 1.
112. *Arizona Journal-Miner*, June 13, 1900, 2.
113. *Salt Lake Herald*, May 29, 1900, 1.
114. *Salt Lake Tribune*, May 29, 1900, 2.
115. *Salt Lake Tribune*, June 8, 1900, 1.

Despite these conjectures, the evidence supports the conclusion that the Arizona, New Mexico, and Utah murders were committed by the same set of men. Witnesses who saw the outlaws ride through Moab prior to the murders or saw them during their flight said they matched the descriptions of the Arizona murderers that were being circulated. Admittedly, most of the published descriptions of the Arizona murderers were sufficiently general that many men could have fit their descriptions. However, it is not the descriptions of the outlaws but the descriptions of their horses—the matching brands and markings—that provide the most persuasive evidence that the same men committed all five murders. The brands on the Arizona outlaws' horses were noted by Beeler and passed on to Utah authorities. Witnesses said the brands on the horses of the men who rode through Moab prior to the murder matched the brands identified by Beeler, as did the horses later abandoned by the outlaws when they fled the Tyler-Jenkins murders. The similarities in the Arizona and Utah murders—each carried out ruthlessly and without warning—lend further support to the conclusion that they were committed by the same men.

Whether just three or five Wild Bunch gang members committed the Utah murders is unclear. Deputy Day thought at least five men had fired on Tyler and Jenkins, but other reports put the number at three to six in the gang.[116] Of course, the outlaws could have split into two groups, as they often had during their flight from Sheriff Beeler. Similarly, it's possible that new Wild Bunch gang members, such as the Sundance Kid or Butch Cassidy, participated in the Utah killings, but insufficient evidence exists to support this assertion other than the initial speculation that Cassidy was involved. Again, the overwhelming evidence—especially the independent identification and verification of the horses' brands—suggests that the same men who murdered LeSueur and Gibbons also murdered Tyler and Jenkins.

After killing the Utah lawmen, three of the outlaws rode hard until their horses gave out about dusk that evening. They dismounted and left all but two of their horses to wander on their own, and they then began helping themselves to horses at a ranch about twelve miles northeast of the murder site. The ranch's owner, Oscar Turner, discovered something was amiss after one of the horses broke loose from the outlaws and appeared at his cabin with a rope around its neck. When Turner and his partner went to investi-

---

116. *Salt Lake Herald*, May 29, 1900, 1–2, contains Day's assertion that there were five outlaws. The *Deseret Evening News*, May 28, 1, initially reported that "there is known to have been at least six in the gang."

gate, they found themselves staring at the barrel end of a Winchester rifle. The outlaws told Turner that "they had had a fight down the canyon and had killed two men and probably three and it would be necessary for them to have four of his horses to carry them out of the country," Turner said.[117]

Recognizing that the outlaws had Sheriff Tyler's horse, Turner asked them where they got it. One of the outlaws replied, "The man who owned it will have no further use for it, so I might as well have it as anyone else."[118]

The outlaws selected four of Turner's horses, but when the rancher protested against their taking one of his favorites, they unsaddled the horse and took another. While saddling up the horses, the men inquired whether Turner knew who had killed Flatnose Currie. Turner's answer was not recorded, but the outlaws' curiosity about Currie's killers, both before and after their ambush of Tyler and Jenkins, fueled suspicion that they had targeted the two lawmen because of their role in Currie's death. The outlaws said they would reimburse Turner for his horses if they made a successful escape, adding that he was welcome to their camp equipment and horses, seven or eight in number, they were leaving behind.[119] They rode off with six horses, two they brought with them and four of Turner's. The talkative outlaws said they planned to ride up Hay Canyon and across the White River. "Just as soon as we get some money we will pay you for the horses, providing we ain't killed," their leader said as the men mounted and left. "One thing is certain, we will never be taken alive."[120]

News of the Tyler-Jenkins killings sparked widespread outrage. "The murder was discussed on the street all day," said the *Salt Lake Herald*, and Utah Governor Wells was overwhelmed by offers from men wanting to help track down the killers.[121] Dozens of men joined posses across the state, including nine officers who took the train from Salt Lake City to Thompson Springs to link up with Sheriff Preece. Men were also sent out to watch Brown's Park and Robbers Roost, known criminal hangouts, while citizens in nearly every settlement and town stood on the alert, with riders ready to gallop to the nearest telegraph station to report any sightings of the outlaws.[122] Posses in Wyoming watched trails leading into Hole-in-the Wall. A dispatch from Price reported that the day after the murders, "the whole

---

117. *Salt Lake Herald*, June 5, 1900, 2.
118. *Deseret Evening News*, May 28, 1900, 1.
119. *Salt Lake Herald*, June 5, 1900, 2.
120. *Deseret Evening News*, May 28, 1900, 1.
121. *Salt Lake Herald*, May 28, 1900, 1; and May 29, 1900, 2.
122. *Salt Lake Tribune*, May 29, 1.

force of blacksmiths are working at their forges at this hour, shoeing horses" that would be sent by train from Price to Thompson Springs for the posses converging there.[123] In addition to the posses, one hundred Ute warriors were closely watching for signs of the outlaws moving across the Uintah reservation. "Jenkins, the murdered deputy, was a warm friend of the Indians, and they are determined to avenge his death," the *Salt Lake Tribune* reported. "The braves have been further worked up by promises of reward."[124] Reporters from Salt Lake City's three daily newspapers accompanied the posse to cover the largest manhunt in Utah history up to that time.[125]

Pinkerton agents working for the railroads continued their own investigations and pursuit of the outlaws. Frank Murray, Assistant Superintendent of Pinkerton's Denver office, had come to Utah after Currie's death to identify the body. Murray was the Pinkerton agent who tracked Cassidy and the Wild Bunch to the WS Ranch in Alma. Murray barely escaped with his own life when the gang discovered who he was. In addition to identifying Currie, Murray was looking for money reportedly cached by Currie following the Wild Bunch's robbery of the Union Pacific the previous June. When Currie's outlaw partners came to Thompson's looking for the stolen loot, they estimated his share to be $8,000. Murray, however, believed that Currie was the treasurer of the outlaw band and so was holding all or most of the holdup money—$28,000, according to Murray— which had not yet been divvied up among the outlaws when he was killed.[126] Whatever the amount, the Pinkertons and Wild Bunch outlaws were vying to be the first to find Currie's loot.

Sheriff Beeler also rushed to join the massive manhunt. Beeler and his deputies had lost contact with the outlaws about two weeks earlier when heavy rains had prevented them from following the outlaws across the swollen San Juan River in northern New Mexico. They subsequently picked up the trail of a man they believed to be James Lowe, and so they pursued Lowe in hopes that he would lead them to the killers. Beeler understood that Lowe was an alias, but he thought Lowe's real name was Mone Kofford,

---

123. *Salt Lake Herald*, May 28, 1900, 1.

124. *Salt Lake Tribune*, June 1, 1900, 1.

125. Smokov, *Harvey "Kid Curry" Logan*, 147; and *Deseret Evening News*, May 28, 1900, 1.

126. *Salt Lake Herald*, May 29, 1900, 1. Murray said the Union Express lost $28,000 in the Wilcox robbery, but some reports said the amount was $50,000.

a man wanted for an 1894 murder of a Utah lawman.[127] Beeler tracked the man to Lee's Ferry, a Colorado River crossing in Northern Arizona; from Lee's Ferry, the man was said to be heading toward the Thompson Springs area with three horses. Given that Beeler never caught up with the man he was trailing, it is unknown whether he really was Lowe—that is, Cassidy— or another man Beeler mistakenly followed. If the man was indeed Cassidy, then he could not have been a participant in the Tyler-Jenkins murders. After receiving news of those murders, Beeler and his deputies took the train from Mancos to Thompson Springs, hoping to join the posses assembling there. By the time they arrived, the Utah posses had already left Thompson's, and so Beeler and his men took the train back to Grand Junction to await further news regarding the murderers' whereabouts.[128]

While waiting to join up with a Utah posse, Beeler talked to a reporter with the *Grand Junction Sun*. The collective reward for capturing the five killers had increased to $15,000, including $5,000 from Arizona counties and individuals. The outlaws were "tough people," resourceful, and hard to track, but if they were captured, Beeler said, he could "identify all by sight and three by name—Capehart, Black and Todd Carver, the latter being minus the forefinger of his right hand."[129] The *Sun* reporter noted that since the day LeSueur and Gibbons were killed, Beeler "has never wearied in the effort to bring the murderers to justice." Beeler acknowledged that the chances of capturing the men were slim, but a desire for vengeance kept him going. "I have stuck to this chase as much for satisfaction as anything else," he said, adding that he earnestly wanted to avenge the deaths of his two friends. "My plan was, had I ever come up with these killers, to ride around them and meet them as they met LeSueur and Gibbons. That is the only way to make a successful clean-up of that kind of cattle."[130] Shortly after the interview, Beeler dispatched three deputies by train to Rock Springs, Wyoming, to help block the outlaws' escape north from Brown's Park, Utah, where it was believed some of them were hiding.[131] The deputies later moved their operations to Baggs, Wyoming, after receiving word that

---

127. *Salt Lake Herald*, June 3, 1900, 12. A description of Kofford's crime can be found in *The Evening Dispatch* (Provo, Utah), July 13, 1895, 1.

128. *Salt Lake Herald*, June 3, 1900, 12.

129. The *Sun* article was reprinted in the *Salt Lake Herald*, June 4, 1900, 2. Jess Black, alias Franks, was Will Carver.

130. *Salt Lake Herald*, June 4, 1900.

131. *Salt Lake Herald*, June 5, 1900, 2. The deputies passed through Salt Lake City on June 4 on their way to Rock Springs.

one of the gang members was hiding there. Beeler stayed in Colorado with the intention of joining Preece's posse in Fruita or Rifle.

Before his arrival in Utah, Beeler had been criticized by one of Utah's newspapers for his decision to mail—rather than telegraph—information about the outlaws to Sheriff Tyler. Several days before Tyler and Jenkins were murdered, a Moab resident spotted the three outlaws riding horses with the same brands and markings described in Beeler's letter. Unfortunately, the letter didn't reach Moab until a day after the murders. "If the Arizona sheriff had notified officers at Moab by telegraph instead of letter they [the murderers] could easily have been captured before they had added more murders to their list and saved the lives of the murdered men," the *Salt Lake Herald* complained.[132] Some also speculated that the outlaws shot Tyler and Jenkins because they thought it was Beeler sneaking up on them.[133] It is curious why Beeler chose to mail the information. Perhaps there was no telegraph service available in the town where he was staying at the time; or maybe he wanted to include more descriptive details than could be reasonably transmitted in a telegraph. Of course, Sheriff Tyler was careless in approaching the outlaws' camp. He was, after all, chasing violent rustlers who might have given him the same deadly welcome. Still, another one of Sheriff Beeler's decisions prompted second guessing due to its seemingly fatal consequences.

With at least six posses scouring mountain passes and guards watching the trails leading in and out of known outlaw hideouts, it would seem only a matter of time before the killers would be flushed out and captured. But seasoned lawmen knew that despite their overwhelming numbers, it was the fugitives who held nearly every advantage: superior weapons and horses; a rugged mountain landscape that made it easy to hide and obscure their tracks; and a long head start. "The robbers know they are being pursued, and the chances are they will see the posse before the posse sees them," said Arthur Pratt, a former Salt Lake City police chief

---

132. *Salt Lake Herald*, May 30, 1900, 1. Supporting the assertion that the horses' brands were noted before the murders, the *Grand Valley Times* (June 8, 1900) reported: "Wiliam [sic] Littleby, who went to the Turner ranch in the north part of the county to identify the horses left by the outlaws who killed Tyler and Jenkins, returned last week and reported that the horses were the same that were driven through Moab by three men from Arizona on the Wednesday before the murders were committed." Reprinted in the *Moab Times Independent*, June 10, 1920, 2.

133. *Salt Lake Herald*, June 13, 1900, 2.

who joined the Salt Lake City posse. "There is almost no chance of their being surprised."[134] Another posse member, Joe Raleigh, echoed Pratt's concerns, saying, "Trailing them up canyons is very dangerous on account of possible ambush."[135] Moreover, the outlaws were desperate men. Their demonstrated willingness to kill, combined with their unwillingness to be taken alive, weighed heavily on the pursuers. "They are all crack shots, and from the formation of the country any posse that may go in there labors under a serious disadvantage," Pratt said. "I fear very much that more of the officers will be killed if they overtake the outlaws."[136]

The outlaws wanted to escape, not shoot it out with lawmen. To this end they had one more advantage: the help of minor Wild Bunch associates and sympathizers, particularly in remote settlements. Such people helped the fugitives hide and provided them with food, fresh horses, and other supplies. The outlaws appeared to vanish in the mountains, leaving the sheriffs simply guessing as to where they might be. "These fellows could never have held out as long as they have, and so successfully eluded the officers, were it not for the fact that they have friends on the 'outside,' who keep them supplied and notified of what is going on," a local informant told the *Deseret Evening News*.[137] One accomplice even falsely reported that he had seen the outlaws riding near Cisco along the Utah-Colorado border, causing lawmen to waste time following up the bogus lead. "The report of three men being seen to cross the railway south of Cisco is a hoax," the *Salt Lake Tribune* reported. "It has been proven that the tracks seen there were made by the man who brought the news into Thompson's, and that it was done to fool the officers."[138]

Sympathizers offered support for a variety of reasons. Some, of course, were criminals themselves, though on a smaller scale than the Wild Bunch. Many small ranchers and homesteaders also resented the power and wealth of the banks, railroads, and large cattle companies, and so drew a measure of satisfaction from the Wild Bunch's rustling and robbing activities. They regarded lawmen as tools of an oppressive elite. When news of Sheriff Tyler's murder reached the Colorado town of Grand

---

134. *Salt Lake Herald*, May 28, 1900, 1.

135. *Salt Lake Tribune*, June 6, 1900, 1.

136. *Salt Lake Herald*, May 28, 1900, 1. Utah County Sheriff Storrs expressed opinions similar to those of Pratt and Raleigh concerning the outlaws' advantages in *Salt Lake Tribune*, May 30, 2.

137. *Deseret Evening News*, May 29, 1900, 1.

138. *Salt Lake Tribune*, June 5, 1900, 1.

Junction, some people said they hoped the murderers would get away. "Tyler had shot unarmed men on more than one occasion, and they were glad he had been given a dose of his own medicine," they said.[139] Probably the main reason gang members enjoyed the support of local farmers and townspeople is that the outlaws treated them well. They typically didn't steal from individuals or small businessmen, and they were generous with those who helped them. In explaining why people in his area tolerated and even assisted the murderers during their escape, Vernal Mayor E. W. Davis told a newspaper reporter, "The presence of desperate outlaws in the country is in no way a menace to the inhabitants. These criminals merely come in there to rendezvous, and they are careful not to arouse the enmity of the settlers by molesting their belongings. When one of those fellows takes anything from a rancher he invariably recompenses him fairly."[140]

Fear undoubtedly motivated some of those who helped the outlaws. Harvey Logan reportedly rode two hundred miles to assassinate a man, Jim Winters, who was helping lawmen track down and arrest him.[141] Whether true or not, it's the type of story that buys considerable cooperation and silence. Within the past twelve months, Wild Bunch members had murdered at least seven lawmen, including two—Sheriff Tyler and Deputy Jenkins—who many believed had been targeted because of their role in killing Flatnose Currie.[142] LeSueur and Gibbons were drawn into an ambush and brutally murdered simply because they were members of a posse. Cassidy and fellow gang members were not Robin Hoods. They didn't give to the poor, but they were generous with their abettors. And those who crossed them paid a high penalty. When asked why no one came forward with information about the Tyler-Jenkins murderers, a local resident said, "Why they can't get anyone to testify, for the reason it is known that it would be as much as a man's life's worth to 'peach.'"[143]

Sheriff Beeler patrolled the eastern portion of Utah during this period, concentrating his efforts in Uintah County's Ashley Valley surrounding Vernal, where some of the outlaws were said to be hiding. Despite many reported sightings of men fitting the outlaws' descriptions—including

---

139. *Deseret Evening News*, May 29, 1900, 1.

140. *Salt Lake Tribune*, June 8, 1900, 1.

141. See pages 250–51 for a description of the murder.

142. For example, Charles Kelly, *The Outlaw Trail: A History of Butch Cassidy and His Wild Bunch*, 263, asserts that Logan murdered Tyler as revenge for killing Currie.

143. *Deseret Evening News*, May 29, 1. "Peach" is slang for snitching or informing.

several people claiming to have seen Butch Cassidy—none of the posses ever saw or engaged the outlaws. About ten days after the Utah posses began operations, state and local authorities reluctantly concluded that the outlaws had escaped the state's borders and so instructed most of the sheriffs and posses to return home.[144] The three sheriffs who remained in the field—Sheriff Swanson of Sweetwater County, Wyoming; Sheriff Preece of Uintah County, Utah; and Sheriff Beeler of Apache County, Arizona—met in Vernal on June 7 to confer on next steps. All three believed that some or all of the outlaws were still hiding in the mountains near Vernal. However, Swanson believed the outlaws were so deeply ensconced in the mountains that "it will take a full regiment of soldiers to capture them."[145] Saying he had other business to address, Swanson broke off his search, but Preece, who knew the area and its residents, agreed to continue operations with Beeler. The two remaining sheriffs formed a rugged pair. Preece, a non-churchgoing Mormon with a square jaw and broad head, was shorter and less talkative than Beeler, but both men were well-built and considered tough but fair lawmen.[146] As they went out in the field, they kept their precise plans to themselves to avoid tipping off the outlaws and their friends.[147]

A newspaper reporter caught up with Beeler a few days later in Vernal. The reporter noted the "ring of determination in his voice," saying, "Sheriff Beeler shows no signs of weakening in his patient pursuit of the gang that are wanted for murder both in Arizona and Utah."[148] Beeler reiterated his desire to achieve a reckoning with the outlaws:

> The boys that these cowardly villians [sic] shot to pieces in the south were my friends and sacrificed their lives to assist me, and I will even up the score. These fellows may as well fight me one place as another, as the time when we meet is bound to come. I know them all, and am as positive of their identity as though they were behind prison bars.[149]

Although Beeler had lost the outlaws' trail, he was confident he could pick it up again, just as he had done before. "What do you propose now?" the reporter asked.

"Follow them to h--l," Beeler replied.

---

144. *Salt Lake Tribune*, June 7, 1900, 1; and *Salt Lake Tribune*, June 8, 1900, 1.
145. *Salt Lake Herald*, June 13, 1900, 2.
146. Preece, "Sheriff 'Billy' Preece," 29.
147. *Salt Lake Herald*, June 8, 1900, 1.
148. *Salt Lake Herald*, June 13, 1900, 2.
149. *Salt Lake Herald*, June 13, 1900.

Five more days of searching yielded no breakthroughs. When Beeler and Preece conferred again on Tuesday, June 12, Preece called it quits, concluding that "the murderers have made good their escape, and that further efforts at present to apprehend them would simply be adding useless expense."[150] Beeler was still convinced that the outlaws, aided by local farmers and ranchers, were hiding close by. He also thought Preece wasn't doing enough to force Vernal citizens to cooperate. After interviewing Beeler, a *Salt Lake Tribune* reporter wrote, "Sheriff Preece, it is believed, was being handicapped by residents in and around Vernal, and that Preece was more afraid of these residents, who are intimidated by the outlaws, than he is of the murderers."[151]

Beeler was undoubtedly the source of this criticism. One can understand his frustration. Normally measured in his remarks, Beeler gave vent after months of mounting disappointment and exhaustion when he complained about Preece and Ashley Valley residents. Beeler was close to finally achieving his quest, but, it appeared, an overly cautious sheriff and cowardly citizens stood in the way. It was widely understood—and even acknowledged by Vernal's mayor—that local residents were aiding the outlaws. Whether Preece could have done more to break through the wall of silence protecting the outlaws is unknown, but as a lawman, he had acquitted himself well. In addition to running down Flatnose Currie, Preece had spent almost as much time in the saddle as Beeler, first pursuing Tom Dilley's gang of rustlers and then the Tyler-Jenkins murderers. He also had stayed on the chase with Beeler longer than any other sheriff from Utah, Wyoming, or New Mexico. "Sheriff Beeler left on the stage Tuesday morning," the *Vernal Express* newspaper reported. "He was badly discouraged as his trip to Vernal was in vain. He neither succeeded in getting track of the outlaws nor in getting any material assistance from local peace officers."[152]

Preece must have wondered at Beeler's refusal to give up the chase. All hope of capturing the outlaws had vanished, and yet the obstinate sheriff wouldn't go home. Beeler's determination was almost certainly rooted in his own feelings of personal responsibility and wounded pride. Beeler had been among the searchers who found the bodies of Frank LeSueur and Gus Gibbons. When he volunteered to stay with the bodies while someone else rode to town to inform the families, Dick Gibbons had

---

150. *Vernal Express*, June 16, 1900, 3.
151. *Salt Lake Tribune*, June 13, 1900, 2.
152. *Vernal Express*, June 16, 1900.

insisted that Beeler himself deliver the news.[153] Beeler organized a posse and quickly left town to pursue the killers, staying on the trail for all but a few days over the next ten weeks. "The grim pursuer," a reporter called him.[154] "My turn will come," Beeler said, a phrase that sounded as much a death wish as a desire for revenge.

Beeler still had three deputies guarding the trails in and around Baggs, Wyoming, but he was now on his own in Utah. After leaving Vernal, he told a reporter in Price that he planned to retrieve his horses in Colorado and return to Ashley Valley to continue the hunt.[155] However, during the midnight train ride between Price and Grand Junction, Beeler finally acknowledged defeat. The game was up. If posses from throughout Utah couldn't track down the outlaws and dislodge them from their hiding places, what hope did he have working alone? Upon arriving in Grand Junction in the early morning of June 13, Beeler announced that he was going to Mancos to get his horses and return home to St. Johns.[156]

As it turned out, one of the Wild Bunch was hiding in Baggs, just as Beeler had suspected. It was Butch Cassidy. After being released from the St. Johns jail, Cassidy had made his way north, probably traveling through Utah, which would explain the Cassidy sightings during the hunt for the Tyler-Jenkins killers. Pinkerton agent Charlie Siringo said that after Cassidy made it to Baggs, he hid in the home of "Mid" Nichols, who owned a saloon there. One day, perhaps while drinking at the saloon, Beeler's deputies took Nichols into their confidence and told him they were trailing the Kid Curry gang. "That night 'Butch' left the Nichols home riding a good horse and saddle and armed to the teeth," Siringo said. "He had to cross a bridge where two of Beeler's men were on guard. They supposed he was a rancher leaving town, and gave him a friendly salute."[157] After that, Cassidy remained hidden in the nearby mountains, well supplied with food and liquor by Nichols's wife, until Beeler's deputies left town.

Sheriff Beeler arrived back in St. Johns on June 25.[158] Since he had begun chasing the outlaws from Springerville on March 26, he had trav-

---

153. Palmer, *Arizona Palmer Family History*, 238.

154. *Salt Lake Herald*, June 13, 1900, 2.

155. *Salt Lake Tribune*, June 13, 1900. See also *Vernal Express*, June 16, 1900, which said Beeler intended to rejoin his deputies in Wyoming.

156. *Salt Lake Tribune*, June 15, 1900, 7.

157. Charles A. Siringo, *A Cowboy Detective: An Autobiography*, 368. Siringo said he got this information from one of Cassidy's friends.

158. Gibbons, "Diary," 273.

eled over 2,400 miles by horse, stage, and rail into Mexico and through five western states and territories, often traversing some of the nation's most rugged mountain and desert terrain.[159] He had spent nearly one thousand dollars of his own money to fund not just his own but also his posse's activities.[160] Beeler dismissed rumors in Utah papers that he would not be reimbursed, saying he fully expected Apache County to pay his expenses.[161] Interestingly, the *St. Johns Herald* had not published any articles about Beeler's activities since May 12 when he arrested and then released one of the alleged murderers, William "Coley" Morris. Other Arizona newspapers occasionally republished articles from Utah papers, including lengthy interviews with Beeler and descriptions of his activities, but the *St. Johns Herald* stayed strangely silent. St. Johns citizens must have been interested in Beeler's progress, but the only reminders the *Herald* provided of the LeSueur-Gibbons murders and Beeler's manhunt were the reward notices that were reprinted on page three of every issue since the March 27 murders. When Beeler finally returned from his three-month pursuit, the *Herald* published a brief two-sentence article that barely acknowledged his absence. The June 30 article was sandwiched between a birth announcement and an advertisement for "Dr. King's New Discovery" cure-all wonder drug. "Sheriff Beeler came in from Utah this week, having business here that required his attention," the newspaper said. "He informs us that at present no posse is in pursuit of the gang he had been following so long."[162]

In interviews with Utah journalists during the manhunt, Beeler had emphasized that Frank and Gus had been his personal friends, that they had died trying to assist him, and that he earnestly wanted to avenge their deaths. Beeler had vowed to stay on the murderers' trail until he ran them down, but he now returned empty-handed. What he said to the LeSueur and Gibbons families when he saw them, or what they said to him, was not recorded in any of their reminiscences. After Beeler's return, the *Herald* stopped printing the reward notices. The paper did not publish any follow-up articles mentioning the murders or Beeler's Ahab-like pursuit of the outlaws during the rest of his term as sheriff.

---

159. *Salt Lake Tribune*, June 15, 1900, 7, provides the estimate of 2,400 miles.
160. *Eastern Utah Advocate*, June 14, 1900, 3.
161. *Salt Lake Tribune*, June 13, 1900, 2. Beeler later said the county reimbursed him for his expenses (*St. Johns Herald*, July 21, 1900, 2).
162. *St. Johns Herald*, June 30, 1900, 3.

CHAPTER 7

CALLED TO ANOTHER MISSION

While Sheriff Beeler was pursuing outlaws across the Western states, the families of the murdered men carried on amid profound grief. The Gibbons family blamed Beeler for leaving Frank and Gus in the field, and a good portion of St. Johns citizens shared this view. Gus's sisters Rhoda and Eva claimed that townspeople came to the LeSueur and Gibbons homes, offering to lynch Beeler. "You can do anything you want as far as I am concerned," J.T. LeSueur reportedly told the mob. Bill Gibbons counseled against hanging the sheriff, saying, "No, it won't bring the boys back and he will get what's coming to him, no matter what is done."[1]

These assertions, made decades later in personal reminiscences, appear highly exaggerated, if not outright false. They are not buttressed by any supporting evidence from other sources. Given what we know about J.T. LeSueur, one cannot believe he would have sanctioned killing Beeler, as Eva contends, nor would the townspeople. Accounts written by LeSueur family members do not express any bitterness toward Beeler. John T. Crosby, J.T.'s grandson, said he "never heard the LeSueurs say anything about Sheriff Beeler being drunk that day [of the murders]." [2]

Still, Frank's murder dealt a hard blow. "His grief stricken mother [Geneva] nearly lost her mind," said her granddaughter, Anona Crosby Heap.[3] The LeSueur's oldest daughter, Alice, returned home early from the Brigham Young Academy to care for the younger LeSueur children and help with household chores while Geneva recovered from illness and heartbreak.[4] J.T. turned some of his grief inward, blaming himself for waiting on the outlaws when they shopped at the St. Johns ACMI store. "He

---

1. Arvin Palmer, *An Arizona Palmer Family History: Selected Sketches Of Arthur Palmer And Evaline Augusta Gibbons Palmer And Their Ancestors*, 143 (Rhoda) and 238 (Eva). The quotes are from Eva's account.
2. John T. Crosby, interview with Carl W. LeSueur, January 16, 2002.
3. Anona Crosby Heap, "Mother of Mine."
4. Alice LeSueur, "My Life History," published in *LeSueur Family History*.

felt remorse for it, for selling them the bullets that killed his son," Crosby said. "But, of course, the men were strangers and how was he to know?"[5]

Bill Gibbons became embittered following his son's murder, angry that God had allowed Gus to be taken in such a brutal manner. How long this bitterness lasted is not known, but at the end of the year, Bill asked to be released from his calling as a counselor to Stake President David Udall. Perhaps his request was unrelated to Gus's murder, but it marked the end of an era for the St. Johns Mormon community. Bill had served as Udall's counselor for twenty years, seven years in the bishopric after the St. Johns ward was established in 1880 and thirteen more years after the St. Johns Stake was organized in 1887.

One of those most deeply affected by the murders was Frank's older brother, James, who was then serving a mission to the British Isles. "Frank and I were like David and Jonathan in our affections," said James.[6] Before leaving on his mission, James had stopped to see his brother in Provo, where Frank was attending Brigham Young Academy. "Just before parting, we held each other's hands and made a covenant that we would follow the Lord's bidding and do anything he desired of us, thus bringing honor to our father's name," James said.[7] Both agreed to devote their lives to a unique Mormon doctrine: redeeming ancestors who had died without an opportunity to hear the gospel of Jesus Christ. "I would gather genealogy on my mission, and we [would] work together for the salvation of our dead relatives," James said regarding their pact.[8] Frank received his mission call in February 1900 but waited to go until after James returned from his mission so the brothers could see each other again. The reunion never occurred. A few days after Frank's death, James received an urgent cable from his mission president informing him of Frank's murder and releasing him to go home.

"I was simply-horror struck," James said. "For a short time this seemingly terrible blow nearly crushed me."[9] But during prayerful contemplation, James said he heard a voice from above say: "Your brother was called for the same purpose as was President Woodruff's son." Mormon President

---

5. Crosby, interview with Carl W. LeSueur, January 16, 2002.

6. James W. LeSueur, "A Patriarchal Blessing," June 29, 1932, published in *LeSueur Family History*.

7. James A. [sic] LeSueur, "A Peep into the Spirit World," published in Michelle R. Sorensen and David R. Willmore, *The Journey Beyond Life*, 147–48.

8. James W. LeSueur, "Regarding Salvation for the Dead," 199.

9. James W. LeSueur, "A Patriarchal Blessing and its Fulfillment," 124; and LeSueur, "Regarding Salvation for the Dead," 199.

Wilford Woodruff, whose teenaged son drowned in a tragic boating accident, said he received assurances from the Lord that his son was taken because he had been called to preach the gospel to deceased souls in the spirit world. For James, the divine voice offered the same reassurance. There was purpose in Frank's death. Later, James would report receiving an even more remarkable confirmation of Frank's new mission: a vision in which James observed Frank, along with other Mormon missionaries, preaching the gospel to deceased LeSueur relatives. Similarly, Gibbons family members reported that Bill was visited by his deceased son, Gus, who said he also had been called to preach to his relatives in the spirit world.

To understand the meaning of these religious experiences for the grieving families, one must understand Mormon beliefs regarding salvation, particularly how salvation is intertwined with Mormon temple rites and genealogical record keeping. The concept of proselytizing among the dead may appear strange to modern Christians, but many early Christian sects believed that their ancestors could gain posthumous salvation, and they engaged in practices aimed at helping the deceased achieve that end.[10] The Catholic Church eventually rejected this belief, and the concept of salvation for the dead remained largely dormant until the early nineteenth century when new American religious movements, including Mormonism, advanced radical ways of reinterpreting conventional mores and Christian teachings. A driving force in this cauldron of revisionism and dissent was a desire to return to original Biblical beliefs and practices. Regarding salvation for the dead, Shakers and Universalists believed that Christ, as a spirit, preached to other deceased spirits.[11] Both groups cited the New Testament scripture, 1 Peter 3:18–20, to support their view:

---

10. For discussions of early Christian beliefs relating to salvation for the dead, see Jeffrey A. Trumbower, *Rescue for the Dead: The Posthumous Salvation of Non-Christians in Early Christianity*; David L. Paulsen, Kendel J. Christensen, and Martin Pulido, "Redeeming the Dead: Tender Mercies, Turning of Hearts, and the Restoration of Authority," 28–51; David L. Paulsen, Roger D. Cook, and Kendel J. Christensen, "The Harrowing of Hell: Salvation for the Dead in Early Christianity," 56–77; David L. Paulsen and Brock M. Mason, "Baptism for the Dead in Early Christianity," 22–49; and Charles R Harrell, *"This is My Doctrine": The Development of Mormon Theology*, 343–60.

11. For developing Christian concepts relating to salvation for the dead prior to the Mormons, see Christopher James Blythe, "Ann Booth's Vision and Early Conceptions of Redeeming the Dead among Latter-day Saints," 112–16;

> For Christ also suffered for sins once for all, the righteous for the unrighteous, to bring you to God. He was put to death in the body but made alive in the spirit, in which He also went and preached to the spirits in prison who disobeyed long ago when God waited patiently in the days of Noah.

In 1800, Universalist Elhanan Winchester argued that Christ would not have preached to the imprisoned spirits if there was no hope for salvation after death. Similarly, seven years before Joseph Smith founded his church, a confessional Shaker work asserted that Christ had initiated ongoing missionary work among the deceased spirits:

> Christ . . . preached the glad tidings of salvation, both in this world and in the world of spirits; and has also commissioned his ministers to do the same. Hence his faithful and true witnesses, after putting off this mortal body, will find a work to do in preaching the gospel to those benighted spirits who never heard its peaceful sound in this world.[12]

The Shakers believed that all people will have a chance to hear and accept Christ's teachings, either in this life or the next. Shaker founder Ann Lee reported having a vision in which she saw Shaker faithful who had passed away preaching the gospel to other deceased spirits in the afterlife.[13]

Beginning in 1830, the Mormon prophet Joseph Smith issued a number of revelations and statements that accepted and elaborated on Christ's mission in the spirit world.[14] At the same time, individual Mormons also reported experiences and visions that affirmed the concept of posthumous preaching. For example, in 1836, future Mormon president Lorenzo Snow received a blessing telling him that he would have "power to preach to the spirits in prison."[15] In 1837, another future Mormon president, Wilford Woodruff, wrote that Zebedee Coltrin prophesied "that I should visit COLUB & Preach to the spirits in Prision [sic] & that I should bring all of my friends or relatives forth from the Terrestrial Kingdom (who had died)

Harrell, *"This is My Doctrine,"* 352–60; and Paulsen, Christensen, and Pulido, "Redeeming the Dead," 33–34. Trumbower examines the meaning of 1 Peter 3:18–20 and related scriptures, such as 1 Peter 4:6, in *Rescue for the Dead*, 44–47.

12. Harrell, *"This is My Doctrine,"* 352.
13. Paulsen, Christensen, and Pulido, "Redeeming the Dead," 33.
14. Harrell, *"This is My Doctrine,"* 352–55.
15. Michael S. Riggs and John E. Thompson, "Joseph Smith, Jr., and 'The Notorious Case of Aaron Lyon': Evidence of Earlier Doctrinal Development of Salvation for the Dead and a Trigger for the Practice of Polyandry?," 116.

by the Power of the gospel."[16] That same year in Guymon's Mill, Missouri, Aaron Lyon told Sarah Jackson he received a revelation that her long-missing husband was actually dead and "preaching to the spirits in prison."[17] A fifteen-year-old boy living in Guymon's Mill also reported having a vision in which he saw Jackson's husband preaching in the spirit prison.[18] The two visions were well known to the Guymon's Mill church members, who readily accepted the idea that a deceased Mormon elder would be preaching to the spirits. As further confirmation of the growing acceptance of this concept, the Mormon *Elders' Journal* stated in a July 1838 article: "All those who have not had an opportunity of hearing the gospel, and being administered to by an inspired man in the flesh, must have it hereafter, before they can be finally judged."[19] Early Christian beliefs pertaining to redeeming the dead, promoted by new American religious movements such as the Shakers and Universalists, had gained acceptance among the Mormons by the time they moved to Nauvoo, Illinois, in 1839.

Joseph Smith added another key piece to the maturing Mormon theology on posthumous redemption when, during a funeral oration in 1840, he introduced the concept of baptism for the dead. Given that baptism is required for salvation, Smith declared that Mormons could fulfill this requirement for their deceased ancestors by being baptized in proxy on their behalf. Asserting that he was restoring a practice of the early Christian church, Smith cited 1 Corinthians 15:29, in which the Apostle Paul writes, "Else what shall they do which are baptized for the dead, if the dead rise not at all? Why are they then baptized for the dead?"[20]

After learning of the concept of baptism for the dead, Mormons enthusiastically began baptizing themselves on behalf of deceased friends

---

16. Grant Underwood, "Baptism for the Dead: Comparing RLDS and LDS Perspectives," 104.

17. Riggs and Thompson, "Notorious Case of Aaron Lyon," 104. After convincing Jackson that her husband had died, Lyon persuaded her to marry him. However, her husband subsequently showed up, and Lyon was tried in a church court for his false revelations.

18. Riggs and Thompson, 114.

19. Riggs and Thompson, 115.

20. In a subsequent letter to Mormon apostles, Smith asserted that baptism for the dead "was certainly practiced by the ancient churches; and St. Paul endeavors to prove the doctrine of resurrection from the same." M. Guy Bishop, "'What Has Become of Our Fathers?' Baptism for the Dead at Nauvoo," 87. See also Trumbower, *Rescue for the Dead*, 34–37, on the ancient practice of baptism for the dead.

and relatives. One researcher counted as many as 6,818 proxy baptisms in Nauvoo in 1841.[21] However, Church leaders had not yet defined the procedures for conducting this new rite. Females were baptized for males and vice versa. In addition, no official records are known to exist.[22] Smith subsequently stated that baptisms for the dead must be performed in a Mormon temple, but Church leaders had not yet devised an administrative policy to track and record proxy baptisms.

The Mormon prophet added yet another layer to his evolving postmortem theology by introducing a temple ceremony, or "endowment," in which participants were said to be endowed with power from on high. In May 1842, seven weeks after being initiated as an apprentice in Freemasonry, Smith introduced the temple ceremony, which closely resembled many of the Masonic rituals, symbols, handshakes, and oaths he had just learned. This was no coincidence. Smith and his followers believed Freemasonry's rituals represented a corrupted form of sacred temple rites dating back to King Solomon. Numerous Mormons asserted that Smith had restored "true Masonry" as practiced in biblical times.[23] Just a month after Smith unveiled the new temple ritual, Mormon Apostle Heber C. Kimball wrote: "Thare is a similarity of preast Hood in masonry. Bro Joseph Ses Masonary was taken from preasthood but has become degen[e]rated, but menny things are perfect."[24]

The new Mormon temple rites eventually would consist of several ordinances, including a washing and anointing ceremony; an endowment ceremony in which men and women solemnly pledge to obey God's commandments, while also vowing never to reveal the temple ceremonies, under the pain of death; and celestial marriage, which "seals" couples together as husband and wife in this life and the next.[25] The sealing rite

---

21. Bishop, "Baptism for the Dead in Nauvoo," 89.

22. Alexander L. Baugh, "'For This Ordinance Belongeth to My House': The Practice of Baptism for the Dead Outside the Nauvoo Temple," 49–50.

23. Cheryl L. Bruno, Joe Steve Swick III, and Nicholas S. Literski, *Method Infinite: Freemasonry and the Mormon Restoration*, 249–52, 319–50. See also David John Buerger, *The Mysteries of Godliness: A History of Mormon Temple Worship*, 35–58.

24. Quoted in Bruno, Swick, and Literski, *Method Infinite*, 250.

25. Originally, celestial marriage meant plural marriage (see, for example, Buerger, *Mysteries of Godliness*, 58–59). And celestial marriage—that is, plural marriage—was a requirement for attaining the highest degree of glory. But after the Mormons abandoned plural marriage, they began to regard celestial marriage and plural marriage as separate concepts, and celestial marriage came to represent

carried special import, because family lineages were also sealed to create a continuous link among ancestors. Smith taught that these rites, including the sealing of children to parents through every generation, are requirements for achieving the highest degree of exaltation. Consequently, Mormons had to perform all the temple rites—not just baptism—in proxy for the dead, a requirement that significantly expanded the scope of their vicarious work.

Persecution forced the Saints to abandon Nauvoo and head west to Utah shortly after the Nauvoo Temple was completed. As a result, they only had time to participate in the temple rites for themselves but not for their deceased ancestors. The proxy work would have to wait until another temple could be constructed. But even after the completion of the St. George temple in 1877, Mormon leaders still had not fully worked out the theology or procedures for redeeming the dead. Although Smith had called for sealing families together, he and Brigham Young also preached an adoption theology that called for living Mormon men (and their families) to seal themselves to Church leaders as adopted children, rather than seal themselves to their own parents.[26] Such adoptions became common during the trek West. The majority of Mormons who were adopted had themselves adopted by—that is, sealed to—Mormon apostles.[27] For example, when the Mormons began organizing for the move to Salt Lake City, Apostle Heber C. Kimball had about two hundred people in his "family" organization, while future Mormon president Wilford Woodruff had forty men, mostly heads of their own families, sealed to him.

Temple adoptions were put on hold after the Saints arrived in Utah, but the completion of the St. George Temple enabled this practice to begin anew. Most Mormons sealed themselves to their own parents, but thousands of living and dead were adopted by Church authorities and other prominent men.[28] Motivating some of those who chose adoption was a fear that their own salvation would be jeopardized if they sealed them-

---

eternal marriage between a husband and wife. Thus, monogamy became sufficient for the highest level of glory.

26. For examinations of Mormon adoption theology, see Samuel M. Brown, "Early Mormon Adoption Theology and the Mechanics of Salvation," 3–52; Gordon Irving, "The Law of Adoption: One Phase of The Development of The Mormon Concept of Salvation, 1830–1900," 1–21; and Jonathan Stapley, "Adoptive Sealing Ritual in Mormonism," 53–118.

27. Irving, "Law of Adoption," 4–5.

28. Irving, 12–13.

selves to deceased parents who rejected the Mormon gospel in the spirit world. Adoption into the lineage of a righteous leader provided greater assurance of heavenly rewards. Adoptions sometimes led to clannishness and hard feelings as members sought connection to high-ranking officials. Historians studying the practice have concluded that Church members were generally confused about the theological underpinnings and policies relating to adoption, as were some of their leaders.[29]

President Wilford Woodruff resolved the issue in April 1894 by directing an end to the practice of adoptions. Woodruff declared,

> We want the Latter-day Saints from this time to trace their genealogies as far as they can, and to be sealed to their fathers and mothers. Have children sealed to their parents, and run their chain through as far as you can get it. When you get to the end, let the last man be adopted to Joseph Smith, who stands at the head of this dispensation.[30]

Woodruff assured the Saints that sealing themselves to their parents, rather than to a top Church leader, would not lower their status in the hereafter. To further alleviate concerns, he also said very few of the deceased, if any, will reject the gospel in the spirit world.

Six months after Woodruff's speech, the Church founded the Genealogical Society of Utah to promote and assist members with the genealogical work required by his proclamation. Mormon leaders asserted that the Saints have a solemn duty to gather the names of their ancestors and submit them to the Church so the saving rites can be performed in proxy for the deceased. The ultimate Mormon goal is that everyone who has lived on earth will be identified and have the vicarious baptism and temple work performed on their behalf before the final judgment, thus giving each person an opportunity for the highest heavenly glory. Church leaders recognized that adopting rigorous genealogical standards for tracing family lineage would be no easy task. After Woodruff announced the new policy, Apostle George Q. Cannon told the Saints not to worry about how long it would take. "We have got a thousand years to do it in," he said.[31]

It was this gathering of family names that James LeSueur vowed to perform during his missionary journey overseas so that he could facilitate the redemption of the LeSueur family dead in the spirit world.

---

29. Irving, 9; and Stapley, "Adoptive Sealing Ritual," 82, 116.

30. Quoted in Irving, "Law of Adoption," 15.

31. James B. Allen, Jessie L. Embry, and Kahlile B. Mehr, *Hearts Turned to the Fathers: A History of the Genealogical Society of Utah, 1894–1994*, 44.

Over the years, Mormon prophets and theologians have formulated increasingly detailed descriptions of the spirit world and the proselytizing that occurs there. Brigham Young described the spirit world, at least for the righteous, as a trouble-free place of transcendent beauty and peace. "In the spirit world we are free from all this [ills and ailments] and enjoy life, glory, and intelligence," he said. "And we have the Father to speak to us, Jesus to speak to us, and angels to speak to us, and we shall enjoy the society of the just and the pure who are in the spirit world until the resurrection."[32] Young also said the spirit world was not located on a distant planet or heavenly sphere, but here on earth. The spiritual and material realms co-exist with only a thin veil separating them. "They are just as busy in the spirit world as you and I are here," Young said. "They can see us, but we cannot see them unless our eyes were opened."[33]

In Mormon theology, the spirit world is divided into two spheres. The righteous spirits dwell in God's presence, often called "paradise," while the rest dwell in a "spirit prison." Deceased beings bring to the spirit world the same level of intelligence and moral capabilities they attained on earth, and they build on those capabilities as they continue learning in the afterlife. The spirit world's busy pace described by Young is driven largely by the need to proselytize. The spirit world is governed by priesthood leaders—chief among them is Joseph Smith—who also watch over and guide the Church's earthly leaders while preparing the way for the Second Coming. "I met a great many of the Apostles and others who are in the spirit world," said the Mormon prophet Wilford Woodruff, "and they all seemed to be in a hurry."[34] For Mormons, the spirit world represents another step in their eternal progression toward divine exaltation.

The St. Johns Mormon community was fully conversant with and immersed in these beliefs. Visions of the spirit world, as well as visitations from those spirits, were not reserved for Church leaders alone, and so it was not uncommon for Mormons to report such experiences in diaries, letters, or church services. At the funeral services for Frank and Gus, several speakers assured the grieving congregation that the young men had been called to serve missions in the spirit world. James LeSueur believed this as well. "I heard a voice as plainly as I had ever heard anything and was

---

32. Bruce Satterfield, comp., "Teachings Concerning the Spirit World," 11.
33. Satterfield, 14.
34. Satterfield, 23.

told that my brother was chosen to take charge of missionary work among my relatives," he said.[35]

James arrived back in St. Johns on April 21, 1900, not quite four weeks after Frank was killed. Although his sorrow had been assuaged, James still had a great desire to see his brother and prayed several times for the privilege of piercing the veil between the earthly and spiritual realms.[36] It speaks volumes about the strength of Mormon beliefs that James felt confident he would be granted this blessing. In May, James and his father made a trip to the mountains south of Springerville and visited the sheep camps where Frank had once worked. After praying again to see his brother, James retired next to his father, who was already asleep. While thinking about Frank, James said his spirit left his physical body, which he could see lying beside his father. A personage dressed in white, whom James understood to be his guardian angel, greeted him and beckoned him to follow. "We traveled with lightning-like speed and in a few moments arrived in a great city in which, I was told, lived the spirits of those who died without hearing the gospel."[37] They came to a building and entered a large room where an estimated ten thousand to twelve thousand spirits were assembled. "The people assembled here are your relatives waiting to hear the Gospel preached to them," the angel said.[38]

James watched as a speaker, also dressed in white, taught the assembled spirits the principles of the gospel: faith in Jesus Christ and his atonement, repentance, and baptism. The speaker told the spirits that baptism would be performed vicariously for them by living friends and relatives who were already gathering their names for that purpose. James marveled that the speaker's arguments and teachings were almost precisely the same as those used by Mormon missionaries. When the speaker finished his address, he turned toward James and "smiled the most joyous smile I had ever witnessed." James saw at once that it was his brother Frank:

> Truly he was filled with joy and I was completely thrilled with ecstacy [sic], and I beheld the transcendent bliss that enveloped him. I thought, "Oh, if I could attain such a supernal joy I would be willing to go through any preparation that the Lord desired for me!"[39]

---

35. LeSueur, "A Patriarchal Blessing and Its Fulfillment," 124.
36. LeSueur, 124.
37. LeSueur, 124.
38. LeSueur, "A Patriarchal Blessing," in *LeSueur Family History*.
39. LeSueur, "A Patriarchal Blessing."

Standing beside Frank was a beautiful young lady with round features and large, piercing eyes. "The young lady is to be his wife," the angel told James, who studied her carefully "that I might know her when I met her again."[40]

The angel led James to two other rooms filled with relatives. In the first, the spirits were being taught to read and write, so they could learn and appreciate gospel principles. James recognized that educating people also represented an important part of missionary service in the spirit world. The last room he visited contained thousands of spirits who were quarreling and fighting, despite the efforts of attending spirits to pacify them. The angel told James that "these also were my relatives who lived on earth during the period of the dark ages, when so much sin, ignorance and war were rampant and when men were held as slaves to cruel masters and wicked potentates."[41] The angel then announced it was time to leave. They traveled back to the camp, where James could see the mountain pines and family sheep below as his spirit descended and rejoined his body.

James told his experience to both his parents, who readily believed his supernatural tale. A few days later, James said, Olena Kempe from the nearby town of Concho visited the LeSueur family. Olena told James's parents that her daughter, Jennie, had died a few weeks earlier. While on her death-bed, Jennie told her mother that she had been visited by Frank's spirit, who asked Jennie to be his wife. Jennie consented and instructed Olena to tell Frank's parents about his visit and obtain their permission to have Frank and Jennie married in a posthumous temple ceremony. After hearing Olena's story, J.T. and Geneva called in James to help decide what to do. James asked to see the photo of Jennie that Olena had brought with her. "I had not seen Jennie for many years, since she was a little girl, in fact, but when shown her picture and getting a full description of her I was quite sure it was Jennie who was with Frank," James said.[42] Jennie Kempe and Frank LeSueur were subsequently sealed together as husband and wife in the Salt Lake Temple.

Bill Gibbons reported having a similar spiritual manifestation. When Bill learned of Gus's brutal murder and saw the badly mutilated corpse, "he was so bitter he thought our Heavenly Father had taken Gus

---

40. LeSueur, "A Patriarchal Blessing"; and LeSueur, "Regarding Salvation for the Dead," 201.

41. LeSueur, "A Patriarchal Blessing."

42. LeSueur, "Patriarchal Blessing and Its Fulfillment," 125.

back to himself," said Bill's daughter Eva.[43] Bill continually talked about the killing, unable to let it go.[44] Finally, one night, while Bill was alone on his sheep ranch, Gus visited his father from the spirit world. "My brother Gus came in and sat on the side of the bed and said, 'Don't feel so bitter.' Then he related to Daddy just all the details of his murder," Eva said.[45] Gus explained that he and Bill's father, Andrew, had been called to preach in the spirit world to his Gibbons ancestors because they were the only family members in the spirit world who held the Melchizedek Priesthood. Gus said he was better prepared than others to perform this mission. Gus's visit comforted and satisfied her father, Eva said, but another family history said Bill still remained bitter about his son's death.[46] Finally, while driving his wagon to the fields, Bill was told—by whom is not stated—that he must stop complaining or the Spirit of the Lord would be completely withdrawn from him. Jolted by this warning, Bill released his anger and became reconciled to his son's fate.

These two experiences—Bill Gibbons's visit from his son and James LeSueur's visit to the spirit world—comforted the grieving families while also strengthening their religious convictions.[47] In later years, James LeSueur recounted his experience not just to his family but also to Mormons throughout the Church. He wrote two separate accounts that were published in Church magazines in 1919 and 1920, while other privately written accounts by James have been published in Church books and online websites.[48] Particularly inspiring to Mormons are its

---

43. Palmer, *Arizona Palmer Family History*, 239.

44. *A Turning of Hearts: William Davidson Gibbons Family History*, 492–93. This Gibbons family history has no single author. Rendol L. Gibbons is listed as the compiler for the chapter on William Hoover Gibbons.

45. Palmer, *Arizona Palmer Family History*, 239.

46. *A Turning of Hearts*, 492–93.

47. Marlene Bateman Sullivan, *Gaze into Heaven: Near-Death Experiences in Early Church History*, Appendix One, 225–48, catalogues the common elements in Mormon near-death experiences. James LeSueur's account is highly consistent with descriptions of the spirit world reported by other Mormons.

48. I have found six different accounts written by James LeSueur about his vision: 1) "A Patriarchal Blessing and its Fulfillment," 122–25; 2) "Regarding Salvation for the Dead," 199–202; 3) "A Patriarchal Blessing," written June 29, 1932, and published in *LeSueur Family History*; 4) "Fulfillment of My Patriarchal Blessing," from James W. LeSueur's "Autobiographical Notes of My Life," which he began in July 1939, 21–24; 5) "A Peep into the Spirit World," an undated manuscript published in Duane S. Crowther, *Life Everlasting: A Definitive Study*

miraculous details. James had not known about the budding romance between Frank and Jennie, nor about Jennie's recent death or their desire to be married vicariously—until Jennie's mother revealed this information to him after his vision. James said it was only when shown Jennie's photo that he recognized her as the deceased spirit standing next to Frank. For Mormons, this helps confirm the reality of James's vision and transforms Frank's brutal murder from an unspeakable tragedy into an inspirational tale of God's endless love and merciful plan for His faithful servants.

This part of James's story, however, is not true. Jennie did not die until April 9, 1902, more than two years after Frank's death. Moreover, Jennie never told her mother, Olena, that she wanted to be sealed to Frank after her death, nor did Olena go to the LeSueur family and ask for that privilege, according to Jennie's family. In fact, Jennie's mother initially recoiled at the thought. "I'd turn over in my grave," Olena Kempe said, if people thought she had asked the LeSueurs to have Jennie married to Frank. Jennie's older sister Lottie, who introduced Frank to Jennie, strongly disputed James's account of Frank and Jennie. "Why, O why, did Jim LeSueur have to say that my mother asked to have this Temple work done, and why print the untruth in church records?" Lottie said.[49]

Who were the Kempes and what accounts for Olena's vehement opposition to the posthumous marriage? And how did Jennie and Frank finally come to be sealed together, despite Olena's initial opposition?

The Kempe family epitomized the thousands of Mormon families who settled the mountain West, toiling in relative obscurity while accepting every call to service and making every sacrifice required. Born in Lutheran Denmark in 1837, Christopher J. Kempe was working as a carriage maker in Sweden when he converted to Mormonism at age twenty-one. He wanted to gather with the Saints in Utah but was continually called on missions to the Scandinavian countries until finally released in 1865. After Kempe told Church leaders he wished to take with him a young girl as a wife,

---

of Life After Death, 288–90; and 6) "A Peep into the Spirit World," an undated manuscript published in Sorensen and Willmore, *The Journey Beyond Life*, 147–56. Although the latter two accounts have the same title, they are not the same. All six accounts are generally consistent with each other, though the timelines vary slightly on some.

49. Ellen Greer Rees, "History of Christopher J. Kempe Family," 162.

They selected and ordered me to marry Anne Ongerod, a young aristocratic lady whom I had previously baptized and who had been desirous for a long time that I should marry her. I told the Brethren as I had before told her that I did not love her, but they were determined and said I would not be blessed if I refused their command and so I did it on condition that she give her money to the poor to emigrate with.[50]

Anne agreed and they were married. She paid the way for seventeen converts in 1865 and left money that enabled others to come the next year. Unfortunately, Anne contracted smallpox during the ocean voyage to the United States and died while crossing the plains. After arriving in Salt Lake City, Kempe married two women, Olena and Anna, whom he had met as a missionary in Norway. He helped build the Tabernacle in Salt Lake City, then moved with his families to Provo, where he again took up carriage making. In 1872, Kempe and his wives moved to Richfield and joined the United Order for three years. Like many Mormons, they did not enjoy or thrive in the Mormon communitarian society, but Kempe blamed the people, not the concept. "The so-called United Order," he said, "[is] one of the most terribly abused organizations ever commenced in the Church, but in reality the best system if carried out correctly, that God ever revealed."[51]

In 1880, the Mormon prophet John Taylor called the Kempes to settle in St. Johns. The two families arrived in September, and the next month, Kempe helped Bishop Udall lay out the town lots. Kempe moved Olena and their children into an unused chicken coop in the Mexican-American part of town, while he set up his other wife, Anna, on their farm across the Little Colorado River. He worked the farm during the day and ran a grist mill at night, but the hardscrabble farmer had little to show for his efforts during the first several years. Olena and Anna took in sewing for extra income. For breakfast, the children often ate nothing but cane seed mush, which was ground in a coffee mill and cooked. "It was flavorless, but nutritious, so the children managed to survive," the Kempe family history said.[52] After Olena gave birth to Charlotte (Lottie) in April 1881, one of her neighbors, Pauline Barth, brought over a plate of food, but Olena refused to eat. When Barth insisted, Olena burst into tears. "How

---

50. Rees, 13.

51. Rees, 20.

52. Rees, 70. Additional details about the family's starving conditions are found in Charlotte Augusta Kempe Magnum, "Life History of Charlotte Augusta Kempe Mangum," 1–3.

can I eat when my children are starving?" Olena cried. "Give the food to them."⁵³ After ensuring that Olena ate, Barth took Olena's children to her home and fed them. Christopher Kempe described his first three years in St. Johns as "the most terrible temporal suffering I have ever known."⁵⁴

The family's situation worsened in 1884 when Kempe was convicted and sentenced to prison for violating federal anti-bigamy laws, leaving his two families to fend for themselves during the two years he served in Detroit's federal penitentiary. Shortly after his return, Kempe was called as bishop of the Concho ward, but Anna, who still had four of her six girls living at home, refused to leave St. Johns, saying she had done enough moving in her life. Christopher and Olena Kempe moved with their children to Concho, while Anna Kempe remained in St. Johns, eventually moving into a house next door to J.T. and Geneva LeSueur. The Kempes' economic prospects improved in Concho, where Christopher planted a thriving orchard of peach trees and ran a general merchandise store, while Olena sewed for the Mexican-American families living in the area. However, Kempe's calling as bishop was not necessarily a happy one. "I soon found however that this was the most disagreeable position I had ever held," he recalled. "To satisfy all parties in a small place was next to an impossibility. My store business however was one of the greatest obstacles. If ever I asked any of the Saints to pay their bills, I was no good, but as long as I could trust them I was a very good Bishop."⁵⁵

A diphtheria epidemic ravaged Concho in 1888 and 1889, killing more than a dozen people. In the Kempe family, Christopher and five of his six children still at home caught it, leaving Olena and nine-year-old Lottie to manage the household, garden, and livestock by themselves. Ten-year-old Eugene died November 27 and his twelve-year-old brother, Otto, died two days later. When a Concho neighbor, Elam Cheney, Jr., brought over a coffin and placed the two boys into it, Lottie was so distraught that she climbed on top of Otto and held on until she was pulled off. She got diphtheria three days later but survived.⁵⁶

---

53. Mangum, "Life History," 2. Mangum said Mrs. Nathan Barth herself recounted this incident to her. Nathan Barth married Pauline Schram (1859–1903) in about 1880.

54. Rees, "History of Christopher J. Kempe Family," 20.

55. Rees, 35.

56. Mangum, "Life History," 5–6. Cheney's family lost three young children to diphtheria in late 1888.

Mormon polygamists typically split time between their households, but after Christopher and Olena moved to Concho, Anna did not allow her husband to live with her in St. Johns. There was no animosity between them. Kempe's two wives, Olena and Anna, got along extremely well, as did their children. Some family members later said that Anna was trying to follow Wilford Woodruff's 1890 Manifesto, which started Mormons on the path to discontinuing polygamy.[57] But Anna began this arrangement several years before the Manifesto, and besides, the Manifesto did not require Mormon men to abandon their plural wives. Anna may have banished her husband to avoid giving government authorities any cause to imprison him again, or perhaps she had grown used to managing the household on her own. She welcomed Christopher's visits and the fruit he brought to the house but would not allow him to stay overnight. Anna supported her family by growing peaches, melons, and other garden fruits and vegetables, and kept milk cows, chickens, and pigs, all of which she sold and used for her own household. She also purchased a sewing machine with an inheritance she received from her parents in Norway and sewed for people in the community.

Anna was not well off and struggled to pay the mortgage on her home while raising her girls. Living next door to the LeSueurs, one of the richest families in the region, only heightened her sense of poverty. Her daughters remembered the LeSueurs as "lovely neighbors," but Anna couldn't help but contrast her circumstances with theirs. Both families had poplar trees lining their property. One evening, Anna came home and told her children that she had been comparing her trees with the LeSueurs' trees. "Theirs are large and bushy and they have plenty of money and an abundance of this world's goods. The trees are like their owners," she said. "My trees are slim and slender and I am poor, not even the last payment on the place made yet."[58]

Christopher and Anna had six children, all girls. He and Olena had ten, but only four of Olena's children, one boy and three girls, survived to adulthood. Kempe's children recalled their bald-headed father as a kind

---

57. For example, the Kempe family history states: "Sometime after [the Manifesto], Anna said, 'I want to live the law, let us not live polygamy any more,' and so she and Christopher lived in separate towns." Ruth L. DeWitt Wake, "Our Heritage Book II: Christopher Jensen Kempe; Wives: Anne Ongerod, Olene Olsen, Anna Dorthea Johnson; Daughter: Ruth Leila (Kempe) DeWitt," 38. See also 51, 69, and 120.

58. Rees, "History of Christopher J. Kempe Family," 124.

man who was popular with the children at Sunday school, a loud snorer who often slept on a table to avoid bed bugs, and a strong man with excellent teeth. "He could hold four or five boys pulling with one end of the rope while he held the other with his teeth," his daughter Amanda said.[59] Kempe's youngest child was Geneva "Jennie" Kempe, who was born to Olena on January 10, 1884, in Concho.

Lottie described her sister Jennie as a "charming, lovely young lady [who] was most gracious and popular."[60] In a photograph probably taken near the time of her death, Jennie poses confidently with the slightest hint of a smile, her dark hair swept back to reveal a pale, open face. Jennie learned the pioneer domestic chores, not just cooking and sewing, but also soap making, wool carding, and quilting. She also danced and served as the church organist in Concho. With only one boy in the family, Jennie and her sisters helped their father build fences, plant the garden and orchards, and herd cows. James LeSueur thought Frank and Jennie met and "kept company together" at Brigham Young Academy, but, in fact, the two were never in Provo together. Frank left for Brigham Young Academy in late August 1897, a few days before his seventeenth birthday, when Jennie was thirteen years old. Frank completed his two years at the academy and returned home in May 1899, just a few weeks before Jennie left Concho to attend the academy.

At the time Frank was killed, Jennie was still attending Brigham Young Academy and living in Provo with her sister Lottie and half-sister Leila. Lottie said she introduced Frank to Jennie at a stake conference dance shortly before Frank was killed. If so, this likely occurred while Jennie and Lottie were home visiting during the 1899 Christmas holidays. Frank was nineteen and planning to go on a mission, while Jennie was fifteen and still completing her first of two years at the academy. They immediately liked each other and spent time together at the dance, but Jennie soon returned to Provo, never to see Frank again. Leila Kempe kept a diary while in Provo and describes several interactions with Frank's sister Alice and his cousin Will LeSueur. However, Leila's diary contains no mention of Frank's murder. This is more than a little surprising, given that Leila grew up next door to the LeSueurs and was good friends with Alice. In addition, Leila was the same age as Frank, so they likely attended school and church together. If Frank's murder caused any heartache or sorrow for

---

59. Rees, 134.
60. Rees, 29.

Jennie Kempe (middle) said that "Frank LeSueur is the swellest guy I ever saw" after they met at a church dance. Although they never saw each other again, Jennie and Frank were "sealed" together as husband and wife in a posthumous ceremony four years after Frank's murder and two years after Jennie's death. Jennie's mother, Olena (left), initially opposed the marriage, saying, "Jennie has died mine, and I'll keep her mine," according to Jennie's sister, Lottie (right). Courtesy JoAnn Stewart Hamblin Descendants.

either Leila or Jennie, Leila did not record it in her diary.[61] Jennie's fleeting night of romance with Frank appears to have been forgotten by Jennie and her family in the intervening years before her death.

After Frank's murder, Jennie continued her studies in Provo, while James went to work at the St. Johns ACMI cooperative store, where his father was a supervisor. James's mother, Geneva, fully believing her son's vision, tried to discover the identity of the deceased girl that James had seen in the spirit world. "When Jim awoke (from the vision or dream), he could not remember who the girl was," Lottie said. "Sister LeSueur said

---

61. Wake, "Our Heritage Book II," contains a typescript of Leila Kempe's diaries, 165–228. Leila's first diary entry after Frank's murder was on page 183 (April 5, 1900), reporting that she was in Salt Lake City for the church conference. Coincidentally, the *Deseret Evening News* had run a front-page story of the murder on April 4.

she wrote every friend she had who had buried a girl Frank's age, but to every photo received, Jim said, 'That is not the girl.'"[62]

Jennie returned home from Brigham Young Academy in May 1901.[63] In Concho, she clerked at a local store for Lee Roy Gibbons, Gus Gibbons's uncle, and helped tend the family farm and garden. On the day before she died, Jennie did some hard riding while helping to drive cows for about seven miles. After chores the next morning, April 9, 1902, she returned to the house complaining of cramps. Jennie suffered excruciating pain for much of the day, though the pain subsided somewhat after a blessing from the elders. She eventually fell into a stupor and died at eleven o'clock that night.[64]

The next day, Amelia Kempe, one of the older Kempe girls from St. Johns, was shopping at the ACMI general store, where she was waited on by James LeSueur. "Jim, Jennie died last night," Amelia said. That's all she said, but for James, it was enough. "My God, that's the girl!" he exclaimed. James hurried from the store, telling Amelia, "Get someone else to wait on you. I must go tell Mother."[65]

Jim rushed home and told his mother that Jennie Kempe had died. "Jim, that's the girl," she said.

Clearly the question of the girl's identity had been a pressing concern for the LeSueurs during the past two years, because James and Geneva promptly hooked up the horses to their buggy and drove fifteen miles to the Kempe home in Concho. Christopher Kempe, Jennie's father, had died the previous September, but Jennie's mother and siblings were present when James and Geneva arrived. Jennie was laid out in the home, perhaps for viewing before the funeral, and so it was "over Jennie's dead body," Lottie said, that James and Geneva proceeded to relate the story

---

62. Rees, "History of Christopher J. Kempe Family," 162.

63. *St. Johns Herald*, May 18, 1901, 4; and June 8, 1901, 4. Of note, the Kempe family history said Christopher Kempe, returning from his mission to Denmark, traveled through Salt Lake City and returned home with Jennie in June. However, the *St. Johns Herald*, April 27, 1901, 4, reported that Kempe returned home in April.

64. Wake, "Our Heritage Book II," 208. Leila, who appears to have written this account of Jennie's death about a month after the event, incorrectly states that Jennie died on April 12.

65. Wake, "Our Heritage Book II," 85; and Rees, "History of Christopher J. Kempe Family," 162.

of Frank's death and James's vision.[66] Geneva told the Kempe family that after the dance where Frank and Jennie met, Frank came downstairs into their kitchen the next morning and said, "Mother, that little Jennie Kempe from Concho is the sweetest girl I ever saw." Geneva also told them she had been writing to the mothers of deceased girls and then, after hearing Jennie had died, realized she was the girl in James's vision.[67] Upon finishing their remarkable story, a story that offered meaning to Jennie's tragic and unexpected death, James and Geneva asked Olena for permission to have Jennie and Frank married in a posthumous ceremony. A temple marriage would seal them together as husband and wife throughout eternity, thus fulfilling the vision James saw in the spirit world.

"No," Olena said, shocking the LeSueurs with her adamant refusal. "Jennie has died mine, and I'll keep her mine." Nothing Geneva or James said could change her mind. Despondent, they returned to St. Johns. After they left, Olena told her children the real reason she had refused their request. "The LeSueurs are rich and we are poor," she said. "As sure as I let them do the [temple] work, they would claim I asked to have the work done, and I'd turn over in my grave if they did!"[68]

Olena's class-conscious rejection of the LeSueurs' request is puzzling. But her response becomes more understandable when understood in the context of how many Mormons approached temple marriage and family sealings in the early days of the Church. When Mormon leaders developed the concept of sealing spouses and families together in eternal bonds, they placed heavy emphasis on creating ties among righteous families. Women were encouraged to enter polygamous marriages with devout men who could assure them a place in the highest heavenly realm. Rather than marry an eligible bachelor their own age, many Mormon women married older men who already had multiple wives, despite the possible emotional and economic hardships of polygamy, because tying oneself to a faithful polygamist offered the promise of eternal reward. This is why so many women wanted to seal themselves as wives to eminent men such as Joseph Smith and Brigham Young, even if they rarely lived with those men as husband and wife. In addition, in the Church's early days, Mormon men would have themselves adopted by Church leaders in temple sealings

---

66. Wake, "Our Heritage Book II," 85.

67. Rees, "History of Christopher J. Kempe Family," 162.

68. This quote combines the quotations from Charlotte's accounts in Wake, "Our Heritage Book II," 85; and Rees, "History of Christopher J. Kempe Family," 162.

that connected them with the righteous lineage of those leaders. And during the height of polygamy, it was not uncommon for Mormon apostles and other leaders to arrange to marry each other's daughters, further creating family ties among God's elite servants. It may have been that Olena didn't want fellow church members to think that she had approached the wealthier, more prominent LeSueurs in hopes of improving her family's eternal status by linking with the LeSueurs through Jennie. She regarded the Kempe lineage as sufficient to gain entrance into heavenly glory.

This is speculation. Lottie didn't elaborate on her mother's cryptic remarks. Clearly, Olena was a proud woman, well aware of her own poverty, and didn't want others to think she was in any way ashamed of her status compared to that of the LeSueurs. She also was distraught, painfully grieving the sudden death of her youngest child. Regardless of whether it was the LeSueurs or any other family making the request, giving Jennie away, even symbolically, was too much to ask on the day after her death. *Who do the LeSueurs think they are?* Olena may have thought to herself. *Barging in while my daughter lies cold on her bed and asking that she be given in marriage to their family, as if they're doing me a big favor.* James and Geneva intended their story to be inspirational and comforting, but in their enthusiasm to claim a wife for Frank, they were insensitive to the feelings of a grieving mother.

The LeSueurs "begged many times" to have Frank and Jennie sealed together, Lottie said.[69] Olena's children also pleaded with their mother to relent, but her opposition continued for more than two years. When Alice LeSueur and John A. Crosby were slated to be married in the Salt Lake Temple in October 1904, the LeSueurs asked again, saying that Alice and John could stand in as proxies for Frank and Jennie after their own ceremony. "With all of us begging, Mother gave in," Lottie said. John and Alice Crosby were married in the Salt Lake Temple on October 12, 1904, and Frank and Jennie were sealed together as spouses the same day.

Charlotte "Lottie" Kempe Mangum provided two known accounts of these incidents approximately sixty years after they occurred. After reading James LeSueur's version in a 1961 Kempe family history, Lottie, then eighty years old, wrote her version in a short piece called "The True Story of Jennie's Sealing to Frank," which was published in a 1991 reprint of the family history.[70] She also wrote or dictated another version, "The TRUE Story of Jennie Kempe," which was published in a different family

---

69. Wake, "Our Heritage Book II," 85.
70. Rees, "History of Christopher J. Kempe Family," 162.

history.⁷¹ Of uppermost concern to Lottie was setting the record straight for her mother. She wanted people to know that the LeSueurs came to Olena and requested the sealing of Frank to Jennie. Olena did not come to them. Because Lottie's accounts were written decades later, they contain some errors in the timing of events. For example, Lottie recalled that Jennie died "nearly a year" after James's vision. In fact, she died almost two years later. Lottie also recalled, incorrectly, that Frank and Jennie were sealed together a year after Jennie died, and that this work was performed by James and his wife, Anna, when they got married. In fact, the work was performed more than two years later—in October 1904—by Alice LeSueur and John A. Crosby. It's interesting to note that James and Anna LeSueur were married May 9, 1902, exactly one month after Jennie's death. When James and his mother visited the Kempes on April 10, James may have asked that he and Anna be permitted to do the sealing during their planned wedding trip to Salt Lake City. This would explain Lottie's confusion about who performed the work.

Despite such errors, Lottie's account is consistent with the chronology of events that occurred after James's reported vision. Unlike James, Lottie knew that Jennie was still very much alive when Frank died. And it wasn't until more than two years after Jennie's death—and four and a half years after Frank's murder—that Olena finally consented to their marriage sealing. How or why James got these crucial facts wrong is a mystery. He wrote his first known account nearly two decades after the incident in the March 1919 issue of the Church's *Juvenile Instructor* magazine, so it's possible he had forgotten the precise chain of events. Or perhaps he streamlined the account for his readers, leaving out the messy details that might have embarrassed the two families and detracted from the story's faith-promoting message. With the passage of time, the LeSueurs forgot the troublesome details. The Kempes did not.

---

71. Wake, "Our Heritage Book II," 84–85.

CHAPTER 8

A RECKONING FOR SHERIFF BEELER

Edward Beeler's final months as Apache County sheriff were uneventful. During his first year in office, Arizona newspapers published numerous articles describing an energetic, well-traveled sheriff. After Beeler returned to St. Johns in June 1900, only one such article appeared, as if little of note occurred.[1] Perhaps the region's criminals were taking an unusual respite, but the more likely explanation is that the months-long pursuit of the LeSueur-Gibbons killers had exhausted Beeler. He needed to recuperate and spend more time at home. In addition, he was no longer auditioning for a second term. Beeler could see that bitterness remained over his role in the young men's death—he probably blamed himself as well—and so he didn't even vie for his party's nomination. Ultimately, his wife's cousin, Duane Hamblin, won the Democratic nomination after serving as Apache County undersheriff and assuming many of Beeler's duties while he had been gone.[2] Hamblin lost the election that November to Leandro Ortega.[3]

As Beeler's term as sheriff was winding down, he entered into a cattle-ranching partnership with his close friend Prime T. Coleman, a Mormon rancher.[4] Following Ortega's election, Beeler began acquiring cattle and

---

1. In the only report of Beeler's activities as sheriff after he returned, the *St. Johns Herald*, November 10, 1900, 2, reported that Beeler led a posse chasing a pair of outlaws who had robbed a man of his ducks. The outlaws were not found.

2. *St. Johns Herald*, May 5, 1900, 3; and September 29, 1900, 3.

3. Apache County Board of Supervisors Minutes, November 19, 1900, 126–27, inserted page. Ortego, who was a sheep owner, won with 53 percent of the votes, 281 to 245. Some writers have incorrectly stated that Beeler lost his reelection bid when, in fact, he didn't run again. See, for example, Larry D. Ball, *Desert Lawmen: The High Sheriffs of New Mexico and Arizona, 1846–1912*, 65–66; and Jody Jensen, "Birth of the Arizona Rangers," 32.

4. Beeler's ranch-related activities over the next several months were reported in the *St. Johns Herald*, November 24, 1900, 3; January 26, 1901, 4; February 16, 1901, 4; March 30, 1901, 4; and April 6, 1901, 4. As of July 1900, Coleman owned fifty head of cattle, according to the Apache County Board of Supervisor

working with Coleman on their ranch, which was located in the Black River valley on property that straddled the Arizona-New Mexico border. Beeler split time between his ranch and his home in St. Johns, where he and Mary continued to reside. Once a cowboy who rode the range for others, Beeler was now building his own herd. Ranching was arduous work but offered Ed and Mary an opportunity to establish a more regular home life and begin raising a family.

On Thursday, January 10, 1901, less than two weeks after relinquishing his sheriff's duties, Beeler rode to Springerville on business. The *St. Johns Herald* noted the trip in its roundup of local news, stating, "Mr Beeler is now free from the cares of official life."[5] This was not entirely true. As sheriff, Beeler had made enemies among those who preferred a less stringent application of the law. One of those was Monterey "Monte" Slaughter, a young cattleman from the Black River valley southeast of Springerville.[6] Monte's father, Pete, was a cousin of famed Texas and Arizona lawman John Slaughter, though Pete and his five sons sometimes rode the other side of the law. The Slaughters were known as a rough bunch, "wild reckless punchers" prone to fighting and violence, especially when drinking.[7] "All the Slaughter boys had hot blood like the one who shot up the dance hall, Christmas, and was fools for trouble," recalled Joseph Pearce, who later served in the Arizona Rangers.[8]

Pete Slaughter moved his family from Texas to Black River in 1881 and became a leading cattleman in the area. The Black River region—and perhaps the Slaughter ranch itself—served as a haven for rustlers and outlaws, including Red Pipkin and Bronco Bill Walters, who were both

---

minutes, July 6, 1900, 84. See also Arvin Palmer, comp., *An Arizona Palmer Family History: Selected Sketches of Arthur Palmer and Evaline Augusta Gibbons Palmer and Their Ancestors*, 143.

5. *St. Johns Herald*, January 12, 1901, 3.

6. "Monte" was the most common spelling used in newspaper articles and documents, though his name was also spelled "Montie" and "Monty."

7. Esther Wiltbank and Zola Whiting, *Lest Ye Forget*, 31, reminiscence of Milo Wiltbank.

8. Joseph Pearce, *Line Rider: A True Story of Stampedes, Gamblers, Indians and Outlaws Written by Arizona Ranger Joseph Pearce 1873–1958*, 117. For other reports of the Slaughter family's violent, troublemaking nature, see *St. Johns Herald*, January 26, 1893, 4; and September 9, 1899, 1, 4; and Wiltbank and Whiting, *Lest Ye Forget*, 7, 188.

friends of the Slaughter family.⁹ In fact, Pipkin worked for the Slaughters in the mid-1890s.¹⁰ Another of Monte's friends was Rufus Nephew, alias "Climax Jim," one of Arizona's most prolific cattle rustlers.¹¹ The *Arizona Bulletin* complained in June 1898 that Bronco Bill's "gang of outlaws and murderers have a rendezvous in the Black River country, and that they are harbored there, fed and furnished, by friends who are no less detrimental to a law-abiding country than 'Broncho Bill' himself."¹² A large ranch like the Slaughter's would have provided a safe place for rustlers to graze stolen cattle before moving them to Mexico or another location for sale—with the Slaughters getting a cut of the action. This is speculation. What is known is that Monte Slaughter seemed especially tight with many Black River outlaws, sometimes posting their bail or appearing as a witness on their behalf.¹³ Monte himself was arrested for defacing brands in 1898, but the charges against him and three others were later dismissed, leading an Arizona newspaper to complain that "such actions will have no good effect on the rustling element of that county."¹⁴

The *St. Johns Herald* would echo these concerns about Black River criminals, and so Sheriff Beeler may have been responding to public clamor when he tried to clean up the Black River country after taking office.¹⁵ Many of Beeler's early arrests targeted men from that region, including Climax Jim, whom Beeler arrested and jailed several times. The energic

---

9. On the friendship of the Slaughters with these gang members, see Karen Holliday Tanner and John D. Tanner, Jr., *The Bronco Bill Gang*, 79, 88, 138, 160–61; Tanner and Tanner, *Climax Jim: The Tumultuous Tale of Arizona's Rustling Cowboy*, 27; and Wiltbank and Whiting, *Lest Ye Forget*, 188. The outlaw Daniel Moroni "Red" Pipkin, born in 1876 in Arkansas, was a Mormon whose family was called to settle Sunset, Apache County, at about the same time the LeSueur and Gibbons families settled St. Johns.

10. Evans Coleman, "Reminiscences Of An Arizona Cowboy," 230–31.

11. Nephew was known as "Climax Jim" because of his copious use of Climax Tobacco. Tanner and Tanner, *Climax Jim*, provide a short biography of Climax Jim and his rustling activities.

12. *Arizona Bulletin*, June 17, 1898, 4.

13. See, for example, *St. Johns Herald*, August 19, 1899, 4; *Arizona Republican*, July 24, 1900, 4; Tanner and Tanner, *Climax Jim*, 27; and Tanner and Tanner, "Revenge: The Murder of Ed Beeler," 3. In addition, Monte's father, Peter, appeared as a defense witness for a man arrested by Beeler for sheep rustling (*St. Johns Herald*, September 2, 1899), 4.

14. *The Oasis* (Arizola, AZ), October 28, 1899, 11.

15. *St. Johns Herald*, October 7, 1899, 4.

Beeler also arrested Monte Slaughter for defacing brands in September 1899, but the charges against Slaughter and other defendants were dismissed a month later, because no witnesses would testify against them.¹⁶ An exasperated editor of the *St. Johns Herald* chastised his fellow citizens, saying if they would just do their duty and appear as witnesses and jurors, "there will soon cease to be a band of Black river bandits."¹⁷ Meanwhile, Monte made additional trouble for himself. Following a disagreement with fellow cattleman Mac McBride, Slaughter attacked him with a knife, slicing up McBride so badly that he looked like "he had been chewed up by a bear" or "had perhaps fell into a threshing machine," according to the *Herald*.¹⁸ Slaughter's arrest for defacing brands, along with Beeler's aggressive prosecution of Climax Jim and other Black River friends, helped fuel a simmering animosity toward the sheriff. "Ed Beeler was a Man with plenty of Guts and the Slaughter Boys were afraid of him," said Grant Hamblin, whose father, Duane Hamblin, told him about their quarrel.¹⁹ The *Holbrook Argus* merely observed that Beeler and Monte Slaughter had "been at enmity a long time" when the two men confronted each other during Beeler's business trip to Springerville.²⁰

At about 2:00 p.m. on Saturday, January 12, Beeler and the twenty-six-year-old Slaughter were playing cards and drinking in Sam Saffell's saloon with a few local citizens, including Slaughter's good friend Claire V. Peery. A well-known cattleman in Black River valley, Peery was also reputed to have mentored outlaw Red Pipkin.²¹ Peery claimed that when he entered the saloon, Beeler was already "jarring or having some words" with Saffell's nineteen-year-old son, Claude. "I took it up with Beeler, and

---

16. *St. Johns Herald*, September 9, 1899, 4.
17. *St. Johns Herald*, October 7, 1899, 4.
18. *St. Johns Herald*, September 9, 1899, 1. The *Graham Guardian* said the dispute between Slaughter and McBride had grown out of the arrest of Climax Jim, but it did not elaborate (September 1, 1899, 1). Interestingly, Slaughter, McBride, and another man had recently posted a bond for Climax Jim, but had it withdrawn. Tanner and Tanner (*Climax Jim*, 35) speculate that the men fought over whether to post another bond.
19. Grant Hamblin to Philip J. Rasch, n.d. Hamblin, whose father had served as Beeler's chief deputy, was the Apache County Sheriff at the time he exchanged letters with Rasch.
20. *Holbrook Argus*, January 19, 1901, 4.
21. Tanner and Tanner, *Bronco Bill Gang*, 160.

Beeler drew his pistol on me," Peery said.[22] After Peery showed Beeler he was unarmed, Beeler handed over his gun for Sam Saffell to put behind the bar. That's when Monte Slaughter joined the quarrel. Given their history, the argument escalated until the two men had to be restrained from going at each other. Slaughter turned to leave, angrily telling Beeler, "I'll be back in a few minutes and I'll fix you."[23]

"I am not armed," Beeler said, having given up his gun.[24]

"Go and arm yourself," Slaughter replied, after which he left with Peery to retrieve a Winchester rifle from his home. Beeler turned to Sam Saffell and asked for his gun, but Saffell declined. "I would not let anyone have a gun when he is drinking," Saffell told the ex-sheriff.[25] The saloon owner then left with one of his patrons, Allen Wardner, just in time to see Slaughter and Peery coming from Slaughter's house. Slaughter held a Winchester. "[We] tried to get Slaughter to drop the matter and let it go," Saffell said, but Slaughter ignored them and stormed up to the saloon, where he stood outside and exchanged more heated words with Beeler through the front door.[26] Beeler again told Slaughter he was unarmed. Peery and Saffell dragged Slaughter away from the saloon and back onto the street, but Slaughter wrangled free and insisted on returning, saying, "he would not shoot anyone who was unprotected but only wished to go over and settle the matter."[27]

While Slaughter's friends worked to calm him down, Beeler looked for a gun. After Saffell left, Beeler turned to Benjamin Slaughter and said, "I have to get a gun."[28] Benjamin, who was Monte's second cousin, knew that Saffell kept a loaded shotgun behind the bar and so removed it from the rack to prevent Beeler from taking it. "Give me the gun," Beeler said, approaching the bar. Slaughter told Beeler to stay away and hid the shotgun in the back room. After that, Benjamin left, leaving Beeler alone in the saloon.

Claire Peery was still holding onto Monte Slaughter, trying to pull him back, when Slaughter pushed open the saloon door. By this time, Beeler had found Saffell's loaded shotgun. Slaughter raised his Winchester and

---

22. Testimony of Clarence V. Peery, in "Inquest held Jan. 12th 1901 over the body of Monte Slaughter" (hereafter Slaughter Inquest).
23. *Holbrook Argus*, January 19, 1901, 4.
24. Testimony of Sam J. Saffell, Slaughter Inquest.
25. Testimony of Benjamin C. Slaughter, Slaughter Inquest.
26. Testimony of Sam J. Saffell, Slaughter Inquest.
27. Testimony of Allen Wardner, Slaughter Inquest.
28. Testimony of Benjamin C. Slaughter, Slaughter.

fired at Beeler but missed. "Get out of the way," Beeler shouted at Peery. "I don't want to have to kill two men."²⁹ As Slaughter took aim for a second shot, Beeler fired two barrels of buckshot, hitting both Slaughter and Peery. Slaughter staggered into the saloon and fell to the floor on top of his Winchester, a loaded cartridge still in the chamber. Perry, who had been struck in the side, was knocked backwards. His wound was painful but not dangerous. "Had it not been for the shot striking his six-shooter handle there would have been two dead men," the *Holbrook Argus* reported.

Sam Saffell retrieved a doctor, who turned Slaughter onto his back and put a pillow under his head, but he was already dead. "We cannot do anything for Montie," a bystander told the doctor. "Let's go and see what we can do for Peery."³⁰

Details of this incident come from two main sources: a formal coroner's inquest held later that day and an account published a week later in the *Holbrook Argus*.³¹ The *Argus* and other newspapers portray Edward Beeler as a man acting in self-defense after being fired upon by an angry Monte Slaughter.³² The four men questioned for the inquest provide a less conclusive description of the shooting, perhaps because they were Slaughter's friends. For example, Sam Saffell saw an empty Winchester shell on the floor but claimed he couldn't say where it came from. Similarly, Saffell and Claire Peery reported that Slaughter said he wanted to go back into the saloon for a drink, as if this had been Slaughter's only intent in returning to the saloon with a loaded rifle after a rancorous argument. It's possible that Slaughter had no intention of shooting Beeler, given that he may have thought Beeler was still unarmed. But when Slaughter walked into the saloon and saw Beeler holding the shotgun, he may have panicked and started shooting in what he considered to be self-defense. Still, it was Slaughter who threatened Beeler, ran off to get a rifle, and warned Beeler to arm himself before bursting back into the saloon. It's not surprising that an afternoon of drinking and contentious words between long-time antagonists armed with loaded weapons resulted in a shooting, regardless

---

29. *Holbrook Argus*, January 19, 1901, 4.

30. Testimony of Sam J. Saffell, Slaughter Inquest. Peery would survive and, in 1903, he married a Mormon, Celia Burke. He died at age sixty-one in Springerville in 1928 and is buried in the Slaughter family cemetery.

31. *Holbrook Argus*, January 19, 1901, 4; and Slaughter Inquest.

32. See, for example, *Arizona Silver Belt*, January 24, 1901, 2; *El Paso Herald*, January 24, 1901, 6; *Graham Guardian*, April 19, 1901, 1; *Holbrook Argus*, January 19, 1901, 4; and *Holbrook Argus*, April 20, 1901, 4.

of whether that was the intention of either party. Following the inquest, Anthony Long, the local Justice of the Peace and acting coroner, issued a warrant for Beeler's arrest.

Beeler promptly gave himself up to local authorities and asked for a trial.[33] Slaughter's friends threatened immediate revenge. According to one report, Beeler barricaded himself with a pistol, rifle, and shotgun on the second floor of Becker's general store in expectation of trouble.[34] An open battle between the Slaughter and Beeler camps was averted when Sheriff Ortega came to Springerville and personally escorted Beeler back to St. Johns on Monday, January 14.[35] At a hearing the following Wednesday, a judge ordered Beeler to stand trial in April and released the ex-sheriff on a $1,000 bond.[36]

Ida Slaughter, Monte's wife, was visiting her family in St. Louis with their infant son at this time. Ida had married Monte a year earlier after a three-week whirlwind romance when Monte was visiting St. Louis. It appears that neither Ida nor her father knew about Monte's criminal associations or past feuds, because they told the *St. Louis Republic* that Beeler and Slaughter were lifelong friends. "None of Slaughter's friends here can understand the shooting," the newspaper said. "He was never known to have carried a revolver, and was known as a quiet, patient man."[37] Ida's father, August C. Dummich, also said that Beeler had frequently dined at his daughter's house in Arizona. This latter assertion may be true, given that Western hospitality and manners obligated folks to treat visitors kindly and offer something to eat, even to those they didn't like.[38]

Beeler's trial was slated for late April. After being released on bail, he and his partner, Prime T. Coleman, continued building up their herd and working their ranch, which was located near the Cienega post office

---

33. *Holbrook Argus*, January 19, 1901, 4.

34. Wiltbank and Whiting, *Lest Ye Forget*, 31. The author of this report, Milo Wiltbank, was born one year after this incident and so had only secondhand information.

35. *Holbrook Argus*, January 19, 1901, 4; and *St. Johns Herald*, January 19, 1901, 3.

36. *Holbrook Argus*, January 19, 1901, 4.

37. *St. Louis Republic*, January 20, 1901, 1.

38. Daniel Justin Herman, *Hell on the Range: A Story of Honor, Conscience, and the American West*, 11–12, describes etiquette and obligations of Western hospitality. See also, Jeff Guinn, *The Last Gunfight: The Real Story of the Shootout at the O.K. Corral—And How It Changed the American West*, 193.

along the Arizona-New Mexico border. The prevailing sentiment was that Beeler, having acted in self-defense, would be acquitted of the murder charge. Grumbling by Slaughter's family and friends continued, but no more trouble ensued between the Beeler and Slaughter camps. The ex-sheriff went about his business as if he did not expect any.

On Thursday, April 11, Beeler spent much of the morning hauling barbed wire across his ranch. After delivering a load along the fence line, he drove his empty wagon back through his property and, about noon, stopped to open a gate. Beeler hopped down and was striding to the gate when two assailants, hiding behind a stone fence sixty feet to seventy feet away, unleashed a fusillade of bullets from smokeless rifles.[39] The first round splintered the gate, but the next round struck Beeler in the shoulder and the hip. He ran for cover in a nearby wash but fell. Four more rounds were fired as he lay on the ground, striking him several times before he could crawl into the ditch. He managed to return fire with his revolver, wounding at least one of the attackers, who fled after firing twelve shots. A posse pursuing his assailants would find blood on the trail.[40]

Later in the afternoon, Henry Thompson and two other men were riding to Coleman's camp when they spotted a team of horses and an empty wagon in a pasture. Upon closer inspection, they saw that it was Prime Coleman's team. One of the horses was standing beside the wagon but the other lay motionless under the wagon's tongue, giving the impression that the horses had become unmanageable and bolted. As Thompson approached the horse that was still alive, he spoke soothingly to keep it calm. "Henry is that you?" a voice called from the gully. Thompson answered yes. "Come quick," Beeler said, groaning. "I am shot all to pieces and am going to die."[41]

Beeler was shot in both shoulders and hips. One horse had been shot and killed. The other had a bullet lodged in its jaw. Beeler asked Thompson if he knew who had shot him. "No," Thompson said. Beeler said he had been so blinded by the gunfire that he could not see who ambushed him.

---

39. Accounts of Beeler's assassination were carried in numerous newspapers. Those providing details for this history are found in: *Florence Tribune*, April 20, 1901, 3; *Graham Guardian*, April 19, 1901, 1; *Holbrook Argus*, April 20, 1901, 4; *Scranton Republican*, April 16, 1901, 1; and *St. Johns Herald*, April 13, 1901, 1.

40. *San Francisco Chronicle*, April 16, 1901, 4; and *Scranton Republican*, April 16, 1901, 1.

41. Quotes from *St. Johns Herald*, April 13, 1901, 1; and *Holbrook Argus*, April 20, 1901, 4.

Thompson placed Beeler in his wagon and drove him to a nearby house. He made the gravely wounded man comfortable while others went to fetch a doctor, but Beeler died at 6:00 p.m. before the doctor arrived.

Coleman and others initially speculated that Beeler was killed by the same outlaws he had pursued after the LeSueur-Gibbons murders, but suspicion soon shifted to Monte Slaughter's eighteen-year-old brother, Pat, and a distant cousin, nineteen-year-old Mal Jowell.[42] In fact, the young assassins made little attempt to conceal their identity, which became common knowledge in Apache County.[43] The pile of cigarette butts found at their hiding spot suggested they hid for hours waiting to murder the ex-sheriff.[44] Once again, friends of both Beeler and the Slaughters took up arms, sparking fears of countywide violence, but the Beeler men joined the sheriff's posse rather than exacting their own justice. Governor Murphy also offered a $500 reward for the capture of the murderers. A posse led by Apache County Deputy Sheriff Sharp tracked the assailants into the Black River country but lost the trail. Separately, Burt Mossman, the future captain of the Arizona Rangers, and another man followed the trail of the suspected murderers into the mountains and tried to surprise the men with a nighttime raid of their camp.[45] The suspects heard Mossman's approach and took off running down a steep, rocky canyon, leaving behind their bedding and a canvas tarp with the name "PAT" printed in capital letters. Mossman continued searching for another week but gave up after failing to pick up the trail. Both Slaughter and Jowell fled the territory. Slaughter hid out with relatives in Texas, while Jowell took off for Sweet Grass County, Montana, where his brother Jason was living.[46]

---

42. Paschal Eldridge "Pat" Slaughter is listed as born on January 4, 1884, on his World War I draft card, but his tombstone lists his birthyear as 1883. Familysearch.org documents and records suggest that 1883 is the correct year of his birth.

Mallie Baxter "Mal" Jowell was born July 17, 1881, in Palo Pinto, Texas. His aunt, Cynthia Ann Jowell, was married to Pat's uncle, Christopher C. Slaughter. Thus, Pat and Mal were each a cousin to the children of Christopher and Cynthia Jowell Slaughter, but they were not cousins to each other.

43. Letter to Albert F. Banta, in the *Arizona Sentinel* (Yuma), April 24, 1901, 3.

44. Lois Hamblin Golding and Delma Golding Johnson, *Our Golden Heritage: The Duane and Addie Noble Hamblin Family*, 82.

45. Frazier Hunt, *Cap Mossman: Last of the Great Cowmen*, 184–85.

46. On Slaughter fleeing to Texas, see Mary Whatley Clarke, *The Slaughter Ranches & Their Makers*, 164–65.

"Mr. Beeler had been one of Arizona's best officials, and his many friends throughout the territory will mourn his loss," said Clifton's *Copper Era* in reporting his murder. "He had many friends in this county, where he was well known and highly respected. He was kind hearted almost to a fault and never failed to respond to the needs of a friend."[47] The *Holbrook Argus* described Beeler as "a brave man and a good one. He knew no such a thing as fear, but was a peace loving citizen."[48] The *Florence Tribune* likewise called Beeler "an able and fearless officer who was badly feared by all outlaws and rustlers."[49] In Utah, the editor of the *Vernal Express* reminded its readers of Beeler's dogged efforts to pry Sheriff Tyler's murderers from their hideouts. "Men who knew him say he was one of the most determined sheriffs in the United States and has done much toward rounding up the outlaw element," the newspaper said.[50]

No such tributes flowed from the *St. Johns Herald*, which published a perfunctory, two-sentence report of Beeler's funeral and burial.[51] Rhoda Gibbons suggests that many in St. Johns had not forgiven Beeler for leaving her brother Gus and Frank LeSueur alone to face the outlaws. "People figured it was the Slaughters" that had murdered the sheriff, she said, "and that Bealer [sic] got what he deserved."[52]

St. Johns Bishop Charles Anderson presided over Beeler's funeral, which was held on Sunday, April 14, in the Beeler home.[53] After the service, a train of carriages, wagons, and footmen followed Beeler's remains to the St. Johns cemetery, where he was buried. Edward and Mary Beeler had been married for four and a half years when he was killed. Ed was thirty-six years old and Mary twenty-eight. They had no children.

---

47. *Copper Era*, April 18, 1901, 3.
48. *Holbrook Argus*, April 20, 1901, 4.
49. *Florence Tribune*, April 20, 1901, 3.
50. *Vernal Express*, April 20, 1901, 2.
51. *St. Johns Herald*, April 20, 1901, 4.
52. Palmer, *Arizona Palmer Family History*, 143.
53. The funeral service is briefly described in Charles P. Anderson, *Journal of Charles P. Anderson: Writings from 1856–1913*, 33; and *St. Johns Herald*, April 20, 1901, 4.

CHAPTER 9

JUSTICE DENIED

Butch Cassidy's movements during the spring and early summer of 1900 have sparked considerable debate among historians. After Cassidy's release from the St. Johns jail on March 31, he tried to rendezvous with the gang, but their frantic flight and the ever-present posses hampered any kind of reunion. Despite speculation at the time that Cassidy participated in the May 26 murders of Utah lawmen Tyler and Jenkins, little evidence links him to the ambush. It was not until Sheriff Beeler and the Utah posses returned home in mid-June that Cassidy and his fellow outlaws were able to reunite and pull off two major robberies at the end of the summer. The outlaws' precise whereabouts before these robberies is uncertain, but a story about Cassidy soon emerged that is both compelling and, when examined closely, highly improbable. After Cassidy eluded Beeler's deputies in Wyoming, he reportedly made his way incognito to Salt Lake City, where he met secretly with Utah Governor Heber Wells and requested amnesty. And when that effort failed, Cassidy's friends tried to persuade Union Pacific Railroad officials to forgive his crimes and hire him as a railroad guard.[1]

The amnesty story began with a sensational front-page *Deseret Evening News* story published just two weeks after Beeler disbanded his posse. "Butch Cassidy, the outlaw, for whose arrest there is a standing reward of $500, offered by the State, is in Salt Lake City ready to give himself up providing Governor Wells can be prevailed upon not to honor extradition papers from Colorado, where he is wanted for breaking jail," the Salt Lake City newspaper reported June 29, 1900.[2] The startling revelation was provided by Salt Lake City Deputy Sheriff Ben R. Harries and "corroborated by at least a half dozen other officers of the law," according to the newspaper. Harries said he

---

1. For an examination of the claims and inconsistencies relating to this episode, see Daniel Buck, "Butch Cassidy Sought Amnesty, Fact or Folklore?," 39–51. Buck concludes that the amnesty story is implausible, while Richard Patterson finds some aspects of the story credible in "Butch Cassidy's Surrender Offer."

2. *Deseret Evening News*, June 29, 1900, 1.

was working through an intermediary to arrange Cassidy's surrender. The next day, the paper published an interview with Cassidy's "supposed" wife, who said the outlaw wanted to surrender but "would never give himself up until the [requested] concessions had been granted."[3]

The purported wife lived on the outskirts of the city with two children she claimed were fathered by Cassidy. She insisted that the outlaw was not a bad man. Cassidy reportedly told her, "Whatever my crimes may have been I have not taken human life, neither have I assisted or encouraged others to kill."[4]

Salt Lake City's other two newspapers, the *Herald* and the *Tribune*, investigated the story and concluded that Deputy Harries had been the victim of a hoax. *Herald* reporters talked with multiple city law enforcement officials and reported that officers "who have run the story down are satisfied that there are nothing but pipe dreams as a basis for the talk about the surrender of the fugitive."[5] In a follow-up story a week later, the *Tribune* quoted an unnamed "gentleman" who claimed Cassidy told him that he had not been in Salt Lake City "for many moons."[6] After reading the *Deseret Evening News* article, Cassidy was "astounded to learn that he had been in Salt Lake unawares," saying he had never even heard of Harries. However, Cassidy said "he was willing to surrender if he would be allowed to make his own terms."

That was the end of the story during Cassidy's lifetime, but it was revived decades later by several writers, including at least one who claimed to have firsthand knowledge of Cassidy's quest for amnesty.[7] Some of these accounts state that Cassidy's appeals to the Utah governor began in 1899, a year before the *Deseret Evening News* article, while others place his efforts in the same time period as the newspaper's. And some imply that Cassidy may have tried twice to strike a deal, first in 1899 and again in 1900. The accounts evolved over time, and often included new details and participants.

The stories begin with a secret trip by Cassidy to Salt Lake City to visit Judge Orlando W. Powers, an influential lawyer who previously defended Cassidy's former bank-robbing partner, Matt Warner. Wild Bunch chronicler Charles Kelly, who gathered his information from Wild Bunch

---

3. *Deseret Evening News*, June 30, 1900, 2.
4. *Deseret Evening News*, June 30, 1900, 2.
5. *Salt Lake Herald*, June 30, 1900, 2.
6. *Salt Lake Tribune*, July 7, 1900, 8.
7. Buck, "Butch Cassidy Sought Amnesty," 49n2, lists the many writers and historians who have provided different versions of Cassidy's efforts to obtain amnesty.

acquaintances and other old-timers, provided a detailed description of Cassidy's conversation with Powers. "I want to quit this outlaw business and go straight," Cassidy reportedly told Powers. "I realize now that it's a losing game. . . . I never killed a man in my life, Judge, and that's gospel. I never robbed an individual—only banks and railroads that have been robbing the people for years."[8]

"What do you want me to do?" Powers asked.

Alluding to Powers's influence, Cassidy said, "I thought maybe you could fix things with the governor to give me a pardon or something so I wouldn't be bothered if I settle down and promise to go straight. I'll give you my word on it."

Powers told Cassidy that the governor had no power to grant amnesty, and he could only pardon the outlaw after he had been convicted of a crime. Additionally, the governor had no authority to pardon or shield Cassidy from prosecution for crimes committed in other states. "No, Mr. Cassidy, I'm afraid you've gone too far to turn back now, at least to settle in any of the western states," Powers said. "The best advice I can offer you is to leave the country and make a new start some place where you are not known."[9]

Disappointed but still determined, Cassidy decided to appeal directly to Governor Wells. Hearing that his friend Sheriff Parley P. Christison of Juab County had arranged a governor's pardon for two young criminals, Cassidy asked Christison to intercede with Wells on his behalf. The governor agreed to a face-to-face meeting, and after talking with Cassidy, Wells said he believed he could arrange a pardon, but only if Cassidy had not committed murder. But when Cassidy and Christison met with Wells a few days later, the governor said he could not extend clemency or immunity because the Utah attorney general had uncovered a murder charge against Cassidy. Neither Christison nor Cassidy could convince the governor that the charge was unfounded.[10]

With a governor's pardon off the table, Judge Powers reentered the story. Convinced of Cassidy's sincerity, Powers contacted Union Pacific Railroad officials and proposed that they forgive Cassidy's robberies and

---

8. Charles Kelly, *The Outlaw Trail: A History of Butch Cassidy and His Wild Bunch*, 267–68.

9. Kelly, 268.

10. Christison's name is often spelled "Christensen," which most of his brothers and sisters went by. Of note, Christison makes no mention of Butch Cassidy or this incident in a two-page memoir he wrote in 1931. He served as Juab County Sheriff from 1897 to 1904. See Parley P. Christison, "A Short Sketch of My Life."

allow him to go straight without the threat of legal harassment. "If Cassidy continues his train holdups it will cost you fellows a lot of money and possibly some lives as well. You stand to be the biggest losers," Powers told the railroad executives. "Here's my proposition: If the railroad will agree to forget all past offenses, I will try to see Cassidy again and with your permission will offer him a permanent job as express guard on your trains, at a good salary."[11]

Union Pacific officials agreed to this plan and authorized Cassidy's attorney, Douglas A. Preston, to contact Cassidy and arrange a deal. Unfortunately, Preston and two railroad officials were delayed in coming to a scheduled meeting with Cassidy, leading Cassidy to believe he had been betrayed. At the remote location where they were supposed to sign a formal agreement, Cassidy left a note under a rock expressing his outrage: "Damn you, Preston, you have double-crossed me. I waited all day but you didn't show up. Tell the U.P. to go to hell. And you can go with them."[12]

Powers wasn't finished trying to assist Cassidy. He next persuaded Governor Wells to authorize Matt Warner, who had been released from prison in January, to bring the railroad's offer to Cassidy. Warner took the train from Salt Lake City to Wyoming in hopes of finding Cassidy, but while he was traveling through Fort Bridger, the conductor handed Warner a telegram: "All agreements off. Cassidy just held up a train at Tipton."[13]

It's not hard to understand why Cassidy—or any outlaw—might want to go straight. Isolation and deprivation stalked the wanted criminal. "You'll never know what it means to be hunted," said Cassidy's outlaw pal Matt Warner. "You can never sleep. You've always got to listen with one ear and keep one eye open. After a while you almost go crazy. No sleep! No sleep! Even when you know you're perfectly safe you can't sleep. Every piss-ant under your pillow sounds like a posse of sheriffs coming to get you!"[14] Climax Jim, the Arizona rustler kept on the run by Sheriff Beeler, concurred, saying, "It don't pay to be an outlaw. A feller eats quail one

---

11. Kelly, *The Outlaw Trail*, 270.

12. Kelly, 271.

13. Kelly, 272. Another version of the amnesty story has Cassidy approaching Judge Powers in 1899, not 1900. In this account, published in 1924 by Frederick R. Bechdolt, the amnesty deal was undermined by the Wild Bunch's holdup of the Union Pacific near Wilcox in June 1899. Cassidy was implicated in the robbery and the murder of a sheriff during the pursuit of the bandits. See Buck, "Butch Cassidy Sought Amnesty, Fact or Folklore?," 43.

14. Kelly, *The Outlaw Trail*, 311.

day and feathers th' next, and your trail is kept warm all the time by officers nowadays."[15] When Flatnose Currie was killed, he didn't have any food with him; Utah lawmen speculated that he hadn't eaten for days. "Currie must have been on the verge of starvation when he was killed," the *Deseret Evening News* reported.[16] And when Cassidy rode north after his release from the St. Johns jail, he had nothing to eat but crackers for many days while he tried to stay clear of the posses chasing his Wild Bunch comrades.[17] Even in seemingly safe locations, outlaws often sat with their backs against a wall, making sure they had a clear view of everything in front of them. "You'll never know what it means to be forever on the dodge," Cassidy reportedly said in explaining his desire for amnesty.[18]

Cassidy also may have become alarmed by the number of bodies piling up on both sides of the law. Over the past twelve months, his gang had murdered at least eight lawmen, while three of his own associates—Lonie Logan, Sam Ketchum, and Currie—had been killed by posses. His best friend in the gang, Elzy Lay, had been badly wounded and sentenced to life in prison. Meanwhile, Cassidy had gotten a taste of normal life while working at the WS Ranch in Alma, where he owned a bar, socialized regularly, had the trust of the ranch foreman, and moved about freely.[19] Given the gang's current troubles, that kind of life probably looked rather good. On May 30, 1900, W.S. Seavey, an agent with the Thiel Detective Agency in Denver wrote to Utah Governor Wells:

> Dear Sir: I desire to inform you that I have reliable information to the effect that if the authorities will let him alone and the U.P.R.R. [Union Pacific Railroad] officials will give him a job as a guard etc: The outlaw Butch Cassidy will lay down his arms, come in give himself up go to work and be a good peaceable citizen hereafter.[20]

Wells likely received this letter a few weeks before the flurry of amnesty stories appeared in the Salt Lake City newspapers. The *Deseret Evening News* reporter who said Cassidy was ready to surrender did not mention this letter, nor did any of the writers who later revived the amnesty story.

---

15. Karen Holliday Tanner and John D. Tanner Jr., *Climax Jim: The Tumultuous Tale of Arizona's Rustling Cowboy*, 1.
16. *Deseret Evening News*, April 23, 1900, 3. See also *Salt Lake Herald*, April 23, 1900, 1.
17. Charles A. Siringo, *A Cowboy Detective: An Autobiography*, 368.
18. Kelly, *The Outlaw Trail*, 269.
19. Richard Patterson, *Butch Cassidy: A Biography*, 158.
20. Quoted in Buck, "Butch Cassidy Sought Amnesty, Fact or Folklore?," 41.

Still, the letter provides further evidence that reports of Cassidy's willingness to surrender and work for the railroad were swirling about in the spring and summer of 1900, a time when Cassidy, now thirty-four years old, may have grown weary of the outlaw life.

Nevertheless, despite the many reasons why Cassidy might have desired amnesty, the historical record provides little evidence that he directly made such a request or that Utah and Union Pacific officials even considered it. The *Deseret Evening News* article that initiated the story contained many questionable facts and assertions. For example, no evidence suggests that Cassidy had a wife, and at least one of his two purported children would have been conceived while he was sitting in a Wyoming prison. He was not wanted for escaping jail in Colorado, as the article reported, but for robbing a bank. Moreover, it is highly improbable that Utah Governor Wells or Union Pacific officials would have entertained a plan to forgive Cassidy's crimes or, in the case of the railroad, make Cassidy a guard. In fact, Wells was not even in Utah when the *Deseret Evening News* first reported that Cassidy wanted an amnesty deal. However, Utah Secretary of State James Hammond, who served as the acting governor in Wells's absence, found the tale comical. "Acting Governor Hammond smiled incredulously yesterday when told the story of Butch Cassiday's [sic] willingness to surrender on terms of his own making," the *Salt Lake Tribune* said. "He declared that no overtures had been made by any one claiming to represent the outlaw."[21] Hammond dismissed the idea of making a deal with Cassidy, saying the only assurance an executive could give the outlaw is that he would receive "equal protection of the law and a fair trial."[22]

It's not implausible that Cassidy would offer to surrender to Utah authorities if he could dictate the terms. What criminal wouldn't? But given Cassidy's lengthy record of crimes, including cattle and horse rustling, bank and train robbery, and murders to which he was at least an accessory, no state executive or law enforcement officer would have acceded to such a demand. Further, the details of the amnesty story—the dates, supporting characters, and locations—changed with each retelling.[23] Finally, the amnesty story leaves unaddressed whether Cassidy had informed fellow gang members of his plan and whether he intended to shoot the Sundance Kid or other friends if they tried to rob the train he was guarding. The tale falls apart under close examination.

---

21. *Salt Lake Herald*, June 30, 1900, 2.
22. *Salt Lake Herald*, June 30, 1900.
23. Buck, "Butch Cassidy Sought Amnesty," 44.

Given the lack of supporting evidence or plausibility, what gives the story its staying power? The tale of Cassidy's ill-fated quest for amnesty plays into the romantic tropes surrounding Western outlaws. Throughout the story, Cassidy and others attest to his essential goodness. He wasn't a murderer, and he never hurt the little guy, only the greedy banks and railroads. A misunderstanding had supposedly led him into a life of crime, and now that he wanted to go straight, fate again conspired against him. A bogus murder charge caused the governor to withdraw an amnesty offer. Bad weather prevented his attorney and railroad officials from arriving on time to a crucial meeting that would have sealed the deal with the Union Pacific Railroad. And finally, when Governor Wells and Matt Warner were trying desperately to salvage the plan, Cassidy undermined their efforts by robbing another train. The latter misfortune was his own fault, of course. Still, he was a good man, well-liked and well-intentioned, but destined to a criminal's life on the run because he just couldn't catch a break. The amnesty story captures Cassidy's meaning in American folklore.

Cassidy and his gang eventually reunited later that summer. The previous year, they had pulled off two robberies netting as much as $120,000 for just a dozen or so bandits and primary accomplices, but they had spent much of their time afterward in desperate flight from trailing posses. Gang members also killed at least eight lawmen during this period, adding to a notoriety that made it even more difficult to travel openly or enjoy their stolen loot. Nevertheless, they remained undeterred. Once Sheriff Beeler and the other posses disbanded, the outlaws began planning their next robberies.

The first robbery occurred August 29, 1900, when five gang members held up the westbound Union Pacific train No. 3 just beyond the Tipton station in Wyoming. The evidence points to Harvey Logan, Ben Kilpatrick, and Bill Cruzan as three of the holdup men, but uncertainty exists as to whether Butch Cassidy and the Sundance Kid were the other accomplices.[24] If Cassidy and Sundance participated in the holdup, this

---

24. Thom Hatch, *The Last Outlaws: The Lives and Legends of Butch Cassidy and the Sundance Kid*, 193–94; and Patterson, *Butch Cassidy*, 163, say Cassidy participated in the Tipton robbery. In contrast, Jeffrey Burton, *The Deadliest Outlaws: The Ketchum Gang and the Wild Bunch*, 275, states that Cassidy and Sundance were in Idaho planning the Winnemucca bank robbery with Will Carver at the time. Bill Betenson, *Butch Cassidy, My Uncle: A Family Portrait*, 143–44, agrees with Burton but believes Cassidy likely helped plan the Tipton robbery.

likely was the first time they teamed together on a robbery, as well as the first time Cassidy participated in a train holdup. But if Cassidy wasn't present, then it's possible that the West's most famous train robber never robbed a train.[25] After blowing up the Union Pacific express car safe, the outlaws gathered up about $55,000 in gold coins and other currency.

The next robbery occurred just three weeks later when three men—Cassidy, the Sundance Kid, and Will Carver—held up the First National Bank of Winnemucca, Nevada. Two of the outlaws carried revolvers and the other a Winchester rifle when they entered the bank and hustled the cashier, three assistants, and a customer into the bank's inner office.[26] Their leader, a man fitting Cassidy's description, placed a cocked revolver at the head of the cashier, George Nixon, and marched him into the vault, where he ordered him to open the safe.[27] When Nixon hesitated, the bandit "drew a murderous looking knife, placed it on my throat and informed me if I did not open the safe immediately, he would cut my throat," Nixon said.[28] Somewhat uncharacteristically, the outlaws robbed the individuals as well as the bank. Altogether, the trio rode away with more than $32,000 in cash, including about $31,000 in $20 gold coins. The bandits did not cover their faces with masks and so, if captured, they could have been identified by the five men they robbed. In fact, based on the witnesses' descriptions and other evidence, the Pinkertons named Cassidy and Sundance as two of the culprits. The Pinkertons reward notice did not identify the third man, Carver, but witnesses said he had a scar on one of his cheeks, hair coloring, and "smelled like a polecat," leading to the conclusion that Carver had a run-in with a skunk shortly before the holdup.[29]

In both robberies, the outlaws eluded pursuing posses with little trouble. Following the Tipton robbery, three of the outlaws—Logan, Kilpatrick, and Cruzan—hid out at a friend's ranch while posses unsuccess-

---

25. Daniel Buck and Anne Meadows, "The Wild Bunch: Wild, but not Much of a Bunch," 30.

26. Details of the bank robbery are provided in a Pinkerton reward circular dated May 15, 1901. Pinkerton's records, Box 87, Folder 2; Betenson, *Butch Cassidy, My Uncle*, 151–53; and Burton, *Deadliest Outlaws*, 276–77.

27. Betenson, *Butch Cassidy, My Uncle*, 152–53. Nixon's description of the group's leader mirrors Cassidy in several regards, such as his small hands and light complexion. Similarly, Sundance was easily identified by his bowlegged walk (see Pinkerton reward circular of February 3, 1902).

28. Betenson, *Butch Cassidy, My Uncle*, 153.

29. Pinkerton reward circular dated May 15, 1901.

fully searched the countryside. After the Winnemucca robbery, Cassidy's trio outran the posses using fresh horses placed at relay stations along their escape route. Once the danger was over, Cruzan headed off on his own, while Logan and Kilpatrick rode to San Antonio, where they met up with Carver and procured the services of local prostitutes. Eventually, Logan, Kilpatrick, and Carver reunited with Butch Cassidy and the Sundance Kid in Fort Worth.

In the past eighteen months, the Wild Bunch had carried out four robberies totaling as much as $200,000, or about $6.2 million in today's dollars.[30] Taking advantage of their anonymity in the relatively large Texas city, the five gang members celebrated their success with lavish spending on alcohol, gambling, women, and fine clothes. Logan and Carver partied with women they brought from San Antonio; Carver, obviously smitten, would soon marry his girl using the alias "Will Casey."[31] On November 21, 1900, the outlaws took a break from their carousing to gather at John Swartz's photographic studio on Main Street and pose for one of the West's most famous photos.

The photograph, often referred to as the Fort Worth Five, features the Sundance Kid, Ben Kilpatrick, and Butch Cassidy seated in the front row, with Will Carver and Harvey Logan standing behind. The five men clearly planned how they wanted to appear. Each wears a fashionable suit coat with vest and tie; each sports a gentleman's derby. A watch and chain hang from several vests. Carver's left hand rests on Kilpatrick's shoulder, his little finger spread slightly to display a diamond ring.[32] The photo gives no hint that the dapper-looking men were among the nation's most wanted criminals, remorseless killers who collectively participated in the murder of fifteen men or more. Cassidy might object to this characteriza-

---

30. In comparison, the sheriffs tasked with running down the outlaws received annual salaries of less than $2,000. Apache County Sheriff Edward Beeler received $1,880 annually for his duties as both sheriff and jailer, while Uintah County Sheriff Bill Preece's sheriff's salary was $800. It is unclear whether Preece received additional money for serving as jailer.

31. Carver and Callie May Hunt were married December 1, 1900, in Fort Worth (Burton, *Deadliest Outlaws*, 280). Donna B. Ernst suggests that Carver's alias of "Casey" was derived from the last name of his stepfather, Walter Causey ("Will Carver alias Will Casey," 24).

32. Carver once told a friend, "Next time you see me I will be wearing diamonds or in a six-foot box," according to John Eaton, *Will Carver, Outlaw*, 62. Eaton believes Carver may have been displaying the diamond ring to highlight the fulfillment of his prophecy. However, Eaton does not cite a source for Carver's quote.

After executing two of their most successful robberies, Wild Bunch outlaws posed for one of the West's most famous photos in Fort Worth, Texas, in November 1900. Sitting (left to right) Harry Longabaugh, alias Sundance Kid; Ben Kilpatrick; and Robert Parker, alias Butch Cassidy. Standing: Will Carver; and Harvey Logan, alias Kid Curry. Collectively, they were responsible for the murders of at least fifteen men, including Frank LeSueur and Gus Gibbons. Courtesy National Portrait Gallery, Smithsonian Institution; gift of Pinkerton's, Inc.

tion, saying that while he may have shot at pursuing lawmen, it was the others who hit their targets.

Noteworthy among Wild Bunch members who did not participate in either the Tipton or Winnemucca robberies were Tom Capehart and Tod Carver. Both men were suspects in the murders of LeSueur, Gibbons, Scarborough, Tyler, and Jenkins, but after spending up to ten weeks on the run from Sheriff Beeler and other posses, they appear to have left the gang. It's possible that neither man was involved in the Utah killings, though some witnesses placed Carver there. In any case, little evidence links either man to the gang's activities after the May 26 killing of Tyler and Jenkins. Capehart's whereabouts are unknown after this time, but Tod

Carver fled south to Texas, likely to San Saba, where he still had family.³³ Carver stayed less than a year in Texas before returning to Arizona and New Mexico, where he previously had worked as a cowboy. Although he was well known in the region, Carver apparently believed he could sidestep trouble if he kept a low profile and waited for public interest in the murders to abate.

One lawman who didn't lose interest was Marshal George "Ed" Scarborough, son of murdered lawman George Scarborough. Just twenty-two years old, Ed was brought into the family business at eighteen when he joined his father's crew of private detectives that patrolled the rangeland for the New Mexico Cattle Protective Organization. Although they worked for a commercial organization, the range detectives held commissions as deputies from the county sheriff, which gave legal authority to their activities. In fact, George (the father) had also held a commission as a federal marshal. Typically, the association's detectives would turn over rustlers and other criminals to the sheriff after making an arrest. After George was murdered, the new head of the cattlemen's detective force, Ed's uncle Frank McMahan, retained Ed on his crew.³⁴ Ed also received a deputy marshal's commission from both county and federal authority, despite complaints about his strong-arm enforcement tactics in enforcing the law.³⁵

Throughout the year after his father's murder, Ed Scarborough had remained on the lookout for the named suspects. Along with fellow marshal Ed Halverson, Scarborough had been quietly tracking Tod Carver's movements for about four months. In the spring of 1901, they received word that Carver had returned from Texas and was lying low in New Mexico.³⁶ After scouting out the area and waiting for a chance to move in, Scarborough and Halverson took possession of Carver's camp while he was away for the day. They hid their horses and waited until Carver

---

33. See 1900 Census, San Saba County, TX, Justice Precinct No. 3, William Hilliard and family.

34. Robert K. DeArment, *George Scarborough: The Life and Death of a Lawman on the Closing Frontier*, 232.

35. *Lordsburg Western Liberal*, January 18, 1901 (cited in DeArment, *George Scarborough*, 250).

36. The precise location of Carver's camp is uncertain. *The St. Johns Herald*, June 29, 1901, 1, states that Carver was captured near the town of Luna in wild country known as Tularosa. However, DeArment (*George Scarborough*, 292n8) points out that Luna actually lies far north of the Tularosa country.

and another man rode into camp late that night. "Up with your hands!" Scarborough yelled as the men approached.[37]

Carver's companion thrust his hands high into the air, but Carver refused, shouting, "Not for any officer."

Scarborough repeated his command and again Carver refused. Scarborough leveled his pistol at the outlaw and said, "Up with your hands or you'll soon be in hell." Carver raised his hands and surrendered without trouble.

The two marshals released Carver's companion and took the suspected murderer to Luna Valley, where they were met by Apache County Deputy Pollard Pearson. The three men escorted Carver to St. Johns, arriving on the morning of Thursday, June 27. "There is not much doubt as to this criminal being one of the murderers of our beloved townsmen Frank Lesueur [sic] and Andrew A. Gibbons 15 months ago today," the *St. Johns Herald* said. "There is a pretty clear case against him. Witnesses are being sent for and justice will get her dues."[38]

The excitement of Carver's arrest soon gave way to fear. Two days after he was brought to St. Johns, a report circulated that a company of armed men was gathering on the outskirts of town with plans to storm the jail and liberate Carver.[39] When shots were heard at about 10:00 p.m. coming from the direction where the men were seen, Scarborough, Halverson, and Apache County Sheriff Leandro Ortega summoned several citizens to help guard the jail, while others were authorized to "keep watch that no stranger might be allowed to come into town."[40] Although the feared jailbreak did not occur, Ortega continued to post extra guards day and night while Carver remained jailed. Among the additional guards was Gus Gibbons's older brother, Will.[41]

Apache County District Attorney Alfred Ruiz called seven witnesses to testify at a preliminary hearing held July 3 before Justice Charles

---

37. *St. Johns Herald*, June 29, 1901, 1.
38. *St. Johns Herald*, June 29, 1901.
39. *St. Johns Herald*, July 6, 1901, 4.
40. *St. Johns Herald*, July 6, 1901. Dick Gibbons states that in early July, while riding into St. Johns after dark, he was stopped by two officers patrolling the roads to prevent a jailbreak by Carver's comrades ("Diary of Richard Gibbons, Copied from His Own Daily Journal and Covering the Time from March 16, 1888 until His Death on January 1, 1924," 287–88).
41. *St. Johns Herald*, July 13, 1901, 4.

Jarvis.[42] The local newspaper said the witnesses "gave strong evidence" against Carver, but the paper provided no details regarding what they said. Two other witnesses were excused before the hearing because they could not identify Carver. After hearing the testimony, Jarvis ordered Carver to be bound over for the Grand Jury and denied the defendant bail for the capital crime.

With Carver's identity confirmed and his safe commitment to jail, the Apache County Board of Supervisors on July 5 voted to pay Marshals Scarborough and Halverson the county's $200 reward for Carver's capture.[43] At the next board meeting three days later, the supervisors rescinded similar $200 rewards previously offered for the other four alleged murderers.[44]

Word of Carver's capture eventually reached Utah, where authorities were eager to have him stand trial there for the murders of Sheriff Tyler and Deputy Jenkins. Grand County District Attorney William Livingston interviewed witnesses and began building a case against Carver. Newspaper articles suggested that the gathered evidence included eyewitnesses who had seen Carver ride through Moab with other gang members prior to the murders, as well as witnesses who had seen Carver at Turner's ranch when three of the murderers stole horses for their getaway. In addition, the outlaws' gear and their horses' brands—which were seen by a key witness when they passed through Moab before the murders—matched the gear and brands of the horses later abandoned by the murderers during their flight. Livingston sent his evidence to Utah Governor Heber Wells requesting that the governor issue a requisition to have Carver extradited from Arizona to stand trial in Grand County for the murders of Tyler and Jenkins. Wells agreed and in late July, Grand County Sheriff A. J. Young and Deputy Ed Thiehoff rode to Arizona with the governor's extradition request. "Our Sheriff will take a man with him who will be able to identify Carver so that there will be no mistake," Governor Wells told Arizona Governor Nathan O. Murphy.[45]

Upon arriving in St. Johns, the unnamed Utah man positively identified Carver as one of the suspected murders, giving Utah authorities con-

---

42. *St. Johns Herald*, July 6, 1901, 4. See also Apache County Jail Record, 3, "T.C. Hilliard alias Tod Carver."

43. *St. Johns Herald*, July 20, 1901, 1. The county also paid $137.50 for sheriff fees and mileage for bringing in Carver, as well as $103.00 for additional guards.

44. *St. Johns Herald*, July 27, 1901, 1.

45. Heber M. Wells, letter to Governor N.O. Murphy, July 31, 1901.

fidence that they had a solid case against Carver. "There was no doubt of Carver's conviction of that crime. The proof was dead against him," Sheriff Young told Apache County authorities when he arrived in St. Johns on Monday, August 5, and showed local authorities the governor's requisition.[46] The Utah lawmen boasted to reporters that "Carver will hang there as sure as fate."[47]

The extradition request presented Apache County authorities with a dilemma. They, as well as all of Arizona, wanted to see Carver punished for his alleged role in the LeSueur-Gibbons murders. However, witnesses' testimony at Carver's preliminary hearing had revealed weaknesses in the prosecution's case. Identifying Carver as one of the five outlaws *and* placing him at the murderous ambush would not be as easy as anticipated. In contrast, Utah authorities confidently believed they had overwhelming evidence against Carver. Consequently, Apache County District Attorney Alfred Ruiz recommended to Arizona Governor Murphy that he comply with Utah's request. Murphy agreed and granted extradition, basing his decision "upon the claims of the Utah officers that Carver could not possibly escape conviction, and also on the showing of the district attorney of Apache county that very little evidence of his guilt for his Arizona crime was available."[48]

Two days after their arrival in St. Johns, Young and Thiehoff departed with their prisoner.[49] At about 7:00 p.m. on Wednesday, August 7, the Utah lawmen shackled Carver and placed him in a carriage that would carry him to the Holbrook train station. A deputy sat next to Carver in the front seat, while Young and Thiehoff sat in the back seat. Apache County Sheriff Ortega and two deputies, including Will Gibbons, accompanied the carriage to the station. During the stopover in Holbrook, Carver apparently spoke with a lawyer, because three days later, Arizona Governor Murphy received a lengthy telegram from a Mr. Jones, who requested that Murphy withdraw his extradition order. Jones, presumably acting on be-

---

46. *Arizona Republican*, August 9, 1901, 1.

47. *Arizona Daily Star*, August 14, 1901, 1. Philip Rasch states that Utah authorities said they would return Carver to Arizona if they failed to obtain a conviction ("Death Comes to St. Johns," 4). However, Rasch did not provide a source for this assertion. Governor Wells did not make this offer in his extradition request, nor could I find evidence of such a promise, though it may have been implicit in the extradition request.

48. *Arizona Daily Star*, January 18, 1902, 2.

49. *St. Johns Herald*, August 10, 1901, 4.

half of Carver, said, "Mr. Carver does not want to be extradited; that he would prefer to be tried in Apache county, this territory, for the murder of Frank LeSeuer [sic]."⁵⁰ The *Arizona Republican* interpreted Carver's request as evidence that the outlaw held in high regard Arizona's ability to render blind justice, but the more likely explanation is that Carver recognized the weakness of Arizona's case against him, making preferable a trial in Apache County. Governor Murphy declined to reverse his order. "There was a fond hope that Carver might be hanged in this territory, but wherever it is done, it will be all the same in a thousand years," the *Arizona Republican* said.⁵¹

Young and Thiehoff escorted Carver to Moab without trouble, arriving August 13.⁵² At a preliminary hearing held nine days later, District Attorney Livingston, along with the county attorney, presented the evidence against Carver, now identified as T.C. Hilliard. Eight witnesses testified for the prosecution, including Herbert Day, who witnessed the murders of Sheriff Tyler and Deputy Jenkins, and William Littleby, who talked with the suspected murderers when he joined them on the trail near Moab. The court record does not contain a transcript of the witnesses' testimony, but an earlier newspaper report said Littleby had "made it his business, he says, to get into conversation with them [the outlaws]. He took particular notice of the stock they had."⁵³ The *Grand Valley Times* summarized the evidence presented as follows:

> The horses and outfits left by the outlaws in escaping was [sic] identified at the time as the same as passed through Moab, connecting the men who had the outfit as the murderers. The testimony introduced by the state went to show that Hilliard was one of the three men. They were seen by a number of people between Mouticello [sic] and Thompson.⁵⁴

Following the witnesses' testimony, the judge bound over Carver for a November trial in the district court. Denied bail for a capital offense,

---

50. *Arizona Republican*, August 11, 1901, 1.
51. *Arizona Republican*, August 9, 1901, 1.
52. *Grand Valley Times*, August 16, 1901, 3.
53. *Salt Lake Tribune*, May 29, 1900, 1.
54. *Grand Valley Times*, August 23, 1901, 1. Similarly, the *Salt Lake Tribune*, August 25, 1901, 5, reported: "The strongest evidence against him is offered by a resident of Moab [likely William Littleby], who claims to have seen the suspect near that place a few days previous to the murder."

Carver was sent in shackles to the state penitentiary in Salt Lake City to await trial.[55]

"Carver stoutly attests his innocence of the murder," the *Deseret Evening News* said after a reporter talked with the defendant.[56] The alleged murderer also "denounced his accusers in strong terms," the *Salt Lake Tribune* reported.[57] Contrary to his portrayal as an outlaw, Carver claimed "his reputation is that of a peaceable man, and he does not on any occasion carry a gun. He denies ever having been in Utah before, and claims he was on the cattle range near his [New Mexico] home at the time of the murder with which he is charged."[58]

Carver's insistence that he was a "peaceable man" was supported by a lengthy letter published a month earlier in Arizona's *Graham Guardian*.[59] The letter writer, Mr. C. B. Martin, scoffed at the idea that Carver committed the murders attributed to him. Martin, a store owner from Clifton in Graham County, said Carver had been traveling and engaging openly in business, not hiding from lawmen.[60] "Carver was at my place three or four days after the St. Johns murder, having brought me a letter from Mr. Mike Wolfe from Tularosa just across the line in N.M.," Martin said. "He had no gun about him and I doubt if he had one when arrested as he seldom carries one." Carver later visited a nearby camp for several days and went to Luna with M.F. McBride, Martin said. After that time, Carver was seen regularly in and around Frisco. Martin also said he had known Carver for ten to twelve years and found it impossible to believe he committed the murders. Martin claimed he did not support outlawry but condemned the *Graham Guardian* and *St. Johns Herald* for publishing articles that "do an innocent man an injustice. I think nearly all the men near Frisco would corroborate the statement I have made about Carver."

---

55. The Grand County Seventh District Court records relating to Carver's preliminary hearing and subsequent release are contained in the Utah State Archives and Records Service, 7th District Court for Grand County, Criminal Case Files, Series 13114. The record states that the defense did not call any witnesses at the preliminary hearing.

56. *Deseret Evening News*, August 26, 1901, 8.

57. *Salt Lake Tribune*, August 25, 1901, 5.

58. *Salt Lake Tribune*, August 25, 1901.

59. *Graham Guardian*, July 26, 1901, 1. The subsequent quotes also come from this letter.

60. The 1900 census for Graham County listed C. B. Martin, age forty-four, as a merchant. He was married with three children living in his household.

Martin, who said he was well known in both Socorro County and Graham County, provided a strong character witness, as well as details that bolstered Carver's claim to be a peaceable man who had nothing to do with the murders. Yet, certain facts don't add up. Carver was publicly identified as a suspect within one or two weeks of the LeSueur-Gibbons murders. In reporting Carver's alleged involvement, a New Mexico newspaper referred to him as "a noted Socorro county desperado," suggesting he already had a well-established reputation as an outlaw.[61] He was subsequently named as a suspect in three additional murders. All five murders—along with the names and aliases of the murder suspects—were reported widely in western newspapers during April, May, and June of 1900. The murders sparked massive manhunts for the killers. If Carver had been working and traveling openly in Clifton, Frisco, and other parts of Arizona and New Mexico, as Martin asserts, how was it that none of the many posses operating across those territories learned of Carver's whereabouts? Carver and his friends would certainly have known that he was named as a suspect. Why didn't he come forward to exonerate himself? Moreover, Carver's missing forefinger clearly marked him as one of the five men who travelled through St. Johns and committed the initial murders. And while Carver was jailed in St. Johns, a witness from Utah identified him as one of the men he'd seen in the area where the Tyler-Jenkins murders occurred. Martin's assertions appear dubious, especially when viewed in light of other evidence linking Carver to criminal activities. Either Martin did not know Carver well or he was lying to help a friend.

Nevertheless, as the case against Carver proceeded, Utah officials discovered that the evidence against Carver wasn't as strong as they had believed. For example, after killing Tyler and Jenkins, three of the outlaws stole horses at Oscar Turner's ranch, where they freely admitted to the murders. But at Carver's preliminary hearing, the ranch hands who had seen and spoken with the outlaws could not positively identify Carver as one of the men.[62] William Livingston, the Grand County district attorney, made a trip to St. Johns in mid-November to gather more evidence against Carver, creating optimism, the *St. Johns Herald* said, that "the conviction of Carver is supposed to be but a matter of time."[63] The approach of Carver's court appearance fueled considerable excitement and speculation

---

61. *Silver City Independent*, April 17, 1900. Article in Philip J. Rasch Collection, box 9, folder 75.

62. *Salt Lake Tribune*, August 25, 1901, 5.

63. *St. Johns Herald*, November 16, 1901, 4.

among local Utah citizens, but when the November 25 court date finally arrived, the prosecution's key witnesses failed to show.[64] Livingston asked for a month-long continuance until the next district court.

Judge Jacob Johnson approved the request, but Livingston was unable to secure his witnesses in the days that followed. Consequently, at the next district court held in Manti on December 27, Livingston asked that Carver be released due to lack of evidence.[65] Johnson approved Carver's release and the Utah prosecution dropped its case.

How did Utah's supposedly airtight case fall apart? An unexpected blow was the inability of Turner's ranch hands to identify Carver. Although at least one Utah witness identified Carver as one of the suspicious men he saw in the Moab-Thompson Springs area, the testimony of the Turner men was crucial to establishing Carver as one of the Tyler-Jenkins murderers. Were the prosecution's witnesses—including the ones who failed to appear in court—intimidated by Carver's criminal associates? While possible, no evidence exists to support this conclusion. It's also possible that Carver split off from the other outlaws after the LeSueur-Gibbons murders, though the preponderance of evidence points to his continued involvement in Utah. As with Arizona's case against Carver, Utah's case rested heavily on circumstantial evidence and, thus, was weaker than prosecutors anticipated.

In contrast to the widespread excitement generated by Carver's arrest, his release garnered little attention. Newspapers that had published front-page stories of his capture buried news of his release among small articles and notices on secondary pages. Perhaps people in Utah and Arizona had already come to recognize that the case against Carver was weak, making news of his release both expected and anticlimactic. It had been nearly two years since the murder spree began, giving friends and family time to address their grief and move forward with their lives. The LeSueur and Gibbons families had found solace in strongly held beliefs that Frank and Gus had been called to important missions in the spirit world. And the unrelenting demands of frontier life forced pioneers to dwell on the present while trusting God to remedy past injustices.

---

64. *Ogden Standard*, November 27, 1901, 4.
65. 7th District Court for Grand County, Criminal Case Files, Series 13114. See also *Arizona Star*, January 18, 1902, 2; *Deseret Evening News*, December 30, 1901, 7; *Graham Guardian*, January 10, 1902, 4; and *St. Johns Herald*, January 11, 1902, 4.

Following Carver's release, the *St. Johns Herald* printed two sentences, a total of twenty-seven words, about the news.[66] More noteworthy, apparently, to the newspaper's editors was the advertisement they placed immediately after news of Carver's release. Partially disguised as a news article and published under the headline "The Secret of Long Life," the ad touted Electric Bitters, a miracle drug guaranteed to work wonders "in curing Kidney Troubles, Female Complaints, Nervous Diseases, Constipation, Dyspepsia, and Malaria"—for just fifty cents a bottle.

Probably the only person who could have positively identified Carver and ensured his conviction in either Arizona or Utah was Sheriff Edward Beeler. During his pursuit of the murderers, Beeler told a newspaper reporter he could identify all five by sight and three by name, including Tod Carver, whom he knew to be missing the forefinger of his right hand.[67] This was not an idle boast. Beeler likely saw all five when they purchased supplies in Springerville and perhaps the next night in St. Johns. He may have also gotten a good look at the outlaws when his posse confronted them at the St. Johns bridge and engaged them in a running gun battle. His long chase of the desperadoes also gave him the opportunity to talk to eyewitnesses in Arizona, New Mexico, and Utah who saw them pass through their communities and towns, further sharpening his ability to identify the men. His knowledge of their horses and brands bolstered his confidence that the five men who killed LeSueur and Gibbons—or a subset of those five men—went on to kill Scarborough, Tyler, and Jenkins. Beeler had already shown himself to be fearless in carrying out his duties as sheriff. There is no reason to believe he would have been intimidated or deterred from testifying against Carver. Besides, he had a large personal stake in seeing the outlaw brought to justice. Not only did Beeler want Carver punished for murdering his two friends, but he also would have wanted to redeem his reputation among the slain men's families and friends. When the Slaughter boys killed Ed Beeler, they effectively killed the best chance of convicting Carver or any of the other four murderers for their crimes.

A month after Utah's case against Carver was dismissed, he was seen working as a laborer on the road between Moab and Thompson Springs, the place where the Utah deputies were slain.[68] Arizona authorities made no known attempts to recapture Carver and return him to Apache County to stand trial for the LeSueur-Gibbons murders.

---

66. *St. Johns Herald*, January 11, 1902, 4.
67. *Salt Lake Herald*, June 4, 1900, 2.
68. Pinkerton's records, Box 89, Folder 5, on Tod Carver.

CHAPTER 10

SERVING AN HONORABLE MISSION

Gusty Gibbons gave birth to her fifteenth child, Nellie, on November 13, 1900. The year had been a rough one for the Gibbons family. After Gus's murder in March, his father, Bill, struggled with his faith. Perhaps needing time to focus on his family, Bill Gibbons resigned as second counselor in the stake presidency a few weeks after Nellie was born.[1] Coincidentally, J.T. LeSueur was selected to take Gibbons's place. Nellie's arrival must have seemed miraculous to the still-grieving Gibbons family. Between 1872 and 1895, Gusty had brought fourteen children into the world, including twelve who survived infancy, but it had been nearly five years since Gusty, now forty-five, had given birth. A young girl would be a welcome addition, a gift, a harbinger of better days to come. Nellie lived just two months. Gusty became pregnant again the next year and bore a son, Joseph, in 1902, but he lived only nine days. "From my earliest recollection I had thorns in my path," Gusty recalled. "I often wonder when they will get rooted out."[2]

Tragedy struck again in September 1904 when the Gibbons's oldest child, Will, was working on the town's threshing machine.[3] Will had driven the threshing machine to a blacksmith shop, possibly to get a part for the machine. While Will was in the shop, something startled the horses and they began to bolt. Will ran back to the street and grabbed the two front horses by their bits but was knocked to the ground. He avoided trampling by the horses but was run over by the threshing machine, breaking three ribs and crushing his chest. Although able to walk one block to his home, Will never recovered. As a result of the accident, a large abscess formed inside his belly, with his pain increasing as the abscess grew. In early 1906,

---

1. St. Johns Stake History, Sunday, December 16, 1900.

2. Arvin Palmer, *An Arizona Palmer Family History: Selected Sketches Of Arthur Palmer And Evaline Augusta Gibbons Palmer And Their Ancestors*, 131.

3. This story is told by Gus's sisters Eva and Rhoda in Palmer, *Arizona Palmer Family History*, 138, 143–44, and 239. Additional information is also found in *Deseret Evening News*, January 18, 1906, 15.

"Oh my God, they have killed my brother," Will Gibbons exclaimed when he discovered Gus's bullet-ridden body. Will stands beside the horse that carried the bodies of Gus and Frank LeSueur from the murder site. He later served as a guard to prevent a jailbreak following the arrest of one of the accused murderers. Courtesy Arizona State Library, Archives and Public Records, Archives Division. No. 97-8567.

Will told his family he was dying, saying he felt as if his insides were going to burst. Will's wife, parents, and siblings gathered at his bedside. "We went [in] and he kissed all of us goodbye," his sister Eva said. "We were all crying but he never had a tear. He just smiled. Even when his wife kissed him he just said 'Goodbye.'"

Bill asked his son if he were afraid of dying, and Will said, "I have taken a drink of liquor when I wanted it and have used tobacco also, but no Dad I'm not afraid to meet my maker. Grandma, Grandad and Gus are all waiting for me."

Shortly after, Will raised himself from his bed and said, "My insides have busted." His family smelled an awful stench, most likely from the abscess bursting. "He waved his hands to all of us and said goodbye, laid down and was gone," Eva said. Will Gibbons, who had seen his father lose a hand to the threshing machine, carried his murdered brother's mutilated body back to St. Johns for burial, and helped guard Tod Carver, one of his brother's alleged murderers, died at age thirty-three, leaving a wife but no children.

Accidents from runaway horses and wagons were not uncommon. Several years before Will Gibbons's accident, Jennie Kempe's father, Christopher, had two accidents caused by runaway horses. In June 1901, while Kempe was riding his cart through Eagar, a runaway resulted in his cart wheel being completely smashed.[4] No one was hurt, but he was not so lucky the next time. On September 19, Kempe was hauling hay in Concho and had just finished weighing his wagon when he stepped from one of his horses to the wagon.[5] While reaching for a rope to pull himself onto the wagon, the sixty-four-year-old man lost his balance and fell to the ground, spooking the wagon team. Across the street in the upstairs schoolroom where she was teaching, Kempe's daughter, Lottie, watched horrified as the frightened horses dragged the wagon and its one-ton load across her father's body, crushing him under its wheels. Lottie ran to where Kempe had fallen, took off her half under-skirt, and placed it under his bleeding head. The blunt force had bent back both his shoulders, torn loose his ribs from his backbone and sternum, and caused severe internal bleeding. Kempe lay bedridden in great pain for eleven days, long enough for all but one of his ten living children and many of his grandchildren to say goodbye. Granddaughter Willamelia, who often rode upon Kempe's shoulders, visited her grandfather on the day he died. Taking Willamelia's hand, Kempe said, "Grandpa will never carry his little darling on his shoulders again."[6]

Christopher Kempe had lived a remarkable life. Following his conversion to Mormonism in Denmark in 1859, he labored six years as a missionary in Scandinavia before immigrating to the United States. He buried his first wife while traveling with a Mormon wagon train to Utah, but married twice more, becoming a polygamist and fathering sixteen children with two wives. Together, they helped settle and build five Mormon settlements: Provo and Richfield in Utah; and St. Johns, Alpine, and Concho in Arizona. Kempe spent two years in the Detroit House of Detention for illegal cohabitation, and at age sixty-one, he was called

---

4. *St. Johns Herald*, June 8, 1901, 4.

5. Descriptions of Kempe's accident can be found in the *St. Johns Herald*, September 28, 1901, 4; and October 5, 1901, 4; *Holbrook Argus*, October 5, 1901, 4; *Salt Lake Herald*, October 6, 1901, 5; Ruth L. DeWitt Wake, "Our Heritage Book II: Christopher Jensen Kempe; Wives: Anne Ongerod, Olene Olsen, Anna Dorthea Johnson; Daughter: Ruth Leila (Kempe) DeWitt," 101; 207 (Leila Kempe's diary); and 275–76; Ellen Greer Rees, "History of Christopher J. Kempe Family," 134; and Willamelia Coleman Smith, Interview, June 3, 1985, 20.

6. Smith, Interview, 20.

away from home to serve another mission in Scandinavia, this time for two years. Upon returning from his mission in April 1901, he had looked forward to spending his last years supporting his families and enjoying the company of his grandchildren, but he had been home just a few months before his accident. Although Kempe worked incessantly, his two families often struggled economically, in part because of his long absences from home and his devotion to his church callings. According to family lore, Kempe had given up an expected $60,000 inheritance from an uncle who disinherited him because he converted to Mormonism. Fortunately, his wives were industrious, tending orchards and gardens with their children and generating income with their sewing and other activities.

Olena was devastated by her husband's death.[7] The sudden passing six months later of her youngest child, Jennie, added to her despair. Overwhelmed with grief, Olena rejected the LeSueurs' request that Frank LeSueur and Jennie be married posthumously. What might have bound the families together became a source of tension. Although Olena later consented to the marriage, the ill feelings apparently remained. There is no evidence the two families had any meaningful contact after the LeSueurs left St. Johns, despite being united through their children's marriage.

The LeSueur family moved to Mesa in 1905 when J.T. was called by the Mormon prophet, Joseph F. Smith, to preside over the Maricopa Stake. J.T. and his wife, Geneva, had moved to St. Johns twenty-five years earlier as part of a Mormon vanguard that included Geneva's mother and J.T.'s brother, William, two sisters, Jane and Harriet, and their spouses and children. Despite early hardship and challenges, J.T. achieved notable success, both in politics and business, and became one of Apache County's leading citizens. Reflecting on the prospect of leaving his long-time home to lead the Maricopa Stake, LeSueur wrote:

> I felt incompetent for such a high responsibility and did not want to move away from St. Johns where I was comfortably situated and had so many dear friends. . . . My wife and I had spent the best years of our lives in St. Johns. We had a good residence and our children were growing up under a good environment with good schools and under good church influence and had several of our relatives in that neighborhood.[8]

Still, a call to service by the prophet was considered a call from the Lord. "I reluctantly accepted the call," J.T. said.[9]

---

7. Wake, "Our Heritage Book II," 101.
8. "Memoirs of John Taylor LeSueur," in *LeSueur Family History*.
9. "Memoirs of John Taylor LeSueur."

The LeSueurs continued to thrive in Mesa. Before his call as stake president, J.T. had already partnered in a general store venture in Mesa with his good friend, Lee Roy Gibbons. The two men foresaw that the building of the Roosevelt Dam would stimulate growth in the Salt River Valley. The initial idea was that Lee Roy, brother of Bill and Dick Gibbons, would run the day-to-day operations of "LeSueur, Gibbons & Co.," while J.T. would provide guidance from St. Johns. But with J.T.'s new church calling, the partners worked together in the Mesa store. They took over the real estate and assets of a struggling cooperative store and soon established a profitable business. While presiding over the Maricopa Stake, J.T. continued investing in multiple business ventures, including sheep, cotton, and the First National Bank of Mesa, where he served as president and a director. He was also elected mayor of Mesa from 1912 to 1914. After all their children had grown and left home, J.T. and Geneva donated their large home to Mesa to be used as the city's first hospital. It became the Southside Community Hospital in 1923.[10]

LeSueur's string of financial successes finally ended with the collapse of cotton prices in 1920. About this same time, a bank panic spread across the United States. During a run on his Mesa bank in 1921, LeSueur paid depositors with his own money, saving the bank and providing customers with needed cash.[11] Although LeSueur's efforts kept the bank solvent, he foresaw that the bank could not survive the deepening economic depression; however, he could not persuade the majority of directors to merge their bank with a more stable bank, and so he sold his bank stock at a discount and severed his connections with the institution, so he would not be liable for future losses.[12] A year later, the bank collapsed and was placed in the hands of a receiver. LeSueur's financial losses during the 1920s eventually reached more than $200,000. He continued working and eventually paid off all his debts, but not before Geneva died of a cerebral hemorrhage on May 27, 1927. LeSueur was profoundly shaken by his wife's death. "The reverses and losses I had suffered in the panic were not comparable to this

---

10. Warren James Mallory, "The Remarkable Memoirs of Warren James Mallory (1868–1945): A Founding Pioneer of Mesa, Arizona, January 18, 1878," A-73; and Alice LeSueur Crosby, "History of Geneva Casto LeSueur," in *LeSueur Family History*. The author's father, John Taylor LeSueur (grandson of J. T. and Geneva), was born April 25, 1923, in the hospital.

11. *Arizona Republic*, December 4, 1945, 3; and "On the Death of Hon. John T. LeSueur."

12. "Memoirs of John Taylor LeSueur."

great calamity and bereavement falling upon me," he said. "Without the faith I have of meeting her again in a future life it would seem to be impossible to endure the sorrow and pangs of this great bereavement."[13]

By this time, LeSueur was nearly seventy-five years old and ready to retire. He had sold his store the year before Geneva's death and wrapped up his financial affairs and debts shortly after. In 1937, while speaking at a celebration commemorating the fifty-year anniversary of the St. Johns Stake, George Crosby reviewed the accomplishments of the town's leading pioneers. As a Mormon lawyer and judge, Crosby had worked closely with LeSueur in both St. Johns and Mesa. J.T. LeSueur, Crosby said, was "in many regards the biggest Mormon that Arizona ever produced and unquestionably the best Latter Day Saint businessman that ever did business in the territory or state."[14]

James LeSueur followed closely in his father's footsteps. When J.T. was called to preside over the Maricopa Stake, James succeeded his father as superintendent of the St. Johns ACMI cooperative store. A year later, James, who was married with two children, sold his sheep and store interests in St. Johns and moved to Mesa, where he invested $10,000 in LeSueur, Gibbons, & Co, becoming a third partner. When J.T. resigned as stake president in March 1912, Church authorities tapped James, only thirty-three years old, to take his father's place. Meanwhile, Lee Roy Gibbons, wishing to return to St. Johns, sold his interest in the store to J.T. and James. Father and son continued working side by side for many years. James and his sister Alice each named a son "Frank" in honor of their slain brother.

James's greatest contribution to the Mormon community was his effort to have a temple erected in Mesa.[15] A month after becoming stake president, James visited Salt Lake City and asked the Church's First Presidency to build a temple in Mesa. It would be just the seventh Mormon temple, and only the third built outside of Utah. A year later, Church leaders expressed a willingness to build a temple in Mesa, and President Joseph F. Smith, along with several other Church authorities, came to Mesa to

---

13. "Memoirs of John Taylor LeSueur."

14. George H. Crosby, speech delivered July 23, 1937, at the fifty-year anniversary of the founding of the St. Johns Stake, published in Crosby, "As My Memory Recalls: Stories of the Colonizing of the Little Colorado River Country," 55.

15. LeSueur describes these activities in "Autobiographical Notes of My Life," 59–63.

select a site. However, after visiting several potential locations, they left without making a decision. Over the next several years, local Mormons began raising funds in anticipation of building the temple, but when Heber J. Grant succeeded Smith as Church president in 1918, prominent members in Southern California began pressing him to build the next temple in the Los Angeles area. James returned to Salt Lake City for another meeting with the First Presidency, who listened to arguments for the Mesa and Los Angeles locations, each of which had backers among the Church's General Authorities. Interestingly, the LeSueurs' good friend, St. Johns Stake President David Udall, opposed building the temple in Mesa because he wanted it in Snowflake. At the conclusion of the meeting, the First Presidency selected Mesa as the next temple site. Church leaders envisioned the new temple as a temple especially designated for Lamanites—that is, for Native Americans and Latin Americans descended from Indigenous People.[16]

The hard work had just begun. Although major decisions were coordinated with—and approved by—Church authorities in Salt Lake City, local members were responsible for raising half of the construction costs and overseeing many aspects of the temple project. James LeSueur headed the temple's six-man Executive Building Committee and served as its treasurer until his father, also an executive committee member, took over as treasurer. James and J.T. performed these tasks while they also tended to their store and other business responsibilities, including addressing the huge personal debts they accumulated during the 1920s. J.T.'s business connections were especially valuable in generating the financial contributions and community support required for such an undertaking. The temple was finally completed in 1927 and dedicated on October 23 of that year. Speaking of the Lamanite people following the dedication, Mormon President Heber J. Grant proclaimed, "The time was very near at hand when this people would be redeemed and fulfill all the promises made to them in the Book of Mormon."[17] The First Presidency selected David Udall as the first temple president, and Udall selected James to be his first assistant. In a private letter to James LeSueur, Apostle Anthony W. Ivins, a counselor in the First Presidency, expressed his personal pleasure at James's new calling. "I have felt from the beginning that to you more than any other individual, the people of Arizona are indebted for the House of the Lord, which is now

---

16. Barry A. Joyce, "The Temple and the Rock: James W. Lesueur and the Synchronization of Sacred Space in the American Southwest," 140–41.

17. Richard O. Cowan, "The Historic Arizona Temple," 104.

finished, and I have felt that you should have a place in it," Ivins wrote.[18] The Mesa Temple is located on 101 South LeSueur Street.

David Udall's calling as president of the Mesa Temple culminated a lengthy career marked by sacrifice and devotion to establishing a Mormon presence in Arizona. Just twenty-eight years old when called to lead the St. Johns mission, Udall and his wife, Ella, gave up promising financial prospects in Utah to lead the Mormon settlement in a town they had never seen and knew little about. As St. Johns's first bishop, he helped Mormon colonizers navigate the severe economic and political challenges of the early years. After serving seven years as bishop, he served another thirty-five years as the St. Johns Stake President, a calling that frequently took him away from his homes and left his business affairs in the hands of his wives and children. Udall estimated that he travelled about 25,000 miles, most of it on horseback or wagon, often through deep snow, to visit each of the stake's wards twice each year.[19] In St. Johns and other Apache County towns, the Udalls achieved only nominal economic success. When Udall sat down with his oldest daughter, Pearl, to write his memoir, he said, "You know, Pearl, I think fate has been against me in financial matters."[20]

Udall described for Pearl the many obstacles and setbacks he encountered in Arizona. An investment in sheep was ruined by low wool tariffs; a farm foundered due to drought. Even financial assistance from J.T. LeSueur and other friends could not prevent the foreclosure and the eventual loss of their farm, a great humiliation and blow to Udall's pride.[21] Seasonal floods that wiped out several dams along the Little Colorado River also, at various times, wiped out fences and swamped his land. "Truly I have had my ups and downs financially," he told Pearl. "Have not the fates seemed against my making money? The 'downs' have been too hard."[22]

Udall praised the contributions of his wives, Ella and Ida, as well as his children, in keeping the family afloat amid their many troubles. "Ella and Ida were always industrious and more than willing to do all they

---

18. A. W. Ivins, letter to President James W. LeSueur, February 3, 1927, in James W. LeSueur, "Autobiographical Notes," 25.

19. David King Udall and Pearl Udall Nelson, *Arizona Pioneer Mormon: David King Udall His story and His family 1851–1938*, 150.

20. Pearl Udall Notes, 31 (summer 1932), in Udall Family Correspondence Collection, 1859–1950.

21. On the impact of the foreclosure, see Maria S. Ellsworth, *Mormon Odyssey: The Story of Ida Hunt Udall, Plural Wife*, 23; and Udall, *Arizona Pioneer Mormon*, 163–65.

22. Pearl Udall Notes, 31.

could to lighten my financial load. At Hunt, Ida cooked for our family and for passengers, during the course of years taking in hundreds of dollars from the latter," said Udall, referring to the stagecoach line between Holbrook and Springerville that he owned. "Ella boarded schoolteachers and students for many years in St. Johns. My womenfolk saved us many dollars by looking after the express and passenger business incident to our mail contracts."[23] Ella also opened up the first millinery shop in St. Johns, while Ida clerked and kept the books for the ACMI cooperative store in Eagar. Over the course of eighteen years, their grown-up daughters taught school in nearby towns and contributed large portions of their salaries to the family's general fund. "It was a great help in maintaining our financial standing and in providing the cash necessities of our family life," Udall said regarding his daughters' assistance.[24]

In the summer of 1903, Ella and her daughters opened an ice cream parlor on St. Johns's Main Street in the Mexican-American part of town.[25] They produced their ice cream with one hundred pounds of ice brought up from Springerville every day by the man who delivered the mail for Udall's postal contract. Ella and her girls made the ice cream in their home, after which twelve-year-old Levi Udall hauled it to the parlor, twelve gallons at a time, in his red wagon. David, of course, knew about the popular ice cream business. He saw that it was paying for the family's groceries and other needs. What he didn't know was that Ella and his children were also diverting some of the parlor's proceeds to pay off a $750 debt hanging over the family's city lot in St. Johns. The man holding the debt, Joseph B. Patterson, was so touched by what Ella and the children were trying to accomplish that he forgave the interest due on the note. When school let out in May, the young women, who were schoolteachers, paid $125 from their salaries to Patterson and then, each week during the summer, paid down the note with cash from their ice cream business. At Udall's fifty-second birthday celebration that September, his family presented him with the cancelled note and the deed to their town lot. "My surprise was so complete," Udall said, "that my knees shook and I could not find my voice."[26]

The essential role played by Udall's wives and daughters in the family's economic affairs was typical of the Mormon families called to colonize St. Johns and other Apache County settlements. Mormon women often

---

23. Udall, *Arizona Pioneer Mormon*, 173.
24. Udall, 173.
25. Udall, 174–75, for Udall's recounting of the ice cream parlor.
26. Udall, 175.

bore the brunt of frontier poverty, especially when their husbands were called away on missions and other church business or, as in the case of Christopher Kempe, imprisoned after an arrest and conviction for polygamy. Kempe's wives and children sewed, served as housekeepers, and clerked at stores to bring in extra cash, while also working their family farms and gardens. Because Kempe had only one son who reached adulthood, his daughters performed much of the farm labor typically assigned to men. His daughter Leila said that in their St. Johns family of six girls, "[w]e all learned to sew, milk, farm, and be generally useful. My earliest recollection is of following behind the thrasher with a little sack tied to my waist and picking up the heads of wheat which were later thrashed and ground on a coffee mill for cereal."[27] As previously mentioned, during the LeSueurs' first two years in St. Johns, Geneva supported the family with her garden, sewing, and other work, never once dipping into the family savings while J.T. was away working on the railroad. Bill Gibbons so admired and appreciated his wife, Gusty, that he wanted to name his first two daughters after her, but she wouldn't agree to it. His third daughter was born eighteen days after Bill lost his hand in a thresher accident and lay near death at his parents' home. When Bill recovered sufficiently to get out of bed, three men helped him walk home to see his wife and new baby girl. "He put his hands on my head and gave me a blessing and a name—Evaline Augusta after my mother. The name I am very proud of," said the daughter, Eva, who added, "I hope and pray I have not been a disappointment to them."[28]

When David Udall touted his wives' valuable contributions to his family's finances, he mentioned his first two wives, Ella and Ida, but said nothing about his third wife, Mary Ann Linton Morgan Udall. In fact, Mary never appears in his memoir. Before marrying Udall, Mary had been married six years to John Morgan, who died suddenly in 1894, leaving Mary to raise three young boys on her own. Mary and Udall's second wife, Ida, had been close friends for many years, even hiding out together when their polygamist husbands were targeted for prosecution by federal agents. At a September 1903 conference in St. Johns, two Mormon apostles, John W. Taylor and Mathias Cowley, counseled Udall to take Mary as a plural wife in order to help raise her boys. Ida approved the marriage but Ella, Udall's first wife, was not interested. Nevertheless, Udall and Mary were married in

---

27. Rees, "History of Christopher J. Kempe Family," 116.

28. The story of Eva's blessing is recounted in Palmer, *Arizona Palmer Family History*, 141 (Rhoda) and 184 (Evaline). Quote is 184.

Salt Lake City during the October 1903 general conference. "Aunt Mary," as she was called, moved in with Ida's family in Hunt, Arizona, where they lived until the spring of 1906, when Mary purchased a nearby house.

Udall's decision to pretend that his third marriage never occurred is not atypical of Mormons who entered polygamy after President Wilford Woodruff's 1890 Manifesto. When Udall began writing his memoir in 1930, the Mormon Church—its top leaders and historians—claimed that Woodruff's Manifesto had officially banned all new polygamous marriages after 1890. This claim was false, but it helped support an important Mormon narrative that its members were law-abiding citizens who abandoned polygamy when it was outlawed by the US government. This was necessary in large part because Mormon leaders had tacitly agreed to end polygamy as a condition of Utah's statehood, which was granted in 1896. Giving up polygamy was also seen as a key step to enable the Mormons to enter the American cultural and political mainstream. Although the pace of new polygamous marriages slowed dramatically after Woodruff's Manifesto, Mormon leaders continued to approve new marriages both inside and outside the United States, but they did so discreetly, so as not to draw attention to their continuing observance of the illegal practice. It was not until April 1904—when Congressional hearings highlighted the Church's deception and threatened to bring more lawsuits—that President Joseph F. Smith officially banned polygamy by issuing the Second Manifesto. However, at the time Udall wrote his memoir, Mormon publications and histories continued to assert that polygamy had ceased in 1890, not 1904. Thus, Udall and Pearl may have decided to omit Mary from Udall's memoir, given that many people, including their fellow Mormons, would have thought he had deliberately violated Church policy when, in fact, high-ranking apostles had endorsed his post-Manifesto marriage.

Pearl's participation in this omission is especially interesting because she entered a polygamous marriage with a Mormon apostle after President Smith's Second Manifesto. Pearl and Frank LeSueur had been sweethearts, according to Maria Ellsworth, who believed they likely would have married had not Frank been killed.[29] After attending Brigham Young Academy, Pearl taught school and contributed to the family's finances. In September 1903, Apostle Rudger Clawson stayed in the Udall home while attending a St. Johns Stake conference, the same conference at which David Udall

---

29. Ellsworth, *Story of Ida Hunt Udall*, 201.

was advised to take a third wife. Clawson, a forty-six-year-old polygamist, was attracted to twenty-three-year-old Pearl and asked her father for Pearl's hand in marriage.[30] Udall left the decision up to Pearl, who, after considerable prayer, agreed to the union. But before the wedding took place, President Smith issued the Second Manifesto permanently banning new polygamist marriages. Nevertheless, Clawson and Pearl married in August 1904 in a ceremony performed by Apostle Cowley.

The marriage placed Pearl in a difficult position. Because it violated both US laws and Church pronouncements, their marriage had to remain a closely guarded secret. She told only her closest family members and friends. Remarkably, Apostle Clawson's family apparently knew nothing about the marriage until a grandson discovered it years after Clawson's death.[31] The demands of secrecy meant that Clawson and Pearl spent little time together, making it a most unsatisfying relationship for Pearl. Finally, nine years into their marriage, the two met secretly in England while Clawson was serving as president of the European Mission, and the apostle agreed to release the unhappy Pearl from their celestial union. In 1919, Pearl, now thirty-nine, married Joseph Nelson, a fifty-seven-year-old Salt Lake City businessman whose first two wives had both died. Nelson married Pearl after receiving assurances from President Heber J. Grant that the Church had annulled Pearl's marriage sealing to Clawson, thus enabling Nelson and Pearl to be sealed together.

Edward and Mary Beeler also had their lives upended by the LeSueur-Gibbons murders. In his first year as sheriff, Ed had won praise for his success in tackling the county's outlaw element. He was ambitious and hardworking, with ties to both the Mormon and non-Mormon communities, and likely would have won a second term as sheriff. But the murders soured the people on Beeler, and perhaps soured Beeler on himself, especially when he failed to capture even one of the killers. His subsequent gunfight with Monte Slaughter after a day of drinking by both men seemed out of character for the disciplined ex-sheriff, leading one to wonder whether lingering guilt or despair over his friends' murders clouded

---

30. Pearl Udall's marriage to Apostle Clawson is described in Roy Hoopes, "My Grandfather, The Mormon Apostle"; and Ellsworth, *Story of Ida Hunt Udall*, 201–2; 220–21, 275n56.

31. Hoopes, "My Grandfather, The Mormon Apostle"; and Ellsworth, *Story of Ida Hunt Udall*, 275n56.

Mary Hamblin Beeler, the attractive daughter of the renowned Mormon Lamanite missionary, Jacob Hamblin, was devastated by the murder of her husband, former Apache County Sheriff Edward Beeler. She remained a widow for fifty-eight years until her death in 1959. Courtesy Marianne E. Loose.

his judgment. Regardless, the murders derailed his career as sheriff. His killing of Slaughter led to his own murder a few months later.

Ed's death devastated Mary. In journal entries written just two weeks after her husband's murder, Mary poured out her heartbreak in anguished lamentations. "Although they have torn my heart from me, and put it in the cold grave, yet I still live and breathe. But how long this will last I know nor care not," she wrote May 1, 1901.[32] Anticipating a life of endless solitude, she wrote, "If I had something to look forward [to], something to hope for, anything but the years of unbroken loneliness that loom up before me. But O! how my heart aches and my frame burns **for I am Alone.**" Mary gave vent to her despair in poetry:

> Just two short months ago today
> The world was full of love;
> The meadow lark sang its gladsome lay
> Then kissed the skies above;
> The lily bent in tenderness
> Its height of graceful slenderness,
> Above the pansy's gentle face–
> My darling thou wert here."

---

32. Mary Elizabeth Hamblin Beeler, Journal.

> The world has lost its smile today,
> And sadly weeps instead;
> The lily wilts and pines away.
> Beside the pansy dead;
> But yet I saw the meadow lark wing
> Its flight to Heaven and gladly sing,
> Loosing [sic] itself beyond the clouds–
> <u>My</u> <u>darling</u> <u>thou</u> <u>art</u> <u>there</u>.

Two months after Ed's death, Mary moved to Nutrioso to live with her mother.[33] Her brother Dudley took charge of Mary's cattle, while she dealt with probate issues related to her late husband's estate.[34] In October, Mary moved back to St. Johns, renting the residence of Francisco Ruiz, so she could keep house for her brother, Carl, while he attended St. Johns Academy.[35] Her grief did not abate. "I am so lonely today, how and what shall I do?" she wrote in a November 7 journal entry. "I dare not stop to think. Just to think that I must face this cold world alone. It is too much O, God! My Father, it is too much."

During her months of anguish, Mary petitioned God for the privilege of seeing Ed again. "Oh, darling! If I could see you for one moment it seems to me I could live and endure so much better," she wrote in a September 10, 1901, journal entry. "O Father in Heaven do not deny me this, for how can I endure life, if you do? 'O, Father! Send me this small ray of light." She made the same plea again in November. After quoting Luke 11:10 ("Everyone that asketh receiveth"), she wrote:

> Oh, darling! My heart is bursting today. Why don't you come to see me? How can you leave me alone so long? I am hungry for one look at your face. Oh! I pray for you, and to you, why don't you hear?
>
> How can I cease to pray for thee? Somewhere In God's great universe thou art today; can He not reach thee with His tender care? Can He not hear me when for thee I pray?

In January, Mary recorded that she had "the first lovely dream I have had about him." After thanking her Heavenly Father for sending the dream, she asked for more. "O Father! Why can't I see him?" she wrote. "Send

---

33. *St. Johns Herald*, June 15, 1901, 4; Myrl Tenney Arrott, "Sarah Priscilla Leavitt Hamblin: Pioneer Midwife," 48.

34. *St. Johns Herald*, June 15, 1901, 1; June 22, 1 and 4; July 13, 1; July 20, 1; and December 21, 4.

35. *St. Johns Herald*, October 26, 1901, 4. Carl was likely Mary's nine-year-old brother, Don Carlos.

him to me just once; let me talk to him, for a few moments. 'I can suffer and be strong' if you will let me have this ray of hope, of cheer more to me than all else."

It wasn't solely loneliness that drove Mary's desire to see her deceased husband. She also worried about his eternal fate. Ed was not a Mormon when he met Mary, and he never joined the Church. The evidence suggests that he was well liked by Mary's large Mormon family. Mary's sister Ella and her husband, Warren Tenney, named one of their sons Edward Beeler Tenney in honor of their slain brother-in-law.[36] Ed also worked closely with J.T. LeSueur and other members of the Mormon community on a variety of projects, and likely attended at least a few Mormon activities with Mary. One of Ed's best friends was Prime T. Coleman, a former Mormon missionary and tough-as-nails cattleman whose roughneck personality helped cement their relationship. The two men were partners in a cattle ranch when Beeler was killed.

Beeler eventually expressed a desire to join the Mormon Church, though it's not known when his interest began. He may have been attending church services with Mary all along, though it's also possible that his soul-searching started when his two friends, LeSueur and Gibbons, were killed, perhaps due to his missteps. The saloon gunfight in which Ed killed Monte Slaughter may have also weighed on his conscience. Ed apparently declared his intention to join the Church while he awaited trial for killing Slaughter. Mormon Bishop Charles Anderson, who conducted Ed's funeral service, recorded in his journal following the burial that Beeler "did not belong to the Church but wanted me to baptize him after court if he had lived."[37]

Mary's journal entries stopped abruptly in February 1902 and did not begin again until January 1929. Did she ever receive the comforting dream or the assurance she desired? Mary doesn't say. But in April 1902, she traveled to Salt Lake City with her brother Dudley, who had been called to serve in Tennessee in the Southern States Mission.[38] While in the city, Mary went through the Salt Lake Temple for the first time, a key rite of passage for Mormon adults. As part of the ceremony, Mary had herself sealed to Ed in a posthumous temple marriage that joined the two

---

36. Edward Beeler Tenney was born January 5, 1903, in Nutrioso, and died April 1, 1975. He named his son Edward Beeler Tenney Jr.

37. Charles P. Anderson, *Journal of Charles P. Anderson: Writings from 1856–1913*, 33 (April 14, 1901).

38. Dudley, age twenty-one, was set apart as a missionary on April 9, 1902, by J. Golden Kimball. He served until October 1904. LDS Missionary Database.

together in the next life. Mormon policy requires people to wait one year before performing temple work for someone who has died. Mary sealed herself to Ed on April 10, 1902, almost one year to the day after Ed was murdered, thus suggesting she had been eager to create this eternal bond. She had probably been thinking about it since the day Ed died.

By linking herself to Ed in the eternities, Mary was severely limiting her chances of remarriage, at least with another Mormon. Mormon men who were marrying for the first time wanted a spouse who would be their companion for "time *and* eternity." A Mormon polygamist or a widower might be interested in a woman who would be his spouse only during this life, given that he already had an eternal mate, but polygamy was on the wane. Those opportunities would be few. By sealing herself to Ed, Mary had embraced the likelihood of continued loneliness in this life, looking ahead to happiness with Ed in the next. It was an act of faith and love.

After the temple ceremony, Mary travelled with Dudley to Tennessee, where she visited with Ed's sisters and other relatives who lived there.[39] She also may have gathered the names of Ed's ancestors for future temple work. Upon her return, Mary and her mother moved to a new house in Eagar. Little is known about her activities for the next two decades, but when her older brother, Jacob, was elected to serve in the Arizona House of Representatives in 1925, Mary accompanied him to Phoenix and got a job in the capitol building. Mary's mother died in 1927, and a year later, Mary left Arizona to serve eighteen months in the Northwestern States Mission. In December 1930, the Arizona governor appointed Mary as the superintendent of Junior Cottage at the Fort Grant State Industrial School for Wayward Boys and Girls, where Jacob Hamblin was the school's superintendent. "Twenty-nine little boys under one roof to be guarded and cared for by two people[,] Albert and myself[,] is no dream," Mary wrote.[40] Somewhat cryptically, she also said, "I am happy in the work if [I] could only forget lifes [*sic*] dark side but dark side or not this is wonderful and we are so grateful." Mary died at age eighty-six on May 12, 1959, fifty-eight years after Ed's death. She never remarried.

In response to the LeSueur-Gibbons murders, Dick Gibbons ran for the territory legislature, pledging to create a force of Arizona Rangers to help rid the territory of outlaws like the men who killed Frank and

---

39. Arrott, "Pioneer Midwife," 48.
40. Mary Beeler, Diary, January 11, 1931.

Gus.[41] In large territories such as Arizona and New Mexico, railroad companies and cattle ranchers, who were the prime targets of Western gangs, protected themselves by establishing private security forces. Large cattle associations employed range detectives to hunt down suspected rustlers. County sheriffs often deputized the detectives, so they carried the weight of the law when performing their corporate duties. The Union Pacific Railroad hired the Pinkerton Detective Agency to break up bandits such as the Wild Bunch and created a special security force to respond rapidly when trains were robbed. However, these privately funded efforts were expensive, and the Pinkertons had an uneven success record.[42] The LeSueur-Gibbons murders, along with several other violent incidents in 1900, made it appear that Arizona's outlaws were gaining the upper hand because of their ability to outrun and outlast local lawmen by fleeing across county borders into the territory's vast expanses. Consequently, Arizona's cattlemen, railroad officials, and newspaper editors began pressuring Arizona Governor Nathan O. Murphy to establish a special territorial force similar to the famed Texas Rangers. "It is a pretty state of affairs when outlaws run loose," the *St. Johns Herald*, "and unless the territory organizes a force of rangers this may go on for an indefinite period of time."[43]

The idea of establishing territorial rangers was not entirely new. Arizona had briefly created a ranger force during the Civil War and again in 1882, but previous legislatures had refused to provide funding to keep the rangers going. After Dick Gibbons won the November 1900 election to the Arizona legislature, he and other representatives began pushing for a ranger force. By this time, Republican Governor Murphy had also become a supporter.[44] Murphy met with Burt Mossman, a rancher with a reputation for successfully battling rustlers, and asked Mossman to work with Frank Cox, head attorney for the Southern Pacific Railroad, to create the outlines for a ranger organization. To avoid arousing opposition, Murphy worked behind the scenes with Rep. Gibbons and other legislators to create a bill and maneuver it through the House committees without drawing attention. Gibbons introduced the bill on March 13, 1901, and the

---

41. Jody Jensen, "Richard Gibbons: Arizona Pioneer."

42. Larry D. Ball, *Desert Lawmen: The High Sheriffs of New Mexico and Arizona, 1846–1912*, 52.

43. *St. Johns Herald*, November 10, 1900, 2. See also, Bill O'Neal, *The Arizona Rangers*, 1–2.

44. The efforts of Governor Murphy, Burt Mossman, and others to establish Arizona Rangers are described in O'Neal, *Arizona Rangers*, 2–4.

legislature approved it eight days later with little opposition.[45] Governor Murphy signed it into law.

Gibbons's legislation created a fourteen-man force of Arizona Rangers with one captain, one sergeant, and twelve privates at monthly salaries of $120 for the captain, $75 for the sergeant, and $55 each for the privates. The men, who enlisted for twelve-month stints, were required to provide their own arms, mounts, and other camp accoutrements, but the territory would replace horses killed in action. The legislation established a tax of five cents on every one hundred dollars of taxable property for a "ranger fund" to pay their salaries and other expenses. Governor Murphy appointed Burt Mossman as the Rangers' captain.[46]

Notable among the Rangers' first recruits was Mary Beeler's cousin Duane Hamblin, who had run unsuccessfully in 1900 to succeed Ed Beeler as Apache County Sheriff. Within weeks of joining, Hamblin and a fellow Ranger, Carlos Tafolla, were leading a posse of Apache County deputies chasing the Bill Smith Gang.[47] One of the posse men was cattleman Henry Barrett. It was the killing of Barrett's cow that had triggered the events leading to the LeSueur-Gibbons murders, and now Barrett was hotly pursuing another band of cattle thieves. On October 8, 1901, the nine-man posse cornered the outlaws in a deep canyon near the source of the Black River. Hamblin, Tafolla, and another posse man, Will Maxwell, approached the outlaws and called for them to surrender.

"All right," Smith said. "Which way do you want us to come out?"[48]

"Come out right this way," Maxwell replied. Smith started walking toward the lawmen as if intending to surrender, dragging his rifle behind him so it couldn't be seen from a distance. When he had closed within range of the lawmen, Smith quickly raised his rifle and opened fire, as did the rest of his gang. Maxwell was killed instantly and Tafolla mortally wounded. Although shot twice in the torso, Tafolla continued firing his Winchester until the magazine was empty. As the gun battle raged, Barrett wounded one or two of the outlaws, enabling Hamblin, who was un-

---

45. Arizona Republican, March 14, 1901, 1; and O'Neal, *Arizona Rangers*, 3.

46. Information about the Arizona Rangers can be found in O'Neal, *Arizona Rangers*; Frank Richard Prassel, *The Western Peace Officer: A Legacy of Law and Order*, 161–63; Ball, *Desert Lawmen*, 296–98; and "History," Arizona Rangers.

47. Details of this incident can be found in Ray McKnight, "The Battleground Shootout—Arizona Rangers Fight Smith Gang," 45–51; and O'Neal, *Arizona Rangers*, 12–17.

48. McKnight, "The Battleground Shootout," 47.

hurt, to maneuver around the outlaws and drive off their horses. Although pinned down, the outlaws, six in number, were able to escape on foot when darkness fell. They subsequently stole horses from a nearby group of cowboys and fled to Mexico.

Will Maxwell was actually a friend of outlaw Bill Smith. When told by the cowboys that he had killed Maxwell, Smith said it was an accident. "When he stood up that way we thought he was Barrett. Barrett was the man we wanted," Smith said. "We feel mighty sorry over killing Will Maxwell. . . . Tell his mother for us that we're very sorry we killed him."[49] Maxwell's brothers picked up his body and carried it back to Nutrioso for burial in the family cemetery, but they left his bullet-torn hat on the ground where Will had been killed. The posse men had left it there, believing it would be bad luck to touch it, and for many years afterward, cowboys working in the area claimed to have seen the hat lying untouched on the ground.

Another member of the initial Ranger force was Ed Scarborough, the man who had arrested Tod Carver and brought him to St. Johns.[50] The *Tucson Citizen* had hailed Scarborough "as one of Captain [Burt] Mossman's best acquisitions," but he proved to be a troublemaker and lasted less than nine months. Mossman discharged Scarborough from the Rangers after he was arrested for starting a fight at the Tombstone courthouse. Scarborough subsequently gained work as a cattle detective and later turned to cow punching, but over the next fifteen years he was charged with numerous crimes, including robbery, assault with a deadly weapon, and horse stealing. None of the charges stuck until he was arrested in 1915 for the murder of a rival rancher, John Clinton. The jury's guilty verdict brought a sentence of ten years to life. However, on the night of May 25, 1917, Scarborough climbed over the prison walls of the Arizona State Prison in Florence and made his escape with two other prisoners. The two prisoners were recaptured the next month, but Ed disappeared into Mexico. He reportedly stayed in Mexico, where he later owned a ranch, but crossed the border occasionally to visit his mother and sisters, who lived in Southern California. He was known to be alive as late as 1945.

Despite some important successes over the years, the Arizona Rangers also stirred up trouble. They were sometimes deployed against workers in labor disputes, and critics contended that the Rangers attracted hardened

---

49. McKnight, "Battleground Shootout," 49.

50. Details of Ed Scarborough's life are found in Robert K. DeArment, *George Scarborough: The Life and Death of a Lawman on the Closing Frontier*, 247–61.

criminals. In addition, county lawmen and prosecutors resented what they perceived as the Rangers' interference in local affairs. These forces led the Arizona Assembly in February 1909 to repeal the act establishing the Rangers. The governor vetoed the repeal, but lawmakers overrode his veto and the Rangers were disbanded.

Henry Barrett had ridden with the Rough Riders in Cuba, chased countless rustlers across Arizona mountains and deserts, and escaped death in the shootout with the Smith Gang, even though Bill Smith was gunning for him. But Barrett's luck ran out when, less than two years after the Smith Gang standoff, he dueled with his longtime friend, Prime T. Coleman.[51] Barrett and Coleman were both well-to-do cattlemen, well known throughout the region, and respected family men with deep roots in Apache County. Barrett, 46, was a non-Mormon, but his wife, Maud, came from a stalwart Mormon family. They had two boys, both under two years old. Coleman, 35, a former Mormon missionary to Great Britain, was married with three children between the ages of three and eight. Despite years of friendship, the two men became entangled in a dispute over grazing rights to a section of land on the Apache Reservation. Coleman claimed he had contracted with the government for the grazing permit and so, when Barrett turned his cattle onto the land, Coleman reported Barrett's infraction to government scouts managing the property. Barrett, however, contended that the grazing rights belonged to him. Enraged by the complaint, Barrett rode into Coleman's camp in the early morning of June 16, 1903, and confronted Coleman while he was cooking breakfast. Barrett carried with him a rope, intending to whip his erstwhile friend for the perceived betrayal.

There is no record of what the two men said to each other when Barrett stepped down from his horse, if they said much at all. Soon they were throwing punches. After Barrett staggered Coleman with a hard blow, both men ran for the rifles—Coleman to his tent and Barrett to his horse. Barrett's horse was closer, but the animal shied just as he grabbed for his gun, giving Coleman time to retrieve and shoulder his rifle at the

---

51. Accounts of the Coleman-Barrett gunfight, which was witnessed by several ranch hands, can be found in the *Arizona Daily Star* (Tucson), June 24, 1903, 1; *Arizona Republican*, June 23, 1903, 8; *Arizona Silver Belt* (Globe), June 25, 1903, 1; *Holbrook Argus*, June 20, 1903, 4; *Weekly Arizona Journal-Miner* (Prescott), June 24, 1903, 1, and July 22, 1903, 1; *Williams News*, June 27, 1903, 1; and Maud Ruth, "Maud Ruth Sherwood Life Story Written By Herself."

same time as Barrett. The ranchers stood about eighty feet apart when they began shooting; the men chased each other around the campsite until they had emptied their rifles, both Mausers. Barrett was shot twice, once in the pit of the stomach and once just below his right ribs. Coleman was hit with four bullets, two in each thigh. When Coleman fell to the ground, Barrett charged and began beating him over the head with his empty gun, eventually knocking Coleman unconscious. "You have killed me, all right, but I will take you to hell with me," Barrett shouted as he pummeled the man.[52] Barrett died almost immediately after delivering his last blow, while Coleman lingered near death for a few days before recovering.

Several cowboys witnessed the fight. Based on their testimony, a grand jury declined to indict Coleman for murder. "It was shown that Barrett was the aggressor, making a most vicious assault on Coleman while he was engaged in cooking over a camp fire," reported the *Weekly Arizona Journal-Miner*.[53] Eighteen months after Henry Barrett's death, his widow, Maud, married Henry's younger brother, Marvin. Maud and Marvin had three children together.[54] Prime Coleman and his wife, Annie, divorced not long after the fight, and Coleman married again in 1905, taking Maud's cousin, LaVerna, as his wife.[55] They had four children. Coleman, who had been Beeler's ranching partner before the ex-sheriff was gunned down, died July 6, 1953, in St. Johns and is buried in the town's cemetery.

Before completing his term in the Arizona territorial legislature, Dick Gibbons was called as a missionary in the southern United States. He had served a two-year mission to New Zealand thirteen years earlier, but he was single then. Now forty-three years old, he was married with four children, including a newborn, but did not hesitate to go. He left in November 1901 and served eighteen months before recurring ear infections and hearing problems forced him to return home. Back in Apache County, Gibbons resumed sheep ranching, growing prosperous while also holding leadership positions within the Mormon community. When the first automobile dealership opened in the area in 1912, Gibbons purchased

---

52. *Weekly Arizona Journal-Miner*, July 22, 1903, 1.
53. *Weekly Arizona Journal-Miner*, July 22, 1903.
54. Maud and Marvin Barrett later divorced, and Maud married again, bearing two more children.
55. LaVerna was a younger sister of Frank LeSueur's childhood friend, Will Sherwood.

a Model-T Ford—one of just two people in St. Johns to do so.[56] After receiving instructions for operating the automobile, Gibbons proudly drove the Model-T home and was nosing it into the garage he had built for the car when he missed the brake pedal. "Whoa!" he yelled, as if the car were a horse, but it kept rolling ahead until it crashed through the back wall of his garage. After regaining his composure, Gibbons circled around and, according to a local history, "parked what was left of his new car in what was left of his new garage."[57] Gibbons had the distinction of having the first recorded auto accident in St. Johns.

In 1913, Gibbons and his wife, Clarissa, moved to Mesa, where they purchased a 160-acre farm. They continued working the farm until Gibbons died at age sixty-five on New Year's Day, 1924. Clarissa died thirteen years later at age sixty-seven on August 23, 1937.

Two weeks after Gus Gibbons was killed, his widow, Pearl, moved back to Snowflake to live with her parents. She had felt close to the Gibbons family, especially to Gus's uncle Dick and aunt Clarissa, but she did not want to remain in St. Johns without Gus. Her brother Hyrum drove the wagon that moved her back to Snowflake. Jesse N. Smith said when his daughter returned to Snowflake "the young woman was much broken up."[58]

Upon leaving St. Johns, Pearl again became "Priscilla," the name by which her family and friends in Snowflake had known her. In July 1900, Priscilla returned to St. Johns to visit the Gibbons families, and she later went on a trip with Gus's parents, Bill and Gusty, to review grazing conditions for the family's herd of sheep.[59] Priscilla, however, was just twenty-three years old and had to make plans for life on her own. In 1902, she travelled to Salt Lake City to take nursing courses at the LDS Hospital in a program sponsored by the Mormon Relief Society organization.[60] To help support herself, she performed house cleaning chores at the home where she stayed. She also attended parties that her host family held in their home, but Priscilla, who once had been the lively "belle of the town of Snowflake," said she now felt "backward" and would leave the parties early

---

56. C. LeRoy Wilhelm and Mabel R. Wilhelm, *A History of the St. Johns Arizona Stake: The Triumph of Man and His Religion Over the Perils of a Raw Frontier*, 135.

57. Wilhelm and Wilhelm, 135.

58. *Journal of Jesse Nathaniel Smith: The Life Story of a Mormon Pioneer 1834–1906*, 434 (April 15, 1900).

59. *St. Johns Herald*, July 14, 1900, 3; and July 28, 1900, 3.

60. Details of Priscilla's nurses training, including the quoted material, are found in Emily S. Parker, "Priscilla Smith Gibbons Smith."

to avoid meeting people. She graduated from the program the next year and was set apart by B. H. Roberts for service as a Relief Society nurse.

While in Utah, she met a second cousin, Jesse Moroni Smith. Although married, Jesse was attracted to Priscilla. "He paid a little attention to me and asked me to a show occasionally," Priscilla said. After finishing her nursing program, Priscilla returned to Snowflake to care for her sister, Sariah, who had just had a baby girl. Soon after, Jesse wrote to Priscilla and proposed. Her father, a polygamist with four wives, told Priscilla he "was willing that I marry in polygamy if that was what I wanted to do," she said. It was. Priscilla travelled by herself on the train to Salt Lake City and on January 5, 1904, she married Jesse M. Smith in a ceremony officiated by Apostle Mathias Cowley and attended by Apostles Abraham O. Woodruff and Marriner W. Merrill. Jesse was forty-five years old, Priscilla twenty-six. Together they had eight children. When Priscilla died at age seventy-six on January 17, 1954, she was survived by six children, eighteen grandchildren, and nine great-grandchildren. Because Priscilla had been sealed to Gus in a temple marriage, she and Jesse were married for this life only, not for the next. However, in a posthumous marriage ceremony performed in 1990 in the Provo Temple, Priscilla and Jesse were also sealed together for eternity.[61]

After Bill Gibbons retired, he and Gusty spent a lot of time in Phoenix, especially in the winter, but kept their home in St. Johns. While in Phoenix, Bill served as a chaplain for the state legislature. The elderly couple had gone through many rugged years together, living in some of the West's most desolate places, constantly moving with their children at the behest of Church leaders. Bill's missionary work often took him away from home for long stretches, which left Gusty to care for and feed their children in his absence. Bill's sacrifices were Gusty's as well. "Many times I wasn't hungry when there wasn't enough to go around so the rest could have it. I couldn't eat for fear they wouldn't have enough," she said.[62] Despite knowing the hardships they would encounter, Gusty said, "I never knew of one instant of my husband ever shrinking or shirking a duty he was called to—church or civic—any time day or night he went where he

---

61. Although Mormon theology allows for men to have multiple wives in the next life, it allows women to have only one spouse. Mormons recognize the theological dilemma created when a woman is sealed to multiple husbands, but they believe such quandaries will be resolved in the afterlife.

62. Palmer, *Arizona Palmer Family History*, 130.

William "Bill" and Evaline "Gusty" Gibbons served colonizing missions throughout the West at the behest of Mormon prophets. The murder of their son, Gus, rocked Bill's faith, but the family steadied and he remained stalwart. "I never knew of one instant of my husband ever shrinking or shirking a duty he was called to—church or civic," Gusty said, adding, "I done every kind of work I could get to help things along." Courtesy Arizona State Library, Archives and Public Records, Archives Division. No. 97-8566.

was wanted."[63] Perhaps feeling as if her husband's accomplishments had been forgotten by the church's younger generation, she added, "But those men aren't looked for now days and take a back seat."

Bill died in Phoenix on January 21, 1925, at the age of seventy-three. His body was taken to St. Johns for a viewing and burial in the town's cemetery. During the viewing, his daughter Eva was in the dining room talking with family members when they heard a loud commotion coming from the front room where Bill's body lay in a casket. During Bill's early years in St. Johns, while serving as a constable, he had faced down a mob of men who had stormed the town jail to hang a young Mexican-American accused of murder. Bill's determined stand prevented the lynching, and the boy was subsequently found innocent. When Eva and the others rushed into the front room, they found an older Mexican-American woman holding Bill's lifeless body with his head in her arms. It was the mother of the young man. Some forty years later, she had not

---

63. Palmer, 131.

forgotten what Bill had done. The woman had "Daddy locked in her arms and had him raised out of the casket," Eva said. "She was kissing him and crying as hard as she could."

Shocked, Eva asked the woman what was going on. "He saved my boy's life and he has always been a friend of the Mexican families all of the time," the woman replied. The boy's father stood beside her, tears filling his eyes.[64]

Eight years to the day after Bill died, Gusty announced that it was time for her to join him. "I am ready to go to Pa," she told her daughter Ione. "I have been lonely. I have my family all raised now."[65] Gusty passed away three days later at age seventy-seven.

Many horses were killed or lost during the shootouts and chases between the Wild Bunch and lawmen. A horse presents a larger target than the man riding it, and so, either by accident or on purpose, it often gets taken down. When the outlaws fled Sheriff Beeler's posse, they would jump onto one of their extra horses if the horse they were riding or trying to mount was shot. John Blevins accidentally killed his brother's horse when he attempted to shoot Sheriff Owens, even though Owens, whom he missed, was standing only five feet away. The two men who murdered Beeler also shot both horses that were pulling his wagon, killing one and hitting the other in the jaw, where the ball lodged. But for the latter horse, which belonged to Beeler's partner, Prime T. Coleman, the story had a happy conclusion. Two and one-half weeks after the horse was shot, Dr. Charles Jarvis, a St. Johns dentist, successfully removed the ball and several small bones from the horse's jaw.[66]

Frank LeSueur's horse also had a favorable outcome. To hasten their escape from posses, the Wild Bunch often stole horses from ranches and farms, riding them hard and letting the horses loose when they gave out. The outlaws also took the horses of the men they murdered, including those belonging to Frank and Gus. No one expected to see the horses again, but nine days after the boys were killed, a man brought Frank's horse back to his family.[67] The ten-year-old bay mare, after being aban-

---

64. Eva offers two accounts of this incident in Palmer, 156, 240.
65. Palmer, 131.
66. *St. Johns Herald*, May 4, 1901, 4.
67. Dick Gibbons notes the horse's return in his contemporary account ("Diary of Richard Gibbons, Copied from His Own Daily Journal and Covering the Time from March 16, 1888 until His Death on January 1, 1924," 265), as does Rhoda Gibbons, Gus's sister, in Palmer, *Arizona Palmer Family History*, 142. The

doned by the outlaws, apparently wandered close enough to St. Johns to be recognized. None of the LeSueurs mention this in their reminiscences, but Joseph Stradling, Jr., a childhood friend of Frank's younger brothers, remembered the horse returning after the murders. "He was black with a white star in the forehead and I have seen Charley, Ray and Leo [LeSueur] ride him many times," Stradling said. Stradling, who later herded sheep for the LeSueurs, saw the horse at the sheep camp during shearings. The horse, he said, "was the pet of the LeSueurs as long as he lived."[68]

Holbrook Argus (April 14, 1900, 5) said the outlaws left a horse stolen from one of the murdered boys in Mangas, New Mexico, about one hundred miles from St. Johns. This could have been Frank's horse.

68. Joseph O. Stradling, Jr. Family Papers, Box 13.

CHAPTER 11

RENDEZVOUS WITH DEATH

A persistent Wild Bunch myth states that the outlaws brought about their own demise by posing for the famous "Fort Worth Five" portrait. According to this story, law enforcement officials discovered the photograph soon after the men left Fort Worth and promptly covered the nation with reward circulars using cropped headshots of the outlaws, making them easy to spot wherever they traveled. Credit for identifying the outlaws has been given to various lawmen, but new evidence suggests that it was Charles R. Scott, chief of detectives of the Fort Worth Police Department, who discovered the portrait. According to Richard F. Selcer, detective Scott saw the outlaws' portrait in the Swartz Studio window and, recognizing two of the men, quickly sent a copy to the Pinkertons. "Within months the Pinkertons had the country blanketed with Wanted posters," Selcer said, concluding that the Fort Worth Five portrait "helped bring down the Wild Bunch."[1]

The outlaws were indeed reckless in posing for the portrait. However, the discovery and distribution of the photo actually played no role in breaking up the Wild Bunch nor in contributing to the arrest of any gang members.[2]

The five outlaws visited Swartz's studio on November 21, 1900. However, their portrait went unnoticed for nearly twelve months. After Ben Kilpatrick was arrested in St. Louis on November 5, 1901, detectives in Fort Worth began searching the boarding houses Kilpatrick and his girlfriend had frequented in their city, looking for additional evidence of his crimes. It was in one of the boarding houses—and not in Swartz's studio—that Detective Scott found the photo of the five outlaws. Scott may have recognized Carver, Harvey Logan, and possibly Kilpatrick, who were known

---

1. Richard F. Selcer, *Photographing Texas: The Swartz Brothers, 1880–1918*, 22, 128.

2. I am indebted to Donna Donnell and Daniel Buck for providing information and insights regarding the discovery and distribution of the Fort Worth Five photo by law enforcement officials. Donnell, who discovered that Detective Scott found the photo in a Fort Worth boarding house, is preparing an article examining the issue in depth.

Texas criminals. The portrait was subsequently sent to St. Louis Chief of Detectives William Desmond, asking if the man they had arrested—that is, Kilpatrick—was one of the men in the photo. Desmond, in turn, gave the photo to the *Daily Globe-Democrat*, which published it on November 21, 1901, exactly one year after the outlaws sat for the portrait.[3] This was the first time the Fort Worth photo was made public. Desmond also provided the outlaws' names to the newspaper, though he misidentified Butch Cassidy as "Dan Cassidy" and the Sundance Kid as "Dan Kilpatrick."

The photo was published the next month in the *Knoxville Weekly Sentinel*, which said the Pinkertons became aware of the photo about the time Kilpatrick was arrested.[4] The Pinkertons were likely alerted by the St. Louis and Fort Worth detectives, who may have asked for help in identifying the outlaws. The police detectives and Pinkerton agents also interviewed women who entertained the outlaws during their visit to Fort Worth the previous year, including Callie May Hunt, the woman who married Will Carver.[5] With the information they gathered, the Pinkertons distributed the first reward circulars using the bandits' headshots in January 1902.[6] By that time, Will Carver had been killed, Ben Kilpatrick and Harvey Logan were both jailed and under arrest, and Butch Cassidy and the Sundance Kid had fled the country. Neither the Fort Worth Five portrait nor the reward circulars caused the breakup of the Wild Bunch. The gang had already disbanded.[7]

---

3. *St. Louis Daily Globe-Democrat*, November 21, 1901, 11. Other newspapers that subsequently published the photo include the *Knoxville Weekly Sentinel*, December 25, 1901, 5; *Denver Daily News*, June 29, 1903; *Leavenworth Times* (Kansas), October 18, 1903, 12; and December 26, 1903, 7; and *New York American*, July 11, 1904.

4. *Knoxville Weekly Sentinel*, December 25, 1901, 5.

5. William Pinkerton memorandum, December 4, 1901. Pinkerton's records, Box 92, folder 2. The memo, which describes in detail an interview with Callie, refers to her both as Callie Casey and Lillie Davis, which was the alias she used when working as a prostitute.

6. Pinkerton's records, Box 89, folder 14.

7. The Fort Worth Five portrait also followed Butch and Sundance to Argentina. In March 1903, the Pinkerton agency sent detective Frank P. Dimaio to Buenos Aires, where Dimaio showed photographs of the outlaws to local authorities. After receiving confirmation that Cassidy and Sundance had been seen in Buenos Aires, Dimaio had the wanted circular with the outlaws' photos translated into Spanish for distribution. However, there is no evidence that Argentine authorities took any action to arrest Cassidy or Sundance based on the circulars. It was only

After posing for the portrait, the five outlaws gambled and caroused with prostitutes and girlfriends for several weeks before splitting up into two groups. Cassidy and the Sundance Kid headed for New York, bringing with them Sundance's girlfriend, Ethel, who is sometimes identified as Etta. From New York, the trio sailed for Buenos Aires, with Sundance and Ethel travelling as Mr. and Mrs. Harry Place. Their plan to relocate to Argentina and give up the outlaw life had been discussed with the gang, but the others weren't interested. In declining, Will Carver reportedly said he would rather "die on dirt I know than live in some jungle."[8] While Cassidy and Sundance made plans to become Argentine ranchers, Carver, Logan, and Kilpatrick started planning another robbery.

The three bandits identified the First National Bank of Sonora, Texas, as their next target.[9] They were in no hurry, and over the course of several months, they stayed in various locations as they refined their plan. Toward the end of March, they took up residence at the Kilpatrick family farm in Concho County with Ben's brothers Boone, George, and Ed. On the morning of March 27, 1901, one of the Kilpatricks' neighbors, Oliver C. Thornton, came over to complain about their hogs, which had strayed onto land he was farming. Bad blood already existed between the Kilpatricks and Thornton, who had appeared as a witness in assault charges against George Kilpatrick four years earlier. When Thornton did not return home, his wife went looking for him. She found him near the Kilpatrick home, dead, lying over a log with a bullet through his forehead and another through his body. Boone and Ed Kilpatrick each offered accounts of Thornton's murder that identified either Carver or Logan as the killer. In one version, the outlaws were playing croquet when Thornton threatened the men with his Winchester, and so he was shot. Another version said the outlaws shot Thornton because they thought he was a spy for law enforcement. That Thornton was the aggressor sounds doubtful. His murder represents another killing that can be attributed to the Wild

---

when the two men came under suspicion for a bank robbery two years later that they were forced to flee the country. See Daniel Buck and Anne Meadows, *The End of the Road: Butch Cassidy and the Sundance Kid in Bolivia*, 7; and Richard Patterson, *Butch Cassidy: A Biography*, 199–200.

8. Jeffrey Burton, *The Deadliest Outlaws: The Ketchum Gang and the Wild Bunch*, 280.

9. The planning of the robbery and other events leading to Will Carver's death, are found in Burton, *Deadliest Outlaws*, 279–95.

Bunch but not to a specific gang member. The outlaws killed Thornton exactly one year after they murdered LeSueur and Gibbons.

The men set Wednesday, April 3, as the day they would rob the Sonora bank. They acquired the necessary ammunition, purchased fast horses, and set up relay stations with fresh mounts along the getaway route. Four men would take down the bank: Carver, Logan, and Ben and George Kilpatrick. On Tuesday, the day before the planned robbery, Carver and George rode into Sonora at dusk to purchase oats for their horses and a few other supplies, but first they rode through the town so George could see the layout of streets and identify possible escape routes. Ben Kilpatrick and Logan waited for them near the edge of town. Unknown to the outlaws, the local sheriff, Elijah "Lije" Briant, had been tipped off about their planned robbery and alerted townspeople to keep a lookout for Carver, who was known in the region.[10] After Carver and George were spotted entering the feed store, the sheriff gathered four deputies and hurried to confront them. Briant left one man outside to prevent an escape through a side door, then he and the other three deputies drew their revolvers and entered the store.

When the lawmen stepped through the door, Carver had just finished purchasing a sack of oats and was bending over by the counter, tying the sack string. George Kilpatrick was standing nearer to the door but was not watching it. The two outlaws were caught by surprise when Briant ordered them to drop their weapons. Carver ignored the command and drew his Colt .45 revolver, but it got tangled in his suspenders. Seeing the outlaw go for his gun, Briant fired and hit the outlaw in the right forearm, causing him to drop his pistol. When Carver reached for his other pistol, a Smith and Wesson, a deputy shot him in the chest, knocking Carver to the floor. The outlaw tried again to grab his Colt, but another deputy rushed forward and kicked it away. Meanwhile, Kilpatrick made no clear movement indicating his intention—to draw or surrender—and so a deputy shot him before he could go for his .38 Army model revolver. With both outlaws lying on the floor, Briant and his deputies continued firing until the wounded men no longer moved. Carver was shot through the right lung, twice in the right arm and twice in the right leg, breaking both the arm and leg in two places. A ball also struck Carver in the left arm and another near his left temple. Kilpatrick received a bullet in his left breast, two in the left arm, one in the left knee, and one in the left

---

10. The tip came after Carver indicated to a former employer, Ed Jackson, that he was planning to visit the Sonora area. Jackson informed a Sonora banker, who warned the sheriff. Burton, *Deadliest Outlaws*, 281.

forehead. When Logan and Ben Kilpatrick heard the gunfire, they galloped out of town.

Carver and George Kilpatrick were taken by stretcher to the courthouse, where doctors attended them. Carver died late that night, April 2, 1901. Along with money, weapons, a watch, and other possessions, Carver carried with him a small photograph of a former girlfriend, Laura Bullion, and another of his late wife, Viana. Enclosed in the locket with Viana's photo was a lock of her hair.[11] Carver was thirty-two years old.

In reporting the outlaw's death, the *San Angelo Standard* said, "Carver was not regarded as a desperate character when he was working in this section of the country as a cowboy and only developed into a desperado the last few years," adding that Carver "was not a Robin Hood character." The newspaper predicted that "the magic of the telephone and telegraph is rapidly making this country unsafe for this sort of gentry, and their ultimate extinction is only a question of a few short years."[12] Wells Fargo awarded Briant $1,000 for killing Carver, who was wanted for the 1897 Steins Pass train robbery.[13] George Kilpatrick would survive his wounds and, three years later, witness the demise of another of the LeSueur-Gibbons killers.

Wild Bunch associate Bruce Weaver was gunned down a week later following a dispute over a young woman. Weaver, like Will Carver and Ben Kilpatrick, had been part of the Ketchum Gang before joining the Wild Bunch. Unlike Carver or Kilpatrick, Weaver hung around the edges of both gangs, carrying messages and holding relay horses after robberies, never fully trusted to be part of the holdup crew. When Apache County Sheriff Beeler arrested Cassidy and Weaver on March 27, 1900, Cassidy, using the alias James Lowe, claimed not to know his companion. Weaver played along and took the fall for the stolen horses they had with them. Apache County authorities released Cassidy and held Weaver until a Socorro County deputy came to get him. Back in Socorro County, both Weaver and Lowe were indicted for horse stealing in April, though only Weaver was present in court.[14] After being set loose, Cassidy had ridden north from St. Johns to Utah, where he was rumored to be seeking amnesty. Weaver eventually gained release on a thousand-dollar bond. Having been paid generously by the Wild Bunch for his services, Weaver spent much of the next ten months enjoying Alma's amenities and, as his former

---

11. Burton, *Deadliest Outlaws*, 293; and John Eaton, *Will Carver, Outlaw*, 47–48.
12. Quoted in Eaton, *Will Carver*, 129–30.
13. *Houston Post*, June 16, 1901, 6; and June 17, 6.
14. See *Socorro Chieftain*, April 28, 1900, 1; May 5, 1; and May 12, 1.

boss at the WS Ranch noted, Weaver used his arrest as cause to "swagger around with his head in the air as became a border hero."[15]

Weaver's troubles began when he became enamored of a young woman.[16] Although Weaver had both time and money to spend on women, his criminal associations had stamped him as someone respectable ladies should avoid. When William "Pad" Hollimon, a relative of the young woman, heard about Weaver's desire to call upon her, he warned the outlaw to stay away, making it clear he thought she was too good for someone of Weaver's low reputation. Angered by Hollimon's interference, Weaver began talking about the woman "in terms not at all complimentary to her character," reported the *Socorro Chieftain*.[17] Tensions escalated until the two men ran into each other at a local store, where Hollimon called Weaver to account for his disrespectful comments. Weaver responded by drawing his six-shooter. Spitting out threats, he shoved the gun in Holliman's face and struck him with an open hand.

"I am unarmed and you have the advantage," Hollimon said. "Give me the chance to get a gun and I'll meet you."[18]

Weaver put away his pistol. "All right. I'll wait," he said. The two men parted without setting a formal date or place for settling their dispute, but Hollimon armed himself for the inevitable confrontation.

The next day, Tuesday, April 9, Hollimon was walking down Alma's Main Street, Winchester in hand, when he saw Weaver coming at him with a drawn six-shooter. Hollimon was quite frightened, given Weaver's reputation, but he continued advancing, as did Weaver. "Stop or I'll shoot you," Hollimon shouted. Accounts vary on what happened next. In one version, both men raised their weapons and fired, each missing, but Hollimon's second shot hit Weaver squarely in the forehead, nearly taking off the top of his head. Another account says that when Hollimon saw Weaver coming at him, he panicked and fired without taking aim, dispatching the outlaw with a lucky shot from the hip. As he was hit, Weaver's hand reflexively squeezed the trigger of his pistol, firing a shot

---

15. Captain William French, *Recollections of a Western Ranchman*, 277–78.

16. Accounts of Weaver's killing can be found in the *Socorro Chieftain*, April 13, 1901, 1; *San Francisco Examiner*, May 5, 1901, 35; *Albuquerque Daily Citizen*, April 16, 1901, 3; and April 19, 1901, 3; *Graham Guardian*, April 26, 1901, 1; and *St. Johns Herald*, May 4, 1901, 1. Hollimon is sometimes spelled "Holliman."

17. *Socorro Chieftain*, April 13, 1901, 1.

18. *San Francisco Examiner*, May 5, 1901, 35.

that grazed Hollimon's shoulder. Weaver then fell lifeless to the ground. "Thus ended another bad man's career," the *Socorro Chieftain* said.[19]

Hollimon surrendered to the local constable. Following a preliminary hearing two days later, he posted a $3,000 bond to appear at the next term of the Socorro County court. On May 24, a grand jury indicted Hollimon for murder, but after several continuances, he received a change of venue to Grant County in December 1903. The final determination of his case is unknown, though few thought he would be convicted. In fact, the *Socorro Chieftain* applauded Weaver's killing:

> Judging from all reports from the vicinity of the tragedy, public sentiment heartily commends Holliman for his action.... [I]f reports are true Holliman should not only be acquitted but should also be paid at least a wolf bounty for ridding Socorro county of a notoriously criminal character.[20]

Weaver was twenty-six years old when he died.[21]

The LeSueur and Gibbons families, along with their St. Johns neighbors, learned of Will Carver's and Red Weaver's deaths from a front-page article in the *St. Johns Herald*.[22] The *Herald* devoted most of its story to the hanging of Tom "Black Jack" Ketchum, leader of the Ketchum gang. Ketchum, whose brother Sam was killed by a posse in 1899, was executed April 26, 1901, in a gruesome public hanging. When Ketchum dropped through the gallows' trap door, the noose severed his head, splattering blood on nearby spectators as the headless body fell to the ground. In reporting the deaths of Carver and Weaver, the *Herald* described the outlaws as "two of the most desperate men in the southwest."[23] William Reno, a Special Agent of the Colorado and Southern Railroad, said, "The killing of Carver and Weaver practically wipes out one of the worst gangs of train robbers ever in the southwest.... There are now not more than three or

---

19. *Socorro Chieftain*, April 13, 1901, 1.
20. *Socorro Chieftain*, April 20, 1901, 1.
21. The identity of the young lady in question remains murky. *The San Francisco Examiner* (May 5, 1901, 35) identified the woman as Anna Swigert, asserting that Hollimon, like Weaver, had a romantic interest in her. In contrast, Philip J. Rasch ("Death Comes to St. Johns," 7) identified the woman as Hollimon's niece, Lydia Sipes. Familysearch.org records show that Hollimon had a nine-year-old sister-in-law named Lydia, but he did not have any nieces old enough to escort to a dance.
22. *St. Johns Herald*, May 4, 1901, 1.
23. *St. Johns Herald*, May 4, 1901.

four of the gang living, and so for [sic] as I know they are separated. I don't think that they will ever again bother the railroads."²⁴

The *Herald's* editor did not mention—he could not have known—that Will Carver was one of the five outlaws suspected of killing LeSueur and Gibbons a year earlier. Sheriff Beeler could have helped the editor make that connection. After spending three months chasing the outlaws, he knew the aliases they used and believed he could positively identify all five. However, Beeler was dead, having been murdered by the Slaughter boys just two days after Weaver was killed. The deaths of Beeler and Weaver eliminated probably the only two men who could have identified the LeSueur-Gibbons killers, aside from the killers themselves.

Railroad agent William Reno spoke prematurely when he asserted that the Wild Bunch had been dispersed and would never again bother the railroads. On July 3, 1901, Harvey Logan, Ben Kilpatrick, and O.C. "Deaf Charley" Hanks held up the Great Northern Coast Flyer No. 3 near Wagner, Montana, making off with $40,500. Hanks was killed a year later in a confrontation with Texas authorities, while Kilpatrick and Logan were subsequently arrested for passing banknotes from the robbery. On December 12, 1901, Kilpatrick pleaded guilty and received a fifteen-year sentence, while his traveling companion, Will Carver's ex-girlfriend Laura Bullion, was sentenced to a five-year term.²⁵

Logan embarked on a spending spree following the Wagner train holdup, but not before he settled an old score. Five years earlier, his older brother John had been killed by Jim Winters during a homestead dispute in Montana. Winters, perhaps fearing retribution from Logan, had recently been helping law officers track him. After the Wagner robbery, Logan travelled to Montana to visit an old ranching partner, Jim Thornhill, and his wife, Lucy, who had once lived with Logan's brother John. On July 25, 1901, Winters, now a well-to-do Montana cattleman, was gunned down as he stepped outside the door of his cabin. The murderer escaped without a trace; but given that Logan was known to be in the vicinity at the time, he was identified as the likely killer. "Winters had some time previous

---

24. *St. Johns Herald*, May 4, 1901.

25. Burton, *Deadliest Outlaws*, 318–21, describes the Wagner holdup and Kilpatrick's arrest and sentencing.

interested himself in locating Harvey Logan, and for revenge Logan killed him," the *Salt Lake Tribune* reported.[26]

Logan later visited an aunt in Missouri and spent some time in Texas and Tennessee with Annie Rogers, a prostitute he had previously known in San Antonio. In September 1901, while in Nashville, Rogers was arrested trying to exchange ten-dollar banknotes from the Wagner robbery. Logan next turned up in Knoxville, exchanging Wagner banknotes and carousing about the town. After a night of heavy drinking and shooting pool at a local bar on December 13, Logan brawled with two local police officers who beat him badly, but he was able to escape after shooting and wounding both. He was captured two days later about thirty miles east of Knoxville. Still bleeding from the pool room fight, he was wearing discarded overalls and a brimless hat as he huddled around a campfire, nearly frozen to death, when authorities found him. "He was almost dead of hunger and exposure and was suffering from scalp wounds from the clubs of the officers whom he shot," the *Nashville American* reported.[27] Logan told the arresting officers that he had not eaten since fleeing Knoxville. Logan was subsequently identified by a Pinkerton agent, while bank notes found in his coat pocket led to criminal charges related to the Wagner holdup.[28]

---

26. *Salt Lake Tribune*, January 19, 1902, 11. The newspaper may have gotten its information from a Pinkerton detective. A Pinkerton memo (September 19, 1914) states that Logan "[k]illed James Winters for revenge as Winters had been assisting the authorities with a view to causing Logan's apprehension." Pinkerton's records, Box 92, Folder 2. An undated Pinkerton history of the Wild Bunch states that "Logan travelled over two hundred miles out of his way to kill James Winters, a well-to-do cattle man, who Logan suspected of having given some information to officers in regard to him" (Box 91, Folder 3).

27. *Nashville American*, December 16, 1901, 1. See also *Knoxville Journal and Tribune*, December 16, 1901, 1. The events surrounding Logan's arrest, trial, and conviction in Knoxville, including his eventual escape from jail, are examined in Sylvia Lynch, *Harvey Logan in Knoxville*; and Mark T. Smokov, *He Rode with Butch and Sundance: The Story of Harvey "Kid Curry" Logan*, 208–77.

28. When Logan was arrested, the Pinkerton agency had not yet published a wanted circular using head shots from the Fort Worth Five portrait. However, in December 1900, a month after the Fort Worth Five photograph was taken, Logan and his girlfriend, Annie Rogers, posed for a portrait in a Denver studio. That photo made its way into the hands of the Pinkertons, who ran it in a November 1901 circular calling for Logan's arrest. The Denver portrait likely helped the Pinkerton agent identify Logan. When the police searched Logan's possessions and found the bank notes from the Wagner holdup, they also found a

As Logan awaited trial in Knoxville, the *Salt Lake Tribune* published a detailed history of his criminal activities based on information provided to the newspaper by Pinkerton General Superintendent James McParland of Denver.[29] McParland said Logan was responsible for the murders of three lawmen, Sheriff Josiah Hazen, Sheriff Tyler, and Deputy Jenkins, and two private citizens, Pike Landusky and Jim Winters. The newspaper also reported that "it is believed Logan and one Tom Capehart killed the two Mormon boys near St. Johns, Ariz., in the spring of 1900."[30] The *Tribune*'s list of possible murders committed by Logan could have also included the names of Deputy Sheriff "Billy" Deane, range detective George Scarborough, and Oliver Thornton. However, in only one instance— Landusky's killing—can the shooting be definitively attributed to Logan.

When Logan was first arrested and brought to Knoxville, two thousand angry citizens had waited at the train station, some threatening violence against the stranger who had shot two local policemen. But after learning the identity of the prisoner, several hundred people called at the jail the next day, just hoping to get a glimpse of the notorious Western outlaw.[31] Jailers allowed the visitors to crowd into the jail in groups of five and six at a time. "Right this way, boys, ten cents a peep," Logan called out, joking with his visitors. But after several men started to lay down dimes, Logan stopped them, saying he didn't need their money. C.E. Lones, the doctor who attended Logan, said "scores of women" had also expressed a desire to see the "nervy" train robber. Nearly all who interacted with Logan, including Dr. Lones and the Knoxville officers, "have expressed admiration of the grit of the prisoner," the *Knoxville Journal and Tribune* reported.[32] Logan's arrest also drew interest from police and prosecutors across the nation. "Since his arrest at Knoxville numerous warrants have been placed against him in the hands of authorities there, and over different sections of

---

copy of the *Saint Louis Daily Globe-Democrat* article that ran the Fort Worth Five photo (*Knoxville Sentinel*, December 17, 1901, 1). While jailed, Logan turned his back and refused a request by the Knoxville sheriff and a Pinkerton agent to be photographed (*Knoxville Sentinel*, December 18, 1901, 1). Logan apparently recognized, too late, that posing for photographs made his identification and capture easier for law enforcement.

29. *Salt Lake Tribune*, January 19, 1902, 11.
30. *Salt Lake Tribune*, January 19, 1902.
31. This incident is described in *Knoxville Journal and Tribune*, December 17, 1901, 2.
32. *Knoxville Journal and Tribune*, December 17, 1901.

the country where he is wanted. He will undoubtedly get a long sentence in Tennessee," the *Salt Lake Tribune* reported.[33]

In March 1902, Logan was convicted of forging and passing stolen banknotes, among other crimes, and was sentenced to 20 to 130 years in the federal penitentiary at Columbus, Ohio. Logan's lawyer appealed, delaying his move to the Columbus prison. While awaiting a decision on his appeal, Logan escaped from his Knoxville jailers.

Logan disappeared for about a year. Rumors and reported sightings provided possible clues to his whereabouts, but he eventually traveled to Texas, where he recruited outlaws Dan Sheffield and George Kilpatrick for new train robbing schemes. George, the younger brother of Ben Kilpatrick, was now recovered from the horrific gunshot wounds he suffered three years earlier in Sonora. On June 7, 1904, the three men held up the Denver and Rio Grande Western train No. 5 westbound near Parachute, Colorado.[34] The amount stolen by the outlaws is uncertain, but it may have been as little as thirty dollars. It didn't matter, at least not to Logan, because he never got a chance to spend it. During a poorly planned getaway, the bandits were forced to steal horses from local ranchers, who telephoned the police and helped the three pursuing posses stay close until they trapped the outlaws in a rocky draw near Glenwood Springs. In the ensuing gun battle, Logan shot the horse from under posse member Rollin Gardner and wounded Deputy Sheriff Elmer Chapman, grazing his cheek. Meanwhile, Gardner, who had taken up a position behind his fallen horse, hit Logan with a bullet that passed through his left arm into his breast, shattering his breastbone and breaking two ribs before burrowing into his right arm.[35]

Kilpatrick or Sheffield called to Logan, using his alias, "Are you hurt, Sam?" or "Come on, Sam."[36]

"Don't wait for me," Logan replied, knowing he was too seriously wounded to flee. "I'm all in and might as well end it right here." As his companions made their escape, he shot himself in the head rather than be

---

33. *Salt Lake Tribune*, January 19, 1902, 11. The newspaper also said that in November, Logan spent some time in Salt Lake City before traveling to Knoxville, showing off reward circulars with his description and offering up to $5,000 for his capture, though there has yet to be found evidence supporting this claim.

34. See Smokov, *Harvey "Kid Curry" Logan*, 286–93, for the Parachute robbery and Logan's killing.

35. Gardner had joined the posse after the outlaws had stolen some of his horses.

36. Smokov, *Harvey "Kid Curry" Logan*, 291.

captured and sent back to prison, likely for the rest of his life. Logan was thirty-six or thirty-seven years old.[37]

The deaths of Will Carver and Harvey Logan, along with Ben Kilpatrick's imprisonment, appeared to vindicate the decision by Butch Cassidy and the Sundance Kid to relocate to South America. For more than four years, the two former outlaws and Ethel—calling themselves James "Santiago" Ryan and Mr. and Mrs. Harry "Enrique" Place—enjoyed relative peace as ranchers in the Cholila Valley in southwest Argentina.[38] By August 1902, they had built a four-room house, chicken house, and stable; acquired 1,500 sheep, 300 cattle, and 28 saddle horses; and had two hired hands working for them, according to a letter Cassidy wrote to a Utah friend.[39] But the Pinkertons continued to pay attention and in March 1903, after hearing reports of the outlaws' relocation to Argentina, sent an agent to investigate. The agent translated into Spanish Pinkerton's reward circulars—with Fort Worth Five headshots—and distributed them to Argentine authorities.

However, it was not the Pinkertons that ultimately caused trouble for Cassidy and Sundance, but rather their own penchant to befriend unsavory characters, including two American outlaws who often stayed at their Cholila ranch. In February 1905, their outlaw friends allegedly robbed a bank in southern Argentina. No evidence indicates that Cassidy and Sundance participated in the holdup, though they may have helped with the planning.[40] The Argentine police, knowing of their ties to the suspected bank robbers, issued warrants for the arrest of both Cassidy and Sundance. Rather than risk arrest, the outlaws sold their ranch and crossed the mountains into Chile, where they became known as James P. Maxwell (Cassidy) and Frank Boyd (Sundance). In August, an intoxicated Sundance shot and killed a twenty-four-year-old policeman in

---

37. There is no record of George Kilpatrick's whereabouts or activities after this robbery, leading to speculation that he might have been mortally wounded during the shootout. See Arthur Soule, "A Tale of Two Georges."

38. For the activities of Cassidy and the Sundance Kid in South America, see Buck and Meadows, *End of the Road*; and Meadows and Buck, "The Last Days of Butch & Sundance," 36–42.

39. Butch Cassidy to Matilda Davis, August 10, 1902, in Bill Betenson, *Butch Cassidy, My Uncle: A Family Portrait*, 180.

40. Buck and Meadows, *End of the Road*, 7, say the likely holdup men were Robert Evans and Herbert Grice.

Antofagasta, but Sundance, claiming the shooting was an accident, escaped prosecution due to the efforts of the United States vice-consul and an apparent payment to the widow by Sundance.[41] The financial settlement may have drained their funds, because in December 1905, Butch and Sundance returned to Argentina and robbed the Banco de la Nación in Villa Mercedes, about four hundred miles west of Buenos Aires. Ethel reportedly participated in the heist but eventually returned to the United States. In late 1906 or 1907, Cassidy and Sundance got jobs guarding payrolls for the Concordia Tin Mine in the Bolivian Andes, but they quit sometime in 1908 after a drunken Sundance bragged about their past criminal exploits.

During this time, Butch had continued looking for another place to resume ranching. In late 1907, while visiting Santa Cruz, he thought he had found the perfect location. Writing to friends in Concordia, Butch said it was "just the place" he had been looking for much of his adult life. "Oh god, if I could call back 20 years . . . I would be happy," he wrote. "If I don't fall down I will be living here before long."[42]

On November 4, 1908, Butch and Sundance robbed a mining payroll of 15,000 Bolivianos (about $6,000).[43] They also took one of the mining company's mules. Three days later, as Cassidy and Sundance arranged for lodging in San Vicente, someone recognized the mule's brand. The two Americans also matched the description of the payroll bandits. Alerted to the bandits' presence, a four-man posse surprised and trapped them in their room. During the resulting gunfight, Cassidy shot and killed an attacker, but Sundance was severely wounded. Seeing no escape, Cassidy shot Sundance and then himself.

Three nights earlier, Cassidy and Sundance had spent the night in Tomahuaico, where Sundance stayed up late talking with an old friend, A. G. Francis, a gold-dredging engineer working in Bolivia.[44] Sundance told Francis about the payroll robbery he carried out with Cassidy earlier that day. He also bemoaned his thwarted plans to go straight, telling Francis that "he had made several attempts to settle down to a law-abiding life,

---

41. This incident is described in Daniel Buck and Anne Meadows, "The Sundance Kid in Chile: Boyds Will Be Boyds," 18–49.

42. Quoted in Buck and Meadows, *End of the Road*, 9.

43. Buck and Meadows, *End of the Road*, 33n39.

44. "A. G. Francis" was likely the pen name of Edward Graydon or his assistant, Harold Holsted, according to Buck and Meadows, *End of the Road*, 14. Graydon was a dredge operator with the Rio San Juan de Oro Company.

but these attempts had always been frustrated by emissaries of the police and detective agencies getting on his track, and thus forcing him to return to the road." Sundance claimed, "he had never hurt or killed a man except in self-defence [sic], and had never stolen from the poor, but only from rich corporations well able to support his 'requisitions.'"[45] Cassidy was forty-two years old, Sundance forty-one when they died.

If they died. Although considerable evidence points to Cassidy and Sundance as the two outlaws killed and buried in San Vicente, no one knows for sure.[46] Their move to South America in 1901 had not quelled reports that they had been seen in Western towns by purported friends and acquaintances. Numerous bank and train robberies committed in the United States were also blamed on one or both of them during the years they lived in South America. These sightings and alleged robberies continued long after the San Vicente shootings. The first known account of the duo's purported deaths was reported in the *New York American* and republished February 6, 1910, in the *Knoxville Daily Journal and Tribune*.[47] The account appears to have escaped the attention of the Pinkertons, but eventually reports of Cassidy's death began circulating in the West. In response, Cassidy's friends sent a man to Bolivia to look into the matter, according to Matt Warner.[48] Their investigator told them the outlaw pair had indeed been killed. A second major account of the outlaws' death,

---

45. A. G. Francis, "The End of an Outlaw," 43. Francis mistakenly referred to the Sundance Kid as Kid Curry and to Butch Cassidy as George Leroy Parker.

46. For discussions and analyses of whether Cassidy and Sundance were killed at San Vicente, see Betenson, *Butch Cassidy, My Uncle*, 207–43; Thom Hatch, *The Last Outlaws: The Lives and Legends of Butch Cassidy and the Sundance Kid*, 273–79; Patterson, *Butch Cassidy*, 219–55; Daniel Buck and Anne Meadows, "Did Butch Cassidy Return? His Family Can't Decide," 24–34, 48; and Buck and Meadows, "Butch & Sundance: Still Dead?," 40–49.

47. *Knoxville Daily Journal and Tribune*, February 6, 1910, 6. The date of the *New York American* article is unknown. Mike Bell, *Butch and Sundance in South America: New Evidence of Their Lives and Deaths*, 38, argues that the *Knoxville Daily* article offers significant evidence that Cassidy and Sundance "were indeed the two men who died in that tiny mining village in November 1908." Recent discoveries by Buck and Meadows in "The Sundance Kid in Chile: Boyds Will Be Boyds," 19, 39, also provide contemporary evidence of their deaths and burials in San Vicente.

48. Matt Warner, *The Last of the Bandit Riders*, 322–23; and Charles Kelly, *The Outlaw Trail: A History of Butch Cassidy and His Wild Bunch*, 314–15.

written by their friend A. G. Francis, appeared in 1913.[49] This time, the Pinkertons took notice, but some refused to credit the report. "I personally believe the whole story to be a fake," William A. Pinkerton, director of the Chicago office, declared after reading Francis's story.[50] The detective agency kept open its files on Cassidy, Sundance, and Ethel for many years afterward, adding information about their reported sightings and alleged ongoing criminal activities. The agency also kept a file on suspects and criminals named James Lowe, making its last known entry in February 1916 to note that a twenty-year-old "James Lowe" was arrested and convicted of bank robbery in Minneapolis.[51]

Historians Daniel Buck and Ann Meadows, who probably have researched the deaths of the two outlaws more closely than anyone, contend that the preponderance of evidence argues that Cassidy and the Sundance Kid died in San Vicente. In contrast, the various reports and sightings of Cassidy and Sundance after 1908—including a claim by Cassidy's sister that the outlaw visited his family in the fall of 1925—suffer from numerous inconsistencies and contradictions. Buck and Meadows have found sixty different anecdotes about the outlaws' deaths on three continents, dating from several years before 1908 to several decades after.[52] Researchers had hoped to remove all doubt about their deaths after identifying the likely gravesite of one of the outlaws in a San Vicente cemetery. In 1991, a NOVA documentary and forensics team exhumed the articulated skeleton and nearby skeletal remains, but DNA analysis showed that the bones belonged to neither Cassidy nor Sundance. Still, this did not stop the San Vicente Museum from displaying the bones as those of the two outlaws.[53] Most researchers agree with Buck and Meadows that the outlaws met their deaths at San Vicente, even if they disagree regarding how the final shoot-

---

49. A. G. Francis, "The End of an Outlaw," 36–43.

50. Wm. A. Pinkerton, letter to Geo. D. Bangs, April 27, 1913. Pinkerton's records, Box 91, Folder 3.

51. Pinkerton's records, Box 92, Folder 5, "James Lowe."

52. Buck and Meadows, *End of the Road*, 30. For decades after the deaths of Cassidy, Sundance, Jesse James, Billy the Kid, and other Western outlaws, imposters assumed their identities and presented themselves to the public as very much alive. "It does not seem to matter if an outlaw dies a disputed and anonymous death, as in the case of Butch and Sundance, or in full view of his family, as with Jesse James. Doubts will linger, and sooner or later, pretenders appear," writes Daniel Buck in "Bandit Resurrections: Who Was the Real Sundance Kid?," 74.

53. Daniel Buck and Anne Meadows, "Wild Bunch Miscellanea," 41.

out unfolded. Nevertheless, a vocal minority contends that Cassidy and Sundance were not the outlaws killed in San Vicente. Cassidy's sister said he returned to the United States and lived a crime-free life until his death in the Pacific Northwest in 1937.[54]

Harvey Logan also refused to stay dead. As with Butch and Sundance, numerous people reported seeing Logan after his purported death, and several robberies were attributed to him. Some people also claimed that he went to South America, where he continued his criminal activities. However, overwhelming evidence points to Logan as the outlaw who committed suicide following the Parachute train robbery in 1904.[55] Multiple people identified Logan, first from photographs taken of the dead man and circulated nationally, and again when his body was exhumed a month later for a more positive identification. Further, the dead man's body matched Logan's height, weight, and other physical characteristics in almost every particular. Again, the Pinkertons were skeptical. On January 15, 1907, Robert A. Pinkerton said, "It is our belief that Logan joined Cassidy and Longbaugh [Sundance] in the Argentine."[56] Scant evidence supports this claim, in contrast to the abundance of evidence that he died by his own hand to avoid capture.[57]

Regardless of whether these three Wild Bunch outlaws really died or lived on under new aliases, their outlaw activities ceased. The bandits known as Butch Cassidy, the Sundance Kid, and Kid Curry vanished. To believe that they lived on also requires believing that the outlaws, after two decades of high-profile murders and thievery, finally kicked their addiction to rustling, robbery, and the adrenaline rush that accompanied the big heist and frantic escape. Of course, they could have moved into other areas of criminal activity, but the flamboyant bank and train robberies suddenly stopped. Cassidy's letters from South America also ceased. The men became rumors and ghosts, yesteryear's legends who materialized suddenly at random moments, offering sly winks and a fleeting glimpse of the Old West before vanishing in the shadows.

---

54. Lula Parker Betenson and Dora Flack, *Butch Cassidy, My Brother*, 195. Buck and Meadows examine the conflicting stories surrounding Butch Cassidy's alleged return to the United States in "Did Butch Cassidy Return? His Family Can't Decide," 24–34, 48.

55. See Smokov, *Harvey "Kid Curry" Logan*, 297–311.

56. "Confidential," January 15, 1907. Pinkerton's records, Box 91, Folder 2.

57. Johnny D. Boggs, "Interview With Author Mark Smokov."

Butch Cassidy's notoriety brought deep shame to his parents, Maxi and Annie Parker. The Circleville newspaper came out twice a week, and each new article detailing Cassidy's latest criminal exploit added to their heartache. Fellow Mormons knew he was their oldest son. "We were humiliated and embarrassed and wished we didn't have to face the townspeople," said Cassidy's sister, Lula.[58] The family even heard reports of his suspected bank robbing activities in South America. "Mother's heart was broken over this wayward son," Lula said. "Even though we were a fun-loving lot, always there was the undercurrent of shame and humiliation."[59] The family didn't talk about Butch, but eventually lawmen learned of his Circleville connection. Pinkerton agent Charlie Siringo travelled under cover to Circleville, where he traced Cassidy to the Parker family. Siringo claims to have made the acquaintance of one of Cassidy's sisters, whom, he said, "I had hard work to keep from falling in love with."[60] Still, Circleville's residents, whatever they knew about Cassidy and his family, revealed relatively little to outsiders, perhaps out of deference to the Parkers. Or perhaps they knew little themselves. After all, by 1900, Butch had been gone more than fifteen years. In later years, Maxi Parker, when questioned about Butch Cassidy, would deny ever having heard of an outlaw by that name.[61]

Butch wasn't the only cause of embarrassment to the family. His brother Dan also engaged in rustling and thievery, but his career ended abruptly in 1891 when he was sentenced to life imprisonment for robbing a stagecoach. Thanks to his parents' lobbying efforts, Dan received a presidential pardon on December 23, 1897, after serving nearly seven years in prison. Following his release, Dan reportedly tracked down his brother and asked to join the gang. Butch turned him down. "You're too damned easy to catch," Butch said.[62]

If this story is true, Butch did his younger brother a favor. Dan eventually settled down and married a Mormon girl, Annice Ann McMullin. They quarreled and didn't always get along, and so he frequently took jobs away from home. Still, he returned home often enough to father ten children. As was the case with his brother, Dan's career as an outlaw was

---

58. Betenson and Flack, *Butch Cassidy, My Brother*, 237.
59. Betenson and Flack, 164.
60. Charles A. Siringo, *A Cowboy Detective: An Autobiography*, 351.
61. See Daniel Buck and Anne Meadows's introduction to Kelly, *The Outlaw Trail*, viii.
62. Kelly, *The Outlaw Trail*, 32.

little discussed, if at all, among family and friends. His sister, Lula, does not mention Dan's criminal activities in her book about Butch. Dan's wife didn't like him talking about his outlaw past. "She didn't want the other children at school to tease them and call them 'little outlaws,'" one of their daughters said.[63]

In one of the letters requesting a pardon for Dan, the Parkers' attorney said that Dan was desperately needed at home to help support the family because his father, Maxi, was seriously ill. "His health is permanently destroyed," the attorney said, adding that Maxi "is now confined to his bed, and no hopes are entertained for his recovery."[64] Perhaps that was Maxi's prognosis at the time, but he lived forty-three more years, dying at age ninety-four in 1938. However, Annie Parker died at age fifty-eight in 1905, just eight years after Dan's pardon. Lula blamed her mother's early death on her anguish over Butch's criminal life. "I have always felt she literally died of a broken heart," Lula said.[65]

What happened to Tom Capehart and Thomas C. "T.C." Hilliard, alias Tod Carver? Capehart melted into the West, leaving behind few clues. One report placed him in South America with Cassidy and Sundance, while another had him dying in a Colorado prison.[66] No evidence supports these or any other Capehart sightings. For many years, some historians believed that "Tom Capehart" was an alias used by either Logan or Sundance, only later realizing that Capehart was a real person. In fact, he worked and was well known on both sides of the Arizona-New Mexico border. Numerous Tom (and Thomas) Capeharts can be found in census records and other documents, but no connection between these men and the outlaw Tom Capehart has yet been uncovered. More research is required.

As for Hilliard, he slipped back into New Mexico and took up cattle ranching with his brothers after Utah authorities dismissed the murder charges against him.[67] Public records and newspaper articles offer fleeting glimpses of Hilliard's whereabouts. He first turns up in February 1904, serving as a witness for a homesteading claim for his brother Samuel in

---

63. Betenson, *Butch Cassidy, My Uncle*, 245–46.
64. Betenson, 94.
65. Betenson and Flack, *Butch Cassidy, My Brother*, 168.
66. Donna B. Ernst, "The Real Tom Capehart," 40.
67. I am indebted to Bob Goodwin for helping me untangle the details of Hilliard's life in New Mexico.

Catron County.⁶⁸ He shows up again in the 1910 census as Towd Hilliard. He and Samuel, both identified as stockmen, appear to have been living together. Two other brothers, Curtis and Prentis, also lived in the area and were stockmen. In 1914, T.C. and Prentis were arrested for assaulting a cattle dealer in El Paso, Texas, following a dispute.⁶⁹ When T.C. registered for the draft in 1918, he listed his name as Thomas C. Hilliard, stating that he was a "stockraiser" in Socorro County.⁷⁰ Two years later, the 1920 census reported that T.C. was living with Samuel's family in Socorro County.⁷¹ Both men identified themselves as "cow ranchers," as did their brothers Curtis and Prentis. He last turns up in the 1940 census for Catron County, where T.C. Hilliard, now sixty-five, was married to a woman named Venia.⁷² These mundane details reveal little about Hilliard's life after his release, but they substantiate that the Tod Carver who was wanted for the LeSueur-Gibbons murders was also the Thomas "T.C." Hilliard who later settled in New Mexico and became a cattleman with his brothers Samuel, Prentiss, and Curtis.

One other Hilliard sighting merits mention. Bert Colter, a cattle rancher born in 1887, says that while working on a cowboy crew, he saw a man named "Tod Hilliard" almost come to blows with Pat Slaughter, one of Sheriff Beeler's suspected killers.⁷³ Colter places the incident in 1905, which would have been four years after Beeler was murdered. Pat Slaughter fled to Texas after the killing, but he returned a year later

---

68. See *Socorro Chieftain*, February 27, 1904, 1; March 5, 1904, 1; and April 2, 1904, 4.

69. *El Paso Herald*, May 29, 1914, 11.

70. "United States World War I Draft Registration Cards, 1917–1918." Hilliard's brothers Samuel and Curtis registered for the draft in the same town on the same day, also listing themselves as "stockraisers." Samuel and Curtis listed their mother as "Amanda," while T. C. identified her as Mrs. William Hilliard, who was still living in their hometown of San Saba, Texas—further verification that T. C. Hilliard, alias Tod Carver, was the son of William and Amanda Hilliard of San Saba County, Texas.

71. U.S. 1920 Census, Precinct 6, Socorro County, NM. Prentis and his younger brother, Curtis, are listed as living together in Alma, New Mexico, in the 1910 census for Socorro County, precinct No. 10. Incidentally, the 1900 census mistakenly lists Prentis as "Princes."

72. U.S. 1940 Census, Precinct 15, Catron County, NM. According to the census, T.C. and Venia Hilliard had been living in the same place since 1935.

73. C. LeRoy and Mabel R. Wilhelm, *A History of the St. Johns Arizona Stake: The Triumph of Man and His Religion Over the Perils of a Raw Frontier*, 173–74.

and turned himself into Socorro County authorities to face the murder charge.⁷⁴ The court records of Slaughter's case have not been found, but Burt Mossman, who was head of the Arizona Rangers at the time, said Slaughter escaped prosecution because of a technicality. Given that Beeler's ranch was located along the New Mexico-Arizona border, Arizona prosecutors could not prove that the murder took place in Arizona.⁷⁵ After his release, Slaughter purchased a home in Springerville and married a twenty-two-year-old Mormon woman, Grace Merrill.⁷⁶ Like other members of the Slaughter family, he became a cattleman. Colter said that during a 1905 cattle roundup, the animosity between Hilliard and Slaughter grew each day until Hilliard criticized Slaughter's cooking, kicking over coffee pots and outdoor ovens as if he were trying to goad Slaughter into a fight. Instead, Slaughter angrily got on his horse and rode out of the camp. Hilliard told Colter he expected Slaughter to come back looking for trouble. "I thought Pat may start something and I wanted to kill him anyway," Hilliard told Colter.⁷⁷

Was "Tod Hillard" the same T. C. Hilliard, alias Tod Carver, who allegedly killed LeSueur, Gibbons, and other lawmen? The evidence strongly points in that direction. As previously mentioned, Hilliard had called himself "Towd" Hilliard in the 1910 census, suggesting that the former outlaw used Tod Hilliard as an alias. In addition, the outlaw Tod Carver was a friend or acquaintance of M. F. McBride, an associate of the Slaughter family.⁷⁸ The man known variously as Thomas C. Hilliard, T.C. Hilliard, and Tod Hilliard lived in the same New Mexico locations where the outlaw Tod Carver lived and worked prior to his arrest in 1901.

---

74. *Arizona Weekly Journal-Miner*, March 5, 1902, 3; *Coconino Sun*, March 8, 1902, 1; *Holbrook Argus*, March 8, 1902, 4; and *Williams News*, March 8, 4. According to Clarke, *Slaughter Ranches*, 165, Pat's older brother Arthur came to Texas and brought Pat back to stand trial.

75. Frazier Hunt, *Cap Mossman: Last of the Great Cowmen*, 186. Along with Mossman, several other sources also assert that Beeler was killed in New Mexico, just across the Arizona border. See, for example, *Coconino Sun*, March 8, 1902, 1; *Holbrook Argus*, April 20, 1901, 4; and John T. Crosby, letter to Philip J. Rasch, December 21, 1978. Crosby, a grandson of J. T. LeSueur, was clerk of the Apache County Superior Court.

76. *Snips & St. Johns Herald*, September 24, 1904, 2. Pat Slaughter resided in Springerville until his death in 1924. Information about Paschal "Pat" Eldridge Slaughter's marriage and death from familysearch.org.

77. Wilhelm and Wilhelm, *History of the St. Johns Arizona Stake*, 174.

78. *Graham Guardian*, July 26, 1901, 1.

It's possible that Hilliard/Carver was not really a Wild Bunch member. No evidence links him to any of the gang's bank or train robberies. He may have been only a minor outlaw or rustler who, for reasons unknown, threw in with the gang for the first time during their fateful ride north from Alma in the spring of 1900. After getting a taste of the desperate, violent life on the run, Hilliard may have decided he wanted to pursue a less exciting occupation. Pat Slaughter returned to the place where he allegedly killed Ed Beeler in cold blood, even marrying and raising a family as if no unpleasantness had occurred. It appears that Hilliard did so too. He led a relatively quiet life, essentially hiding in plain sight after avoiding prosecution for the LeSueur-Gibbons and Tyler-Jenkins murders.

Ed Beeler's other alleged assassin, Mal Jowell, did not settle into a quiet life, at least not for another twenty years. Arizona Ranger Joseph Pearce claimed Jowell was a nice young man who unfortunately got caught up in the Slaughter-Beeler feud.[79] Nothing could be further from the truth. Born in Palo Pinto, Texas, Jowell herded cattle in Texas before moving to Arizona and working as a cow puncher on the Slaughter ranch. Just nineteen years old when he helped kill Beeler, Jowell fled to Montana, where his brother Jason was living with his in-laws in Sweet Grass County. Before long, Mal and Jason were rustling cattle and stealing horses, leading to their arrest and imprisonment at the Montana State Prison in Deer Lodge. Mal received an eight-year sentence.[80] Released from prison in late 1910 or 1911, he soon returned to stealing cattle and horses, gaining notoriety as the leader of the "Jowell Gang" and Western Montana's "king of the cattle rustlers."[81] On November 16, 1911, Jowell shot and killed a Sweet County deputy sheriff in Melville and then fled by holding bystanders at bay with a six-shooter. He eluded pursuers by hiding at night in snowbanks, nearly freezing to death, and rode eighteen different horses—many

---

79. Joseph Pearce, *Line Rider: A True Story of Stampedes, Gamblers, Indians and Outlaws Written by Arizona Ranger Joseph Pearce 1873–1958*, 117–21. Little of what Pearce says about Jowell—or about his conversation with Jowell while he hid from lawmen—appears trustworthy.

80. The 1910 Census shows that both Mal and Jason Jowell were inmates at the Montana state prison in Deer Lodge in May 1910. I have been unable to find the length of Jason's prison sentence, but both brothers served several terms at Deer Lodge for horse stealing, according to the *Harlowton News*, November 17, 1911, 3.

81. *Anaconda Standard*, November 21, 1911, 3; and *Laurel Sentinel*, November 7, 1912, 7.

stolen, some provided by friends—until he reached Phoenix, Arizona. A month later, Jowell was captured after his prostitute girlfriend turned him in for the $1,000 reward. Armed guards brought him back to Montana to stand trial for murder.[82]

Montana's newspapers emphasized that the six-foot-tall Jowell was a well-built, handsome man known for his gallantry and popularity with the ladies. During his trial, many women came ninety minutes early to make sure they got seats in the crowded courtroom, passing the time knitting while they waited for the day's proceedings to begin.[83] Reporters noted that more women than men attended the trial. Jowell took the stand, pleading self-defense in shooting the sheriff, but the jury found him guilty of second-degree murder, despite his good looks. The judge gave him a twenty-two-year sentence.[84]

Just three months into his sentence, Jowell and another prisoner, while shackled together, jumped out the bathroom window of a train traveling an estimated thirty to forty miles per hour. The two men managed to get free of their chains, but Jowell was arrested a short time later in Nevada and convicted of horse stealing. He served three years in a Nevada prison and when that sentence was completed, prison officials escorted him back to Montana. Although he was not eligible for parole until 1924, the governor commuted Jowell's sentence to eight years on the recommendation of the prison warden, who said Jowell had saved the lives of many prisoners by nursing them during a flu epidemic. Jowell was paroled in March 1919 with the stipulation that he never again enter Sweet Grass or Park counties, whose citizens had protested his release. Jowell returned to his home state of Texas, married in 1922, and lived an apparently trouble-free existence, farming and raising a family in Swisher and nearby counties. He died in September 1966 at the age of eighty-five, survived by his widow,

---

82. Jowell's crimes, escape, trial, and imprisonment are detailed in dozens of Montana newspaper articles, including the *Anaconda Standard*, November 17, 1911, 12; November 28, 1911, 8; January 7, 1912, 7; May 4, 1912, 1; May 5, 1912, 1; May 8, 1912, 1; September 20, 1915, 6; *Butte Daily Post*, August 12, 1912, 3; *Butte Miner*, November 21, 1911, 1, 4; November 28, 1911, 9; December 6, 1911, 2; *Harlowton News*, November 17, 1911, 3; *Independent Observer* (Conrad), February 13, 1919, 7; *Helena Independent*, December 31, 1918, 8; *Laurel Outlook*, December 27, 1911, 1; and *Laurel Sentinel*, November 7, 1912, 7.

83. *Anaconda Standard*, May 8, 1912, 1; and *Butte Miner*, May 9, 1912, 8.

84. Jowell entered the Montana state prison on May 15, 1912. Montana Prison Records, Mal B. Jowell, accessed August 2, 2021.

five children, three stepchildren, thirty-six grandchildren, and four great-grandchildren.[85] He outlived Ed Beeler by more than sixty-five years.

Ben Kilpatrick, the last of the Fort Worth Five outlaws, met his death at the hands of a mild-mannered Wells Fargo agent during a failed train robbery. Nothing about David A. Trousdale, a railroad messenger for the Well Fargo Express Company, suggested he would become an overnight sensation and hailed as a hero throughout the United States.[86] In March 1912, Trousdale was thirty-four years old, single, of average height and weight, quiet and unassuming, seemingly ordinary in every way.[87] He had grown up in Columbia, Tennessee, but persistent health problems prompted him to move to Texas at the recommendation of his doctors. He eventually settled in San Antonio, where in 1902 he landed a job with Wells Fargo Express and steadily worked his way up from a clerk to a Wells Fargo messenger.[88]

On March 13, just after midnight, Trousdale and his assistant, G.K. Reagan, were sitting in the express car when the engineer banged on the

---

85. Jowell's obituary was published in the *Odessa American* (Odessa, TX), September 22, 1966, 2.

86. Detailed accounts of Trousdale and his role in thwarting the attempted robbery of Southern Pacific Sunset Express No. 9 are found in *Houston Post*, March 14, 1912, 1, 8; March 15, 1–2; March 17, 11; *San Francisco Call*, March 14, 1912, 3; and *St. Louis Dispatch*, March 12, 1912, 1; April 21, 59. In addition, John Boessenecker wrote about this incident in *Shotguns and Stagecoaches: The Brave Men Who Rode for Wells Fargo in the Wild West*, 286–300.

Some of the precise details of the incident are difficult to pin down because contemporary newspaper accounts—which are the main sources of information—do not agree on all the facts, even though they all cite Trousdale as their source. For example, in some accounts, Trousdale is quoted as saying that Kilpatrick roughed him up with his pistol, but in others he said Kilpatrick prodded him with his rifle. In some accounts, Trousdale is quoted as saying he grabbed the ice mallet and immediately clubbed Kilpatrick on the head, while others state that he hid the ice mallet under his coat before striking the outlaw. The amount of reward money and gifts Trousdale later received also vary.

87. This physical description comes from Trousdale's 1917–1918 Draft Registration Card and *Houston Post*, March 14, 1912, 1. In *Shotguns and Stagecoaches*, 286, Boessenecker states that Trousdale was born September 20, 1876. However, Trousdale's Draft Registration Cards for both World War I and World War II say he was born September 20, 1877, so I used the latter date in calculating his age.

88. Boessenecker, *Shotguns and Stagecoaches*, 287.

door and asked them to open up. The train had stopped a few miles outside of Dryden, Texas, so the engineer apparently had some news, such as a report of engine trouble. But when Trousdale and Reagan opened the door, they found themselves staring at an "ugly looking rifle" wielded by a masked bandit.[89] The outlaw, a man about six feet tall and weighing 210 pounds, had already rousted the mail clerk, M.E. Banks, from the mail car. He gruffly ordered Trousdale and the others to march back to the engine, where another masked bandit, this one considerably shorter, was holding a gun to the other enginemen. Trousdale saw something about the outlaws that marked them as inexperienced, especially the big man. "These fellows are green," he whispered to Banks. "We'll watch our chance and get them, sure."[90]

The so-called "green" big man was Ben Kilpatrick, one of the Old West's most infamous highwaymen. Kilpatrick had managed to stay alive longer than the leaders of his first gang, Sam and Tom Ketchum. He had also outlasted the other members of the Fort Worth Five: Will Carver, killed in 1901; Harvey Logan, killed in 1904; and Butch Cassidy and the Sundance Kid, killed in 1908. Kilpatrick's longevity cannot be attributed to superior intellect or cunning but largely, if not solely, to his having spent most of the last decade in prison. Sentenced to a fifteen-year prison term in December 1901, he had started out as a rebellious, troublemaking inmate but eventually became a model prisoner and a good worker on the stonecutting gang, making him eligible for early release—to which the Pinkertons objected. "Every effort should be made, I think, by the Railroad Officials and others, to prevent the release of Kilpatrick from the Penitentiary at Atlanta," wrote William A. Pinkerton, head of the agency, on January 13, 1911. "He is a very bad man to have at large."[91]

Despite Pinkerton's concerns, Kilpatrick's good behavior won him release just five months later on June 11, 1911.[92] He was immediately rearrested by Texas authorities for the murder of Oliver Thornton at the Kilpatrick home ten years earlier, but insufficient evidence forced prosecutors to drop the case before it came to trial. At some point, Kilpatrick began working at a ranch on the Pecos River, telling friends in San Angelo

---

89. *Houston Post*, March 17, 1912, 11.

90. *Houston Post*, March 17, 1912.

91. William A. Pinkerton, letter to Geo. D. Bangs, January 13, 1911. Pinkerton's records, Box 90, Folder 8.

92. For Kilpatrick's time in prison and subsequent release, see Burton, *Deadliest Outlaws*, 329–30.

that he intended to settle down and give up the criminal life. "I'm going down on the Pecos to try to get a piece of good land and a little bunch of sheep and make a good living," he said.[93]

Kilpatrick's professed good intentions were a ruse. Less than five months after his release, Kilpatrick teamed up with one of his friends from the Atlanta penitentiary, Ole Beck, to pull off a series of train robberies in Arkansas, Oklahoma, and Texas.[94] Their last holdup began just after midnight on March 13, 1912, when they boarded the Southern Pacific Sunset Express No. 9 after the train stopped in Dryden to take on water. The outlaws swung onto the engine, brandished their rifles, and instructed the engineer to continue until they told him to stop about ten miles outside of Dryden. There they ordered Trousdale and the other railroad men to march to the engine while the porter decoupled the combination and express cars from the passenger cars.[95] The engine then pulled the combination and express cars about a half mile up the track until they stopped again. The outlaws had carefully picked this location for looting the train's packets and packages. Mexico lay just twenty miles away across the Rio Grande River, and they had horses positioned nearby to make their escape through a mountainous territory that would make them hard to catch before they crossed the river onto foreign soil. While Beck kept the engineer and fireman covered, Kilpatrick forced Trousdale, Reagan, and Banks to accompany him back to the combination and express cars to help him find the most valuable packages. As the men walked through the cars, Kilpatrick repeatedly poked Trousdale, taking brutal pleasure in jabbing Trousdale forcefully with his pistol. "I had no thought of resisting the robber until he began punching me with his pistol," Trousdale said. "But the fellow made me madder all the time. On the pretext that I was not holding my hands high enough, he amused himself by prodding me in the ribs. It hurt."[96]

Despite his growing anger, Trousdale remained calm, all the while looking for an opportunity to turn the tables on the outlaw. Kilpatrick kept his pistol carefully trained on Trousdale as he searched the satchels and packages, so Trousdale tried to put him at ease with friendly banter and flattery. He also assured the outlaw he didn't intend to risk his life for

---

93. *Daily Advocate* (Victoria, TX), March 21, 1912, 1. According to Burton, *Deadliest Outlaws*, 330, Kilpatrick told a newspaper editor he intended to lease some land near Sheffield, which is close to the Pecos River.

94. Burton, *Deadliest Outlaws*, 330–31.

95. The combination car includes both mail and baggage.

96. *St. Louis Dispatch*, April 21, 1912, 59.

his paltry salary of just $100 a month. "I am not going to scrap with you all," he said. "I'm not getting 'fighting wages.'"⁹⁷

As Kilpatrick rifled through packages in the express car, Trousdale noticed a wooden ice maul lying on top of an oyster barrel. Shaped like a croquet mallet, the ice maul's handle was as thick as that of a hatchet and its head even heavier, making it a formidable weapon. Trousdale also noticed that Kilpatrick was no longer guarding him with his revolver. Meanwhile, Kilpatrick was becoming visibly frustrated because he hadn't yet found any packages of significant value, and so Trousdale offered to show him some valuable packages. Kilpatrick willingly followed him toward the oyster barrel, where Trousdale casually kicked at a small box on the floor. "Why don't you pick up that package?" he said. "It's worth more than all the stuff you've got."⁹⁸

Kilpatrick leaned his rifle against the wall and knelt to get a closer look. While he was stooped over, absorbed in the package, Trousdale quietly picked up the ice maul and bashed the outlaw over the head. Kilpatrick collapsed on the floor, groaning. Trousdale delivered two more blows, the second crushing Kilpatrick's skull and splattering blood and brains across the train's wall.

Trousdale and the mail clerk, Banks, seized Kilpatrick's weapons, taking a .40 caliber rifle and two pistols. Although Trousdale had a shotgun on his desk, he kept Kilpatrick's rifle, while Banks and Reagan took the pistols. After turning out the gas lights in the express car, they waited in the dark for Beck to come looking for his partner. They had decided that Trousdale would take the first shot and if he missed, Banks and Reagan would open fire. Nearly an hour passed with no sign of Beck, and so Trousdale fired a single shot through the roof of the car, which soon brought the outlaw. Beck poked his head into the darkened car. "Frank," he said, calling Kilpatrick by his current alias. Beck stepped back before Trousdale could take aim. "Frank," he called again and began climbing through the door. Trousdale fired once, killing Beck instantly with a shot one inch above the left eye.

When the three railroad men examined Beck, they discovered that he was carrying six sticks of dynamite, a bottle of nitroglycerin, and fuses in case Trousdale had refused to open the car door. "I shudder when I think of what our finish might have been had Trousdale's shot struck that dynamite and nitroglycerin on the robber's person instead of tearing the

---

97. *San Francisco Call*, March 14, 1912, 3.
98. *San Francisco Call*, March 14, 1912, 3.

The bodies of outlaws Ben Kilpatrick (left) and Ole Beck (right) are stood up for display at the Sanderson, Texas, train station. David Trousdale, the Wells Fargo Express railroad messenger who killed both men to thwart a robbery, stands behind Kilpatrick, holding up his head. Photo taken March 13, 1912, courtesy of Library of Congress Prints and Photographs Division, Washington, D.C.

top of his head off," Banks said.[99] The *Amarillo Daily News* speculated at the probable outcome: "Had the bullet struck his body there might have been no one left to tell the tale. . . . The two cars would have been blown to splinters."[100]

The railroad men loaded the outlaws' bodies onto the baggage car. The engineer backed up the engine and two cars, recoupled the train with the passenger cars, and steamed to the next scheduled stop at Sanderson, where they stood up the bodies on the station platform and took a photo of the dead men. News of the thwarted robbery spread quickly. Trousdale became an instant hero as newspapers from coast-to-coast published banner headlines and laudatory accounts of the night's events, including the photograph of the slain robbers.[101] Passengers told the *St. Louis Dispatch* that Trousdale's action was "the most daring exploit in the railroad history of the Southwest."[102]

---

99. *Houston Post*, March 17, 1912, 11.
100. *Amarillo Daily News* (TX), March 17, 1912, 5. The paper said the robbers also stashed almost a hundred pounds of dynamite near the scene of the holdup.
101. *St. Louis Dispatch*, April 21, 1912, 59.
102. *St. Louis Dispatch*, March 13, 1912, 1.

It wasn't just Trousdale's cleverness in foiling the robbery that caused a sensation. The killing of the "notorious and dangerous train robber" Ben Kilpatrick also stirred widespread interest.[103] Many newspapers noted Kilpatrick's lengthy criminal career riding with both the Ketchum and Hole-in-the-Wall gangs. His death brought down the curtain on two of the most feared Western gangs from a fast-fading era.

Congratulatory telegrams and letters poured into Trousdale. He began receiving movie and vaudeville offers "almost before the train reached the next station," said one newspaper with only a little exaggeration.[104] Among the stage offers, the Texas Vaudeville Circuit offered Trousdale a guaranteed package that included $100 a week for twenty weeks of touring in Texas and another ten weeks at $200 a week touring in other states, plus expenses. Several motion picture companies also sought to capitalize on Trousdale's fame. The Texas Film Company offered him $1,000 to re-enact the holdup in a movie, plus a lecture tour at the same rate as the vaudeville offer. Under the latter deal, Trousdale would earn more than four years' worth of salary in less than a year. He turned down every offer.

"Theatrical stunts are not in my line," he said. "None of these propositions hold any interest for me. Besides, I don't want the notoriety."[105]

As it turned out, Trousdale would eventually receive gifts and rewards totaling $8,000—more than $200,000 in today's currency.[106] The Southern Pacific railroad gave him $3,000 and Wells Fargo added $2,000 for killing the two bandits who had been plaguing railroad lines along the Mexican border. In addition, the citizens of Sanderson and San Antonio raised $1,500 each through popular subscriptions. These awards may or may not have included the value of a $250 gold watch and chain presented to Trousdale by Wells Fargo and $100 raised by the train passengers after learning of Trousdale's heroics. Wells Fargo also promoted Trousdale, making him the supervising messenger between San Antonio and Houston—regarded as the company's best run—and raising his annual salary from $1,200 to $2,000.[107]

Trousdale intended to leave Wells Fargo and use the reward money to purchase a ranch in west Texas, which would enable him to enjoy the

---

103. *St. Louis Dispatch*, April 21, 1912, 59.
104. *Houston Post*, March 17, 1912, 11.
105. *Waco Morning News* (TX), March 16, 1912, 8.
106. *St. Louis Dispatch*, April 21, 1912, 59.
107. *Belvidere Daily Republican*, April 15, 1912, 1.

outdoor life prescribed by his doctors.[108] It appears that he never followed through on this plan. Census records and draft registration documents for World War I and World War II indicate that he stayed in San Antonio and remained employed with Wells Fargo and its successor companies until he retired in 1945. His fame also garnered him numerous marriage proposals from women throughout the United States. He turned them all down. But two years after the attempted robbery, he married Allie B. Lester, and together they had two boys, David and William. A few years after retiring, Trousdale and his wife moved to his hometown of Columbia, Tennessee, where he died at age seventy-five. As for Ben Kilpatrick, he and Ole Beck were wrapped in sheets and buried together in a single box in a Sanderson cemetery.[109] Kilpatrick was thirty-eight when he died.

The outlaw life, Butch Cassidy reportedly said, was a losing game—despite the outlaws' numerous advantages. A meticulously planned robbery allowed them to strike at the time of their choosing. Strategically stationed horse relays enabled them to outrun posses. The threat of deadly ambush kept pursuers from trailing too closely. Associates and sympathizers provided food and provisions, helped conceal their whereabouts, and even sent posses in the wrong direction. Vast forest and mountain expanses offered myriad places in which to disappear until pursuers gave up. All these advantages, combined with a little luck, made capture nearly impossible. But luck wasn't always on their side. Butch Cassidy was identified in each of his first two bank robberies. He got away but was forever a wanted man, constrained in his movements, always looking over his shoulder and sitting with his back to a wall, warily watching the door. Despite their efforts to plan carefully, Wild Bunch outlaws sometimes got sloppy—and paid the price. After Will Carver told an acquaintance he was planning to visit Sonora, the information reached the local sheriff, who surprised Carver in the town's feed store and shot him to death. Harvey Logan failed to put in place sufficient relays of fresh horses after his train robbery near Parachute, Colorado, leading to his shooting and suicide. In Bolivia, Cassidy and Sundance carried their stolen loot using a mule from the mining company they had just robbed. The mule's brand alerted authorities to the outlaws' location and led to their deaths in a shootout. Ben Kilpatrick's greed and inattention during his last train rob-

---

108. *St. Louis Dispatch*, April 21, 1912, 59.
109. Arthur Soule, "The Tall Texan: The Story of Ben Kilpatrick."

bery resulted in his ignominious death. Western outlaws who lived long lives—for example, Matt Warner, Elzy Lay, Tod Carver, Dan Parker, and Mal Jowell—were those who got out of the business, often after a prison sentence extinguished their desire to continue testing their luck. Keep rolling the dice and eventually they will turn up snake eyes, no matter how slim the odds. Outlaws who continued robbing banks and trains eventually ended up captured or dead, no matter how careful the planning. That's the story of the Western desperado.

AFTERWORD

Outlaws could sometimes point to a bad break or misunderstanding that led to their life of crime. Tom Capehart joined the Wild Bunch after being beaten and jailed for a crime he said he did not commit. Will Carver turned to drink and outlawry after becoming despondent over the death of his young wife and baby. When Harvey Logan was eight or nine, he and other siblings were given over to be raised by an aunt and uncle after his mother died, a circumstance that may have contributed to his dissolute life. No one complained more loudly about bad breaks than Butch Cassidy and the Parker family. They didn't dispute his well-deserved reputation as a rustler and bandit; yet, whenever he got caught, the Parkers cried misunderstanding or frameup. He was tripped up, they said, by false accusations, first for cattle rustling when he left home in Circleville, then for horse stealing that led to his imprisonment in Wyoming, and later for murder that scuttled a rumored amnesty deal. And when Cassidy and Sundance tried to use their stolen money to settle down and live quiet lives as ranchers in Argentina, Pinkerton agents and Argentine lawmen wouldn't stop hounding them, eventually forcing the duo to return to a life of crime.

When working as cowboys, Wild Bunch members often drew praise for their skills and even friendliness. Capehart and Elzy Lay impressed employers with their ability to break horses. Will Carver was considered an excellent roper and horseman, while Flatnose Currie's former ranch boss called him "the best he ever saw." Both Carver and Currie were well-liked by fellow cowboys. Most popular of all gang members was Cassidy. Many stories told by people who knew him highlight his good humor, generosity, and sympathy for the little guy. If the personable young Mormon wasn't stealing your livestock or sticking a gun to your head (and demanding money), he was a pleasant, cheerful companion. Charles Kelly, who interviewed many people who knew Cassidy, said, "Among cowboys and cattlemen of the old frontier his name stood for daring, courage, resourcefulness, and a certain chivalry."[1] Cassidy's sister, Lula Betenson, claimed her brother was bitter that his attempts to go straight in South America had failed. "When a man gets down, they won't let him up. He never quits paying his price," Cassidy reportedly told his family.[2] That Cassidy actually returned to Utah and made this remark is doubtful, but it certainly reflects how Betenson and other family members viewed the matter. "Butch was not afraid of hard work on ranches," said Cassidy's great-nephew Bill Betenson. "In fact most employers gave him praise, but each time he tried to live an honest life, the law seemed to catch up with him."[3] Based on the observations of people like William French, Cassidy's boss at the WS Ranch, Cassidy demonstrated genuine intelligence and a talent for leadership. He could have made something of himself had he not been an outlaw.

Wild Bunch gang members weren't really the victims of bad breaks. In Cassidy's case, for example, he chose a criminal life and continually returned to it even when presented with opportunities to go straight. Many of the stories told about Cassidy follow the predictable character and plot lines of popular outlaw folklore. One of the most persistent tropes of Western outlaws portrays them as social bandits fighting on the side of society's disenfranchised against the rich and powerful.[4] Popular lore contends that such bandits were driven to outlawry by injustice or persecution, but, being good men, they trained their vengeance on the wealthy (such as banks and railroads) and gave to the poor. These "good badmen" never killed except in self-defense, were polite and kind—especially to

---

1. Charles Kelly, *The Outlaw Trail: A History of Butch Cassidy and His Wild Bunch*, 4.
2. Lula Parker Betenson and Dora Flack, *Butch Cassidy, My Brother*, 182.
3. Bill Betenson, *Butch Cassidy, My Uncle: A Family Portrait*, 139.
4. Among those examining the myths and traditions surrounding so-called Robin Hoods or social bandits: Eric Hobsbawm, *Bandits*; Frank Richard Prassel, *The Great American Outlaw: A Legacy of Fact and Fiction*; Kent L. Steckmesser, "Robin Hood and the American Outlaw," 348–55; Steckmesser, *Western Outlaws: The "Good Badman" In Fact, Film, and Fiction*; Stephen Tatum, *Inventing Billy the Kid: Visions of the Outlaw in America, 1881–1981*; and Richard White, "Outlaw Gangs of the Middle Border: American Social Bandits," 387–408.

White's *"It's Your Misfortune and None of My Own": A History of the American West*, 613, describes the dominant place the mythic West held within American popular culture in the mid-twentieth century: "By 1958, Westerns comprised about 11 percent of all works of fiction published in the United States, and Hollywood turned out a Western movie every week. In 1959 thirty prime-time television shows, including eight of the ten most watched, were Westerns."

women and children—and revered their mothers. Stories told about the James-Younger gang, Dalton gang, and Billy the Kid, among others, conform to this pattern. So too do many of the stories surrounding Butch Cassidy. The Cassidy of legend eschewed killing, treated women honorably, adored his mother, shared his riches with poor homesteaders (even paying a widow's mortgage), exuded good cheer and optimism, and never got drunk. Such stories can be traced to English tales of Robin Hood, the quintessential good badman. These same English stories subsequently attached themselves to many American outlaws in succeeding generations. Such folk narratives rely largely on oral traditions divorced from the historical record. That record—as contained in newspapers, court records, etc.—presents a markedly different picture of Western bandits. "The American outlaws are grimmer and more violent characters than the Robin Hood of the ballads," states Kent Steckmesser regarding outlaw mythology. "Robin's half-friendly bouts with friars and plough-men bear little resemblance to the inevitably fatal gun battles which mark the careers of American outlaws."[5] Frank Prassel concurs, stating, "Badmen were greedy, violent brigands transformed into heroes after death by journalists fulfilling roles once occupied by minstrels and balladeers."[6] Cassidy and his Wild Bunch cohorts stole cattle and horses, robbed banks and trains, and murdered lawmen not to help others but to help themselves.

Telling the outlaws' stories from the victims' perspective, as this history does, upends other aspects of outlaw mythology as well. Rather than engaging adversaries in even odds and fair fights, Wild Bunch outlaws preferred to ambush their victims, as they did LeSueur and Gibbons in Arizona, and Tyler and Jenkins in Utah. Those who fled were shot in the back. This perspective also offers a necessary corrective to historians and biographers who, perhaps unconsciously, identify too closely with the outlaws. In his investigation of the LeSueur-Gibbons murders, Philip Rasch suggests that the outlaws had good cause for shooting them. "While it may appear callous to say so, the young men were armed and presumably quite willing to take the lives of five men who could be charged only with suspicion of having killed a cow. The best of causes confers no immunity upon its adherents," Rasch said.[7] Rasch is mistaken in asserting that the outlaws' only alleged crime was killing a cow. They had also fired upon Sheriff Beeler and his deputies with an intent to kill while resisting arrest.

---

5. Steckmesser, "Robin Hood and the American Outlaw," 353–54.

6. Prassel, *Great American Outlaw*, 327.

7. Philip J. Rasch, "Death Comes to St. Johns," 3.

But regardless of whether their crimes were minor or severe, Rasch's position would suggest that law officers who carry weapons make themselves fair game for suspected criminals because, after all, the officers might use their weapons in making an arrest.

Frank LeSueur and Gus Gibbons encountered the historical Western outlaws, not those of imagination and myth. They truly caught a bad break. It was only a matter of luck that they were summoned by the sheriff to join the posse. Frank had just come down from the family's sheep camp and was purchasing supplies in Springerville when the sheriff asked for his assistance. Gus was summoned while collecting the morning mail. He was the last to join the posse. That their posse failed to meet up with Sheriff Beeler's posse represented another piece of bad luck. The two posses should have crossed paths as one was going out and the other coming in. When that didn't happen, Beeler should have immediately gone back out on the trail—or sent someone—to tell the LeSueur-Gibbons group that he was no longer pursuing the outlaws. He might not have reached them in time, but he still should have tried. His belief that they would never catch up with the outlaws proved to be dead wrong. Dick Gibbons, Gus's uncle, also deserves a measure of blame. It was his decision to split the eight-man posse into two groups and send four young men on their own. He wrongly assumed they were following the sheriff's posse, even though they had not once seen the sheriff during an entire day of tracking. A shepherd told Dick that the four boys were hot on the trail of the outlaws, but he did not mention seeing the sheriff's posse. Similarly, the four boys, especially Frank and Gus, also erred in thinking the sheriff's posse was riding just ahead. Again, the shepherd said only that the outlaws, not the sheriff, had ridden past on the trail. Gus initially wanted to go back with Antonio and Francisco, but given Frank's determination to press on, Gus may have agreed to continue—perhaps against his better judgment—simply so Frank wouldn't be tracking alone. Once that decision was made, common sense should have told them to proceed carefully. Any competent tracker would have known not to walk up that mesa draw. Their inexperience led them into an ambush.

Still, Frank and Gus posed little threat to the outlaws. One wonders what might have happened if Butch Cassidy, who was trying to catch up with his Wild Bunch comrades, had been present at the top of the mesa. Would Cassidy have persuaded the others not to kill the young men, just as he reportedly had done when the outlaws wanted to kill a Pinkerton agent in Alma? They could have robbed Frank and Gus of their guns and horses, and then turned them loose to make their way on foot back to the sheep camp, where they would arrive long after dark—and long after the outlaws had made their escape. But Cassidy wasn't there, and the outlaws were in an unforgiving mood, given that several of their gang, including Harvey Logan's brother, had recently been slain by posses. Frank and Gus were done in by a bad break. They never had a chance to make something of themselves.

The St. Johns Mormons had bad breaks too, lots of them. Floods, drought, frost, high winds, poor crop yields, cattle rustling, rampant lawlessness. But the Mormons didn't let the bad breaks deter them from their mission. Hunger and destitution could not drive them from their chosen path. Except in rare instances, they moved away only when "honorably released." The mission assigned them was punishing, even cruel. But like Job, many Mormon colonizers viewed their hardship and suffering as a test, one that would perfect their faith; and like Job, come hell or high water, they were determined to demonstrate their faith, though they often felt as if they got both hell *and* high water. After pondering the difficulties encountered by those called to the St. Johns region, Christopher Kempe concluded, "God has a good reason for allowing the Saints to suffer in this manner from year to year." As for why, he said, "I for one am unable to answer."[8]

In June 1905, the Mormon Prophet Joseph F. Smith officially released the St. Johns Saints from their colonizing mission. The final straw was the May 2 collapse of the Salado Dam, an earthen structure that provided irrigation water for cultivating the large plain between St. Johns and the McIntosh Hills.[9] Located on the Little Colorado River about six miles upstream from St. Johns, the Salado Dam was the largest dam on the river at the time. Following several years of drought, a heavy snow runoff filled the dam beyond its capacity until the walls gave way. The cascading water destroyed the Zion Dam about twenty miles downstream and the Woodruff Dam in Navajo County, flooding St. Johns and other locations while imper-

---

8. C. J. Kempe to My Dear Wife and Children, undated letter, written from Norway, published in Ellen Greer Rees, "History of Christopher J. Kempe Family," 56.

9. For details about the many dams built by the Mormons on the Little Colorado River, including the collapse of the Salado and Lyman Dams, see William S. Abruzzi, *Dam That River! Ecology and Mormon Settlement in the Little Colorado River Basin*, 121–42; Cameron Udall, *Images of America: St. Johns*, 53–60; C. LeRoy and Mabel R. Wilhelm, *A History of the St. Johns Arizona Stake: The Triumph of Man and His Religion Over the Perils of a Raw Frontier*, 60–71; and Robert Lucas, "St. Johns: Town of Friendly Neighbors Had Unfriendly Start."

iling crop production for miles along the Little Colorado River corridor. A month later, President Smith and his counselors granted honorable releases to everyone in the St. Johns Stake, informing Stake President David Udall:

> We are in receipt of a couple of letters from brethren of your stake asking to be released from the mission given to them to settle permanently in St. Johns.
>
> For your information, and the information of your people, we desire you and them to know that we had already taken this matter under consideration, and had concluded to write you to the effect that, under the circumstances, we could not feel to ask any member of the St. Johns Stake to dwell there any longer against their own inclination, and it was therefore the unanimous decision of the First Presidency and Apostles in council assembled, that all of the people of the St. Johns Stake, including each member of the presidency thereof, together with the bishoprics, might consider themselves honorably released from the mission given to them to settle in and build up that country, with permission to leave whenever it may suit their own convenience to settle wherever they may desire to.
>
> In taking this action however we particularly desire you and your people to know that in our deliberations we deeply sympathized with you, and felt grateful for the faith manifested by all those of our brethren and sisters who have so manfully contended against the great difficulties confronting you in the settlement of that region of country.
>
> We desire you to know also that in giving one and all this honorable release, it was not done for the purpose of breaking up and abandoning the places upon which so much labor has been spent; neither was it done in the spirit and feeling that the country is not worth redeeming and holding, but it was done so that all who desire to move away may feel perfectly free in changing the place of their residence; and it was done too in the belief that by far the greater part of the people would continue the struggle which they have so admirably carried on. Therefore to all who may conclude to leave we would say, Brethren and sisters, you have our love and blessing and fullest confidence, believing without the shadow of a doubt that you are entitled to the approbation and blessing of our Heavenly Father wherever you may go; and upon all who remain we shall continue to invoke the blessing of the Lord, both upon themselves and their labors, and all that pertains to them.[10]

The mission release did not prompt a mass exodus of Saints from St. Johns and the surrounding settlements, but a sizable number took advantage of the freedom granted to move on. Between 1905 and 1910, the Mormon population in St. Johns declined from 566 to 455.[11] In later

---

10. Joseph F. Smith, John R. Winder and Anthon H. Lund, letter to Prest. D. K. Udall and Counselors, June 13, 1905.

11. Abruzzi, *Dam That River!*, 139, n. 25.

years, many retirees moved to the Mesa-Phoenix area, so they could perform vicarious work for the dead in the Mesa Temple. Those who remained continued building dams, including the massive Lyman Dam, which was almost double the size of the Salado Dam. Completed in 1912, the walls of the Lyman Dam collapsed in April 1915, releasing a ferocious deluge that killed eight people as it carved a wide swath of destruction.[12]

The LeSueur-Gibbons murders played an indirect role in the selection of Mesa for a temple site. As Maricopa Stake President, James LeSueur was the leading voice in persuading Church authorities to build the temple in Mesa rather than Los Angeles, as many wanted. After Mesa was chosen, he played a vital role in financing and overseeing the temple's construction. He later said it was his vision of the spirit world following Frank's death that inspired and drove his efforts.[13] That vision also sustained James's lifelong passion for genealogy. In order to perform work on behalf of deceased ancestors, Mormons require not only their names, but also birth and death records, as well as the names of spouses and children, to ensure reliability, avoid duplication, and make certain all family members are sealed together. As a leading voice for genealogical research, James traveled throughout the western states gathering names, training local genealogists, helping build genealogical libraries in Mormon congregations, and encouraging Church leaders to call women as genealogists. James also led ten genealogical excursions to Denver, Salt Lake City, and Los Angeles during the 1930s, bringing along family members and fellow Mormons to scour government records, libraries, and other sources for information about their ancestors. James estimated that he and his family members found 168,265 new ancestors during these trips, while other participants found 182,000, for a total of more than 350,000 names to deliver to Mormon temples for vicarious baptisms and other ordinances.[14] His son, James K. LeSueur, said regarding his father's

---

12. Mormon Joseph Pearce observed that despite God's apparent support for their efforts, the Saints could not tame the "ugly temper" of the Little Colorado River. "Like one of the Elders prayed at the dedication of a dam: 'O Lord, we pray that this dam may stand if it be thy will—if not, let Thy will be done.' And the Lord's will was done over and over again" (Joseph Pearce, *Line Rider: A True Story of Stampedes, Gamblers, Indians and Outlaws Written by Arizona Ranger Joseph Pearce 1873–1958*, 1–2).

13. James Warren LeSueur, "Autobiographical Notes of My Life," 24.

14. LeSueur, "Autobiographical Notes," 64–65. These are corrected totals, as the numbers were added incorrectly in LeSueur's text.

enthusiasm for tracking down ancestors, "How well I remember his coming home after a long day of genealogical research and joyously saying, 'I found a new ancestor today' with more happiness than if he had found a million dollars."[15]

The Arizona Saints made sure they performed the temple rites for non-Mormon friends who had helped them settle the territory. One of those noteworthy friends was Commodore Perry Owens. Many Mormons believed that Owens's election as Apache County Sheriff was a literal answer to their prayers, and that his aggressive pursuit of lawbreakers during his term in office enabled them to stay in Arizona. Owens died May 10, 1919, at age sixty-six, in Seligman, Arizona. On June 8, 1920, Mark E. Karchner, a Mormon who had served as one of Sheriff Owens's bondsmen, was baptized on his behalf in the Salt Lake Temple. The next day, John Bushman, who believed that God had brought Owens to Arizona to protect Mormons, performed other temple ordinances on Owens's behalf. "Men like Sheriff Owens did as good a job of building as did others with their herds, teams, and ploughs," said George Crosby, a Mormon friend of Owens.[16]

Today, Latter-day Saints make no judgments regarding the worthiness of the people for whom they are vicariously baptized. Whether a person deserves a second chance in the spirit world is left to God. And so it is that Wild Bunch gang members who robbed banks and trains, murdered lawmen, and killed Frank LeSueur and Gus Gibbons, have had—or, eventually, will have—temple work performed on their behalf.[17] The same holds true for Robert LeRoy Parker, alias Butch Cassidy, and Harry Alonzo Longabaugh, alias the Sundance Kid. If the Mormons' conception of the afterlife is true, then I like to think that when these outlaws met their deaths and were ushered into their first indoctrination session, their instructors were Frank and Gus, perhaps teaching an introductory course on basic gospel principles and the Ten Commandments, including no. 6, "Thou shalt not kill."

---

15. From "Compiler's Preface," in LeSueur, "Autobiographical Notes."

16. Quoted in Della Crosby Smith, *The George Henry Crosby Family*, 65.

17. Genealogical records on the Mormon website, familysearch.org, show that the temple work has been completed for Will Carver, Ben Kilpatrick, Harvey Logan, and Harry Longabaugh. George LeRoy Parker's ordinances are not available for viewing on the website. Because of incomplete genealogical data, it is unclear whether temple work has been performed for Tom Capehart or Thomas C. Hilliard.

Afterword

From whence springs this desire to serve the dead? From the earliest times and across virtually every culture, the living have devised rituals that invest human remains with existential importance.[18] Modern humans fully embrace these traditions, despite our scientific understanding of the natural processes that break down the disenchanted body. We especially abhor the desecration of the corpse, such as Achilles dragging the body of Hector over the plains of Troy or the followers of General Mohamed Aidid dragging the body of a dead American soldier through the streets of the Somali capital. Even at great risk, the living will seek to retrieve a body atop a mountain or fallen in battle, though the dead themselves are beyond feeling or caring. "There seems to be a universally shared feeling not only that there is something deeply wrong about not caring for the dead body in some fashion, but also that the uncared-for body, no matter the cultural norms, is unbearable," says Thomas W. Laqueur, author of *The Work of the Dead: A Cultural History of Mortal Remains*. "The corpse demands the attention of the living."[19]

The manner in which the living pay that attention takes many forms. We build structures to house the dead, conduct rites to ease their transition into the next world, bury them in sacred clothes and sacred places, bury and honor them where they have fallen in battle, and gather their names and place them on lists and memorials. And so the dead live on. They live in our imaginations. They work, even in death, to give our lives meaning. "They dwell in us—individually and communally," Laqueur says.[20]

The Mormons' devotion to genealogical research and temple work, while not centered on the dead body, reflects the same universal impulse. Individual Mormons may spend hundreds of hours compiling the names of their ancestors. The Church likewise allocates significant administrative resources to verifying and organizing those names, and dispersing them to their temples, now approaching two hundred in number, where the vicarious ordinances take place. The spirits of the deceased, Mormons contend, are clamoring for the living to perform this work on their behalf.

The Church of Jesus Christ of Latter-day Saints is now the world's leading organization in promoting and shaping the practice of genealogy. FamilySearch International, the successor organization of the Church's

---

18. Thomas W. Laqueur, *The Work of the Dead: A Cultural History of Mortal Remains*, examines how and why the living have cared for the dead. For my discussion, see especially pages 1–9.

19. Laqueur, 8.

20. Laqueur, 17.

Genealogical Society of Utah, oversees a massive crowdsourcing effort aimed at tracing and mapping the entire family of humankind. Free and accessible to both Latter-day Saints and those once referred to as Gentiles, the familysearch.org website had more than twelve billion searchable names in its database as of January 2023, up from one billion names in 2010.[21] Users continually add new records to their ancestors' webpages—more than one million each day—in the form of birth and death certificates, marriage licenses, census data, and other government and church documents. Equally significant, people are also attaching photographs, letters, diaries, memoirs, newspaper articles, family histories, and other personal artifacts to their ancestors' webpages. This represents a treasure trove for the historian, though it also requires regularly monitoring familysearch.org webpages to keep up with the constant stream of new biographical information. Mormons have gone beyond merely documenting an individual's existence to recreating it and keeping the deceased alive. The dead dwell in them.

My interest in writing this history began when I learned that members of the Wild Bunch gang had murdered my great-uncle Frank LeSueur. Their notoriety drew me in. I knew relatively little about my LeSueur ancestors, except for the story told by James about seeing Frank preaching in the spirit world. I could not have found St. Johns on a map. But as I investigated Frank's murder, I became fascinated by the LeSueurs' story. And not just their story, but also the stories of the Gibbons, Kempes, Udalls, and other Mormon families called to settle one of the West's most lawless and unforgiving regions. Their diaries, letters, reminiscences, and other records provide an extraordinary window into their everyday lives, particularly into their struggle to build a lasting community. Is historical research and writing—the recreating of lives—also the work of the dead? As I read the pioneers' accounts, I felt their isolation and deprivation, their determination to succeed, their bewilderment at constant setbacks, their sorrow at tragic deaths, and their joy in small pleasures and warm friendships. I admired their resourcefulness, perseverance, and wry humor that carried them through grim times. And I wept, as they must have wept with both sadness and relief, when I read the First Presidency's letter honorably releasing them from their colonizing mission after twenty-five years of faithful sacrifice. They dwell in me.

---

21. "FamilySearch.org Facts," FamilySearch.org. In addition to its online resources, the church also has more than 5,700 Family History Centers throughout the world staffed with volunteers to assist people in their genealogical research.

The St. Johns Mormons ardently believed the end of the world was fast approaching. Morris K. "Mo" Udall, a grandson of Bishop David K. Udall, offered a unique perspective regarding their proximity to the world's end. Born in 1922 and raised in St. Johns, where he played basketball and football, Mo Udall and his brother Stewart rose to national prominence in American politics. Stewart served as Secretary of the Interior under Presidents John F. Kennedy and Lyndon B. Johnson from 1961 to 1968; Mo served thirty years as a U.S. Representative from Arizona and was a leading contender for the Democratic presidential nomination in 1976. Regarding the isolated frontier town where he grew up, Mo Udall observed, "St. Johns is not the end of the world, but you sure as hell can see it from there."[22]

St. Johns's desolate, end-of-the-world appearance did not go unnoticed by Church authorities from Salt Lake City. When Apostle Rudger Clawson visited St. Johns for the first time in 1900, he was accompanied by fellow Apostle Heber J. Grant and J. Golden Kimball, one of the seven presidents of the Council of Seventy. While stopped at the Holbrook train station waiting for a carriage to take them to St. Johns, the three men talked about the many out-of-the-way Mormon settlements along the Little Colorado River. Clawson said he "wondered how the saints ever found all these nooks and corners."[23]

"When you see them you will wonder how they live there," Grant replied.

Kimball was impressed by what he saw. Eight years later, while speaking at the Church's semiannual conference in the Salt Lake City Tabernacle, he offered this assessment of the St. Johns Saints:

> I would like to take you on a trip down to Arizona, in the St. Johns country. I preached Faith there once, but I want to tell you I haven't got enough faith to stay in such undesirable country. You talk about good people; you talk about righteous people; I tell you there are people in this city who are not worthy to unlatch their shoestrings. That hard country, and their obedience to the Priesthood of God, has made those men great characters. You can't discourage them. They will build a dam across the Colorado River every five years, if it washes out the next day; and live on dry bread and molasses. Yet, that is their home; and that is their country; and there they worship God. . . . I tell you that the Almighty is not pleased with some of the rising generation. They stick up their noses at these homely men. It is such homely men and

---

22. Tom Beal, "St. Johns Hardships Legion, but Mormons Stood Firm."
23. Joseph Fish, "The Life and Times of Joseph Fish, Mormon Pioneer," 416.

women of character who have made this country, and this Church, what it is today, and I say God bless them.[24]

The Mormons who settled the St. Johns region were not without flaws. Although they moved into an established community, they sought to keep themselves apart from their Mexican-American neighbors. Their opinion of their neighbors, at least at first, was no less prejudiced than their neighbors' opinion of them. Many Church leaders feared that mixing with Gentiles would lead to apostasy. Such clannishness did not serve them well, particularly in a town and county with a large non-Mormon population. With regard to polygamy, the Mormons were unrepentant lawbreakers who viewed polygamy prosecutions as undisguised religious persecution. In their reminiscences, Mormon men and women often said they recoiled in horror when the concept of polygamy was first introduced to them. Yet they refused to believe that non-Mormon opposition to the practice could arise from the same strongly held cultural and religious mores. That's not to say that political opportunists didn't cynically whip up anti-polygamy fervor to their advantage, especially to label the Mormons' practice of polygamy as a clear sign that "they" do not accept "our" American values. Mormon clannishness strengthened this perception. Much of the political and legal opposition directed at the St. Johns Mormons dissipated when they started working with the Mexican-American and gentile communities to address common problems. Relations also improved after the Mormon prophet issued the 1890 Manifesto that significantly scaled back the number of new polygamous unions, though prosecutions for illegal cohabitation continued into the twentieth century. Those who settled St. Johns, both Mormons and non-Mormons, were rugged individuals. Nevertheless, it was not rugged individualism but community and collaboration that enabled them to survive.

The Mormons' closer relationship with the non-Mormon community served to undermine Mormon values to some degree, though not in the way Church leaders feared or even recognized. By aligning themselves with Apache County's law-and-order movement, the Mormons became supporters of extralegal methods to enforce the law. Their stance is understandable, given that local sheriffs and judges had been unable to rein in the outlaw gangs that excited real fears and inflicted significant economic losses on the Mormon community. But as a result, the Mormons be-

---

24. Bonnie Taylor, ed., *The Sermons of J. Golden Kimball, December 1891-April 1938*, 101–2, April 1908 General Conference.

came cheerleaders for the violent expulsion of people merely suspected of wrongdoing. They appear to have been untroubled by the lynching—essentially, murder—of three cowboys. Even the ever-conscientious Bishop Udall accepted the violence against their enemies as necessary and justified, though he was careful to point out that it was not done by Mormons. The Mormons did not recognize the irony that they once had been victims of extralegal violence aimed at defending law and order. In Missouri and Illinois, everyday citizens, believing the Mormons to be lawbreakers and a cancer on respectable society, drove the Saints from their homes when legal means proved incapable of defending community values.

When the Mormons began settling St. Johns in 1880, the town's existing population numbered about 400 people, nearly all Spanish-speaking people of Mexican descent.[25] Forty-two of the working residents in the Mexican-American community, about 30 percent, were farmers. In 1900, the St. Johns census district consisted of nearly 850 people, of which slightly less than 400 were non-Mormons of Mexican or other descent. In addition, the number of Mexican-American farmers had declined to just nine, or about 8 percent of the working population in that community. Interestingly, the number of Mexican-American sheepherders experienced an offsetting increase from nine sheepherders in 1880 to forty-two in 1900, with many of them working for Mormon sheep owners such as J.T. LeSueur. In short, the Mexican-American population remained roughly the same size in 1900 as it had been in 1880. The Mormons had not pushed aside their neighbors, but their emigration into St. Johns had the precise effect the Mexican-Americans had feared: the Mormon influx effectively prevented further growth of their community.

One may wonder why some Mormons prospered while others did not. J.T. LeSueur and Bill Gibbons, for example, had the advantage of being among the first to arrive. Fewer opportunities awaited those who came in later years. In addition, LeSueur and Gibbons had multiple sources of income. Gibbons initially hauled freight and farmed after arriving in St. Johns, but he also raised sheep and served as constable, as county treasurer, and on the county board of supervisors. LeSueur was even more diversified, investing in multiple businesses, including a pharmacy, a newspaper, a cooperative store, and sheep raising. Both families planted vegetable and fruit gardens. Gibbons also had fruit trees, and LeSueur may have as well. Most families, if not all, raised vegetables and fruits. Many also had

---

25. These statistics are drawn from St. Johns census records for 1880 and 1900.

chickens and cows. It appears that a large portion of those who struggled were farmers. Droughts, short growing seasons, grasshoppers, and other challenges made farming a precarious undertaking. The region could not support a large number of farmers, certainly not the additional one hundred families sent to colonize St. Johns in 1884. LeSueur, who grew quite wealthy, claimed not to have any special business acumen. "I had most always been lucky in all places where I had lived," he wrote, stating that his success was "not because of any particular financial ability."[26] LeSueur's assertion betrays a touch of false modesty, but it also reflects a lifetime of watching many equally hardworking families fail economically. It also reflects his own experience losing nearly everything in the 1920s to bank failure amid an economic depression. Mormons who successfully established themselves in St. Johns might have been tempted to attribute their good fortune to personal righteousness. After all, the scriptures teach—and their leaders preached—that God rewards His people for their faith and good works, both spiritually and temporally. But experience taught them that good fortune was as unpredictable as the weather, their piety notwithstanding. They dared not tempt God by suggesting they possessed divine favor or were more resolute than the families forced by poverty to abandon their missions. Those who persevered may have felt some measure of pride in their accomplishment—and deservedly so—but the people who left the colonizing mission were not typically shunned or scorned. Just the opposite. The families that left often received a warm sendoff and heartfelt best wishes from those who remained.[27]

What impact did the killings have on the Wild Bunch? In the short run, the outlaws were forced into perilous lives on the run. Posses from Arizona, New Mexico, Utah, and Wyoming scoured Western mountains and trails, and staked out known hideouts in an effort to capture the suspected murderers. Cassidy, who was sitting in the St. Johns jail when news of the LeSueur-Gibbons murders reached town, had a front-row seat to the unfolding human consequences of his gang's activities. These weren't faceless railroad and bank executives but innocent young men who stumbled

---

26. "Memoirs of John Taylor LeSueur," in *LeSueur Family History*.

27. For example, when H. J. Platt and his family left St. Johns to seek better opportunities in southern Arizona's Gila valley, his Mormon friends held a party "to give him a good 'send off,' as we do to all who leave us," said a local correspondent for the *Deseret Evening News*. "Many remarks were made, showing that Brother Platt was appreciated by his neighbors" (*Deseret Evening News*, January 31, 1900, 7).

into an ambush. He would have heard discussions between Sheriff Beeler and his deputies about finding the murdered boys, and perhaps even overheard or saw distraught family members who came to the jail to consult with Beeler. But whatever Cassidy and his fellow outlaws may have felt about the murders, once the posses disbanded, they began planning their next robberies. To be sure, Tod Carver and Tom Capehart appear to have left the gang, but Harvey Logan, Will Carver, and Ben Kilpatrick, along with Butch Cassidy and the Sundance Kid, pulled off two of the gang's most successful heists in August and September of 1900. They proceeded with business as usual, as if their murderous rampage and near capture had never occurred.

We don't have to speculate regarding how the murders affected the Mormon community. Newspaper accounts described a town enveloped in gloom, and a chapel echoing with the wails and cries of the bereaved. Even as far away as the Church's Salt Lake City headquarters, the young men's death "came as a fearful shock to us all," Apostle Heber J. Grant said.[28] On March 27, 1901, exactly one year after Frank and Gus were killed, Bill Gibbons and James LeSueur erected five-foot high stone cairns where each of the young men's bodies were found, and placed stone tablets on the cairns describing the circumstances of their murders. "Long shall the citizens of this country remember the bravery with which these young martyrs met their death trying to establish law and order," the *St. Johns Herald* wrote regarding the commemoration.[29]

Bill and Gusty Gibbons lost not only their son, but also, ultimately, their daughter-in-law. Pearl Gibbons left St. Johns and returned home, later remarrying and raising a family in Utah with another man. Gus's murder rocked Bill's faith for a time, but he steadied, and the family endured, though their lingering heartbreak found expression in their animosity toward Sheriff Beeler. Beeler recognized that he had failed the community, particularly the murdered men's families. His obsessive quest to capture the killers was driven, at least in part, by a sense of responsibility, even guilt. The murders derailed his once-promising career as a lawman. The LeSueur family persevered, finding strength in James LeSueur's vision of Frank safe in God's presence. J.T. LeSueur believed firmly in the reality of this vision. In his memoir, J.T. said he received a visit from his deceased wife, Geneva, further affirming his belief in the afterlife. But such faith could not erase the pain of Frank's death. Their once wild and

---

28. Heber J. Grant, letter to David K. Udall, April 11, 1900.
29. *St. Johns Herald*, March 30, 1901, 1.

rebellious son had finally found his footing, only to die on the cusp of manhood. Even thirty-eight years later, J.T. would say of Frank's murder, "It was a shock and a blow to us that we cannot overcome in our lives."[30]

More than a century of wind and rain have eroded the soil and carved deep gullies into the mesa draw where Frank and Gus were killed, but the two cairns erected by Bill Gibbons and James LeSueur still rise above the prairie grass to mark the spots where searchers found the young men's bodies. Family members periodically hike to the place and replenish the stones so their lives—and deaths—are not forgotten.

---

30. "Memoirs of John Taylor LeSueur," (written June 1, 1938).

ACKNOWLEDGMENTS

I started researching the LeSueur-Gibbons murders nearly a decade ago after I volunteered to give a short presentation about the episode at a family reunion. I became so fascinated by the topic that my planned twenty-minute talk swelled into a two-hour PowerPoint presentation replete with photographs, maps, bullet-point chronologies, and outlines of family trees. I was subsequently encouraged to write more about the subject but advised not to give any more presentations without a strictly enforced time limit.

I have been helped along in my research by librarians and archivists from numerous libraries and institutions, both in person and via email. Those deserving my thanks include the following:

- Rachel Black and Perri Pyle, Archivists & Librarians, Arizona Historical Society
- Janelle Breedveld, Federal Documents Librarian, State of Arizona Research Library
- Wendy Goen, Lead Reference and Photograph Archivist, Arizona State Archives
- Julia Huddleston, Archivist, Special Collections, J. Willard Marriott Library, University of Utah
- Dena Hunt, Senior Archivist, State Archives of New Mexico
- Susan M. Irwin, vice president of Library and Archives, Arizona Historical Society
- Ryan K. Lee, Curator, 19th Century Mormon and Western Manuscripts, L. Tom Perry Special Collections, Brigham Young University
- Gwendolyn Sherwood, LDS Family History Center, St. Johns, Arizona
- Heidi Stringham, Reference Staff, Research Center of the Utah State Archives & Utah State History
- Suzi Taylor, Reference Archivist, Wyoming State Archives
- Tyson Thorpe, Reference Coordinator, LDS History Library, Salt Lake City

I was also assisted by librarians and other staff members at the Library of Congress Manuscript Division and the library's Duplication Services. In St. Johns, I received assistance from employees with the Sheriff's Office and Clerk of the Court in Apache County, Arizona.

Daniel Buck, who has written extensively about Butch Cassidy and the Wild Bunch, patiently answered many questions and generously shared his knowledge, offering both encouragement and insight. Also helpful in examining various aspects of Western outlaw history and lore were Bob Goodwin, Mike Bell, and Donna Donnell.

Family members from the LeSueur and Gibbons families shared research materials and photographs. Carl W. LeSueur, Don L. LeSueur, and Leo M. LeSueur of the LeSueur Family organization were especially helpful in this regard. Don compiled an excellent LeSueur family history of recollections, letters, and photographs. Arvin Palmer, a descendant of Gus Gibbons's younger sister, Eva, gave me insight into the Gibbons family. Arvin, who is now deceased, compiled and edited an invaluable Gibbons family history.

Nonie Harmon shared with me a photograph of Edward Beeler and a typescript of Mary Beeler's journal begun shortly after her husband's murder. Nancy E. Brown shared with me her research into Beeler's life.

St. Johns resident Rick Pearce guided me to the LeSueur-Gibbons murder site, where stone cairns still mark the place where the young men's bodies were found. Rick has helped many individuals and groups of relatives who have journeyed to the murder site.

A special thanks goes to Abner Hardy, who created the maps under the supervision of Dr. Brandon Plewe at ThinkSpatial, BYU Geography.

The website familysearch.org proved to be an invaluable source of genealogical information, as well as a source for family histories, reminiscences, and legal documents. Maurine Clift Nuttall, a genealogist and family historian, helped me navigate the website and understand how to use its resources.

Also deserving thanks is Loyd Isao Ericson, managing editor of Greg Kofford Books. Loyd has been enthusiastic and supportive, provided excellent guidance and suggestions, and responded quickly to questions and concerns along the way. The journey from the submission of my manuscript to its publication has been swift and easy.

As is the case with any historical work, I benefited immensely from the efforts of historians who preceded me. Even when I disagree with and offer corrections to some of their conclusions, I recognize that their research has contributed to my own. I have also had the advantage of new source materials now available, including those that have become more accessible due to the rise of digital technologies. You will find the names of these historians in the footnotes and bibliography.

Finally, I was fortunate to have friends and scholars read and critique drafts of my manuscript. They are Daniel Buck; Bob Goodwin; Steve Gregory; Craig Jolley; Carl W. LeSueur; Jeffrey C. LeSueur; Gregory A. Prince; Kathy Reeder; and Dean Rehberger. All offered insights and recommendations, asked needed questions, and overall sharpened my thinking and writing, as well as alerted me to potential errors. Of course, I am responsible for this history, including any errors, but these people contributed to whatever merit readers may find in this book.

One of those who read my manuscript is my wife, Kathy Reeder. Kathy not only reviewed drafts of the book, but she also read and critiqued short articles about these events, sat through numerous presentations, accompanied me to St. Johns and nearby locations, and listened to me talk endlessly about the book. I relied extensively on her feedback and advice.

WORKS CITED

Abruzzi, William S. *Dam That River! Ecology and Mormon Settlement in the Little Colorado River Basin*. Lanham, MD: University Press of America, 1993.

Allen, James B., Jessie L. Embry, and Kahlile B. Mehr. *Hearts Turned to the Fathers: A History of the Genealogical Society of Utah, 1894–1994*. Provo, UT: BYU Studies, 1995.

Alverson, Leonard. "Reminiscences of Leonard Alverson," as told to Mrs. George F. Kitt, October 8, 1938. Typescript. Leonard Alverson Personal Correspondence, 1933–1939. Arizona Historical Society, Tucson.

Anderson, Charles P. *Journal of Charles P. Anderson: Writings from 1856–1913*. N.p.: Gilbert Publishing Co., 1975.

Apache County Board of Supervisors Minutes. State of Arizona Library and Archives, Phoenix.

Apache County Jail Records, Arizona.

"Arizona Line of Duty Deaths." Officer Down Memorial Page, accessed August 17, 2022. https://www.odmp.org/search/browse/arizona.

Arnett, Susan Inez Sherwood, ed. "The Life History of William Wellington and Erma Udall Sherwood & Their Descendants." Typescript. Familysearch.org.

Arrington, Leonard J., and Davis Bitton. *The Mormon Experience: A History of the Latter-day Saints*. New York: Alfred A. Knopf, 1979.

Arrington, Leonard J. *Great Basin Kingdom: An Economic History of the Latter-day Saints 1830–1900*. Salt Lake City: University of Utah Press and Tanner Trust Fund, 1993 [1958].

Arrott, Myrl Tenney. "Sarah Priscilla Leavitt Hamblin: Pioneer Midwife." Typescript. The Church of Jesus Christ of Latter-day Saints Church History Library, Salt Lake City.

Axford, Joseph "Mack." *Around Western Campfires*. Tucson: University of Arizona Press, 1969.

Bair, JoAnn W., and Richard L Jensen. "Prosecution of the Mormons in Arizona Territory in the 1880s." *Arizona and the West* 19, no. 1 (Spring 1977): 25–46.

Ball, Larry D. "Commodore Perry Owens: The Man Behind the Legend." *The Journal of Arizona History* 33, no. 1 (Spring 1992): 27–56.

———. *Desert Lawmen: The High Sheriffs of New Mexico and Arizona, 1846–1912*. Albuquerque: University of New Mexico Press, 1992.

Barnes, Will C. *Apaches and Longhorns: The Reminiscences of Will C. Barnes*. Edited by Frank C. Lockwood. Tuscon: University of Arizona Press, 1982.

Baugh, Alexander L. "'For This Ordinance Belongeth to My House': The Practice of Baptism for the Dead Outside the Nauvoo Temple." *Mormon Historical Studies* 3, no. 1 (Spring 2002): 47–58.

Beal, Tom. "St. Johns Hardships Legion, but Mormons Stood Firm." *Arizona Daily Star*, September 18, 2011.

Beeler, Mary Elizabeth Hamblin. Journal. Typescript in author's possession.

Bell, Mike. *Butch and Sundance in South America: New Evidence of Their Lives and Death*. London: The English Westerners' Society, 2021.

———. "Butch Cassidy and the Great Western Horse Thief War." Unpublished paper.

———. *Incidents on Owl Creek: Butch Cassidy's Big Horn Basin Bunch and the Wyoming Horsethief War*. Leeds, West Yorkshire, UK: Book Empire, 2013.

———. *Wyoming Outlaws: Butch Cassidy in Wyoming, 1889–1896*. London: The English Westerners' Society, 2020.

Betenson, Bill. *Butch Cassidy, My Uncle: A Family Portrait*. Glendo, WY: High Plains Press, 2014.

———. *Butch Cassidy, The Wyoming Years*. Glendo, WY: High Plains Press, 2020.

Betenson, Lula Parker and Dora Flack. *Butch Cassidy, My Brother*. New York: Penguin Books, 1976.

Bishop, M. Guy. "'What Has Become of Our Fathers?' Baptism for the Dead at Nauvoo." *Dialogue: A Journal of Mormon Thought* 23, no. 2 (Summer 1990): 85–97.

Blythe, Christopher James. "Ann Booth's Vision and Early Conceptions of Redeeming the Dead among Latter-day Saints." *BYU Studies Quarterly* 56, no. 2 (2017): 105–22.

Blythe, John. "History of John A. Blythe." Typescript. Brigham Young University Harold B. Lee Library, L. Tom Perry Special Collections, Provo, UT.

Boardman, Mark. "A Tall Order? What We Don't Know about Wild Bunch Member Ben Kilpatrick." *True West: History of the American Frontier*, March 13, 2010. https://truewestmagazine.com/article/a-tall-order.

Boessenecker, John. *Shotguns and Stagecoaches: The Brave Men Who Rode for Wells Fargo in the Wild West*. New York: Thomas Dunne Books, 2018.

Boggs, Johnny D. "Interview with Author Mark Smokov." *Historynet*, March 3, 2013. http://www.historynet.com/interview-with-author-mark-smokov.htm.

Brown, Errol G., comp. *The Greer Family and A Look Into The Past*. Kanab, Utah: Quality Printing Company, n.d.

Brown, Lorenzo. "The Journal of Lorenzo Brown, 1823–1900." Typescript. The Church of Jesus Christ of Latter-day Saints Church History Library, Salt Lake City.

Brown, Samuel M. "Early Mormon Adoption Theology and the Mechanics of Salvation." *Journal of Mormon History* 37, no. 3 (Summer 2011): 3–52.

Bruno, Cheryl L., Joe Steve Swick III, and Nicholas S. Literski. *Method Infinite: Freemasonry and the Mormon Restoration*. Salt Lake City: Greg Kofford Books, 2022.

Buck, Daniel. "Bandit Resurrections: Who Was the Real Sundance Kid?" *Appendix* 2, no. 1 (January 2014): 70–75.

———. "Butch Cassidy Sought Amnesty, Fact or Folklore?" *Wild West History Association Journal* 5, no. 6 (December 2012): 39–51.

Buck, Daniel, and Anne Meadows. "Butch & Sundance: Still Dead?" *Quarterly for the National Association of Outlaws and Lawmen History* 30, no. 2 (April–June 2006): 40–49.

———. "Butch Cassidy and the Sundance Kid." In *The Mythical West: An Encyclopedia of Legend, Lore, and Popular Culture*, ed. Richard W. Slatta, 63–70. Santa Barbara: ABC-CLIO, 2001.

———. "Did Butch Cassidy Return? His Family Can't Decide," *Western Outlaw and Lawmen Association Journal* 6, no. 3 (Spring 1998): 24–34, 48.

———. *The End of the Road: Butch Cassidy and the Sundance Kid in Bolivia*. London: The English Westerners' Society, 2017.
———. "The Sundance Kid in Chile: Boyds Will Be Boyds." *Wild West History Association Journal* 15, no. 4 (December 2022): 18–49.
———. "The Wild Bunch: Wild, but not Much of a Bunch." *True West* 49, no. 8 (November/December 2002): 29.
———. "Wild Bunch Miscellanea." *Wild West History Association Journal* 8, no. 4 (August 2015): 35–41.
Buerger, David John. *The Mysteries of Godliness: A History of Mormon Temple Worship*. San Francisco: Smith Research Associates, 1994.
Burton, Jeffrey. *The Deadliest Outlaws: The Ketchum Gang and the Wild Bunch*. Denton, TX: University of North Texas Press, 2012.
Campbell, Eugene E. *Establishing Zion: The Mormon Church in the American West, 1847–1869*. Salt Lake City: Signature Books, 1988.
Carlock, Robert H. *The Hashknife: The Early Days of the Aztec Land and Cattle Company, Limited*. Tucson, AZ: Westernlore Press, 1994.
"Charles Godfrey DeFriez Jarvis." Typescript. Familysearch.org.
Christison, Parley P. "A Short Sketch of My Life." Typescript, 1931. Familysearch.org.
Clarke, Mary Whatley. *The Slaughter Ranches & Their Makers*. Austin, TX: Jenkins Publishing Company, 1979.
Coleman, Evans. "Do You Remember." Evans Coleman Papers. Arizona Historical Society, Tucson.
———. Letter to The Arizona Pioneer's Historical Society, January 22, 1953. Evans Coleman Papers. Arizona Historical Society, Tucson.
———. Letter to The Arizona Pioneer's Historical Society, February 7, 1953. Evans Coleman Papers. Arizona Historical Society, Tucson.
———. "Nesters, Rustlers and Outlaws." *The Journal of Arizona History* 14, no. 3 (Autumn 1973): 177–84.
———. "Reminiscences of an Arizona Cowboy." Edited by Frank C. Lockwood. Typescript. Evans Coleman Papers, Arizona Historical Society, Tucson.
———. "Saint Johns Purchase." Typescript. Mormon Settlements in Arizona Collection, 1857–1986. University of Utah J. Willard Marriott Library Special Collections, Salt Lake City.
Compton, Todd M. *A Frontier Life: Jacob Hamblin, Explorer and Indian Missionary*. Salt Lake City: University of Utah Press, 2013.
Cooper, Dona Lucile Johnson. "A Combination of Simple Biographies, Autobiographies and Histories of the Areas They Settled and the Part They Played in Opening Up the Arizona Territory." For Benjamin Samuel "Sam" Johnson; Susan Elvira Martineau; Reddin "Frank" Reddick Allred; Mary Matilda Park; Samuel "Jodie" Joseph Johnson; Cora May Allred, 2011. Typescript. Familysearch.org.
Cowan, Richard O. "The Historic Arizona Temple." *Journal of Mormon History* 31, no. 1 (Spring 2005): 99–118.
Crigler, Winkie. *Beans 'N' Things*. Mesa, AZ: Mead Publishing, 1993.
Crosby, George H. "As My Memory Recalls: Stories of the Colonizing of the Little Colorado River Country." Compiled by Laprele Crosby Nunnery. Typescript. The Church of Jesus Christ of Latter-day Saints Church History Library, Salt Lake City.

Crosby, John T. Interview by Carl W. LeSueur, January 16, 2002. Transcript in author's possession.
———. Letter to Philip J. Rasch, December 21, 1978. Philip J. Rasch Collection. Arizona Historical Society, Tucson.
Crowther, Duane S. *Life Everlasting: A Definitive Study of Life After Death*. Bountiful, UT: Horizon Publishers, 1998 [1967].
Dalton, Rodney Garth. "From Knights to Dreamers: The Journey of Our Utah Dalton Family from Early 1100 AD to 2007 AD and Beyond," 5 vols. Typescript. Available at https://www.daltondatabank.org/DaltonChronicles.htm.
Davisson, Lori. "Arizona Law Enforcement: A Survey from the Collections of the Arizona Historical Society." *The Journal of Arizona History* 27, no. 3 (Autumn 1986): 315–48.
DeArment, Robert K. *George Scarborough: The Life and Death of a Lawman on the Closing Frontier*. Norman and London: University of Oklahoma Press, 1992.
Eaton, John. *Will Carver, Outlaw*. San Angelo, TX: Anchor Publishing Co., 1972.
Ellsworth, Maria S., ed. *Mormon Odyssey: The Story of Ida Hunt Udall, Plural Wife*. Urbana and Chicago: University of Illinois Press, 1992.
Ernst, Donna B. "A Deadly Year for St. Johns Lawmen." *Quarterly of the National Association for Outlaw and Lawman History, Inc.* 25, no. 1 (January–March 2001): 18–21.
———. "The Real Tom Capehart." *The Journal of the Western Outlaw-Lawman History Association* 9, no. 2 (Summer 2000): 38–41.
———. "Unraveling Two Outlaws Named Carver." *The Journal of the Western Outlaw-Lawman History Association* 7, no. 2 (Fall 1997): 30–32.
———. "Will Carver alias Will Casey." *Old West* 32, no. 1 (Fall 1995): 22–25.
"FamilySearch.org Facts." FamilySearch.org, updated January 2023. https://www.familysearch.org/en/newsroom/company-facts.
Fish, Joseph. "History of the Arizona Territory." Typescript. Joseph Fish Papers, Arizona Historical Society, Tucson.
———. "History of the Eastern Arizona Stake of Zion and of the Establishment of the Snowflake Stake." Typescript. Familysearch.org
———. "The Life and Times of Joseph Fish, Mormon Pioneer." Typescript. Familysearch.org.
Folkman, Kevin H. "'The Moste Desert Lukking Plase I Ever Saw, Amen!' The 'Failed' 1873 Arizona Mission to the Little Colorado River." *Journal of Mormon History* 37, no. 1 (Winter 2011): 115–50.
Francis, A. G. "The End of an Outlaw." *The Wide World Magazine* (May 1913): 36–43.
French, William. *Recollections of a Western Ranchman*. Silver City, NM: High-Lonesome Books, 1990 [1928].
Fritz, Scott E. "Merchants of St. Johns, 1876–1885: A Study In Group Formation, Bigoted Rhetoric, And Economic Competition." Arizona Historical Convention papers, 2009. Arizona Historical Society, Tucson.
Garcia, Vince. "The Wilcox, Wyoming Train Robbery—As It Happened." *Wild West History Association Journal* 13, no. 2 (June 2020): 65–84
Gibbons, Andrew A. Letter to Wilford Woodruff, July 28, 1897. First Presidency missionary calls and recommendations, 1877–1918. The Church of Jesus Christ of Latter-day Saints Church History Library, Salt Lake City. Available at https://catalog.churchofjesuschrist.org/record/5a1b20a1-9b49-40af-ae42-26161f8e479e/0.
Gibbons, Clarissa Isabell Wilhelm. "A Short Sketch of My Life." Written January 18, 1934. Typescript in author's possession.

Gibbons, Richard. "Diary of Richard Gibbons, Copied from His Own Daily Journal and Covering the Time from March 16, 1888 until His Death on January 1, 1924." Typescript. Familysearch.org.
Golding, Lois Hamblin, and Delma Golding Johnson. *Our Golden Heritage: The Duane and Addie Noble Hamblin Family.* N.p., 1977.
Grant, Heber J. Letter to David K. Udall, April 11, 1900. Udall Family Correspondence Collection, 1859–1950. The Church of Jesus Christ of Latter-day Saints Church History Library, Salt Lake City.
Grasse, David. *A Killer is What They Needed: The True, Untold Story of Commodore Perry Owens, a Sheriff of the Arizona Territory.* Santa Ana, CA: Graphic Publishers, 2013.
Greer, Robert. "San Juan Dia 1882." Typescript. David K Udall Papers. University of Arizona (Tucson) Libraries Special Collections.
Guinn, Jeff. *The Last Gunfight: The Real Story of the Shootout at the O.K. Corral—And How It Changed the American West.* New York: Simon & Schuster Paperbacks, 2012.
Hamilton, Patrick. *The Resources of Arizona. Its Mineral, Farming, Grazing and Timber Lands; Its History, Climate, Productions, Civil And Military Government, Pre-Historic Ruins, Early Missionaries, Indian Tribes, Pioneer Days, Etc., Etc.* San Francisco: A. L. Bancroft & Company, printers, 1884.
Harrell, Charles R. *"This is My Doctrine": The Development of Mormon Theology.* Salt Lake City: Greg Kofford Books, 2011.
Hartley, William G. "Coming to Zion: Saga of the Gathering," *Ensign,* July 1975. Available at https://www.churchofjesuschrist.org/study/ensign/1975/07/coming-to-zion-saga-of-the-gathering.
Hastings, Amanda. "Memorandum." Amanda Christina Kempe Hastings Collection, Brigham Young University Harold B. Lee Library, L. Tom Perry Special Collections, Provo, UT.
Hatch, Lorenzo Hill. Journal. *Typescript.* Brigham Young University Harold B. Lee Library, L. Tom Perry Special Collections, Provo, UT.
Hatch, Thom. *The Last Outlaws: The Lives and Legends of Butch Cassidy and the Sundance Kid.* New York: New American Library, 2013.
Heap, Anona Crosby. "Mother of Mine." Typescript. Familysearch.org.
Herman, Daniel Justin. *Hell on the Range: A Story of Honor, Conscience, and the American West.* New Haven & London: Yale University Press, 2010.
"History." Arizona Rangers, accessed April 3, 2023. https://azrangers.us/history/.
Hobsbawm, Eric. *Bandits.* New York: Pantheon Books, 1981.
Hoopes, Roy. "My Grandfather, The Mormon Apostle." *American Heritage* 41, no. 1 (February 1990): https://www.americanheritage.com/content/my-grandfather-mormon-apostle.
Horan, James D. *The Authentic Wild West: The Outlaws.* New York: Gramercy Books, 1995 [1977].
Hunt, Frazier. *Cap Mossman: Last of the Great Cowmen.* New York: Hastings House, 1951.
"Inquest held Jan. 12th 1901 over the body of Monte Slaughter." Apache County Courthouse, St. Johns, AZ.
Irving, Gordon. "The Law of Adoption: One Phase of The Development of The Mormon Concept of Salvation, 1830–1900." *BYU Studies* 14, no. 3 (Spring 1974): 1–21 (reprint).
Jensen, Jody. "Birth of the Arizona Rangers." *Old West* (Spring 1982): 30–33.

———. "Richard Gibbons: Arizona Pioneer," *Ensign*, September 1982. Available at https://www.lds.org/ensign/1982/09/richard-gibbons-arizona-pioneer.

Jenson, Andrew. *Latter-Day Saint Biographical Encyclopedia*, 4 vols. Salt Lake City: Deseret News, 1941; rpt, Salt Lake City: Greg Kofford Books, 2012.

"John and Caroline LeSueur Family." Typescript. The Church of Jesus Christ of Latter-day Saints Church History Library, Salt Lake City.

Joyce, Barry A. "The Temple and the Rock: James W. Lesueur and the Synchronization of Sacred Space in the American Southwest." *Journal of Mormon History* 43, no. 2 (April 2017): 131–48.

Kelly, Charles. *The Outlaw Trail: A History of Butch Cassidy and the Wild Bunch*. Lincoln and London: University of Nebraska Press, 1996 [1938].

Laqueur, Thomas W. *The Work of the Dead: A Cultural History of Mortal Remains*. Princeton and Oxford: Princeton University Press, 2015.

Leerhsen, Charles. *Butch Cassidy: The True Story of an American Outlaw*. New York: Simon and Schuster, 2018.

LeSueur, Don L., comp. *LeSueur Family History: Descendants of John T. LeSueur and William F. LeSueur*. Mesa: n.p., 1990.

LeSueur, Frank. Letter to President Lorenzo Snow, February 18, 1900. First Presidency missionary calls and recommendations, 1877–1918. The Church of Jesus Christ of Latter-day Saints Church History Library, Salt Lake City. Available at https://catalog.churchofjesuschrist.org/record/5a1b20a1-9b49-40af-ae42-26161f8e479e/0.

LeSueur, J. T. Letter to Elder George Reynolds, July 12, 1897. First Presidency missionary calls and recommendations, 1877–1918. The Church of Jesus Christ of Latter-day Saints Church History Library, Salt Lake City. Available at https://catalog.churchofjesuschrist.org/record/5a1b20a1-9b49-40af-ae42-26161f8e479e/0.

———. Letter to Elder George Reynolds, July 29, 1897. First Presidency missionary calls and recommendations, 1877–1918. The Church of Jesus Christ of Latter-day Saints Church History Library, Salt Lake City. Available at https://catalog.churchofjesuschrist.org/record/5a1b20a1-9b49-40af-ae42-26161f8e479e/0.

LeSueur, James Warren. "Autobiographical Notes of My Life." Typescript. The Church of Jesus Christ of Latter-day Saints Church History Library, Salt Lake City.

———. "A Patriarchal Blessing and its Fulfillment." *Juvenile Instructor* (March 1919): 122–25.

———. "Regarding Salvation for the Dead." *Relief Society Magazine* (April 1920): 199–202.

"Letters Written by Ed Beeler to His Family in 1887 & 1898." RoundValleyAZ.com, accessed May 5, 2023. https://www.roundvalleyaz.com/beeler1.html.

Long, Genevieve J. "Laboring in the Desert: The Letters and Diaries of Narcissa Prentiss Whitman and Ida Hunt Udall." PhD Dissertation: University of Oregon, December 2002.

Loomis, John A. *Texas Ranchman: The Memoirs of John A. Loomis*. Chadron, NE: The Fur Press, 1982.

Lucas, Robert. "St. Johns: Town of Friendly Neighbors Had Unfriendly Start." *Arizona100—An Arizona History Blog*, May 21, 2011. http://arizona100.blogspot.com/2011/05/st.html.

Lyman, Edward Leo. "Elimination of the Mormon Issue from Arizona Politics, 1889–1894." *Arizona and the West* 24, no. 3 (Autumn, 1982): 205–28.

Lynch, Sylvia, *Harvey Logan in Knoxville*. College Station, TX: Creative Publishing, 1998.

Lyon, William H. "Live, Active Men, With Plenty of 'Push': Arizona's Territorial Immigration Commissioners." *The Journal of Arizona History* 37, no. 2 (1996): 149–62.

Mallory, Warren James. "The Remarkable Memoirs of Warren James Mallory (1868–1945): A Founding Pioneer of Mesa, Arizona, January 18, 1878." Edited by Mario "M" Holland, 2011. Typescript. Familysearch.org.

Mangum, Charlotte Augusta Kempe. "Life History of Charlotte Augusta Kempe Mangum." Typescript. Familysearch.org.

McClintock, James H. *Mormon Settlement in Arizona: A Record of Peaceful Conquest of the Desert.* Phoenix, AZ: The Manufacturing Stationers Inc., 1921.

McKnight, Ray. "The Battleground Shootout—Arizona Rangers Fight Smith Gang." *Bulletin of the American Society of Arms Collectors* 94 (Fall 2006): 45–51.

Meadows, Anne, and Daniel Buck. "The Last Days of Butch & Sundance Kid." *Wild West* (February 1997): 36–42.

Miller, Mark E. "St. Johns's Saints: Interethnic Conflict in Northeastern Arizona, 1880–85." *Journal of Mormon History* 23, no. 1 (1997): 66–99.

Moy, Thomas B. "Butch Cassidy in Wyoming State Prison." *Wild West History Association Journal* 13, no. 3 (September 2020): 56–63.

New Mexico Territory vs. Bruce Weaver and James Lowe, April 27, 1900, "Larceny of horses." Records of the United States Territorial and New Mexico District Courts for San Miguel County, Civil Records. Serial #18118, Collection 1976-031, Case 1733. New Mexico State Records Center & Archives.

O'Neal, Bill. *The Arizona Rangers.* Austin, TX: Eakin Press, 1987.

"On the Death of Hon. John T. LeSueur." Arizona House of Representatives, Resolution No. 1, April 25, 1946.

Oveson, Ove C. "Sketch of the Life of Ove Christian Oveson." Typescript. The Church of Jesus Christ of Latter-day Saints Church History Library, Salt Lake City.

Palmer, Arvin, comp. *An Arizona Palmer Family History: Selected Sketches of Arthur Palmer And Evaline Augusta Gibbons Palmer And Their Ancestors.* Taylor, AZ, Palmer Publications, 1994.

Parker, Emily S. "Priscilla Smith Gibbons Smith." Typescript. The Church of Jesus Christ of Latter-day Saints Church History Library, Salt Lake City.

Patterson, Richard. *Butch Cassidy: A Biography.* Lincoln and London: University of Nebraska Press, 1998.

———. "Butch Cassidy's Surrender Offer." *Wild West* (February 2006). [Republished by HistoryNet, January 29, 2002. https://www.historynet.com/butch-cassidys-surrender-offer-2.htm.]

Paulsen, David L., and Brock M. Mason. "Baptism for the Dead in Early Christianity." *Journal of Book of Mormon Studies and other Restoration Scripture* 19, no. 2 (2010): 22–49.

Paulsen, David L., Kendel J. Christensen, and Martin Pulido. "Redeeming the Dead: Tender Mercies, Turning of Hearts, and the Restoration of Authority." *Journal of the Book of Mormon and Other Restoration Scripture* 20, no. 1 (2011): 28–51.

Paulsen, David L., Kendel J. Christensen, Martin Pulido, and Judson Burton. "Redemption of the Dead: Continuing Revelation after Joseph Smith." *Journal of the Book of Mormon and Other Restoration Scripture* 20, no. 2 (2011): 52–69.

Paulsen, David L., Roger D. Cook, and Kendel J. Christensen. "The Harrowing of Hell: Salvation for the Dead in Early Christianity." *Journal of the Book of Mormon and Other Restoration Scripture* 19, no. 1 (2010): 56–77.

Pearce, Joe, and Richard Summers. "Joe Pearce—Manhunter: Some Adventures of an Arizona Ranger." *The Journal of Arizona History* 19, no. 3 (Autumn 1978): 249–60.

Pearce, Joseph. *Line Rider: A True Story of Stampedes, Gamblers, Indians and Outlaws Written by Arizona Ranger Joseph Pearce 1873–1958*. N.p.: Lost Boys Ink, 2013.

Peterson, Charles S. "Arizona, Pioneer Settlements In." In *Encyclopedia of Mormonism*, ed. Daniel H. Ludlow, 5 vols., 1:66–67. New York: Macmillan, 1992.

———. *Take Up Your Mission: Mormon Colonizing Along the Little Colorado River 1870–1900*. Tucson, AZ: University of Arizona Press, 1973.

Pinkerton's National Detective Agency Records. Library of Congress Manuscript Division, Washington, D.C.

Prassel, Frank Richard. *The Great American Outlaw: A Legacy of Fact and Fiction*. Norman: University of Oklahoma Press, 1993.

———. *The Western Peace Officer: A Legacy of Law and Order*. Norman: University of Oklahoma Press, 1972.

Preece, Colleen Pitt. "Thomas William Preece aka Sheriff 'Billy' Preece." Typescript. Familysearch.org.

Rasch, Philip J. "Death Comes to St. Johns." *Quarterly of the National Association and Center for Outlaw and Lawman History*, 7, no. 3 (Autumn 1982): 1–8.

Rees, Ellen Greer, comp. "Greer Men and Ellen C. Greer." Typescript, 1953. Familysearch.org.

———. "History of Christopher J. Kempe Family." Typescript, 1961; rprt. 1991. Familysearch.org.

Riggs, Michael S., and John E. Thompson. "Joseph Smith, Jr., and 'The Notorious Case of Aaron Lyon': Evidence of Earlier Doctrinal Development of Salvation for the Dead and a Trigger for the Practice of Polyandry?" *The John Whitmer Historical Association Journal* 26 (2006): 101–19.

Satterfield, Bruce, comp. "Teachings Concerning the Spirit World." N.p., accessed May 1, 2023. https://emp.byui.edu/satterfieldb/PDF/SpiritWorld.pdf.

Selcer, Richard F. *Photographing Texas: The Swartz Brothers, 1880–1918*. College Station, TX: Texas A&M University Press, 2019.

Sherwood, Maud Ruth. "Maud Ruth Sherwood Life Story Written By Herself." Typescript. Familysearch.org.

Siringo, Charles A. *A Cowboy Detective: An Autobiography*. Chicago: W. B. Conkey Company, 1912.

Smith, Della Crosby. *George Henry Crosby Family*. Austin, TX: Historical Publications, Inc., 1998.

Smith, Jesse N. *Journal of Jesse N. Smith: The Life Story of a Mormon Pioneer: 1834–1906*. Salt Lake City: Deseret News Publishing Co., 1953.

Smith, Joseph. *History of the Church of Jesus Christ of Latter-day Saints*, 7 vols. Salt Lake City: Deseret Book Company, 1978.

Smith, Joseph F., John R. Winder and Anthon H. Lund. Letter to D. K. Udall and Counselors, June 13, 1905. Udall Family Correspondence Collection, 1859–1950. The Church of Jesus Christ of Latter-day Saints Church History Library, Salt Lake City.

Smith, Oliver R., and Williams, Dorothy H., eds., *The Family of Jesse Nathaniel Smith, 1834–1906*. Snowflake, AZ: Jesse N. Smith Family Association, [1978].

Smith, Pauline Udall. "The Memoirs of Pauline Udall Smith." Typescript. The Church of Jesus Christ of Latter-day Saints Church History Library, Salt Lake City.

Smith, Willamelia Coleman. Interview by Marsha C. Martin, June 3, 1985. Typescript. LDS Family Life Oral History Project, Charles Redd Center for Western Studies. Brigham Young University Harold B. Lee Library, L. Tom Perry Special Collections, Provo, UT.

Smokov, Mark T. *He Rode with Butch and Sundance: The Story of Harvey "Kid Curry" Logan*. Denton, TX: University of North Texas Press, 2012.

Sorensen, Michelle R., and David R. Willmore. *The Journey Beyond Life*. Midvale, UT: Sounds of Zion, 1992 [1988].

Soule, Arthur. "A Tale of Two Georges." Unpublished paper, 2019.

———. "The Tall Texan: The Story of Ben Kilpatrick." *Texas Escapes Online Magazine*, accessed May 1, 2023. http://www.texasescapes.com/FEATURES/Arthur_Soule/Ben_Kilpatrick_Texas_train_robberies.htm.

———. *The Tall Texan: The Story of Ben Kilpatrick*. Deer Lodge, MT: TrailDust Publishing Inc., 1995.

St. Johns Ward General Minutes. The Church of Jesus Christ of Latter-day Saints Church History Library, Salt Lake City.

Stapley, Jonathan. "Adoptive Sealing Ritual in Mormonism." *Journal of Mormon History* 37, no. 3 (Summer 2011): 53–118.

Steckmesser, Kent L. "Robin Hood and the American Outlaw." *The Journal of American Folklore* 79, no. 312 (April–June 1966): 343–55.

———. *Western Outlaws: The "Good Badman" In Fact, Film, and Folklore*. Claremont, CA: Regina Books, [1983].

Stradling, Joseph O., Jr. Family Papers. Brigham Young University Harold B. Lee Library, L. Tom Perry Special Collections, Provo, UT.

Sullivan, Marlene Bateman. *Gaze into Heaven: Near-Death Experiences in Early Church History*. Springville, UT: Cedar Fort, Inc., 2013.

Tanner, Karen Holliday, and John D. Tanner Jr. *The Bronco Bill Gang*. Norman: University of Oklahoma Press, 2011.

———. *Climax Jim: The Tumultuous Tale of Arizona's Rustling Cowboy*. Tucson, AZ: Arizona Lithographers, 2005.

———. "Revenge: The Murder of Ed Beeler." *The Journal of the Western Outlaw-Lawman History Association* 13, no. 1 (Summer 2004): 2–7.

Tate, John W. "Journal of John W. Tate, October, 1880 to July, 1881." Typescript. University of Utah J. Willard Marriott Library Special Collections, Salt Lake City.

Tatum, Stephen. *Inventing Billy the Kid: Visions of the Outlaw in America, 1881–1981*. Tucson, AZ: University of Arizona Press, 1997.

Taylor, Bonnie, ed. *The Sermons of J. Golden Kimball, December 1891–April 1938*. N.p.: Latter-day Publishing, 2007.

Tinsley, Jim Bob. *The Hash Knife Brand*. Gainesville: University Press of Florida, 1993.

Toronto, LaReah H., comp. "To These, Our Grandparents." Typescript. The Church of Jesus Christ of Latter-day Saints Church History Library, Salt Lake City.

Trumbower, Jeffrey A. *Rescue for the Dead: The Posthumous Salvation of Non-Christians in Early Christianity*. Oxford: Oxford University Press, 2001.

A Turning of Hearts: Williams Davidson Gibbons Family History. Orem, UT: Remember When Histories Journals, 1981.

Udall Family Correspondence Collection, 1859–1950. The Church of Jesus Christ of Latter-day Saints Church History Library, Salt Lake City.

Udall, Cameron. *Images of America: St. Johns*. Charleston, SC: Arcadia Publishing, 2008.

Udall, David King, and Pearl Udall Nelson. *Arizona Pioneer Mormon: David King Udall His Story and Family 1851–1938*. Tucson: Arizona Silhouettes, 1959.

Underwood, Grant. "Baptism for the Dead: Comparing RLDS and LDS Perspectives." *Dialogue: A Journal of Mormon Thought* 23, no. 2 (Summer 1990): 99–105.

"United States World War I Draft Registration Cards, 1917–1918." FamilySearch, accessed April 2, 2023. https://familysearch.org/pal:/MM9.1.1/KXTC-676.

Wake, Ruth L. DeWitt, comp. "Our Heritage Book II: Christopher Jensen Kempe; Wives: Anne Ongerod, Olene Olsen, Anna Dorthea Johnson; Daughter: Ruth Leila (Kempe) DeWitt." 2004. Familysearch.org.

Warner, Matt. *The Last of the Bandit Riders*. Caldwell, ID: The Caxton Printers, Ltd., 1940.

Wells, Heber M. Letter to Governor N. O. Murphy, July 31, 1901. Governor Wells Correspondence, Series 235, microfilm reel 20, p. 28. Utah State Archives and Records Service, Salt Lake City.

White, Richard. *"It's Your Misfortunate and None of My Own": A History of the American West*. Norman and London: University of Oklahoma Press, 1991.

———. "Outlaw Gangs of the Middle Border: American Social Bandits." *The Western Historical Quarterly* 12, no. 4 (October 1981): 387–408.

Wilhelm, C. LeRoy, and Mabel R. *A History of the St. Johns Arizona Stake: The Triumph of Man and His Religion Over the Perils of a Raw Frontier*. Orem, UT: Historical Publications, 1982.

Wilson, Gary A. *The Life and Death of Kid Curry: Tiger of the Wild Bunch*. Guilford, CT, and Helena, MT: TwoDot, 2016.

Wiltbank, Esther, and Zola Whiting. *Lest Ye Forget*. Arizona [no city]: Apache County Centennial Committee, 1980.

Woodruff, Wilford. Letter to Brother [Ammon] Tenney, November 24, 1879. Typescript. Mormon Settlements in Arizona Collection, 1857–1986. The Church of Jesus Christ of Latter-day Saints Church History Library, Salt Lake City.

Woodworth, Jed. "Public Schooling in Territorial Arizona: Republicanism, Protestantism, and Assimilation." *The Journal of Arizona History* 46, no. 2 (Summer 2005): 95–134.

ADDITIONAL RESOURCES

Collections

Becker Family Papers, 1870–1959. Arizona Historical Society, Tucson.
David K. Udall Papers. University of Arizona (Tucson) Libraries Special Collections.
Evans P. Coleman Papers, 1883–1959. Arizona Historical Society, Tucson.
Jack A. Becker Collection. Available at http://www.roundvalleyaz.com/index.html.
James Warren LeSueur Papers, 1874–1939. Arizona Historical Society, Tucson.
Joseph Fish Papers, 1840–1926. Arizona Historical Society, Tucson.
LDS Missionary Database. Available at https://history.churchofjesuschrist.org/landing/missionary-database.
Mormon Settlements in Arizona Collection, 1857–1986. University of Utah J. Willard Marriott Library Special Collections, Salt Lake City.
Philip J. Rasch Collection, Box 8 ("Death Comes to St. Johns"), Arizona Historical Society, Tucson.
St. Johns Ward record of land purchases, 1879–1886. The Church of Jesus Christ of Latter-day Saints Church History Library, Salt Lake City.
St. Johns Stake manuscript history. The Church of Jesus Christ of Latter-day Saints Church History Library, Salt Lake City.
St. Johns Stake Academy student records. The Church of Jesus Christ of Latter-day Saints Church History Library, Salt Lake City.

Genealogical Information

The bulk of genealogical information, as well as a wealth of documents, reminiscences, family histories, etc., can be found at www.familysearch.org and www.ancestry.com.

Government Documents

Apache County Court Records, Arizona.
Grand County, Utah, Seventh District Court, Utah State Archives and Records Service, Criminal Case Files.
Montana Prison Records (Ancestry.com).
San Miguel County District Courts, Civil Records. Records of the United States Territorial and New Mexico District Courts. New Mexico State Records Center & Archives.
United States Census Records.

Newspapers

Chronicling America: Historical American Newspapers, U.S. Library of Congress. Available at https://chroniclingamerica.loc.gov.
Digital collections of U.S. newspapers can be found online on these sources:
Newspapers.com.
Utah Digital Newspapers. Available at https://digitalnewspapers.org.

Reminiscences, Diaries, Journals, Letters, etc.

George A. Brown. "The Wagon." Typescript (written November 28, 1949). The Church of Jesus Christ of Latter-day Saints Church History Library, Salt Lake City.
Crosby, George H. "A Stake Historical Sketch Written and Read by George A. Crosby Jr. on July 23, 1917." Typescript. The Church of Jesus Christ of Latter-day Saints Church History Library, Salt Lake City.
Frost, Allen. Reminiscences and Journals, 1874–1901, vol. 8, "1899 July–1901 February." The Church of Jesus Christ of Latter-day Saints Church History Library, Salt Lake City.
George, William. Letter to President [John] Taylor, July 21, 1885. Typescript. Mormon Settlements in Arizona Collection, 1857–1986. University of Utah J. Willard Marriott Library Special Collections, Salt Lake City.
Hamblin, Dudley. "My Story," written October 19, 1959. Typescript. Familysearch.org.
Larsen, Joseph J. "A Sketch of My Life." Typescript. The Church of Jesus Christ of Latter-day Saints Church History Library, Salt Lake City.
LeSueur, James Warren. "How Saint Johns was Settled." Typescript. University of Utah J. Willard Marriott Library Special Collections, Salt Lake City.
Udall, Stewart L. "Human Values and Hometown Snapshots: Early Days in St. Johns." *American West* (May–June 1982): 26–33.

Family Histories

Flammer, Gordon H., ed. "The Life Stories of Joshua Smith Gibbons & Nancy Louisa Noble Gibbons and of Five of Their Children Who Lived to Raise Families (Including Descendancy Charts)." 2001. Familysearch.org.
Lundberg, Anna. "Biographical Sketch of William George, Jr." Typescript, 1927. Familysearch.org.
Savage, Levi Mathers. "Family History Journal: First entry, March 28, 1876; Last entry, August 2, 1935." Brigham Young University Publication Services, 1955.
Wert, Edith, and Ruth Wake. "Descendants of Ruth Leila Kempe DeWitt Daughter of Anna Dorthea Johnson and Christopher Jensen Kempe." 1996. Familysearch.org.

Books and Articles about the Mormons, Arizona, and St. Johns

Becker, Jack A. "Sheriff from 1887–1888: Commodore Perry Owens Helped Clean Up Early Years of Apache County." RoundValleyAZ.com, accessed May 1, 2023. http://www.roundvalleyaz.com/owens2.html.
Bitton, Davis. "'These Licentious Days': Dancing among the Mormons." In *The*

Ritualization of Mormon History and Other Essays. Urbana and Chicago: University of Illinois Press, 1994.

Blue, Martha. *Indian Trader: The Life and Times of J. L. Hubbell*. Walnut, CA: Kiva Publishing, 2000.

Compton, Todd. "Civilizing the Ragged Edge: The Wives of Jacob Hamblin." *Journal of Mormon History* 33, no. 2 (Summer 2007): 155–98.

Ellis, Catherine H. "'Arizona Has Been Good to Me': Routes and Recollections of Latter-day Saint Settlement in Arizona." *The Journal of Arizona History* 54, no. 1 (Spring 2013): 1–32.

Ellis, Catherine H., and D. L. Turner. *Images of America The White Mountains of Apache County*. Charleston, SC: Arcadia Publishing, 2010.

Ewing, E. Jack. "Mormon Colonization of St. Johns, Arizona." The Church of Jesus Christ of Latter-day Saints Church History Library, Salt Lake City.

Greenwood, N. H. "Sol Barth: A Jewish Settler on the Arizona Frontier." *The Journal of Arizona History* 14, no. 4 (Winter 1973): 363–78.

Hayes, Alden. *A Portal to Paradise*. Tucson: The University of Arizona Press, 1999.

Herman, Daniel J. "The Rim Country War Reconsidered: Honor Rustling, Vigilantism, and How History Got Remembered." *The Journal of Arizona History* 58, no. 1 (Spring 2017): 1–62.

Jackson, Richard H., ed. *Mormon Role in the Settlement of the West*. Provo: Brigham Young University Press, 1978.

Jennings, James R. *Arizona Was the West*. San Antonio: The Naylor Company, 1970.

Lavender, David. *The Southwest*. Albuquerque: University of New Mexico Press, 1980.

Leone, Mark P. "The Evolution of Mormon Culture in Eastern Arizona." *Utah Historical Quarterly* 40, no. 2 (Spring 1972): 122–41.

Sherlock, Richard. "Mormon Migration and Settlement after 1875." *Journal of Mormon History* 2 (1975): 53–68.

Shumway, Wilford J. *St. Johns Arizona Stake Centennial: 1887–1987*. N.p., 1987.

Sletten, Carol, and Eric Kramer. *Story of the American West: Legends of Arizona*. Pinetop, AZ: Wolf Water Press, 2010.

Smiley, Winn Whiting. "Ammon M. Tenney Mormon Missionary to the Indians." *The Journal of Arizona History* 13, no. 2 (1972): 82–108.

Tanner, George S., and Richards, J. Morris. *Colonization on the Little Colorado: The Joseph City Region*. Flagstaff, AZ: Northland Press, 1977.

Books and Articles on Outlaws, Sheriffs, and the American West

Agnew, Jeremy. *Creation of the Cowboy Hero: Fiction, Film and Fact*. Jefferson, NC: McFarland & Company, 2015.

———. *Crime, Justice and Retribution in the American West, 1850–1900*. Jefferson, NC: McFarland & Company, 2017.

———. *Old West in Fact and Film: History versus Hollywood*. Jefferson, NC: McFarland & Company, 2012.

———. *Smoking Gun: The True Story about Gunfighting in the Old West*. Lake City, CO: Western Reflections, 2010.

Baker, Pearl. *The Wild Bunch at Robbers Roost*. Lincoln and London: University of Nebraska, 1989 [1965].

Bartholomew, Ed. *Kill or Be Killed.* Houston: The Frontier Press of Texas, 1953.
Beckstead, James H. *Cowboying: A Tough Job in a Hard Land.* Salt Lake City: University of Utah Press, 1991.
Brands, H. W. *Dreams of El Dorado: A History of the American West.* New York: Basic Books, 2019.
Ernst, Donna B. *The True Story of Will Carver.* Sonora Texas: Sutton County Historical Society, 1995.
Gordon, Kathryn Jenkins. *Butch Cassidy and Other Mormon Outlaws of the Old West.* American Fork, UT: Covenant Communications, 2013.
Hamblin, John Ray. *Outlaws of the Last Frontier: Retold Stories from Apache County, Arizona.* Orem, UT: Likes Publishing, 2002.
Hunsaker, Gordon A. *Gunfights & Gunfighters: Reflections from a Phoenix Police Officer.* Bloomington, IN: iUniverse Inc., 2010.
Jameson, W. C. *Butch Cassidy: Beyond the Grave.* Lanham, MD: Taylor Trade Publishing, 2012.
Metz, Leon Claire. *The Encyclopedia of Lawmen, Outlaws, and Gunfighters.* New York: Facts on File, 2013.
Pointer, Larry. *In Search of Butch Cassidy.* Norman: University of Oklahoma Press, 1988 [1977].
Rutter, Michael. *Outlaw Tales of Utah: True Stories of Utah's Most Famous Rustlers, Robbers, and Bandits.* Guilford, CT: TwoDot, 2011.
Riffenburgh, Beau. *Pinkerton's Great Detective: The Amazing Life and Times of James McParland.* New York: Viking Penguin, 2013.
Selcer, Richard F. *Hell's Half Acre: The Life and Legend of a Red-Light District.* Fort Worth: Texas Christian University Press, 1991.
Selcer, Richard and Donna Donnell. "Last Word on the Famous Wild Bunch Photo." *Wild West Magazine* (December 2011). [Republished by HistoryNet, September 21, 2022. http://www.historynet.com/last-word-famous-wild-bunch-photo.htm.]
Streib, Daniel T. "Butch Cassidy and the Wild Bunch." In *Outlaws of the Old West*, ed. Charles D. Anderson. Los Angeles: Mankind Publishing Company, 1973.
Tanner, Karen Holliday, and John D. Tanner Jr. "Red Pipkin: Outlaw from the Black River Country." *Wild West* 16, no. 3 (October 2003): 30–36, 71.
Trimble, Marshall. *Arizona Outlaws and Lawmen: Gunslingers, Bandits, Heroes and Peacekeepers.* Charleston, SC: The History Press, 2015.

Books and Articles on Mormon Temples, the Spirit World, and Salvation for the Dead

Allen, James B., and Jessie L. Embry. "'Provoking the Brethren to Good Works': Susa Young Gates, the Relief Society, and Genealogy." *BYU Studies* 31, no. 2 (Spring 1991): 115–38.
Barlow, Philip L. "To Mend a Fractured Reality: Joseph Smith's Project." *Journal of Mormon History* 38, no. 3 (Summer 2012): 28–50.
Barton, John. *A History of the Bible: The Story of the World's Most Influential Book* (New York: Viking, 2019).

Bennett, Richard E. "'Line upon Line, Precept upon Precept': Reflections on the 1877 Commencement of the Performance of Endowments and Sealings for the Dead." *BYU Studies* 44, no. 3 (2005): 38–77.

Harris, Amy. "A Genealogical Turn: Possibilities for Mormon Studies and Genealogical Scholarship." *Mormon Studies Review* 5 (2018): 73–88.

Peterson, Evan Tye, comp. *The Ninth Temple: A Light in the Desert.* Orem, UT: Granite Publishing and Distribution, 2002.

Stephenson, Johnny, and H. Michael Marquardt. "Origin of the Baptism for the Dead Doctrine." *John Whitmer Historical Association Journal* 37, no. 1 (2017): 132–46.

INDEX

A

adoption theology, 171–72, 184–85
Alma, New Mexico
   Weaver gunned down in, 247–49
   Wild Bunch at, 31, 43–47, 141, 145–46, 201
Anderson, Charles P., 28n80, 86, 90, 103, 106, 120, 196, 231
Apache County, Arizona
   anti-Mormon fervor in, 23–25
   cattle raising in, 65–66
   lawlessness and violence in, xii, 57–61, 66–72, 82–83, 130–31, 188–90, 234–35, 277
   population, 130
   sheep raising in, 7
Arizona Cooperative Mercantile Institution (ACMI), 11–12, 23, 27, 89, 165, 182–83, 222, 225
Arizona Rangers
   disbanded 235–36
   established, xi, 232–34
Armijo, Antonio
   member of LeSueur-Gibbons posse, 93–96, 122–24
   returns to town, 99, 101, 123n58, 276
Aztec Land and Cattle Company
   conflict with Mormons, 65–67, 75
   expels outlaws, 71–72
   known as Hashknife, 65
   outlaws work for, 49, 66
   sells cattle business, 83

B

baptism for the dead, 169–74, 279–80
Barrett, Henry
   character of, 58
   chases Bill Smith Gang, 146, 234–35
   gunfight with Prime T. Coleman, 236–37
   posse member, 89–90
Barth, Morris, 5–6, 20–23
Barth, Nathan, 25, 179n53
Barth, Pauline, 178–79
Barth, Solomon "Sol"
   leader of St. Johns Ring, 23–25, 75, 82n88, 83
   mediates San Juan Day gunfight, 65
   sells St. Johns land, 5–6, 20–23
Beck, Ole, 267–71
Beeler, Edward
   ambushed and killed, 193–96
   Apache County Sheriff, xi, xiii
   arrests Cassidy and Weaver, 97–98
   asks to join LDS Church, 231
   cattle ranching, 187–88
   criticism of, 89–90, 97, 127–28, 158, 165, 196, 276, 287
   early life, 128–30
   kills Monte Slaughter, 188–93, 228–29
   organizes posse 57–58, 87, 92, 103, 118
   pursues LeSueur-Gibbons murderers, 133–64, 215
   pursues outlaws, 89–91, 93, 96
   searches for murdered men, 99–100
Beeler, Mary Elizabeth Hamblin
   life after Ed Beeler's murder, 228–32
   marries Ed Beeler, 129–30, 132, 196
   posthumous sealing to Ed Beeler, 231–32
Betenson, Lula Parker
   on Cassidy, 32, 37, 274
   on Cassidy as embarrassment to family, 259–60, 274
   on Cassidy as social bandit, 41–42
   on Cassidy's death, 258
Birchfield, Walt, 138–39

Blevins, Andy (Andy Cooper), 75–78, 82
Blevins, John
  convicted of attempted murder, 78
  pardoned, 79–80
  wounded by Sheriff Owens, 76
Blevins, Sam, 77
Book of Mormon
  name of church derives from, xiv, 1
  and Native Americans, 14–16, 223
Briant, Elijah "Lije," 246–47
Brighton, Jonas
  accused of vigilantism, 81
  kills Clanton and Renfro, 74–75
Brown, John W.
  on LeSueur-Gibbons murders, 112, 117, 121, 136
  St. Johns Academy principal, 102
Brown's Park, 35, 39–40, 135, 155, 157
Bullion, Laura, 247, 250

C

Cannon, George Q., 4, 172
Capehart, Tom
  activities after murders, 206, 260
  assists Folsom train robbery, 45
  early life, 47–49, 273
  killing of Scarborough, 139
  LeSueur-Gibbons murderer, ix, 136, 145–47
  physical description of, 49, 145
Carver, Tod. *See* Thomas C. Hilliard.
Carver, William "Will" (G.W. Franks)
  early life, 52–54, 273
  Fort Worth Five photograph, 205–6, 243–44
  killed, 245–47, 271
  LeSueur-Gibbons murderer, ix, 146, 249
  member of Wild Bunch and Ketchum Gang, 41
  physical description of, 53, 145
  robs train, 44–45
  robs bank, 204–5
  vicarious temple work for, 280n17
Cassidy, Butch. *See* Robert LeRoy Parker.
Cassidy, Mike, 33–35
Church of Jesus Christ of Latter-day Saints, The
  known as Mormon Church, xiv
  millennial expectations, 1–2
  settling of Arizona and St. Johns, 4–29
  settling of the West, 2–3
Clanton, Ike, 60, 74, 81
Clanton, Phineas, 60, 74, 80–81
Clawson, Rudger
  polygamous marriage to Pearl Udall, 227–28
  prays for St. Johns colonizers, 86
  visits St. Johns, 283
Coleman, Evans
  on crime in Apache County, 60–61, 67–68
  on farming in St. Johns, 9n22
  on Sheriff Beeler's character, 132n23
  wild youth, 115
Coleman, Prime T.
  elected to county office, 83
  gunfight with Henry Barrett, 236–37
  partnership with Ed Beeler, 187–88, 193–94, 231, 241
colonizing missions
  calls were binding, 2, 10, 22, 86, 286
  St. Johns colonizers released, 277–78
Cooper, Andy. *See* Andy Blevins.
Crosby, Ben, 91–94
Crosby, George
  on J.T. LeSueur, 26–27, 222
  on Sheriff Owens, 81, 280
Crosby, John T., 165–66
Cruzan, Bill, 203–5
Currie, George "Flatnose"
  excellent cowhand, 148, 273
  killed, 147–50, 201
  member of Wild Bunch, 41
  robs train, 44

D–F

dams
  collapse of, 8, 10, 277, 279
  Mormons build for irrigation, 10
Davis, Jane LeSueur, 7
Day, Herbert
  testifies at Hilliard hearing, 211
  witnesses Tyler-Jenkins murder, 151–54
Deane, William "Billy," 148, 252
Deseret (proposed US state), 2–3

Index

Evans, Billy (Ace of Diamonds, Jack of Diamonds, and Timberline)
  killed, 74–75
  kills James Hale, 68
Farr, Edward J., 45
Fish, Joseph
  on anti-Mormons, 61n7, 67, 68n34, 70
  on conflict over water, 18
  criticism of Sheriff Beeler, 127
  on lynchings, 79
  praises Sheriff Owens, 81–82
  on San Juan Day gunfight, 62–63, 65, 69
Fort Worth Five photograph, 205–6, 243–44, 251n28, 254
Francis, A.G., 255–57
French, William
  learns Jim Lowe is Cassidy, 45–46
  praises Cassidy, 43–45, 274
  vouches for Cassidy, 97–98, 134, 141–42, 247–48

G

genealogy
  in service of the dead, 281–82
  James LeSueur efforts, 166, 279–80
  promoted by LDS Church, 281–82
  Mormons urged to save ancestors, 172
Gibbons, Andrew, 67, 83n90, 103, 120, 128
Gibbons, Andrew Augustus "Gus"
  body found, 99–100
  early life, 105–10
  funeral of, 120–21
  murder of, 121–25
  physical description of, 108–19
  serves on posse, 91–96, 118–19
  stone cairn erected for, 287
  with family, 20
Gibbons, Clarissa Isabell Wilhelm
  criticizes Sheriff Beeler, 90, 127
  death of, 238
  on pursuit of the outlaws, 91–93, 96–98, 101–2
Gibbons, Eva
  criticizes Sheriff Beeler, 127, 165
  father's funeral, 240–41
  on Gus Gibbons, 105–6
  with family, 20

Gibbons, Evaline Augusta Lamb "Gusty"
  early struggles of family, 13–14, 18–20, 26
  last years, 217, 239–41
Gibbons, Lee Roy, 83n90, 183, 221–22
Gibbons, Loman, 20, 101
Gibbons, Priscilla Smith "Pearl"
  Gus's murder, 91–92, 96–98, 100–101, 119
  marries Gus, 107–10
  remarriage, 238–39, 287
Gibbons, Rhoda Ann
  on Beelers, 130
  criticizes Sheriff Beeler, 165, 196
  on Hopi people, 17
  relationship with Gus, 105, 108, 110
  with family, 20
Gibbons, Richard "Dick"
  and Arizona Rangers, ix, 232–34
  last years, 237–38
  leads posse, 91–95, 98, 118, 276
  searches for murdered men, 98–103, 162–63
  visits murder site, 121–25
Gibbons, William H. "Bill"
  erects stone cairn for Gus, 287
  Gus's murder, 103, 165–66
  last years, 217, 239–41
  leader in St. Johns, xiv, 17–20, 25–26, 69, 83, 285–86
  missionary to Native Americans, 13–14, 17
  vision of Gus, 175–76
Gibbons, William "Will"
  death of, 217–18
  jail guard, 210
  searches for murdered men, 99–102
  with family, 20
  at youth picnic, 84–85
Grant, Heber J.
  annuls Pearl Udall's plural marriage, 228
  counsels St. Johns Mormons, 86–87
  on LeSueur-Gibbons murders, 287
  and Mesa temple, 223
  on Mormon colonizers, 283
Greer cowboys
  feud with Mexican-Americans, 61–62
  protect Mormons, 69
  San Juan Day gunfight, 62–65

Greer, Dick, 121, 125
Greer, Harris, 65
Greer, Nathan "Nat"
   bodyguard for Bishop David Udall, 69
   businesses, 84
   country treasurer, 83
   on San Juan Day gunfight, 62–65

H

Hainer, Al, 35–37
Hales, James, 68
Hall, Mark, 8
Halverson, Ed, 207–9
Hamblin, Duane, 129, 187, 190, 234–35
Hamblin, Dudley, 230–32
Hamblin, Jacob Jr., 129, 232
Hamblin, Lyman "Duane," 57–58, 89
Hanks, O.C. "Deaf Charley"
   member of Wild Bunch, 41
   robs train, 250
Hashknife Cattle Company. *See* Aztec Land and Cattle Company.
Hatch, Hyram "Hi," 63–64
Hazen, Josiah, 44, 148–49, 252
Hilliard, Thomas C. (Tod Carver and Todd Hilliard)
   arrested for murder, 206–9
   case against dismissed, 214–15
   early life, 49–50, 66
   extradited to Utah, 209–14
   later life, 260–63, 272
   LeSueur-Gibbons murderer, ix, 47, 144, 146
   physical description of, 49, 145
Hole-in-the-Wall, 39, 135, 155
Hollimon, William "Pad," 248–49
Houck, James, 72, 78–79
Hubbell, John Lorenzo
   Apache County sheriff, 67, 72, 74–75
   member of St. Johns Ring, 25, 82n88, 83

J–K

Jarvis, Charles, 83n90, 102–3, 208–9, 241
Jenkins, Samuel
   early life, 147–48
   identity of killers, 153–55, 158, 197
   killed by outlaws, 150–53
   kills Flatnose Currie, 149–50

Jowell, Mallie Baxter "Mal"
   flees to Montana, 263
   kills deputy sheriff, 263–64
   kills Ed Beeler, 194–96
   settles in Texas, 264–65, 272
Kempe, Anna, 178–80
Kempe, Charlotte "Lottie" (married name Mangum)
   on Frank LeSueur and Jennie Kempe, 113–14, 116–17, 177
   on Jennie's death, 182–86
Kempe, Christopher J.
   death of, 219–20
   on hardships, 277
   imprisoned for polygamy, 179
   settles in Apache County, 177–81, 226
Kempe, Geneva "Jennie"
   romance with Frank LeSueur, 113–14, 116–17, 175, 177, 181–83
   sealed to Frank LeSueur, xiii, 175, 185
Kempe, Leila, 181–82, 226
Kempe, Olena, 175, 177–86, 220
Ketchum, Sam
   robs train, 44–45, 56, 201, 249
   runs gambling saloon, 52
Ketchum, Tom, 48–49, 52, 56, 66, 249
Kid Curry. *See* Harvey Logan.
Kilpatrick, Ben (Johnny Ward and Mack Stein)
   early life, 51–52
   Fort Worth Five photograph, 205–6, 243–44
   imprisoned, 205
   killed, 265–71
   LeSueur-Gibbons murderer, ix, 146
   member of Wild Bunch and Ketchum Gang, 41
   physical description of, 52, 145
   robs train, 44–45, 203–4
   vicarious temple work for, 280n17
Kilpatrick, George
   disappears, 253, 254n37
   wounded, 244–47
Kimball, Heber C.
   adoption theology, 171
   on temple ceremony and Masonry, 170

Index

Kimball, J. Golden
  on faith of colonizers, 283–84
  promises success to St Johns colonizers, 86
Knight, Jesse, 38

L

Lamanites. *See* Native Americans.
Landusky, Pike, 55, 252
Lay, Elzy (alias William "Mac" McGinnis)
  member of Wild Bunch, 40–41
  robs bank and mine payroll, 42–43
  robs train, 44–45
  sentenced to prison, 45, 56, 201
  at WS ranch, 43, 273
Lee, Bob, 44, 56
LeSueur, Alice, 27, 105, 113, 165, 185–86, 222
LeSueur, Frank
  body found, 99–100, 103
  early life, 12, 27–29, 105, 110–18, 120
  in posse, 92–96, 118–19
  funeral of 120–21
  James's vision of, 174–75
  murder of, 121–25
  physical description of, 111
  posthumous marriage to Jennie Kempe, 185–86
  return of horse, 241
  romance with Jennie Kempe, 113–14, 116–17, 181–82
  romance with Pearl Udall, 105, 113, 117
  stone cairn erected for, 287
LeSueur, Geneva
  donates house as first Mesa hospital, 221
  early life in St. Johns, 11–12, 27–29, 226
  Frank's murder, 98, 165, 220
  and Jennie Kempe, 175, 182–85
LeSueur, James
  on criminals in Apache County, 59–60
  erects stone cairn for Frank, 287–88
  Frank's murder, 166–67
  genealogical work, 279–80
  and Kempe family, 183–86
  and Mesa temple, 222–24, 279
  praises Sheriff Owens, 81–82
  relationship with brother Frank, 28, 110–13, 115–18, 166

  vision of spirit world, xi–xiii, 172–77, 181–82
  with family, 27
LeSueur, John Taylor "J.T."
  community leader, xii, 26–29, 72, 83, 217, 285
  early years in St. Johns, 10–13
  fights outlaws, 61, 65, 69
  on Frank's wild nature, 114–15
  Frank's murder, 89, 98, 165, 288
  leader in Mesa, 220–23
  moves to St. Johns, 6–7
LeSueur, William, 7, 10–11
Littleby, William, 158n132, 211
Livingston, William, 209, 211, 213–14
Logan, Harvey (alias Kid Curry)
  allegedly kills Jim Winters, 160, 250–52
  arrest in Knoxville, Tennessee, 250–53
  death of, 253–54, 258, 271
  early life, 54–56, 273
  Fort Worth Five photograph, 205–6, 243–44
  kills Pike Landusky, 55, 252
  leader in Wild Bunch, 41
  LeSueur-Gibbons murderer, ix, 47, 145–46
  in popular culture, viii
  physical description of, 55–56
  possible murders by, 42, 54, 148, 160, 245, 250, 252
  robs train, 44, 203–5, 250
  vicarious temple work for, 280n17
Logan, Lonie
  killed, 56
  member of Wild Bunch, 41
  at Wilcox, WY, train robbery, 44
Longabaugh, Harry (Sundance Kid, Harry Place, and Frank Boyd)
  death of, 255–58
  Fort Worth Five photograph, 205–6, 243–44
  kills Chilean policeman, 254–55
  member of Wild Bunch, 41
  in popular culture, x–xi, 46
  robs bank, 203–5
  robs train, 44, 149
  in South America, 245
  vicarious temple work for, 280n17

Love, Henry M., 45
Luna, New Mexico, 57, 135
lynching of suspected outlaws, 17–18, 59, 65, 78–79, 240, 285

M

Mallory, Warren James, 9, 18n48, 101
Martin, C. B., 212–13
McCarty, Tom, 35
McParland, James, 252
Meeks, Henry "Bub"
 member of Wild Bunch, 41
 robs bank and mine payroll, 42–43
 sentenced to prison, 56
Mexican-Americans
 conflict with Mormons, 20–25, 284
 first settlers of St. Johns, xii, 4–5
 gunfight with Greer cowboys, 61–65, 69
 Mormons work for, 11, 179
 population in St. Johns, 285
 work for Mormons, 84, 285
Mormons. *See* The Church of Jesus Christ of Latter-day Saints.
Morris, William "Coley"
 released, 143–45, 164
 suspect in LeSueur-Gibbons murder, 134, 140–41
Mossman, Burt
 leads Arizona Rangers, 233–35
 tracks Ed Beeler's killers, 195, 262
Murphy, N. Oakes
 approves extradition of Hilliard, 209–11
 endorses Arizona Rangers, 233–34
 offers reward for Ed Beeler's murderers, 195
 offers reward for LeSueur-Gibbons murderers, 134
Murray, Frank
 investigates stolen bank notes, 45–46
 saved by Cassidy, 46
 searches for stolen money, 156

N–O

Native Americans
 friend of Jenkins, 148, 156
 Mesa temple built for, 223
 in Mormon theology, 2, 14–15
 relations with Mormons, 13, 15–17

Nephew, Rufus "Climax Jim"
 arrested for cattle rustling, 189–90
 on life on the run, 200–201
O'Day, Tom, 41
Ortega, Leandro, 187, 193, 208, 210
Overson, David, 103
Oveson, Ove C., 59n2, 63
Owens, Commodore Perry
 Apache County sheriff, 72–75
 controversy, 79–81
 kills Andy Cooper, 75–78
 posthumous baptism of, 280
 praised by Mormons, 81–82

P

Parker, Ann Gillies, 31–33, 39, 259–60
Parker, Dan
 convicted of robbery, 38–39
 later life, 259–60, 272
 robs bank, 35
Parker, Maximilian "Maxi," 31–33, 39, 259–60
Parker, Robert LeRoy (Roy Parker, George Parker, George Cassidy, Butch Cassidy, James "Jim" Lowe, James "Santiago" Ryan, and James P. Maxwell)
 adopts alias "Butch Cassidy," 35
 arrested in St. Johns, ix, 97–98, 134, 141–43, 247, 286–87
 complains of bad breaks, 273–74
 Fort Worth Five photograph, 205–6, 243–44
 hides in Baggs, WY, 163
 imprisoned for horse stealing, 37–39
 leaves home, 33–34
 Mormon upbringing, 31–34
 physical description of, 34, 36, 43, 98
 prevents killing of Pinkerton official, 46
 reputation as social bandit, x–xii, 41–42, 160, 274–75
 robs bank, 35, 42–43, 204–5
 seeks amnesty, 197–203
 in South America and death, 245, 254–58
 steals horses, 46–47
 trail boss at WS Ranch, 43–45
Patterson, Joseph B., 101, 225

Index

Pearce, Joseph
  describes tracking technique, 123–24
  on Little Colorado River dams, 279n12
  on Mal Jowell, 263
  on Slaughter family, 188
Peery, Claire V., 190–92
Perkins, E.S., 102, 120–21
Pinkerton National Detective Agency
  describes Logan's crimes, 252
  hired to break up Wild Bunch, 44
  identifies Logan, 251
  refuses to believe Cassidy, Sundance Kid, or Logan died, 257–58
  uncovers Cassidy at WS Ranch, 31, 56
  warns against releasing Kilpatrick from prison, 256
Pipkin, Dan "Red," 47, 60, 188–90
Place, Ethel (also known as Etta)
  girlfriend of Sundance Kid, 245, 257
  in South America, 254–55
Pleasant Valley War, 71, 75, 78, 82–83
polygamy
  1890 Woodruff Manifesto, 180, 227, 284
  1904 Smith Manifesto, 227
  Mormons imprisoned for, 24–25, 226
  opposition to in Arizona, 22–24, 69, 83, 284
  post-Manifesto plural marriages, 227–28, 239
posse comitatus
  danger of tracking outlaws, 123–24, 140, 158–59, 271
  sheriff's posses in the West, 118–19
Powers, Orlando W., 198–200
Preece, William
  hunts Tyler-Jenkins murderers, 151, 155, 158
  joins forces with Sheriff Beeler 161–62
  kills Flatnose Currie, 149
  salary of, 205n30

R

Renfro, Lee, 75, 81
Reward notices for LeSueur-Gibbons murderers
  description of murderers, 133–34, 139–41, 145, 164
  reward amounts, 134, 157

reward for capture of Hilliard, 209
reward withdrawn, 209
Rogers, Annie, 55, 251
Richards, William A., 38
Robbers Roost, 39, 44, 135, 155
Roberts, Mose, 76–77
Roundy, Lorenzo, 4
Ruiz, Alfred
  investigates alleged LeSueur-Gibbons murderers, 143–44, 208–9
  member of St. Johns Ring, 25, 82n88
  recommends extraditing Hilliard, 210
  worries about posse, 97
Ruiz, Francisco
  member of LeSueur-Gibbons posse, 93–96, 122–24
  returns to town, 99, 101, 123n58, 276

S

Saffell, Sam, 190–92
San Juan Day gunfight, 61–65
Scarborough, George (father)
  identities of killers, 139, 150, 153, 206, 215, 252
  killed by outlaws, 137–39
  roughs up Capehart, 47–48, 137
Scarborough, George "Ed" (son)
  arrests Hilliard, 207–9
  joins Arizona Rangers, 235
Scott, Charles R., 243
sheepherding
  among Mexican-Americans, 5, 21, 285
  among Mormons, xiv, 12, 26–27, 87, 110, 221, 224, 237
  in Apache County, 7
  conflicts with cattlemen, 62, 69, 71, 83–84
Sherwood, William "Will"
  friendship with Frank LeSueur, 119–20
  searches for murdered men, 99–101
Siringo, Charlie, 46, 163, 259
Slaughter, Ida, 193
Slaughter, John
  cousin of Pete Slaughter, 188
  leads posse, 139–40
Slaughter, Monterey "Monte"
  criminal associations, 188–90
  killed by Ed Beeler, 190–93, 228, 231

Slaughter, Paschal Eldridge "Pat"
  kills Ed Beeler, 194–96, 215, 250
  returns to Apache County, 261–63
Slaughter, Pete, 188
Smith, Bill, 47, 58, 60, 90, 146, 234–36
Smith, Jesse N.
  declines to settle in St. Johns, 5
  fasts and prays for peace, 70–71
  father of Priscilla Smith Gibbons, 107, 108, 238
Smith, Joseph F.
  on Mesa temple, 222–23
  releases St. Johns colonizers, 277–78
  Second Manifesto, 227–28
Smith, Joseph Jr.
  and Lamanite curse, 14n35
  restoration of Christ's church, xii, 1–2
  on spirit world and temple work, 168–72, 184
social bandits
  outlaws' reputations as, x, 41
  rejection of "Robin Hood" myth, 160, 247, 274–75
spirit world
  James LeSueur's vision of, 173–75
  Mormon conception of, 167–73, 280
Springerville
  Beeler kills Monte Slaughter in, 190–92
  Frank LeSueur called to posse in, 118
  frequented by Clantons, 60–61
  James Hale killed in, 68
  Pat Slaughter moves to, 262
  Wild Bunch purchase supplies in, 57, 92
Stanley, Ebin, 78
St. Johns, Arizona
  early settlement of, 4–6
  landscape and harsh environment of, xii, 7–10, 84–86, 277
  Mormon colonizers released from mission, 277–78
  population, 5, 130, 278, 285
St. Johns "Ring"
  anti-Mormon activities, 24–25
  deaths of members, 82
Stott, Jamie, 78–79
Stover, Ebenezer S., 21n53, 59n2, 65, 82n88
Stradling, Joseph O. Jr., 121, 242

Sundance Kid. *See* Harry Longabaugh.

T–V

temples
  building of Mesa temple, 222–24, 279
  ceremonies, 170–71
  Lamanites and temple work, 16, 223
  vicarious work for outlaws, 280
Tenney, Ammon, 5–6
Tenney, Nathan, 63–65
Thornton, Oliver C., 245, 252, 266
Trousdale, David A., 265–71
Turner, Oscar
  and Hilliard hearing, 209, 213–14
  horses stolen, 154–55, 158n132
Tyler, Jesse
  early life, 147–48
  identity of killers, 153–55, 158, 197
  killed by outlaws, 150–53
  kills Flatnose Currie, 149
Udall, David King
  conflict in St. Johns, 21–22, 25, 67, 69–71, 81–83, 285
  on LeSueur-Gibbons murders, 102, 120
  Mesa temple president, 223–24
  partnership with J.T. LeSueur, 12
  praises wives and daughters, 224–25
  polygamy, 226–27
  St. Johns bishop, 10
  St. Johns stake president, 17, 224
Udall, Morris K. "Mo," 283
Udall, Pearl
  Frank LeSueur's girlfriend, 105, 113, 117
  marries into polygamy, 227–28
Vaughan, James, 63–64
Vernal, Utah, 160, 162

W

Walters, "Bronco" Bill, 60, 146n81, 188
Warner, Harriet LeSueur, 7
Warner, Matt
  convicted of murder, 42–43
  friendship with Butch Cassidy, 34–35
  investigates Cassidy's death, 256
  on life on the run, 200
  robs bank, 35
Weaver, Bruce "Red"

arrested in St. Johns, 97–98, 134, 141–43
assists in robbery, 45
charged with horse stealing, 143
implicated in LeSueur-Gibbons murders, 142, 146
killed, 247–50
physical description of, 98
rides with Cassidy, 46–47, 90
Wells, Heber M., xi, 151, 197, 199–202
Wild Bunch
   assisted by sympathizers, 159–60, 163–64, 204
   Idaho's Montpelier Bank robbery, 42–43
   kills Deputy Deane, 148
   kills George Scarborough, 137–39, 150, 153
   kills Oliver Thornton, 245
   kills Sheriff Farr and Deputy Love, 45
   kills Sheriff Josiah Hazen, 44
   kills Sheriff Tyler and Deputy Jenkins, 150–53
   LeSueur-Gibbons murderers, ix, 47, 145–46
   life on the run, 44, 200–201, 251, 271–72
   members of, 40–41
   origin of name, 39–40
   payroll robbery in Castle Gate, UT, 43
   praised for cowboy skills, 45–48, 52, 148, 273
   train robbery near Folsom, NM, 44–45
   train robbery near Tipton, WY, 203–4
   train robbery near Wagner, MT, 250–51
   train robbery near Wilcox, WY, 44
   Winnemucca Bank robbery, 203–5
   at WS Ranch, 43–47
Winters, Jim, 160, 250–52
Woodruff, Wilford
   1890 Manifesto, 180, 227, 284
   on adoption theology, 171–72
   on Laminates, 16
   millennial prediction, 1
   on settling St. Johns, 5, 106
   on spirit world, 166–69, 173
WS Ranch
   horses stolen at, 140n56
   Pinkerton agent tracks Wild Bunch to, 45–46, 56, 156
   Wild Bunch hideout, 44, 56, 201
   Wild Bunch works at, 31, 43–46

Y

Young, Brigham
   adoption theology, 171
   attitude toward Native Americans, 15–17
   description of spirit world, 173
   efforts to colonize West, 2–3
Young, Brigham Jr., 70–71
Young, John, 8
Zion, xiv, 1–2

Also available from
GREG KOFFORD BOOKS

Mormonism in Transition: A History of the Latter-day Saints, 1890–1930, 3rd ed.

Thomas G. Alexander

Paperback, ISBN: 978-1-58958-188-3

More than two decades after its original publication, Thomas G. Alexander's Mormonism in Transition still engages audiences with its insightful study of the pivotal, early years of the Churcah of Jesus Christ of Latter-day Saints. Serving as a vital read for both students and scholars of American religious and social history, Alexander's book explains and charts the Church's transformation over this 40-year period of both religious and American history.

For those familiar with the LDS Church in modern times, it is impossible to study Mormonism in Transition without pondering the enormous amount of changes the Church has been through since 1890. For those new to the study of Mormonism, this book will give them a clear understanding the challenges the Church went through to go from a persecuted and scorned society to the rapidly growing, respected community it is today.

Praise for Mormonism in Transition:

"A must read for any serious student of this 'peculiar people' and Western history." – STANLEY B. KIMBALL, *Journal of the West*

"Will be required reading for all historians of Mormonism for some time to come." – WILLIAM D. RUSSELL, *Journal of American History*

"This is by far the most important book on this crucial period in LDS history." – JAN SHIPPS, author of *Mormonism: The Story of a New Religious Tradition*

"A work of careful and prodigious scholarship." – LEONARD J. ARRINGTON, author of *Brigham Young: American Moses*

"Clearly fills a tremendous void in the history of Mormonism." – Klaus J. Hansen, author of *Mormonism and the American Experience*

The Annals of the Southern Mission: A Record of the History of the Settlement of Southern Utah

James Godson Bleak
Edited by Aaron McArthur and Reid L. Neilson

Hardcover, ISBN: 978-1-58958-652-9

James G. Bleak's *Annals of the Southern Mission* (1900–1907) number 2,266 loose and lined pages and represent the finest early history of Southern Utah stretching from its initial Mormon settlement in 1849 into the early years of the twentieth century.

Bleak submitted the first portion of the history, numbering over 500 pages, to the Church Historian's Office in April 1903. He submitted additional increments of the manuscript when he visited Salt Lake City, usually for general conferences. He delivered the final installment of his Annals to the Historian's Office in October 1907. The complete holograph manuscript has been in the continuous custody of the Church History Department (formerly the Church Historian's Office) ever since.

Carefully transcribed and annotated by Aaron McArthur and Reid L. Neilson, this important work provides a detailed historical, ecclesiastical, agricultural, governmental, and cultural record of Southern Utah in the latter half of the nineteenth century.

Praise for *The Annals of the Southern Mission*:

"Professional historians and lay readers will be inspired by this vivid account of the pioneer experiences mostly before statehood or modernization. Developing water systems, establishing schools, creating courts and laws, constructing civic and commercial building and homes, raising food and animals promoting the arts, and generating faith and community harmony in some forty villages in Southern Utah and nearby Nevada and Arizona are all captured by James G.. Bleak. We will all be indebted to Brandon Metcalf for the fine Introduction and to Aaron McArthur and Reid Nielson for their brilliant editing of this important and extensive document." —Douglas Alder, Professor Emeritus and Former President of Dixie College

Excavating Mormon Pasts: The New Historiography of the Last Half Century

Newell G. Bringhurst and Lavina Fielding Anderson

Paperback, ISBN: 978-1-58958-115-9

Special Book Award - John Whitmer Historical Association

Mormonism was born less than 200 years ago, but in that short time it has developed into a dynamic world religious movement. With that growth has come the inevitable restructuring and reevaluation of its history and doctrine. Mormon and non-Mormon scholars alike have viewed Joseph Smith's religion as fertile soil for religious, historical and sociological studies. Many early attempts to either defend or defame the Church were at best sloppy and often dishonest. It has taken decades for Mormon scholarship to mature to its present state. The editors of this book have assembled 16 essays addressing the substantial number of published works in the field of Mormon studies from 1950 to the present. The contributors come from various segments of the Mormon tradition and fairly represent the broad intellectual spectrum of that tradition. Each essay focuses on a particular aspect of Mormonism (history, women's issues, polygamy, etc.), and each is careful to evenhandedly evaluate the strengths and weaknesses of the books under discussion. More importantly, each volume is placed in context with other, related works, giving the reader a panoramic view of contemporary research. Students of Mormonism will find this collection of historiographical essays an invaluable addition to their libraries.

Mormon Polygamous Families: Life in the Principle

Jessie L. Embry

Paperback, ISBN: 978-1-58958-098-5
Hardcover, ISBN: 978-1-58958-114-2

Mormons and non-Mormons all have their views about how polygamy was practiced in the Church of Jesus Christ of Latter-day Saints during the late nineteenth and early twentieth centuries. Embry has examined the participants themselves in order to understand how men and women living a nineteenth-century Victorian lifestyle adapted to polygamy. Based on records and oral histories with husbands, wives, and children who lived in Mormon polygamous households, this study explores the diverse experiences of individual families and stereotypes about polygamy. The interviews are in some cases the only sources of primary information on how plural families were organized. In addition, children from monogamous families who grew up during the same period were interviewed to form a comparison group. When carefully examined, most of the stereotypes about polygamous marriages do not hold true. In this work it becomes clear that Mormon polygamous families were not much different from Mormon monogamous families and non-Mormon families of the same era. Embry offers a new perspective on the Mormon practice of polygamy that enables readers to gain better understanding of Mormonism historically.

"Swell Suffering": A Biography of Maurine Whipple

Veda Tebbs Hale

Paperback, ISBN: 978-1-58958-124-1
Hardcover, ISBN: 978-1-58958-122-7

Maurine Whipple, author of what some critics consider Mormonism's greatest novel, *The Giant Joshua,* is an enigma. Her prize-winning novel has never been out of print, and its portrayal of the founding of St. George draws on her own family history to produce its unforgettable and candid portrait of plural marriage's challenges. Yet Maurine's life is full of contradictions and unanswered questions. Veda Tebbs Hale, a personal friend of the paradoxical novelist, answers these questions with sympathy and tact, nailing each insight down with thorough research in Whipple's vast but under-utilized collected papers.

Praise for *"Swell Suffering"*:

"Hale achieves an admirable balance of compassion and objectivity toward an author who seemed fated to offend those who offered to love or befriend her. . . . Readers of this biography will be reminded that Whipple was a full peer of such Utah writers as Virginia Sorensen, Fawn Brodie, and Juanita Brooks, all of whom achieved national fame for their literary and historical works during the mid-twentieth century"
—Levi S. Peterson, author of *The Backslider* and *Juanita Brooks: Mormon Historian*

Villages on Wheels: A Social History of the Gathering to Zion

Stanley B. Kimball and Violet T. Kimball

ISBN: 978-1-58958-119-7

The enduring saga of Mormonism is its great trek across the plains, and understanding that trek was the life work of Stanley B. Kimball, master of Mormon trails. This final work, a collaboration he began and which was completed after his death in 2003 by his photographer-writer wife, Violet, explores that movement westward as a social history, with the Mormons moving as "villages on wheels."

Set in the broader context of transcontinental migration to Oregon and California, the Mormon trek spanned twenty-two years, moved approximately 54,700 individuals, many of them in family groups, and left about 7,000 graves at the trailside.

Like a true social history, this fascinating account in fourteen chapters explores both the routines of the trail—cooking, cleaning, laundry, dealing with bodily functions—and the dramatic moments: encountering Indians and stampeding buffalo, giving birth, losing loved ones to death, dealing with rage and injustice, but also offering succor, kindliness, and faith. Religious observances were simultaneously an important part of creating and maintaining group cohesiveness, but working them into the fabric of the grueling day-to-day routine resulted in adaptation, including a "sliding Sabbath." The role played by children and teens receives careful scrutiny; not only did children grow up quickly on the trail, but the gender boundaries guarding their "separate spheres" blurred under the erosion of concentrating on tasks that had to be done regardless of the age or sex of those available to do them. Unexpected attention is given to African Americans who were part of this westering experience, and Violet also gives due credit to the "four-legged heroes" who hauled the wagons westward.

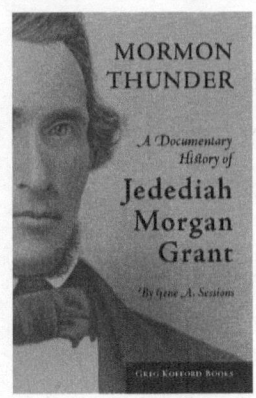

Mormon Thunder: A Documentary History of Jedediah Morgan Grant

Gene A. Sessions

Paperback, ISBN: 978-1-58958-111-1

Jedediah Morgan Grant was a man who knew no compromise when it came to principles—and his principles were clearly representative, argues Gene A. Sessions, of Mormonism's first generation. His life is a glimpse of a Mormon world whose disappearance coincided with the death of this "pious yet rambunctiously radical preacher, flogging away at his people, demanding otherworldliness and constant sacrifice." It was "an eschatological, pre-millennial world in which every individual teetered between salvation and damnation and in which unsanitary privies and appropriating a stray cow held the same potential for eternal doom as blasphemy and adultery."

Updated and newly illustrated with more photographs, this second edition of the award-winning documentary history (first published in 1982) chronicles Grant's ubiquitous role in the Mormon history of the 1840s and '50s. In addition to serving as counselor to Brigham Young during two tumultuous and influential years at the end of his life, he also portentously befriended Thomas L. Kane, worked to temper his unruly brother-in-law William Smith, captained a company of emigrants into the Salt Lake Valley in 1847, and journeyed to the East on several missions to bolster the position of the Mormons during the crises surrounding the runaway judges affair and the public revelation of polygamy.

Jedediah Morgan Grant's voice rises powerfully in these pages, startling in its urgency in summoning his people to sacrifice and moving in its tenderness as he communicated to his family. From hastily scribbled letters to extemporaneous sermons exhorting obedience, and the notations of still stunned listeners, the sound of "Mormon Thunder" rolls again in "a boisterous amplification of what Mormonism really was, and would never be again."

Lot Smith: Mormon Pioneer and American Frontiersman

Carmen R. Smith and Talana S. Hooper

Paperback, ISBN: 978-1-58958-692-5
Hardcover, ISBN: 978-1-58958-720-5

Lot Smith: Mormon Pioneer and American Frontiersman is the comprehensive biography of Utah's 1857 war hero and one of Arizona's early settlement leaders. With over fifty years of combined research, mother and daughter co-authors Carmen R. Smith and Talana S. Hooper take on many of the myths and legends surrounding this lesser-known but significant historical figure within Mormonism.

Lot Smith recounts the Mormon frontiersman's adventures in the Mormon Battalion, the hazardous rescue of the Willie and Martin handcart companies, the Utah War, and the Mormon colonization of the Arizona Territory. True stories of tense relations with the Navajo and Hopi tribes, Mormon flight into Mexico during the US government's anti-polygamy crusades, narrow escapes from bandits and law enforcers, and even Western-style shoot-outs place *Lot Smith: Mormon Pioneer and American Frontiersman* into both Western Americana literature and Mormon biographical history.

Praise for *Textual Studies*:

"An excellent and effective example of a 'life-and-times' biography, this history of the legendary Lot Smith as an imposing figure in the Mormon settlement of the West provides a fresh and very interesting retelling of that story. In the hands of two family members, the treatment is understandably friendly but remarkably thorough and complete. We follow Smith not only through his remarkable role as leader of the guerrilla force that harassed and delayed the U.S. Army during the Utah War but also his involvement in such other adventures as the Mormon Battalion, the Handcart Rescue, service in the Union Army, extensive involvement in polygamy, and an ambitious sortie into Navajo country that led to his death. This is a fascinating book worthy of a truly fascinating nineteenth-century frontiersman." —Gene A. Sessions, professor of history at Weber State University and author of *Mormon Thunder: A Documentary History of Jedediah Morgan Grant*

www.ingramcontent.com/pod-product-compliance
Lightning Source LLC
Chambersburg PA
CBHW030008240426
43672CB00007B/875